Proceedings of the Fifth European Conference on
Computer Supported Cooperative Work

W0232248

Proceedings of the Fifth European Conference on Computer Supported Cooperative Work

Edited by

John A. Hughes
Lancaster University, U.K.

Wolfgang Prinz
GMD-FIT.CSCW, Germany

Tom Rodden
Lancaster University, U.K.

and

Kjeld Schmidt
Risoe National Laboratory, Denmark

Cover Design by Roger Bonninck

SPRINGER-SCIENCE+BUSINESS MEDIA, B.V.

A C.I.P. Catalogue record for this book is available from the Library of Congress.

ISBN 978-94-015-7374-0   ISBN 978-94-015-7372-6 (eBook)
DOI 10.1007/978-94-015-7372-6

Table of Contents

Formalisms and Mediation

Objects, Spaces and Bodies

Sharing: Information and Process

The Influence of Devices and Environments

Cooperation and Access Coordination

From the Editors

This volume represents the proceedings of ECSCW'97, the 5th European Conference on Computer Supported Cooperative Work. The conference provides an international forum for research activities from various technical and social disciplines. The conference alternates with the ACM international conference on CSCW to provide annually a principal point of focus for CSCW research.

The programme of technical papers presented here is the result of a difficult review process. This year the conference received 111 submissions of very high quality from which the 24 papers making up the technical programme were selected. Both the number of submissions and the quality and diversity of the programme presented here are testimony to the health of the CSCW community. We are sure that you will enjoy the papers in this proceedings.

The technical papers in this volume are only one aspect of a diverse and dynamic event such as ECSCW. The technical paper programme is complemented by tutorials, workshops, demonstrations and posters reflecting some of the most exciting and novel aspects of CSCW. These activities are essential to the success of the conference and the continued growth of the community.

This conference could not have taken place without considerable enthusiasm, support and encouragement as well as sheer hard work. Many people have earned the thanks of those who attended and organised ECSCW'97. In particular, we would like to gratefully thank:

- All those who submitted to the conference. This year saw the highest number of submissions to this conference. The standard was extremely high and reflects well on the research work in the community.
- All of those who contributed to the conference through workshops, tutorials, posters, demos and paper presentations.
- All of those who contributed to the organisation of the conference. Planning a major international conference is a complex endeavour and many people made significant contributions to realising a successful conference.
- All of the local conference management team and the Student Volunteers who work so tirelessly during the conference to ensure things run smoothly.
- Those members of the Conference and Programme Committees who gave so freely of their time and energy to ensure that the conference was both smoothly run and of high technical quality. The many individuals we owe our thanks to are listed elsewhere in this volume.
- The many sponsors and supporters of ECSCW'97 for their contributions to the conference and to the CSCW community generally.

We would also like to acknowledge the organisers of the ACM CSCW conference for the support and encouragement they extend to this conference. The close cooperation between ECSCW and the ACM CSCW conferences allows us to continue the growth of a truly international research community tackling the problems core to CSCW. Between both conferences we have been able to establish an annual international conference on CSCW for the last decade charting the development and maturity of the discipline. These proceedings represent the start of the next decade of international CSCW research and the further development of our research community. The future appears to hold considerable promise for us all.

John Hughes, Wolfgang Prinz, Kjeld Schmidt, and Tom Rodden

ECSCW '97 Conference Committee

Conference Co-Chairs
    Tom Rodden, Lancaster University, UK
    John Hughes, Lancaster University, UK
ECSCW'95 Past Chair: Yngve Sundblad,
    KTH, Sweden
Programme Chair: Wolfgang Prinz, GMD,
    Germany
Organisation Chair: Jacqui Forsyth, Lancaster
    University, UK
Proceedings Chair: Kjeld Schmidt, Risø
    National Lab, Denmark
Tutorials Chair: Mike Twidale, Lancaster
    University, UK
Workshops Chair: Carla Simone, University
    of Torino, Italy
    (Local Arrangements: Gareth Smith)
Demos Chair: Paul Dourish, Apple
    Computer, Inc., USA
    (Local Arrangements: Andy
    Colebourne)
Videos Chair: Steve Benford, University of
    Nottingham, UK
Posters Chair: John Mariani, Lancaster
    University, UK
    (Local Arrangements: Jonathan Trevor)
Student Volunteers Chair: Stephen Viller,
    Lancaster University, UK
Doctoral Colloquium Chair: Yvonne Rogers,
    University of Sussex, UK
Technical Support Chair: Jon O'Brien,
    Lancaster University, UK

Liaison outside Europe

N. American Liaison: Prasun Dewan,
    University of North Carolina, USA
Australian Liaison: Simon Kaplan,
    University of Queensland, Australia
Asian Liaison: Hideaki Kuzuoka, University
    of Tsukuba, Japan

ECSCW '97 Programme Committee

Sponsors

ECSCW '97 is grateful for the generous support of the following sponsors:

Apple Computer, Inc.

Bell Laboratories, Lucent Technologies

Holdens Computer Services Ltd.

And also for the support of:

National Westminster Bank plc.

The Production of Order and the Order of Production: Possibilities for Distributed Organisations, Work and Technology in the Print Industry

Graham Button
Rank Xerox Research Centre, Cambridge

Wes Sharrock
University of Manchester

Abstract.

Drawing on a fieldwork study, this paper considers different design options for the development of a system for facilitating distributed organisation and distributed working within a sector of the print industry. The relationship between the design of the system and the design of the organisation is also examined. It is concluded that if organisations are to practically benefit from the continued evolution of communication infrastructures, CSCW should attend to the *appropriate* development of information and work co-ordination systems. It is also concluded that CSCW should develop measures of the value of proposed systems for organisations and users.

Introduction

The advent of digital technology in the print industry has ushered in many changes in working practices and organisational configurations. Networking distributed production sites suggests the possibility of yet further changes. This is because networking offers various alternative technological and organisational possibilities to those that currently exist. Past research in CSCW on the introduction of networks into working environments (Bowers, 1994, Orlikowski, 1992, Rogers, 1992) suggests that it is necessary to develop better understandings of the work and the organisational context into which networks are introduce if they are

1

J. Hughes et al. (eds.), Proceedings of the Fifth European Conference on Computer Supported Cooperative Work, 1-16.
© 1997 Kluwer Academic Publishers.

to be optimally used to support the work of the organisation. In this spirit we have been engaged in a study of a UK commercial printer who is contemplating networking twenty Print Centres through ISDN links. This will provide the company with the opportunity to print-to-order a document that has been originated at, or submitted to one site, at another site. We are interested in understanding what order of organisational issues have to be addressed in the development of the network and the determination of what could be its optimal use by the company.

It has been suggested to the organisation that there are commercial advantages to be gained from such a move, for example, load-balancing, maximisation of resources, and enhanced services, (Bowers, Button and Sharrock, 1994). Currently, production is managed on a site-by-site basis. Thus, for instance, each site has its own job acquisition and scheduling procedures. Networking the sites, however, provides the opportunity to redesign the organisation. It has been suggested that in order to unlock the envisioned commercial advantages the twenty sites could be run as one large 'virtual' print factory within which the management of production across the network is centralised, with, for instance, centralised job acquisition and job scheduling.

At least two options thus exist for the way in which the management of production is controlled in the future. Should the company reconfigure itself as a large virtual print factory, the production activities of each site would be centrally determined and managed. This would require that production information about, for example, machine state and run progress is centrally gathered to determine not just which print machine a job will run on, but which geographic site will be used. The network could thus be used to distribute centrally acquired jobs according to a centrally determined schedule. Alternatively, if the sites are organised on a site-by-site basis then, although locally controlled, they can use the network to co-ordinate their production with one another. For example, passing jobs on to one another should they be overloaded; passing a job to another site if the intended destination for the job is actually nearer to that site than they are, or passing a job on to another site because a vital machine has gone down.

Not only does the possibility of networking sites open up different organisational options for the company with respect to the control and management of production, choosing between these options is also consequential for the design of systems used to facilitate the management of networked production. Thus, for example, should an organisational configuration of co-operating sites be established, production information about each site may need to be accessed by all sites in order to determine when a job may be passed from one site to another, or which site a job should be passed to. All sites may, then, need to be mutually aware of each other's real-time production status. This awareness may, however, only extend to the status of the scheduling of other sites so that the commissioning site can establish a priority listing of sites that could receive the job. Should, though, a centrally organised system be contemplated, awareness of production status between the sites would not be necessary, but the detail of production states may need to be deeper and extend to production matters such as individual job status, stock status, and machine and personnel status.

There is a direct relationship between the design of the organisation and the design of the network and production management systems. Should the network be centrally designed, for example, it will pre-dispose the organisation to become more centrally dominated in order to be able to effectively and optimally use the network. However, should the organisation remain de-centralised then the network will be crossing different organisational procedures such as different pricing policies and will have to be designed accordingly. The designers of such networked systems and the organisational toolsmiths (Bittner, 1965) thus confront a dilemma concerning both the design of the network and the design of the organisation.

We maintain that contemplating the technical and organisational possibilities for networked factory production printing can be facilitated through an understanding of the methods and practices by which production is currently ordered. It is to the task of describing the production of order in Factory Production Printing (FPP) that the bulk of this paper is dedicated.[1] We go on to suggest that the design decision to produce a centrally or de-centrally managed network can be taken in a methodic fashion and how this in turn affects the design of networked information and co-ordination technologies for use in production management. The issues this study raises for the design of information and work co-ordination technologies are of general relevance for CSCW if the promised benefits for organisations from the growth of communication infrastructures are to be fully realised. This, however, begs the questions: 'how are organisations to measure and assess the benefits?', and 'how can a determination of what may be an optimal system for their purposes be made?' We conclude by suggesting that CSCW may find answers to these questions in understanding the nature of the entwined relationship between technology and organisations.

The Ordering of Factory Production Printing

FPP is large volume printing, for example, the production list for one day at one of the organisation's Print Centres recorded 141 jobs covering a total of 2,754,801 printed documents - let alone pages. Production is organised as a chain of processes through which a job passes, run according to a schedule and against a deadline. The print factories within the organisation we have examined were known as Print Centres (PC) and the persons allocated the responsibility of managing production were the Print Centre Manager (PCM); the Administration

---

[1]   We are presenting a case study, for which we make no apologies. Establishment Printers is not, however, just a randomly selected firm, it is one of the largest and oldest European printers, and, at least in the UK, it is recognised to be a depository of 'industry wisdom'.

Manager (AM); and the Production Manager (PM). It is their work of production management that is the focus of this present examination.[2]

The work of production management displays an orientation to the order of production. Personnel make determinations such as: 'is this job on time?'; 'is this job going to be late?'; 'how late will the job be?'; 'what do we have to do to get the job out on time?'; 'do we have the necessary resources -the right paper in the right quantities, the necessary inks and toners, enough memory, money in the overtime budget?'; 'can we take this job on in the light of our other commitments?"; "how are we going to cope now this machine has broken down?'

These questions are formulated in the light of two imperatives for FPP: i) a maximum ten day turn around from the receipt of an order to delivery, and, ii) keeping the plant at full production, (Bowers, Button and Sharrock, 1995). The former is a contractual obligation entered into with their customers, and the latter maximises profitability. Personnel engage in a number of activities that are designed to achieve an order to PC production that is accountable to these imperatives.

The Production of a Schedule

The AM attends to the imperatives of production printing in working out a production order for the printing machines from out of the daily and contingently presented customer job requests using a 'forward-loading-board'. This organisational artefact is used to turn a circumstantially produced collage of job requests into an order of printing that is tractable to the imperatives of FPP. The PC is presented with a circumstantially produced collage of jobs because not all job requests can be anticipated. At best, the AM may know that a job can be expected because a customer has informed him that they are placing an order. However, on just what day the order will arrive is not always known in advance of its actual arrival. There is always the possibility that it will not arrive at all because even when a customer promises a job for a given day, past experience dictates that jobs do not always automatically follow such a commitment.

Consequently, the internal mail through which the postal and courier services are channelled presents the AM with a new array of jobs each working day. One way in which production on these may begin is by merely printing them in the order in which they arrive on the print room floor and at a time when a machine becomes available. Such a procedure, however, is unlikely to result in compliance with the imperatives of print production to turn the job around in ten days and to work to full capacity. For example, one large job may tie up one machine, but there may be insufficient demand for other machines that day which thus remain

---

[2] For the sake of brevity the details of our description are drawn from fieldwork at just one site, though the issues addressed are to be found throughout Establishment Printers. We should also distinguish our ethnographic approach from the Operations Management literature which has extensively examined production management, especially production scheduling. Cf. Scott (1994). This work, however, emphasises mathematical modelling whereas we are interested in the embodied practices and oriented to features of production work and organisation.

idle. Working up a production order in the face of *this* contingency by splitting the job between machines would then not only complete the job more quickly, it would also ensure all machines are working to full capacity.

Working up a production order in the face of a contingently presented array of jobs thus displays an orientation to the imperatives of print production. The AM must make decisions about which machine will print which job, about splitting a job across machines, about how long a job will take so that upon the completion of that job the next one is ready to go. In taking these decisions a new job must be interlaced into an existing history of production decisions. Past decisions thus constrain the decisions that can now be taken with regard to a new job. However, past decisions can be revised in the light of new jobs. In order to make these decisions the AM must be able to make *calculations* as to the effects that his decisions will have upon production. He must, therefore, be able to turn the daily array of jobs into objects upon which he can perform calculations. This will allow him to make decisions as to when a job will be printed and on what machine, what consequences this may have for past decisions and what degree of freedom it allows him with respect to future decisions.

The forward-loading-board is an organisational artefact that is used to work up the daily array of jobs into a rational production order and by means of which the AM is able to perform his necessary calculations. The board consists of a vertical axis made up of machines aligned against weeks, and a horizontal axis of the number of hours in a week, from 0 to a maximum of 100.

The AM knows from the job order form how many copies of a document are required. He knows from past experience the hourly production capacity for each machine and he is thus able to calculate how long a job will take if it is printed on any given machine. He can then give over a machine for a number of hours to a particular job. He blocks out that machine for the requisite number of hours and assigns the job name to the machine. In this way he is able to see, for example, if printing the job on that machine will extend the production beyond the point at which it should be delivered if it is to meet its ten-day turn-around target. It thus allows him to see if he needs to place the job on two machines.

Through the forward-loading-board the AM is able: i) to project ahead, ii) to see the consequences of past decisions; iii) play 'what if' games and examine the consequences of different production orders; iv) fine tune production, and v) establish the timings for a job with respect to its arrival on the print room floor from the prior origination process, and its progression to the next process such as finishing.

The AM is thus able to make rational decisions as to: i) can the print centre take on another job this week?; can it be accepted?; must it be turned down?; should the job be outsourced?, or should the customer be approached and asked if they would accept the job on a different time-cycle?; ii) is a job late, progressing to schedule, or early?; iii) the re-ordering of production should a production contingency such as a machine going down arise; iv) whether the PCM should be advised that over-time may be required, and v) in what order should the jobs be printed in? The forward-loading-board is thus an organisational artefact that is used to make production a calculable phenomenon and to furnish data through which rational decisions as to the order of production can be made. Through the forward-loading-board a schedule of jobs for the print machines is constructed, and through the forward-loading-board a particular order to the production process is in part constituted.

Sequential Order

The AM and the PC editors are responsible for entering a job into the production system. In so doing they orient to a sequential order in the production process. First, they draw out the sequentially dependent relationship between processes in situatedly configuring for the job at hand a process profile from out of a range of possible profiles. Second, they provide a means through which the sequential imperative of 'first-things-first' can be met in the production life cycle. Third, they furnish a partial resource through which different parts of the production process can be co-ordinated one with another. It may seem to be a truism to suggest that in managing a production process one is managing a sequential order and that one of the primary rules is to ensure 'first-things-first'. However, arranging matters so those first things actually do come first in unproblematic ways is by no means an easy task.

Sequential Dependency

The activities required for the production of a particular job within the PC can be configured from out of a range of possible activities within each of the production processes: 1) *Origination*: authentication; composition; artwork; layout; bar codes; ISBN assignment; proofing; plate making; scanning. 2) *Printing*: signatures, highlights, grey tones, colour, over printing, embossing, inserts, covers. 3) *Finishing*: trimming, folding, cutting, stitching, binding, perfect binding, spiral binding. 4) *Dispatch*: tying, boxing, wrapping, customer distribution, client distribution. For each job a process/activity profile is configured from out of the above range of possible processes and activities a job can be subjected to. In discussions with the customer and using information retrieved from the order request form submitted by customers, the AM and the editors make up a specification for the job on a 'work-ticket'. The work-ticket is affixed to a 'work-bag' that contains the job request form, hard copy, electronic file, and artwork.

The work-ticket is a second organisational artefact that is used in ordering the production. In entering the process/activity profile in a section of the work-ticket entitled *Component Details*, the AM and the editors orient to the sequential order of the processes and make this a visible feature of working on the job. For example, they enter a numbered list of activities the job should go through, each number corresponding to a production activity. Thus any particular job will have a list of numbered production activities configured for it. The numerical hierarchy thus makes transparent the sequential order in which the activities are to be performed.

Accordingly, users of the work ticket are able to tell what has to be done next, and where that job should be sent once they have completed work on it. For example, following 'printing' the job may have to go to 'finishing' where it will be trimmed to size. However, trimming is only one of a possible number of activities that might relevantly be engaged in next as part of the finishing process. It could, for example, be folded or it could by-pass the finishing processes altogether and go straight to packing. Thus any one activity (with the exception of the activities associated with the last process) has a range of possible next activities that are relevant, and the work ticket constitutes a particular activity as the relevant next activity for *this* job. Accordingly, a resource is constituted for answering the question 'what next?' by making manifest the *defacto* sequential order to the production processes.

First-Things-First

The second orientation to the order of the work is displayed in the use of the work-ticket to attend to the issue of 'first-things-first' in the production process. The work-ticket furnishes a resource whereby users can determine what needs to be done before what. Thus, for example, the work ticket is examined by the Stock Controller to determine the type and quantity of paper required for the job. Should the necessary paper not be available from stock, or should there be an insufficient quantity, the stock controller is able to order the required paper. Unless the required stock is available then printing cannot begin, thus the work ticket is a means through which 'first-things-first' can be attended to: first ensure the stock required for printing is available before printing is to begin. The Stock Controller can thus order the required paper, should that be necessary, while the job is in origination.

Work Co-ordination

The third orientation to the order of the work that is displayed in the use of the work-tickets and work-bags is to the co-ordination of the work done on a job. An 'abbreviated work-bag' is made up at the same time as the main work-bag. It only provides information relevant for the actual printing of the job such as the type and colour of ink and the amount and type of paper required. The production work-bag is sent to the PM. From the information contained within the work-bag the PM can determine how to set up the machines for printing. For example, if a conventional printing machine is to be used, whether it needs to be 'washed', or if a job is to be printed on an electronic printer, which files need to be loaded? The PM also uses the production work-bag to determine what inks or toners are required and what paper is to be used. With this information he can drawn the required resources from the appropriate stocks and have them ready to hand behind the machines in anticipation of the arrival of the job. This means that when the job arrives from origination, the actual printing can proceed with the minimal delay. The production work-bag is thus a device the PM can use to co-ordinate the work of printing with the work of origination.

An orientation to the sequential order of production makes the work of production management accountable to one of the imperatives of production printing: a stringent deadline on turn-around. For example, having the necessary resources to hand so that printing may commence upon the arrival of a job from origination minimises the amount of time involved in moving the job on from one process to another. This contrast with a situation in which the job, having finished with one process has to wait before the next processes can be begun. Attending to 'first-things-first' guards against delays caused by the discovery that, at the time it is required, the necessary stock is not in store. Providing a resource for solving the problem of 'what next?' allows the job to be smoothly moved on to its next process so that the minimum of time is lost in the transfer. Attending to the sequential order of the work is thus a way in which time is saved and the possibility of meeting the deadline maximised.

Demand-Monitoring

The AM orients to the achievement of a smooth flow of work through the print room by working to make the consequences of his forward loading activities visible for the demand on printing machines and other machines involved in subsequent production stages. He is concerned with detecting the potential for log-jams in the production cycle that his prior decisions may cause but which, as he is making them, may not be detectable. To do so he uses another device he has designed to make production actives amenable to calculation.

A smooth flow of work through the PC is desirable within FPP because it attends to the imperatives of maximising production and meeting targets, (Bowers, Button and Sharrock, 1995). The mangers within the PCs are concerned with moving jobs on from one process to another with the minimum of delay. Thus, once a job has been printed it is stacked in front of the machine in an aisle way, awaiting collection by personnel involved in the next process. However, although a smooth flow of work from one process area to another is desirable it can be a problematic state to achieve for two reasons. First, one printing machine may become overloaded with the consequence that jobs stack up for that machine and their printing becomes delayed. Second, loading jobs onto printing machines in a certain order may result in similar jobs coming off numerous printing machines at the same time which are all destined for the same next process, for example, trimming. This may mean that a log-jam for this process develops and that jobs may have to wait rather than moving onto the next process.

In his forward loading operations the AM can exacerbate these problems and thus, while attending to one problem involved in the production of an order of production, scheduling, he may make decisions that adversely affect another, a smooth flow of work. The manger uses a device for calculating the load on a machine and processes in order to make the consequences of his forward loading decisions for the smooth flow of work from one process to another visible. This device consists of a board for each machine into which paper strips can be inserted. The details of a job are written on a strip, which is then inserted into the board. It is thus possible to display a sequential list of jobs for each machine. As a job is finished the strip is taken out and moved to the next machine that will be used in the production process such as one of the folding machines, and the rest of the jobs on the ladder are moved up. The AM is, consequently, able to monitor the load that is building for each machine. The device does not so much allow him to project in advance what will be the consequences of his forward loading, but it does allow him to monitor the building up of pressure on certain machines and the potential for a log-jam of work. This, in turn, allows him to make remedial decisions such as re-ordering the work by swapping it to other machines or extending the production day through the use of over-time.

Recognising the Order

A pre-requisite for maintaining a smooth flow of work is that the jobs are identifiable to those who must move them on from one process to another, and by those who must ensure that they are moved on. It is also important that the job is moved in its entirety and not just some part of the job. Both matters can be more complex than might appear from outside of the work of the PC, for at any time the process areas can contain many pallets of printed paper in various stages of production. Pallets of printed paper are lined up in the aisles behind the printing machines, and one job may occupy numerous pallets. Pallets of printed paper are also placed in aisles in the finishing area and in the dispatch area. One job may be comprised of several pallets of printed paper and the pages may run on in order across a number of pallets. To move the jobs onto the next process it is necessary for those involved to be able to know which job it is and what parts make up that job. The problem they face is to bring into prominence the particular pallets on which the job resides from amongst the array of pallets on the floor, to identify just those pallets they require and all the pallets they require. To the inexperienced roving eye the jobs can all look alike, and the sheer quantity of the jobs can act to camouflage any one job.

Those involved have to, to paraphrase Melinda Baccus (1986), extract the animal from the foliage, and one method for so doing is to make jobs self-evident with respect to their identity. A device that is used to do this is the 'job-flag'. This is a large piece of paper that is inserted into the piles of printed paper sitting on the pallets and which displays the job title, number of copies and the number of pallets that make up the job and the sequential position of the particular pallet. The flags announce the identity of the job and are thus a device through which those involved are able to differentiate the contents of one pallet from that of another pallet. They are thus a resource that can be used in moving the entire job on to the next process.

Tracking the Job

The PM displays a pre-occupation with the order of work in attending to the interrelated questions: 'where in the production cycle is the job?', and 'is the job progressing according to the production schedule?' He constantly reviews the jobs in the production areas with these questions 'in mind'. Thus any job as it, for example, lies on pallets or sits in the in-files of machine operators, may be examined under the auspices of these questions. To answer these questions the PM needs to satisfy himself as to: i) the identity of a job; ii) what has been done on the job and what remains to be done, particularly what is next to be done, and iii) the projected times by which work has to be done.

Jobs are made self-evident with respect to the first two questions through two devices. First, the work-bag remains with the job at all times, whatever form the job is currently in. The work-ticket on the front of the work-bag can thus be consulted in order to answer the question 'what has been done to the job?' for each of the manufacturing processes are laid out on the work-ticket and are signed off as completed. Thus, the PM can quickly ascertain what has been done, what has not been done, and what is to be done next, by consulting the work-ticket. Second, once printed, the job-flags inserted into the piles of printed paper allow the PM, as he makes regular passes through the production areas, to immediately ascertain the identity of the job. The PM can then match the jobs against the production-sheet and ascertain, for example, that the job is behind schedule because it has not yet gone into the folding process and thus may be in danger of missing its target completion date.

By making all jobs subject to the above questions and through using the three devices to answer them, the PM is able to monitor the flow of work from one production process to another. He is thus able to detect if a job is slipping behind its schedule, and look into the cause of the problem in order to take remedial action. Accordingly, the PM is able to explore the possibility that a job has been overlooked, or the possibility that there is a log-jam building for a particular process despite the best efforts of the AM. He may then be able to take remedial action by, for example, taking personnel from one production process to temporally help out in the execution of the process under pressure, or scheduling overtime and weekend working or, as a last resort, outsourcing the process.

Remedial action is often taken in collaboration between the PM, the PCM and the AM. A further organisational artefact that is used in this respect is the 'work-list-report'. This document is compiled at the beginning of the working day and lists all jobs currently being worked on. It contains information on their run length, run type, delivery times and dates, and status. Each job is examined in turn. For most jobs this is a simple matter of noting that it is progressing to schedule but for some jobs it is an opportunity to mark problems. For example, a job may be experiencing production problems because the printers are finding it difficult to match a particular colour. The PM may use the occasion to mark that a potential workflow problem may be in the offing should this problem not be effectively attended to. Contingency plans may then be drawn up. For example, the AM may take this into account when forward loading machines and possibly open up a space on another printing machine, which would allow the job to be spread over two machines if it is necessary to make up lost time. Those involved use the work-list-report to reach agreement on particular production strategies to enable the smooth flow of work and to co-ordinate their work.

Production Management

In using the locally designed production management artefacts of the forward-loading-board, demand-monitor, work-ticket, work-bag, production-work-bag, production-sheet, job-flags, and work-list-report, those involved individually work, and collectively collaborate, to produce an order to production that is tractable to the imperatives of FFP.[3] These organisational artefacts are used as devices through which questions as to the various ways in which the sequential integrity of the process of production and the smooth flow of work can be answered. Thus, for example, questions such as 'what has been done to this job and what is to be done next?'; 'what is the next job to print?', and 'is this job going to be completed on time?' can be methodically answered. These and other questions are asked in the course of production so as to attend to both the progression that is being made with respect to a particular job and with respect to the load on the PC. They display that the work of production management is an ongoing accomplishment, the details of which are attended to during the course of production. This suggests that the uses of these artefacts orient to two features of the production of order: i) it is revisable in the light of the unfolding circumstances of production, and ii) it is visible in the products it provides for.

The Revisability of the Order of Production

A fieldwork anecdote is revealing in this respect. Half an hour into one working day the anxious AM conferred with the PM over a job, the proofs of which had been promised by the customer for delivery that morning. The production schedule relevant for that day had been constructed around this promise and one of the large presses which was due to come to the end of a million sheet run had been scheduled to pick up the job by mid-afternoon. Projecting backwards from that time, the AM had estimated that the proofs had to be in the PC by 10 o'clock in order to complete the necessary origination processes and to have the job ready for printing at the time the machine in question became vacant. Any later than this

---

3   A reviewer was surprised that we made no mention of computer-assisted production systems that have been around for many years. The organisation we studied is, to stress, a repository of industry wisdom and at the forefront of many technical innovations, yet it uses these simple paper based tools, not the CSCW technologies the reviewer champions. Perhaps this, in itself, informs us of the practical utility of these systems. If not a sufficient comment, see a previous study (Bowers, Button and Sharrock, 1995) that details the chaos that ensued when just such a computer assisted production technology was introduced by Establishment Printers. A lesson we may draw from their experiences is that designers and developers should not become complacent about existing technology, and assume that just because there are systems that address production problems they have actually solved them. One thing that can be learnt from studying technology-in-use is that there is often a shortfall between the technology and its reputation.

and the scheduled machine would be idle for an indefinite time. The required proofs had not yet been delivered; the customer had been contacted and had assured the AM that the proofs would be hand delivered by 10 o'clock. Nevertheless, the AM was sceptical. The AM and PM developed a strategy to guard against this contingency which involved re-working the production order. Although this required some complicated calculations it was notable from reviewing the tape recordings made of their deliberations how quickly they arrived at their decision.

As this anecdote testifies, the order of production is a revisable order that is sensitive to the unfolding contingencies of FPP. The AM and the PM were able to revise the order of production in a very short time because, in the words of the PM, they had the production order 'in their heads'. By having the forward-loading-board in hand, and conducting their conversation around the production board they were able to readily consult these artefacts and confirm for themselves the order of production they were working to and view the opportunities for re-working that order. With a short walk to the plate room to consult work-tickets they were able to confirm where in the process two other relevant jobs were, and thus placed themselves in a position whereby they could make a decision to revise the order of production. The revisability of the order was done in the use of the artefacts that made production a rationally accountable activity. The forward-loading-board and production board are not only instruments through which an order to production can be initially constituted but are also instruments through which, and in conjunction with others, that order can be revised. Thus, the order that is achieved in scheduling and sequencing production is an order that is open to revision, and the tools through which that revision can be accomplished are the same tools with which the order is initially produced.

The At-A-Glance Visibility of Order

The revisability of order resides in the extent to which the order is visible to those who must revise it. As the above example suggests, the artefacts were a means by which the AM and PM could view the order of production 'at-a-glance'. They are publicly available and on public display. They sit at specified centres from which production is managed. Thus the forward-loading-board and load monitor sit on the AM's desk, the production boards on the PM's two desks (one on the print room floor the other in origination) and the work-tickets and job-flags sit on the jobs themselves. The only exception is the work-list-report. Although, involving particular peoples' desks, these centres of control are, however, public places. They are open and inspectable to all, not just to those whose desks they nominally are. As the PCM, AM and PM make their passes around the PC they can review the order of production by glancing at these devices, as they lie on each other's desks and on the jobs, and they can amend them as required. Not only are they used by the three managers they are also used by the process charge hands and process operators who consult them to remind themselves as to what jobs are upcoming, or where a job has to go next, and when it has to be there by.

The at-a-glance visibility of order afforded by the public nature of these arte-facts is not only a resource in the revision of a production order but also in maintaining a production order, for the public availability of work-tickets and job-flags allows the relevant people to move the jobs on. Thus, at a glance, operators can see which jobs have to be shifted and, at-a-glance, a delay in production can be detected. The at-a-glance visibility of order is not, of course, a unique feature of the order of printing, it is a methodical feature of social order per se. The point we are making is how the at-a-glance visibility of order is achieved for the work of print production.

Conclusion: Deciding Between Options for the Network and the Organisation

The work of production management is thus oriented to providing for a revisable and visible order to the order of production. At the beginning of this paper we suggested that one possibility that is being seriously considered is a centralised system that will create a virtual PC with, for example, centralised job acquisition and scheduling.[4] We are suggesting that this consideration can be reviewed in the light of our explication of production management. This explication can be viewed as domain knowledge. It provides a rationale for making design decisions concerning the control of production management that are grounded in the exper-tise of those involved in the management of FPP. It thus allows the designer to use the organisations' expertise in FPP, an expertise not possessed by the de-signer, as a resource in their own designing work.

On the face of it there might be much to commend a centralised view, for it might seem that the use of resources could be maximised and the organisation rationalised. However, as we have described, although production management involves the organisation of a production schedule, the order of production that is embodied in that schedule is one that has to be ongoingly worked at to achieve and maintain, and one that is open to revision at a moments notice. The resources for so doing, however, are locally assembled and locally deployed. A virtual PC would then require the replication of these local resources within a generalised context. For example, as the local arrangements provide for the order of produc-tion to be 'in the heads' of the relevant local personnel, so too would ways be required to have the order of production within the virtual PC 'in the heads' of the relevant central personnel. Further, as there are ways of making the order visible to local personnel, at a glance, so too ways would be required to make the order visible, at a glance, centrally.

Alternatively, production management can be locally organised, and the transmission of a job from one PC to another could be folded into the order of production in the manner of any job submission. The network would then be used

4   The issue of centralisation in technology has been extensively examined elsewhere. Cf. Zuboff (1984).

to co-ordinate the work of one PC with another by providing access to the production status of each site on the network. AMs would thus be able to scan the network in order to off-load work to other, more lightly loaded sites. A job that might otherwise have to be turned down could thus be accepted. Currently, contacting other sites for this purpose is not systematic. The AM of one site might have to ring around all the other sites with the attendant problems associate with trying to contact the right people at just the time they are needed. Access to the forward-loading-boards would allow the AM to know which sites have a spare capacity. With an added service of being able to directly place the job into the job acquisition and work-ticket phase of production management, make a rational decision over the production of the job in the manner that can be currently made within individual PCs.

Although our examination has been concerned with just one organisation it does, nevertheless, suggest two general points of interest for CSCW: i) the need for CSCW to strenuously address the issue of appropriate information technologies and the co-ordination of work in the light of the evolution of communication infrastructures, and ii) the extent to which CSCW might develop measures of the value of proposed systems for organisations and users that trades on the entwined relationship between technology and organisations.

Communication Infrastructures and the Co-ordination of Work

The development of communication infrastructures and the concomitant proliferation of networking facilities for information technologies means that increasingly networks of organisations such as the one that has figured in this examination, may be developed into complex relationships of customers, suppliers, collaborators (even competitors) and outsourcers. Inevitably, again as this study suggests, this development will lead to increasing demands on the co-ordination of information systems. Current information technologies, however, are mainly concerned with insuring the interoperability of information systems predicated on the continued evolution of communication infrastructures. Thus, although the exchange of information will, seemingly, become increasingly easier, they will not, however, provide support for, nor make co-ordination easier. Consequently a situation that current information systems will engender, the increased need for co-ordination, is not addressed in the design of information systems.

Concomitantly, technologies that currently exist for the co-ordination of work and information do not provide for the easy communication of those involved, and have been strenuously criticised for their centralised and rigid approach to work order (Suchman, 1994). Consequently, it appears that there are no current co-ordination systems through which the co-ordination of work can be realised in a revisable and flexible manner. Thus organisations such as the one that figures in our examination are faced with a very real dilemma. There are clear business advantages to the organisation in capitalising upon the rapid growth in communication infrastructures. However, these infrastructures will result in a situation that will require the co-ordination of complex activities across different parts of the organisation. Seemingly, neither the infrastructures, nor the current work co-ordination technologies, are capable of allowing the organisation to address this situation. However, the development of technologies intended to do this also confronts a dilemma, a centralised/decentralised information and co-ordination system. With respect to the latter, the entwined relationship between the design of the systems and the design of the organisation must be considered. It may just not be feasible for an organisation to maximise the benefits of enhanced communication infrastructures if the new information and work co-ordination systems necessities the re-design of the organisation in ways that compromise the very work that it carries out.

Technology and Organisational Design

The acknowledgement that there is an entwined relationship between technological infrastructure and organisational structure is widespread in sociology and organisational studies, and is now also quite commonplace within CSCW. Business Process Re-engineering obviously uses technology as a major force in the re-design of organisations and increasingly there are designers who recognise that new technologies impact upon the organisation and the work of those in organisations into which the technology is introduced. In addition, there are those 'toolsmiths' within the organisations themselves who use technology as a significant resource in their re-structuring activities, especially communication and information technologies. A question that members of these groups are held accountable to either by organisations employing their services, those they report to in the organisation, or the persons within the organisations who must now use new technology and orient to new processes is: 'how do we measure the success of the new organisational design?' For instance, should the organisation we have been involved with be 'sold on' a technology that would require it to re-design itself as a virtual PC within which existing local decision making with respect to job pricing; job acceptance; job acquisition; job scheduling; job pacing, and job distribution being transferred to a central controlling agency, the question that could be raised is: 'what measures can the organisation invoke to determine the value to be gained from such a re-design before going to the actual lengths of re-designing themselves?'

Put another way, those who are designing a new system will have to satisfy the organisation that any new organisational configuration it will necessitate is of exceptional value to the organisation. How can designers of the system do that? One type of answer that has been very common amongst designers is too ephemeral for many commercial organisations. It is one that theoretically postulates the value to be derived from technology developments, requiring organisations to make leaps of faith and share the designers' vision of the future. It is a measure of value that is derived more from the vaulting expectations of designers rather than the realities of trading, and as the studies to which we referred at the beginning suggest, designers expectations are often thwarted by the realities of organisational life. Designers of commercial systems thus need to be able to develop measures of value that their systems can create for organisations that will satisfy the organisations' own methods of accounting. Although the difficult of measuring the business value of technology has been well document (cf. Brown and Remenyi, 1994), nevertheless designers need to be able to access and deploy benchmarks, standardised procedures, forms of solutions and the like, rather than unsubstantiated projected gains.

We are suggesting that one way in which the design of a distributed print factory can progress in this respect is through an understanding of the order of practices we have defined as the local management of print production. Making this the woof and warp of the design, we are arguing, will allow designers to measure the value of their intended system. We have here only been able to gesture at what this involves and do not underestimate the problem. However, even a gesture suggests that there may be less value to be derived by the organisation from following the original design path that envisioned a centralised system and organisation than there would be in designing a 'light-weight' system grounded in the current and highly successful organisational structure.

Acknowledgements

We are extremely grateful to Establishment Printers, James Pycock, Bob Anderson, John Bowers and Remo Pareschi. Wes Sharrock acknowledges the support of an ESRC Senior Research Fellowship No. H524700895.

References

Baccus, M.D. (1986): Multipiece Truck Wheel Accidents and their Regulations. In H. Garfinkel (ed.), *Ethnomethodological Studies of Work*. London: Routledge and Kegan Paul.

Bittner, E. (1995): The Concept of Organisation. *Social Research*, vol. 32, 239-55.

Brown, A and Remenyi, D. eds., (1994). *Proceedings of the First European Conference On IT Investment*. Birmingham: Operational Research Society.

Bowers, J. (1994): The Work to Make a Network Work: Studying CSCW in action. *Proceedings of CSCW'94, Chapel Hill, USA*. New York: ACM Press.

Bowers, J., Button, G., and Sharrock, W.W. (1994): *Networking Reprographic and FM Sites at Establishment Printers*. Consultation Document presented to Establishment Printers.

Bowers J., Button, G. and Sharrock, W.W. (1995): Workflow From Within and Without: Technology and Co-operative Work on the Print Industry Shopfloor. In *Proceedings of ECCSW'95*, Dordrecht: Kluwer Academic Publishers.

Orlikowski, W.J. (1992): Learning From Notes: Organisational Issues in Groupware Implementation. *Proceedings of CSCW'92, Toronto*. New York: ACM Press.

Rogers, Y. (1992): Ghosts in the Network: Distributed Troubleshooting in a Shared Working Environment. *Proceedings of CSCW'92, Toronto*. New York: ACM Press.

Scott, B. (1994): *Manufacturing Planning Systems*. London: McGraw-Hill Book Company.

Suchman, L. (1994): Do Categories Have Politics? The Language/Action Perspective Reconsidered. *Computer Supported Work (CSCW)*, vol. 2 no. 3.

Zuboff, S. (1984): *In The Age Of The Smart Machine: The Future of Work And Power*. New York: Basic Books.

Plans as Situated Action: An Activity Theory Approach to Workflow Systems

Jakob E. Bardram
Computer Science Department, Aarhus University and Kommunedata I/S,
Denmark.
bardram@daimi.aau.dk

Abstract: Within the community of CSCW the notion and nature of workflow systems as prescriptions of human work has been debated and criticised. Based on the work of Suchman (1987) the notion of situated action has often been viewed as opposed to planning work. Plans, however, *do* play an essential role in realising work. Based on experiences from designing a computer system that supports the collaboration within a hospital, this paper discusses how plans themselves are made out of situated action, and in return are realised *in situ*. Thus, work can be characterised as *situated planning*. This understanding is backed up by Activity Theory, which emphasises the connection between plans and the contextual conditions for realising these plans in actual work.

Introduction

The issue of workflow systems has been addressed by several authors as ways of routing information objects among users, and to specify automatic actions to be taken in that routing typically according to certain process models (Medina-Mora et al., 1992; Abbott and Sarin, 1994; Schäl, 1996). A process model is typically understood as a computerised (i.e. formal) representation of work procedures that controls the order in which a sequence of tasks are to be performed. These workflow systems for the coordination of activities in organisations have drawn much attention, but have been subject to much controversy and criticism for their rigid representation of work in process models (Suchman, 1994; Winograd, 1994; Bowers et al., 1995; Heath and Luff, 1996). The potential danger with current

17

J. Hughes et al. (eds.), Proceedings of the Fifth European Conference on Computer Supported Cooperative Work, 17-32.
© 1997 *Kluwer Academic Publishers.*

workflow systems is that their design is predictated entirely by formal procedures – ignoring (and even damaging) the informal practice (Symon et al., 1996).

Suchman (1987) shows the importance of differentiating between work and representations of work like plans and process models. Plans are representations of situated actions produced in the course of action and therefore they become resources for the work rather than they in any strong sense determine its course. Suchman emphasises action as essential situated and *ad hoc* improvisations, which consequently make plans rational anticipations, before the act, and *post hoc* reconstructions, afterward. The theoretical work on situated action, and the studies underlying it, seems to have attained so much attention that the importance of plans and protocols as guidance of work has been neglected. Recently, at the CSCW '96 conference in Boston, Suchman herself commented that an unfortunate, but typical, mis-reading of her work was that plans do not exist. Plans do exist and should be viewed as "an artifact of our *reasoning about* action, not ... the generative *mechanism* of action." (p. 39, emphasis in original).

Nevertheless, in medical work, *pre-hoc* representations of work like plans, checklists, schedules, protocols, work programmes etc. have proved extremely valuable as mechanisms giving order to work. Such plans support handling complex work situations, involving coordination and collaboration among several health professionals. For example, the patient's diagnosis and the associated treatment plan are essential coordination mechanisms, which convey information to the involved staff about the nature of the illness and how the treatment should proceed. Without this plan, extensive communication has to take place in order to inform all involved personnel about the patient, his illness and how the physician in charge intends to cure it. Thus, plans as pre-scriptions of activity are valuable, and indeed used, within organisations like hospitals to carry out work. This makes Schmidt and Simone (1996) raise the rhetoric question to Suchman of "What is it that makes plans such as production schedules, office procedures, classification schemes, etc. useful in the first place? What makes them 'resources'?" (p. 169).

These studies of work seem to leave us with what can be called the *planning paradox*: On the one hand, due to the contingencies of the concrete work situation work has an ad hoc nature. Plans are not the generative mechanisms of work, but are 'merely' used to reflect on work, before or after. On the other hand, we find that plans, as more or less formal representations, play a fundamental role in almost any organisation by giving order to work and thereby they effectively help getting the work done. Within a hospital context this tension between informal practice and formal procedures for work is also discussed by Symon et al. (1996):

> "[A]ny investigation of work coordination should look beyond formal procedures to consider contextual factors (i.e. factors that may give rise to informal practices), while *at the same time* taking into account the use and influence of formal procedures" (p. 3, emphasis in original).

This planning paradox is addressed in this paper. First, the theoretical understanding of human activity based on Activity Theory shows how a concept of planning does not necessarily mean total pre-handling and control of work, but can be achieved in the course of activity. The false dichotomy between plans and situated action is removed and it becomes possible to talk about, and thus support by computers, *situated planning*. This theoretical insight is then supported by empirical insight into the working of a Danish hospital by illustrating the important role, which planning plays within hospital work and how a computer system was designed to support planning without emphasising rigid matches between plans as representations of work and work itself. Finally, the paper concludes by arguing that a workflow system often exists in a tension between supporting a smooth flow of work within a work practice and the organisational needs for accounting for this work, and that this tension needs to be considered in design.

Activity Theory

Activity Theory originated in the former Soviet Union as part of the cultural-historical school of psychology founded by Vygotskij, Leontjev and Lurija. The theory is a philosophical framework for studying different forms of human praxis as developmental processes, with both the individual and social level interlinked. Within the HCI community, Activity Theory has recently attained increased attention (Bødker, 1991; Nardi, 1996) and has been proposed as a basis for CSCW research too (Kuutti, 1991). Here I will focus on certain core concepts of the theory, which are fundamental in understanding the role of technology and human activity as guided by plans. The following is based on the writing of Vygotskij (1978), Leontjev (1978; 1981), and Anokhin (1973; 1976).

   The fundamental unit of analysis is the *human activity* which has three basic characteristics; firstly, it is directed towards a material or ideal *object* which distinguishes one activity from another; secondly, it is *mediated* by artifacts (tools, language, etc.); and thirdly, it is social within a *culture*. In this way, computer artifacts, like all other artifacts, mediate human activity within a practice. By acting in the world, human beings meet the objective world, which is experienced through the activity. Thus, human knowledge about the world is *reflection* obtained through activity, constituting the basis for expectations, and desires about activities in this world. This describes the basic dialectical relationship between the human being and the world, the subject and the object.

The Structure and Development of Human Activity

Human activity can be described as a hierarchy with three levels: *activities* realised through chains of *actions*, which are carried out through *operations*. Human activity is always directed toward a material or ideal object satisfying a need and the subject's reflection of, and expectation to, this object characterises the *motive* of the activity.

Human activity is carried out through actions, realising objective *results*. These actions are controlled by the subject's conscious *goals*, which are the anticipation of the future results of the action. The activity exists only as one or more actions but the activity and the action are not identical and cannot be reduced to each other. For example, for a physician the activity of diagnosing a patient can be realised in several ways. He can trust the diagnosis stated by the general practitioner on the referral papers. Or he can establish his own diagnosis by obtaining the necessary clinical data, like blood sugar level, X-ray pictures, etc, using the service departments at the hospital. Or he can use a computer-based patient record system to see if such data are already available. These are different actions, mediated by different tools, which all realise the activity of diagnosing the patient. On the other hand, the same action can be a part of realising different activities: The action of requesting an X-ray examination at the radiology department can be part of the diagnosing activity or it can be part of preparing for surgery, thus realising a total different activity. Furthermore, actions are usually *polymotivated*; two or more activities can temporarily merge, motivating the same action, if the goal is part of reaching the motives of several involved activities simultaneously.

Even though the goal of the action can be represented in the human mind independently of the situation in which it has to take place, the practical process of realising the action cannot be detached from the conditions of the concrete situation. Therefore, actions are realised through a series of operations; each accommodated to the concrete physical *conditions* of the action. While the analytical level of actions describes the intention of an activity – what results should be obtained – operations describe the operational level – how the action is realised, adjusted to the actual material conditions of the action. For example, the way the phone is used to order an X-ray examination depends entirely on how the phone works, the phone number of the radiology department, the physical surroundings of the phone, etc. Operations are performed without thinking consciously but are oriented in the world by a non-conscious *orienting basis* of the operation. This orienting basis is established through experience with the concrete material conditions for the operation, and is a system of expectations about the execution of each operation controlling the operation, in the process of the activity. Again, the action and the operations realising the action are not identical and cannot be reduced to each other: an operation can be part of several actions (together with other operations) and the same action can be realised through different operations.

Planning Recurrent Actions through Anticipatory Reflection

At all three levels the human activity is guided by anticipation. This anticipation is the motive of the activity, the goal of the action and the orienting basis of the operation, respectively. The anticipation of future events is the fundamental principle of *anticipatory reflection* as developed by Anokhin. The classical example of anticipatory reflection is Anokhin's rethinking of Pavlov's discovery of the conditioned reflex: When a dog salivates in response to the ringing of a bell, it is not because saliva is needed to digest the bell but because the dog anticipates food to appear *in the future* which has to be digested. The anticipatory reflection guides the activity by making an *afferent synthesis* between a *perception* of the environmental state of the activity, and *memory* (i.e. the cumulated experience of the person). This afferent synthesis forms an anticipation of the future state as a result of the activity about to be performed. When the activity is performed there is a feedback mechanism which compares the result of the activity with the prediction, and any incongruence (i.e. a breakdown) gives rise to a learning situation (i.e. the experience of the person is expanded). This model of anticipatory reflection based on the afferent synthesis between perception and memory is a general model for all levels of the activity.

The basic principle that makes the anticipatory reflection possible is the recognition of *recurrent structures* in the world. The existing of all living beings and their reflection of recurrent structures, which repeat themselves over time, is the indispensable prerequisite for prediction. Pavlov's experiments also illustrate this because the response is mutually correlated with the amount of training sessions.

Artifacts as Mediators and Crystallisation of Work

Describing human activity as actions realised through operations helps to understand the fundamental role, which plans play in human cognition and activity. Based on prior experience the plan anticipates future results of the actions realising the activity, but these plans, or anticipations, have to be implemented through operations which are adjusted to the material conditions of the situation. The afferent synthesis explains how human activity indeed is planned, i.e. anticipated, and at the same time situated, i.e. contextual.

Now one could ask what plans, as cognitive constructs have to do with material artifacts like checklists, production lists and workflow systems? However, within the cultural-historical school there is no such differentiation between ideal (i.e. cognitive) and material artifacts: plans as artifacts are used to mediate activity regardless of whether they exist on e.g. paper or are memorised. Human work is characterised by the collaborative production of artifacts; each made with the purpose of mediating a certain activity. The mediating characteristics of an activity is therefore *crystallised* (or objectified) (Bærentsen, 1989) into these artifacts, and through use, the artifacts are continuously modified and shaped to meet the evolving human needs. For example, the radiology order form used at AAS is a product of years of experience in ordering X-ray examinations, containing fields that prompt for certain important information. Therefore, the cognitive plans and their material counterpart are mere reflections of each other because they are both resources for, and products of, human activity.

The SAIK project: Developing Computer Support for Clinical Work

The SAIK[1] project was launched as the experimental part of redesigning a national-wide mainframe-based Hospital Information System. The aim was to investigate the coordination and planning of patient care within hospitals and based on these investigations to develop a prototype – called the PATIENT SCHEDULER – illustrating how coordination of patient care within hospitals can be supported by computer technology.

This participatory design process took a 24-bed specialised medical (endocrinological) ward as point of departure for investigating the work and collaboration among departments within the hospital for the County of Aarhus (AAS). Typical patients at the ward are diabetics or elderly patients with osteoarthritis. AAS is a middle size Danish hospital with 1700 employees and 370 beds. It has 7 medical and surgical specialised departments, each with 2 - 4 wards, several out-patients' clinics, and several service departments – e.g. radiology, laboratory, and pathology. Historically, Danish hospitals, including AAS, have become increasingly specialised and centralised (Vallgårda, 1992). This has resulted in large hospitals with a large number of specialised departments. Because of this specialised nature of medical work, collaboration across departmental and professional borders is patient treatment and care *per se*, making the hospital an excellent place for investigating issues in computer support for people cooperation closely. For example, the daily treatment of all patients admitted to the ward is based on data from e.g. blood tests and X-ray pictures, which involves frequent communication and coordination with the laboratory and radiology departments, respectively.

A fundamental statement within the participatory design tradition is that a profound understanding of the users' work practice is a pre-condition for designing computer support. This understanding of the work at AAS was done as workplace studies based on qualitative methods such as qualitative interviews; workshops; participative observations of daily work at the ward and service departments, meetings and conferences; and studies of different documents, records and other tools. Based on this understanding the PATIENT SCHEDULER was developed and used for further participatory design sessions at AAS. The PATIENT SCHEDULER aims at providing flexible support for requesting, booking and scheduling examinations, tests, etc. on different departments within the hospital.

---

[1] SAIK is a Danish abbreviation for "Collaborative Informatics in Clinical Practice"

Planning as a Central Activity of Clinical Work

Treatment of patients within a hospital can clearly be characterised as specialised and informal skills that have to take the contingencies of the concrete situation into account. Nevertheless, clinical work is subject to a large degree of planning and plans play a central role in guiding and recording work at a hospital. Let us consider three examples from the hospital: A central planning tool widely used within medical work is **protocols of treatment**, or Standard Operating Procedures (Strauss et al., 1985), which prescribe a standard treatment for a standard disease for a standard patient. Such protocols are developed by the clinical team who uses them, and they are supported by general policies and guidelines of use. A central part of such a protocol is often the **unravelling program**, which prescribes which initial examinations and tests should be ordered to state a precise diagnosis. Hence, the unravelling program provides a plan for obtaining the necessary clinical data for further treatment. Another planning tool applied at the ward is the **24-hour-care plan** made every afternoon by the nurses on duty. This plan describes the care of each patient within the next 24 hours and functions as a "boundary object" (Star, 1989) by carrying information between three working shifts in a standardised way. This plan is made according to the overall plan of treatment (the protocol) by taking into consideration the patient's condition in the concrete situation. By analysing the use of these planning tools from an Activity Theory perspective on CSCW, the following characteristics of plans emerged:

Plans as Socially Constructed and Used Artifacts

Documents used in daily work are *socially constructed* in and through the intersubjective understanding and use of members in a community. A document is not 'just' a document, but a certain document like the medical record (Hughes and King, 1993). Thus a certain document (record) is an artifact reflecting certain work activities and the socially defined purpose of these activities. For example, all departments within the hospital, like the medical, surgical and anaesthetic departments, have their own patient files and records, made to suit their special activities and needs. Similarly, plans are socially used and constructed as part of the ongoing work activities at the hospital. The production of the different unravelling plans used at the ward is an on-going activity closely connected to the treatment of patients. Thus, these plans are crystallisations of a historically developed sociocultural knowledge of how to treat different kinds of diseases and patients. An implication of this is that plans and protocols change over time, and thus have a historicity. At the ward this is most evident in the continuous making of 24-hour-care plans by the nurses, but also unravelling plans and medical protocols for treatment of patients are changed to reflect the results of the latest research within the international medical community.

The Difference between the Plan and the Instantiation of the Plan

There is a fundamental distinction between a plan and an *instantiation* of the plan, i.e. the actual performance based on the plan. Building on prior experience, plans become resources, detached from the concrete and situated real-world activities, which later might implement and carry out the plan. The strength of the plan is the anticipation of future ways of performing activities, detached from, but still taking into account, the conditions of the real-world settings. When applying a plan to a concrete problem, the situated actions performed in the activity often mirror the plan, but are adjusted to the concrete details and conditions of the context. For example, the unravelling plan for an osteoarthritis patient might state that an X-ray image of the hip is necessary. But when applying the plan to Mr. Jones, who doesn't have any problems with his hips, this part of the plan may be skipped – and other examinations, like a blood test, might be added to Mr. Jones' unravelling plan. Thus instantiations of plans have *fuzzy boundaries*. When applying an unravelling plan at AAS, the actual use is reflected in the patient's *examination card* that contains an overview of all examinations ordered or performed. Hence, the unravelling plan reflects the plan and the examination card reflects the instantiation of the plan.

Plans as Means of Dividing Work

Plans are used to organise the work, and when several people are involved in this work, the plan reflects the responsibility of the involved actors. Even if the plan does not contain a formal description of who is doing which part of the plan, this responsibility either refers to the wider organisational division of work or is clarified when the plan is instantiated. The nurses' 24-hour-care plan, for example, is divided into sections that reveal the care to be undertaken by each workshift, thus explicitly reflecting the responsibility of each shift. On the other hand, when a medical protocol states that the temperature of a patient has to be measured twice a day, the protocol does not explicitly state who should do this, because this is the job of the nurse in charge of the particular patient within the particular workshift.

Plans as Status Overviews

As a result of carrying a division of labour, a plan works as a *status overview*, like a checklist, revealing the state of the work according to the prescribed plan. The characteristic of checking off items on a checklist becomes essential when several interdependent actors work together using plans to coordinate work. The 24-hour nursing plan helps coordinate the work across working shifts because the different tasks listed in it are marked done when performed. Similarly, the examination card reflects the status of the unravelling programme of a patient, containing information on the status of each test, whether they are prescribed, ordered, or carried out.

Plans as Records

Often when plans are used in work settings, like a hospital, the interesting issue is not to follow the plan but the *deviation* from the plan. Deviating from a plan is a breakdown and therefore a potential learning situation. This fact is well recognised within medical work, where the use of problem-oriented records is becoming more widespread. Problem-oriented records are based on general medical protocols for treatment of a disease, like diabetes or appendicitis, and when a patient is treated, only deviations from this protocol are recorded. This makes problem-oriented records very powerful tools, because they contain only potential learning material compared to the standard protocol and, at the same time, they are extremely effective in both production and use.

The PATIENT SCHEDULER

The PATIENT SCHEDULER is based on requesting, booking and scheduling services, like examinations, tests, etc. as *patient appointments* (see Figure 1). These appointments involve different *resources* within the hospital like equipment, examination rooms, physicians and patients. These resources belong to different organisational units, like the service department or the requesting ward. In principle, anything can be named a resource. In contrast to traditional booking and calendar systems supporting the task of scheduling within the service department, the prototype aims to facilitate a more direct collaboration between the employees at the different wards and service departments. Based on the analysis of the work practices at the ward and service departments, support for collaboration in the PATIENT SCHEDULER has been divided into three areas: communication, sharing and planning:

Communication: A request for a patient appointment can be sent to another department, team, or whichever organisational unit set up to receive appointments at the hospital. When received, appointments can be sorted into different intrays (both manually and automatic) and scheduled according to different *resource calendars*. The status (requested, scheduled, performed, halted, etc.) of each appointment is generally accessible for inspection.

Planning: When requesting future examinations of a patient a *deadline* can be added to the request, indicating the latest acceptable time for examination. If the service department cannot comply with this deadline, a message can automatically be routed back to the sender on his request. Furthermore, the tool supports the creation of an *examination programme* (see Figure 1) consisting of several *templates* for patient appointments. Such a programme could be an unravelling programme and can be built up in the process of using the PATIENT SCHEDULER. A patient appointment can at any time be made into a template and added to a programme. These programmes and templates are in return available for use within the department (organisational unit) and can be instantiated on a particular patient.

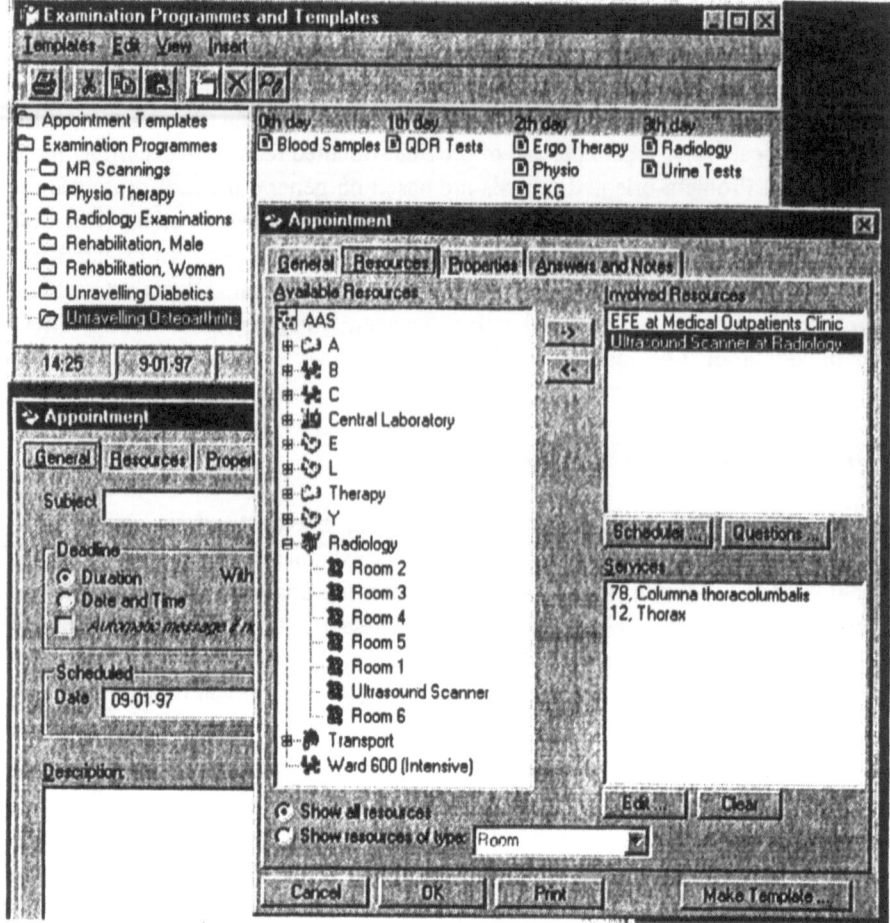

Figure 1: The Examination Programmes and an Appointment involving several resources.

When instantiating a template or a programme the user can modify the resulting appointment(s) before sending it (them) to a recipient. Unnecessary appointments, e.g. the hip examination, can be skipped if desired.

Sharing: The *sharing mechanism* makes the scheduled appointments accessible within the hospital. By looking into this shared pool of appointments, the PATIENT SCHEDULER can generate different *comprehensive views* on patient appointments – e.g. a view on appointments involving a certain department, ward or physician; day calendars showing appointment 'with the CT-scanner'; and, most important, a *shared calendar for each patient* at the hospital. This shared patient calendar gives an overview of the status of the patient's trajectory and enables the users to schedule the treatment of the patient according to the patient's other appointments. The different service departments, like radiology, can share (part of) their resource calendars, hence enabling other departments to *directly book* trivial examinations that need no approval from a radiologist. This opens up for considerable time-saving in the daily routine examinations. Finally, appointment templates and examination programmes can be shared enabling e.g. the ward to use templates and programmes made at the radiology department.

Rethinking Workflow as Situated Planning

A typical workflow system helps to define, execute, coordinate and monitor the flow of work within an organisation. In order to do this a workflow system must contain a computerised representation of the structure of the work procedures and activities. Such a computerised representation has often been a sequential or hierarchical decomposition of an activity into tasks and are built separate to the execution of the activity. As stated by Schäl (1996):

"Workflow management technology is composed of a workflow modelling component and a workflow execution component. The workflow modelling component enables administrators, users and organisational analysts to define working processes, so that processes and activities are defined, analysed, simulated and allocated to people (roles)" (p. 90)

These computerised representations cannot take into account unforeseen events and breakdowns. The decomposition into tasks builds on several assumptions concerning the conditions of future work and the typical problems with a workflow system arise when these assumptions break down. Hence, exception handling has attained considerable attraction within workflow management technologies, and questions on how to handle unforeseen situations and how to 'design for unanticipated use' are often raised. The central point of this paper, however, emphasises that breakdown situations are *not* exceptions from work activities but are a natural and very important part of any activity which forms the basis for learning and thus for developing and enhancing plans for future action. When synthesised with the current conditions, the plan is a central resource in the realisation of any activity and is subsequently enhanced based on the experience obtained during this activity. Of course, it is important to consider exactly who is allowed to use, alter and save plans within a work practice, but this is a question of division of work and corresponding access rights within the computer system – not a separation of the planning and execution of work.

A New Understanding of Plans Based on Activity Theory

Based on Activity Theory a plan can be defined as *a cognitive or material artifact which supports the anticipatory reflection of future goals for actions, based on experience about recurrent structures in life.* As an artifact, the plan is socially constructed, is eventually crystallised into a material form, is shared among the actors in the work practice, is used to mediate work, and constitute a central part of the organisation's material conditions for work. A plan is a series of expectations to future results under certain conditions and the execution becomes an afferent synthesis between the plan and the conditions of the concrete situation. The fundamental feedback loop in the course of an activity forms the basis for a learning process embedded in the activity. This learning process creates and enhances the plan, which was originally the guiding principle for the activity.

Characteristics of Computer Tools Supporting Planning

According to the above understanding of planning as a central part of human activity, a major challenge for planning tools is to support the anticipation of recurrent events in working life and in turn to use this anticipation in the course of work. Based on this conceptualisation of human activity some characteristics of computer support for planning can be drawn from our analysis of medical work and from designing the PATIENT SCHEDULER. These characteristics can be read as guidelines for design.

Producing and Altering Plans in the Course of Work

The experience of using a plan to guide an activity under certain conditions is obtained during the activity itself. So, in order for plans to become resources for the future realisation of an activity, the plan should be made as part of this activity – *situated planning*. Thus, it is important that the planning tool allows for the ongoing creation and modification of a plan based on obtained experience in realising the plan. The PATIENT SCHEDULER supports this in a simple way by allowing any appointment, expected to be used in the future, to be transformed into a template and added to an examination programme. These examination programmes can in turn be modified by sharing, moving and copying templates within and between programmes.

Sharing Plans Within a Work Practice

The use of the 24-hour-care plan at the ward illustrates how central the sharing of plans are, when they are used as coordination mechanisms among several actors involved in an activity. When all involved personnel has access to use the shared plan, the need for communication is considerably reduced. This enables the involved actors to act as a collective subject with a common motive. In the PATIENT SCHEDULER the underlying access mechanism controls who has access to plans enabling plans to be shared among employees and/or departments at the hospital.

Executing Plans According to the Conditions of the Work

The difference between plans as anticipated results of actions and the realisation of these actions as operations according to the conditions of the situation should be considered when designing a planning tool. Because anticipation will always be imperfect any instantiation of a plan should be malleable. For example, in the PATIENT SCHEDULER every appointment made on the basis of an examination programme can be altered or skipped according to the need of the user.

Inspecting Plans and their Potential Outcome

First of all, an overview of the available planning artifacts within a work practice is clearly a prerequisite for using plans in the first place. The PATIENT SCHEDULER supports this in the 'examination programme window' (Figure 1). Secondly, to avoid pure trial-and-error use of plans, the tool must reveal the *potential outcome* from applying a particular plan. This can be accomplished in many ways. In the PATIENT SCHEDULER, the appointment templates within a programme are listed according to a time axis, revealing, in a rudimentary fashion, the temporal order of the resulting appointments from applying the plan. As discussed at AAS, another way of revealing the result of instantiating a plan, is a simulation mechanism: being able to simulate the plan and alter the resulting scheduling of patient appointment, before 'letting them loose' within the hospital. This simulation part of the prototype has not yet been implemented. Finally, the overview of plans should reveal the condition under which the plan is useful and helps establish whether some concrete conditions match the conditions of the plan. This is supported in a very rudimentary way in the PATIENT SCHEDULER, where an examination programme contains a textual description of the premises of the plan, leaving it to the user to establish the connection between this description and his current conditions.

Monitoring the Execution of Plans

Having an overview of the unfolding of activities is essential to all work. However, when the work is initiated on the basis of a plan, it becomes important to monitor the progress in work *according to the plan*. Thus, recognising any *deviation* from the plan is particularly important and should be supported by the planning tool. This monitoring of any deviation from a plan also encompasses any initial deviation when instantiating the plan, as emphasised in the above guideline. This part has not yet been implemented in the PATIENT SCHEDULER. When the user has instantiated an examination programme the resulting appointments cannot be traced backward to the original programme. This functionality, however, was raised and discussed as a central requirement during several prototyping sessions.

Conclusion: Plans as Situated Actions or Technologies of Accountability

This paper has re-entered into the discussion on how to support ways of planning and prescribing work by providing a new conceptualisation of the role of plans and prescriptions in work activities. By analysing the work within a hospital and designing computer support for planning work, it was illustrated that planning is not to be viewed as opposed to work *in situ*. Plans as chains of anticipated goals, are a central part of human activity, but are realised accommodated to the contextual conditions. The core point is to recognise the function of plans as ways of anticipating and pre-handling events in (working) life based on their recurrent nature, and be able to save and later reuse the experience obtained in handling these events. Winograd and Flores (1986) make the same argument by showing how many patterns of action within organisations are designed to anticipate and cope with such recurrent structures. This is especially evident within a hospital; plans for handling all kinds of recurrent events, from receiving injured people involved in car accidents to ordering food for patients at the ward daily, have been made and constitute the operational backbone of the hospital. This understanding of plans as central assets in work has some implication for the issue of workflow systems: instead of supporting routing information around in organisations according to a workflow process model, the computer should be a tool mediating the anticipatory reflection of recurrent events in working life. Hence, such a planning tool should support *situated planning* – building, altering, sharing, executing, and monitoring plans within the cooperative work activities.

Based on this conceptualisation it becomes possible to make a planning tool that does not emphasise a rigid match between process models and work. However, it is central to understand why such formal process models are made and embedded in workflow systems in the first place. Often – e.g. in the area of Business Process Reengineering – workflow systems are viewed as the 'enabling technologies' for turning the modern firm into a process organisation with greater opportunities for efficiency and cost reduction (see e.g. Abbott and Sarin, 1994). Thus, workflow systems are conceived as organisational infrastructure used and designed for meeting organisational goals (e.g. customer satisfaction) (Schäl, 1996). When viewed from this overall organisational perspective, workflow systems are often used to keep track of the work according to these organisational goals. This means that a workflow system is not just mediating the workflow (which has been the premise for this paper so far), but is used for additional managerial purposes. Hence, the workflow system becomes a 'technology of accountability' as defined by Suchman (1994):

> "By technologies of accountability I mean systems aimed at the inscription and documentation of actions to which parties are accountable [...] in the sense represented by the bookkeeper's ledger, the record of accounts paid and those still outstanding" (p. 188).

In this sense the actions realised by the workflow system are *polymotivated*. On the one hand, the system is used to give order to the unfolding of work within the organisation by making some top-down decomposition of the organisational goals into work processes. On the other hand, the system is a 'technology of accountability' by recording the progress of work according to such process models.

The idea of many workflow systems is to consider this polymotivated nature of organisational work and try to integrate (at least) these two motives within the organisation in one system. Unfortunately, this often ends up in having the organisational and administrative activities setting the agenda for the work activities. For example, Bowers et al., (1995) describe a workflow system that embeds the motive of management of keeping track of print-work at the expense of the motive of the employees at the shopfloor of 'maintaining a smooth flow of work'. Similarly, Heath and Luff (1996), reporting from a case study in the Healthcare sector in the UK, illustrate how a workflow system is designed to satisfy the motive of the pharmaceutical firms to record the amount of used medication, at the expense of the motive of the medical practitioners to structure their medical record according to 'descriptive economies'.

The point to be emphasised here is that such problems with existing workflow systems should not be understood merely as conflicting motives and goals within the organisation which could easily end up in a conclusion saying that either you design for accountability or you design for work support. It is important to recognise that an organisation, like a hospital, is not merely 'getting the work done', e.g. curing patients, but is doing this work in a visible, inspectable, documentable and accountable way (Bowers et al., 1995). An organisation is not only engaged in the activity of producing a product, or curing patients. An organisation has to be viewed as a collection of multiple activities, each realising different needs. Some of these activities are directed toward the 'object' of the organisation, like curing patients, and others are directed toward an organisational accountability of work. From an Activity Theory perspective this means that the polymotivated nature of actions involved in a plan should be considered so that motives of all involved actors, responsible for different areas of the work within the organisation, are recognised – and satisfied if possible.

Acknowledgements

Thanks to the employees at AAS and to Trine Grundahl with whom the workplace studies were done and discussed.

References

Abbott, K., and Sarin, S. (1994): "Experiences with workflow management: Issues for the next generation", In *Proceedings of the Conference on CSCW, Chapel Hill, USA*. ACM, p. 113-120.

Anokhin, P. K. (1973): "The forming of natural and artificial intelligence", *Impact of Science on Society* XXIII (3).

Anokhin, P. K. (1976): "The Philosophical Importance of the Problem of Natural and Artificial Intellects", *Soviet Studies in Philosophy* XIV (4), p. 3-27.

Bærentsen, K. (1989): "Mennesker og Maskine [Man and Machine]", In Hedegaard, Hansen, and Thyssen (eds.): *Et virksomt liv [An active life]*. Aarhus: Aarhus Universitets Forlag, p. 142-187.

Bødker, S. (1991): *Through the Interface: A Human Activity Approach to User Interface Design*. Hillsdale, NJ: LEA.

Bowers, J., Button, G., and Sharrock, W. (1995): "Workflow from within and without: Technology and Cooperative Work on the Print Industry Shopfloor", In *Proceedings of the Fourth European Conference on CSCW, Stockholm, Sweden.* Kluwer Academic Publishers, p. 51-66.

Heath, C. and Luff, P. (1996): "Documents and Professional Practice: 'bad' organisational reasons for 'good' clinical records", In *Proceedings of the Conference on CSCW, Boston, Massachusetts USA.* ACM, p. 354-363.

Hughes, J. and King, V. (1993): "Paperwork", In S. Benford and J. Mariani (Eds.): *COMIC D4.1: Requirements and Metaphors of Shared Interaction,* Lancaster: Lancaster University.

Kuutti, K. (1991): "The concept of activity as a basic unit of analysis for CSCW research", In *Proceedings of the Second European Conference on CSCW, Amsterdam.* Kluwer Academic Publisher, p. 249-264.

Leontjev, A. (1978): *Activity, Consciousness, and Personality,* Englewood Cliffs NJ: Prentice-Hall.

Leontjev, A. (1981): *Problems of the Development of Mind.* Moscow: Progress Publishers.

Medina-Mora, R., Winograd, T., Flores, R. and Flores, F. (1992): "The action workflow approach to workflow management", In *Proceedings of the Conference on CSCW, Toronto, Canada.* ACM, p. 281-288.

Nardi, B. A., (ed.) (1996): *Context and Consciousness: Activity Theory and Human-Computer Interaction.* Cambrigde, MA: MIT Press.

Schäl, T. (1996): *Workflow Management Systems for Process Organisations.* Berlin: Springer Verlag.

Schmidt, K. and Simone, C. (1996): "Coordination mechanisms: Towards a Conceptual Foundation of CSCW Systems Design", *Computer Supported Cooperative Work* 5, p. 155-200.

Star, S. L. (1989): "The Structure of Ill-Structured Solutions: Boundary Objects and Heterogeneous Distributed Problem Solving", In L. Gasser and M. Huhns (Eds.): *Distributed Artificial Intelligence,* London: Pitman, p. 37-54.

Strauss, A., Fagerhaugh, S., Suczek, B. and Wiener, C. (1985): *Social Organization of Medical Work.* Chicago and London: University of Chicago Press.

Suchman, L. (1987): *Plans and situated actions. The problem of human-machine communication.* Cambridge: Cambridge University Press.

Suchman, L. (1994): "Do categories have politics? The language/action perspective reconsidered", *Computer Supported Cooperative Work* 2 (3), p. 177-190.

Symon, G., Long, K., and Ellis, J. (1996): "The Coordination of Work Activities: Cooperation and Conflict in a Hospital Context", *Computer Supported Cooperative Work* 5, p. 1-31.

Vallgårda, S. (1992): *Sygehuse og sygehuspolitik i Danmark: Et bidrag til det specialiserede sygehusvæsens historie 1930-1987. [Hospitals and hospital politics in Denmark: A contribution to the history of the specialised hospital sector 1930-1987].* København: Jurist- og Økonomforbundets Forlag.

Vygotskij, L. S. (1978): *Mind and Society.* Cambrigde, MA: Harvard University Press.

Winograd, T. (1994): "Categories, diciplines and social coordination", *Computer Supported Cooperative Work* 2 (3), p. 177-190.

Winograd, T. and Flores, F. (1986): *Understanding Computers and Cognition: A New Foundation for Design.* Norwood, New Jersey: Ablex Publishing Corp.

Rethinking CSCW systems: the architecture of MILANO

Alessandra Agostini, Giorgio De Michelis
Cooperation Technologies Laboratory, DSI - University of Milano, Italy
{agostini, gdemich}@dsi.unimi.it

Maria Antonietta Grasso
Rank Xerox Research Centre, Grenoble Laboratory, France
Antonietta.Grasso@Grenoble.RXRC.Xerox.com

Abstract: After eleven years, CSCW is a well recognized research field which has generated, among other things, some new theoretical findings on work practices and cooperation and some new systems that are successfully applied by several organizations. The evaluation of successful applications from the point of view of the above recalled CSCW theories indicates some requirements (openness, continuity, contextualization and language-action integration) that the new generation of CSCW systems should satisfy. The prototype of the MILANO system is a working example of how those requirements can be met and of the challenges a full development of the CSCW potential poses to system designers and developers.

Introduction

Over the eleven years since the first CSCW Conference in Austin Texas, the CSCW field has grown and matured in America, Asia and Europe without having lost its primary characteristics: that of being an interdisciplinary research field involving people from both computer and human sciences.

Two facts have occurred during these eleven years that deserve attention:

1. while many failure cases have been reported and discussed in the literature (Grudin, 1988), some CSCW platforms, offering to its users a well equipped workspace, have been successfully applied and they are currently having a large diffusion in the market (the most relevant example is LOTUS NOTES,

33

J. Hughes et al. (eds.), Proceedings of the Fifth European Conference on Computer Supported Cooperative Work, 33-48.
© 1997 *Kluwer Academic Publishers.*

followed by LINKWORKS and other Workflow Management Systems): we have therefore real feedback from users (Orlikowski, 1992; Bowers, 1994; Rogers, 1994; Rouncefield et al., 1994; Bowers et al., 1995; Ciborra, 1996; Prinz & Kolvenbach, 1996; Whittaker 1996);

2. it is becoming ever clearer to CSCW practitioners and designers that new CSCW systems should reflect the understanding of work practices developed over these years by anthropologists, organizational theorists and social scientists (Winograd & Flores, 1986; Swenson et al., 1994; De Michelis & Grasso, 1994; Bogia & Kaplan, 1995; Dourish et al., 1996).

In the process of developing new CSCW systems or prototypes, therefore, the crucial step is not testing a new cooperative application in some (semi)-real experimental work setting, but designing it so that it overcomes the limitations and drawbacks of existing CSCW platforms emerging from the analysis of their applications. From this point of view, it is crucial to analyze the existing platforms (in particular the successful ones, because their limitations are better distinguishable as the users do not express them through a radical refusal of the whole platform) in order to understand the new requirements to be met by the system to be designed.

In this paper we present the rationale and architecture of the new CSCW system prototype we have developed at the Cooperation Technologies Laboratory of the University of Milano, called exactly MILANO, in the context of a general discussion of the requirements a new generation of CSCW platforms should satisfy. Our point of view is rather general and can be considered our synthesis of the understanding we get through CSCW theoretical work (mainly the ethnographic and sociological research) of some successful applications of two CSCW systems - LOTUS NOTES, the only CSCW system with a massive worldwide diffusion (Ciborra, 1996; Whittaker, 1996), and LINKWORKS, whose application at a German Ministry is a surprising success (Prinz & Kolvenbach, 1996). Our choice has also been influenced by the fact that both systems are generic platforms (integrating various CSCW and traditional applications) for supporting work processes, like MILANO.

The theoretical perspective from which we observe work practices can be considered a situated language/action perspective, since it merges the situated action approach (Suchman, 1987; Lave & Wenger, 1991; Brown & Duguid, 1991) with the language/action perspective (Winograd & Flores, 1986). Work practices have the shape of cooperative processes, where people act and interact in order to do the required performance. Cooperative processes are performed by groups of people (communities) who share an experience of action, communication and learning. The community performing a cooperative process is a social aggregate constituted by all the people participating in it (both performers and customers); it is not a well defined organizational structure. The reader may look at (De Michelis, 1995, 1996, 1997) for further details on our theoretical approach to cooperative processes.

From the above perspective we synthesize the evaluations of some real cases of successful application of LOTUS NOTES reported in the literature (Ciborra, 1996;

Whittaker, 1996) and of the already mentioned application of LINKWORKS at a German Ministry (Prinz & Kolvenbach, 1996).

Based on the above analysis, we have defined four general requirements - openness, multimedia continuity, contextualization and integration of communication and action - new CSCW systems should meet as completely as possible, since their limited satisfaction in the above systems are responsible for both the success and limitations of the above cases. We have complemented them with a fifth requirement - personalized and selective workspace interfaces - that is not emerging from the above cases, but that we think will be increasingly more relevant as, and if, CSCW systems shape the workspaces of their users.

In this paper, after the discussion of the above requirements, we present the architecture of MILANO and its most relevant features. The conclusion is devoted to the discussion of some open problems and of our future research directions.

Some Requirements for a New Generation of CSCW Systems

As anticipated in the previous section, some general findings about CSCW systems, the analysis of some successful applications of LOTUS NOTES and of LINKWORKS and their conceptualization within the cooperative process theoretical perspective have led us to define four requirements for a new generation of CSCW systems. The presentation of the four requirements that follows is rather short and general: the references to the literature allow the reader to deepen her understanding of each.

Openness

Membership in a community is intrinsic and in many senses dynamic (Beck & Bellotti, 1993; Whittaker, 1996).

On the one hand, during the time interval within which a cooperative process is performed some members leave it while some new members join it. On the other, different members have different levels of engagement in it at different moments; finally, others participate in it occasionally. There is therefore a continuous movement between central and peripheral participation (Lave & Wenger, 1991) in the cooperative process.

The CSCW system supporting a cooperative process should adapt itself to current membership with the maximum degree of plasticity in order to avoid constraining the behavior of the community members. In order to do so, it should first and foremost be able to support the interaction between those having it and those not having it. LOTUS NOTES is going in this direction with its INTERNOTES module.

Multimedia Continuity

Communities performing a cooperative process are distributed in space and time. Their members communicate through different media not only because at any moment one of them can use only some media, but also because she needs to choose the best available medium for the communication she needs to do. They need therefore to be supported by a system not only making available a large set of communication media, but also allowing them to switch almost continuously from one medium to another so that they can choose at any time and in any situation the best available medium (Reder & Schwab, 1990; Whittaker, 1996; G. Patriotta in (Ciborra, 1996)). The application of LINKWORKS at the German Ministry has widely extended it in this direction (Prinz & Kolvenbach, 1996).

Contextualization

A cooperative process is a history of mutually related communication and action events. Any communication (action) event logically follows some communication and/or action events, except for the event starting a new cooperative process; and it triggers other communication and/or action events. The ordering among the events of a cooperative process therefore selects within the temporal evolution of the events the links defining a dependence relation. Thus the context of a cooperative process is mirrored by the partial order of communication and action events representing its history. The actors of a cooperative process are immersed in its history and need to refer to a representation of it in order to act effectively (Orlikowski, 1992; Prinz & Kolvenbach, 1996; Whittaker, 1996; W. Orlikowski in (Ciborra, 1996)). Sometimes they need the context to be transparent, other times visible (Agostini et al., 1996). LOTUS NOTES supports partially contextualization through the possibility of attaching a conversation to a document, while LINKWORKS offers a greater assistance with its capability to create a folder for any cooperative process where the documents created during its execution are stored and mutually linked.

Integration between Communication Flow and Action Flow

Within a cooperative process people communicate and act. Both communication and action flows define the basic units of cooperative work: respectively, conversations and workflows.

On the one hand, within the communication flow of a cooperative process we can observe various distinct conversations; i.e., various partial orders of mutually related communication events (Bullen & Bennett, 1990). On the other, within the action flow of a cooperative process we can distinguish various types of structures of mutually related action events:

- partial orders of actions performed in agreement with a plan designed outside the process (let us call it a procedure);
- partial orders of actions performed in agreement with a plan designed inside the process (project);
- partial orders of actions created step by step (evolutionary workflow).

Plans for both projects and procedures are resources for actions (Suchman, 1987): they must be simple, open to exceptional paths and/or to changes (Abbott & Sarin, 1994; Swenson et al. 1994, Dourish et al., 1996; Ellis et al., 1995).

Communication events and action events (and, therefore, conversations and workflows) are mutually related since actions are agreed, delivered and declared (un)successful within conversations, whereas conversations can be generated (as a reaction to a breakdown) while performing an activity. A CSCW system supporting a cooperative process should provide its users a support to both conversations and workflows and to their integration. Both LOTUS NOTES and LINKWORKS are partially meeting the above requirement since they allow users to create conversations within workflows but not vice versa.

Personalized and Selective Workspace

Many intensive users of workstations experience problems managing the objects they have created, received and/or manipulated in their workspaces. In order to give order to them, they continuously create new folders, folders of folders, and so on. Names of objects and/or folders become important for retrieving them; after a while previous names of folders and/or objects lose meaning, and finding things needed becomes increasingly more difficult. The situation becomes more difficult if and when the workspace is populated also by objects the user shares with other people - as in the case of CSCW systems - giving the user the impression that the situation is beyond her control. The user has, in fact, to manage not only the objects she has located somewhere but also the objects created by other users and located by the system automatically, so that she is no longer aware of her workspace. In our opinion, this fact will create a major obstacle to the diffusion and use of CSCW systems. A CSCW system supporting a community should, at any moment, bring forth to any of its users all and only the objects she needs at that particular moment. A reasonable criterion for choosing what to display at a particular moment to a particular user is to relate the distance of an object in the workspace (Rodden, 1996) to the time distance of the cooperative process to whose context it belongs from the current activity performed by the user.

This requirement is not sufficient *per se*, since the context of a cooperative process is a complex issue. The actors of a cooperative process are, in fact, immersed in a unique history. But due to their different roles in the process they have different views of that history; i.e., of the past events of the process in which they are participating (Malone et al., 1992; Trigg & Bødker, 1994). Moreover, within her personal view of the past events of the process, each participant at any time is looking at a part of it, depending on what she is currently doing. The personal view of each member of a community mirrors the context in which she is acting and interacting. A CSCW system supporting a cooperative process should provide all its users with the right context for their participation, increasing their awareness of it. Users sometimes need the context to be transparent, other times visible (Agostini et al., 1996).

Shaping the workspace offered by a CSCW system through the capability of providing its users with personalized views and automatic filtering mechanisms is a rather difficult task. The workspace becomes in some sense alive, since it changes automatically reacting to what its user is doing and to the communication of the other users. There is, however, the risk that it confuses the user as much as traditional interfaces do, even if in a different way. The problem is therefore to design the workspace in a 'natural' way, so that its behavior does not capture the attention of the user who can act transparently in it. This is a typical 'design' problem in the sense described by Terry Winograd (1996).

While the MILANO system (as will be shown in the next section) has been conceived to meet to a certain degree the four previous requirements, research in regard to the design of its workspace is still at an exploratory stage. New solutions are under development in cooperation with Marco Susani of Domus Academy.

Let us conclude this section summarizing in Table I at which degree both LOTUS NOTES and LINKWORKS achieve the above listed requirements. We claim that the successful LOTUS NOTES cases rest on its approach to the openness issue and on its capability to link the communication events to the outcomes of the actions (even if the two flows are not completely integrated). In reference to LINKWORKS, as used and extended in the Politeam project (Prinz & Kolvenbach, 1996), we believe that its strong points are based on devoting considerable care to the multimedia issue, as well as on providing their users with the historical context of the process; moreover, the integration of the action flow with the documents related to communication events allows a medium level of integration between communication and action.

Requirements	Low	Medium	High
Openness	LINKWORKS		LOTUS NOTES
Multimedia Continuity	LOTUS NOTES	LINKWORKS	
Contextualization		LOTUS NOTES	LINKWORKS
Integration between Conversation and Action Flows		LOTUS NOTES, LINKWORKS	
Personalized and Selective Workspace	LOTUS NOTES, LINKWORKS		

Table I. Comparative evaluation of LOTUS NOTES and LINKWORKS

The Architecture of the MILANO System

The currently developed MILANO system prototype is a CSCW platform integrating in the user workspace a workflow management system (MWMS) with a multimedia conversation handler (MCH), and, finally, an object repository (MOR).

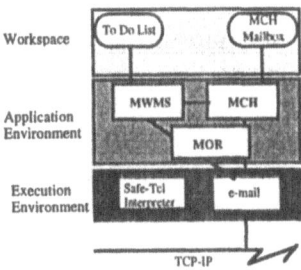

Figure 1. The overall architecture of the MILANO system

MILANO, evolving from previous mail-based CSCW systems (THE COORDINATOR (Winograd & Flores, 1986), INFORMATION LENS (Malone et al., 1986), CHAOS (De Cindio et al., 1986), STRUDEL (Shepherd et al., 1990), UTUCS (Agostini et al., 1994), CONVERSATION BUILDER (Bogia & Kaplan, 1995)), is based on the computational mail (through the Safe-Tcl environment see the next section). Future developments will be: on the one hand, the extension of the existing components and, in particular, a newly conceived workspace interface; on the other, the development of the links integrating MILANO with the organization information system (De Michelis et al., 1996).

The openness of the MILANO system architecture

As pointed out in the previous section, CSCW platforms need to be open with respect to both the integration of any software application and the cooperation with other systems. The latter requirement in particular finds its natural environment in the Internet. Openness of cooperative processes on the Net, we think, can be reached at a maximal degree through the enabled mail model. Enabled mail is an active medium, where messages are automatically manipulated when they are sent and/or received. E-mail is often recognized as one of the most successful groupware applications (after fax and telephone). At a functional level, it matches the way people work; it is asynchronous, easy to learn, and ready to be electronically stored. At a technical level, it runs on heterogeneous environments from its very beginning. Moreover, the use of e-mail as a distribution model makes the group boundaries inherently *dynamic*, providing contemporaneously different degrees of participation. E-mail is, therefore, a natural candidate to be the middleware for groupware, that is, its enabling technology. This capability increases significantly with enabled mail. An example of enabled mail is BEYOND

MAIL. Based on the INFORMATION LENS (Malone et al., 1986), it basically adds a rule engine to the mail agent, in such a way that users can define rules to be applied to the messages and to the documents routed in the system. Within the enabled mail family the term computational mail is used when the enabling of e-mail comes specifically from the embedding of programs within electronic mail messages (Borenstein, 1992). With computational mail, for example, messages can bring the execution environment necessary for reacting to them, providing the receiver with whatever she needs to be effective in the cooperation.

MILANO uses the computational mail model to obtain openness. In particular, the Safe-Tcl environment (Borenstein, 1994) has been used. Let us discuss this. The Safe-Tcl interpreter is based on an existing language called Tcl (Ousterhout, 1993) and on its graphical extension Tk. Safe-Tcl enriches the original Tcl primitives adding to them some commands to handle MIME messages; it also inherits the Tk primitives to design portable interfaces. Moreover, the security issue has been carefully considered designing a particular mechanism of safe interpretation. Finally, a mechanism of safe extendibility has been designed in such a way that the system can be aware of 'safe sites' on the net where it can look for extension scripts not found locally; the interpreting mechanism allows their use in 'real-time', avoiding the need to recompile the entire system.

MILANO makes great use of active software objects; i.e., self-contained, concurrently executing software processes, encapsulating some states and being able to communicate with other agents via message passing (Wooldridge & Jennings, 1995).

Within MILANO we distinguish three different kinds of active software objects: mail-robots, agents and applets. *Mail-robots* are specialized portions of code which are executed, without directly involving the user, either at delivery time or at receipt time. They are devoted to filtering the mail, to synchronizing information, and so on. In turn, *agents* are multipurpose and event-driven portions of code devoted to handling the objects of the system and their relationships. Both agents and mail-robots have full access to the user's resources. Finally, the *applets* - their name refers to Java applets, even if Safe-Tcl allows MILANO's applets to have a much broader set of functionality (Wayner, 1996) - are mobile and support interaction between MILANO users and those without the system installed at their site. An applet is a portion of code that can be inserted in a message and is executed at *activation* time, when the user reads it.

The above features allow MILANO to support, with different levels of service, cooperation between three types of actors: those having the MILANO system; those having the Safe-Tcl interpreter; and those just using e-mail (see Figure 2).

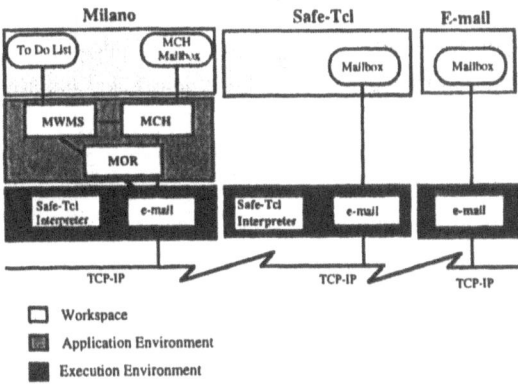

Figure 2. The multi-level user architecture of the MILANO system

While two actors both having MILANO can obviously cooperate using the full set of services offered by it; the other cases require further discussion. The actor having a Safe-Tcl interpreter is still provided with a meaningful subset of functionalities, since MILANO's messages embed data and source code that the interpreter executes on destination sites for interacting with MILANO users. Some of the functionalities provided are: notification of activities to be performed; visualization of the context of an activity; complete handling of the action flow (calculation of the next step, routing of the involved data, etc.); access to both the missing parts of a conversation and, more generally, to the state of the running cooperative process. This is done by the applet (see above) issuing back a request on the sender machine to the agent who is in charge of handling the conversations or the cooperative processes, as appropriate.

For her part, the actor who just uses common e-mail is also provided with useful information and can easily be involved in an ongoing cooperative process. In this case, in fact, any program embedded in a message cannot be executed so the user can only read it. This is why messages always contain a 'textual' part giving all relevant information, such as the description of the activity to be executed, the information to be produced and so on. In case of a user having a MIME compliant reader the 'textual' part of messages is actually hypermedial. Moreover, in order to handle the flow of information, messages embed forms for filling in some information to be returned to the sender, so that MILANO does not see any difference with respect to the other two cases.

The MILANO Object Repository (MOR)

The MILANO system reflects and represents the history of a cooperative process linking any new (communication or action) event to the events to which it is reacting: a reply is linked to the message to which it is replying; an action is linked either to the communication event where its performance was agreed upon or to the previous action within a plan; etc. Through these links the system automatically creates for any cooperative process a partial order, selectively offering the user access to the appropriate resources, tools, information and documents she needs to act effectively.

Figure 3 offers some hints about the representation of the history of a cooperative process in the MILANO system. The context presentation of its interface is currently under development along similar lines.

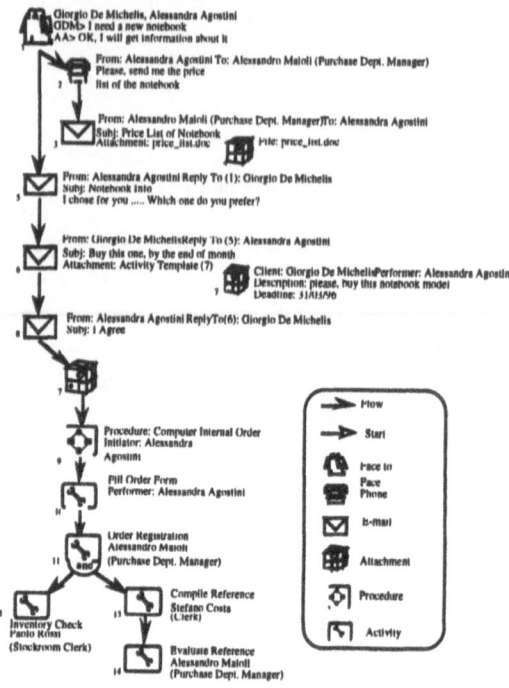

Figure 3. A sketch of the history of a cooperative process

The partial order of Figure 3 contains both communication and action events. The links relating them are distinguished between those connecting objects of the same type (Flow arrows) and those connecting objects of different type (Start arrows). Flow arrows single out from the history of the cooperative process the representation of conversations and plan instances, while Start arrows represent the integration between conversations and workflows.

Finally, it has to be recalled that MOR is a fully distributed component, based on both the user workstations and on the Web server of the whole community: the former contain the personal archives of each user, while the latter contains the object base where each user can search for the objects she does not have in her archive (see the subsection on Workspace below).

The MILANO Conversation Handler (MCH)

Conversations are the basic unit of communication in MILANO (De Michelis & Grasso, 1994): any communication event (message, meeting session, phone call, etc.) is always part of a conversation, within which it gets its sense. Milano conversations are unstructured, multipersons, multimedia; and allow any type of attachment.

A conversation acts as a folder collecting communication events from a group of participants which can been modified as needed. The communication events can be created by a complete range of communication media: from synchronous to asynchronous, supporting distant or close communication (only a subset of these possibilities is currently implemented in MILANO, but extensions are foreseen). Each event is characterized by the possibility of attaching enclosures of various types.

The MILANO Workflow Management System (MWMS)

As observed in the previous section, workflows may be either plan instances (procedures or projects) or evolutionary workflows. With respect to plans, the MWMS allows its users to design them even if they have little or no experience with computer science, programming, formal languages, etc., providing them with a design framework for defining simple plan models: a user can in fact design the plan as a partial order of progressing activities (steps), disregarding at the design phase any exception and/or breakdown which may occur during its execution. Given a plan definition, the set of possible exceptional paths is computed when needed. In general the exceptional paths allow the user to roll back, to jump forward, to execute unforeseen activities, etc. Moreover, exceptional paths are distinguished on the basis of the different levels of responsibility that can authorize them.

The workflow management component of the MILANO system embeds a part of the theory of Elementary Net Systems (Rozenberg & Thiagarajan, 1986; Nielsen et al., 1992) allowing an elegant treatment of both static and dynamic changes (Ellis et al., 1995). Therefore, the MWMS offers a framework for effectively supporting both procedures and projects.

Finally, the MILANO workflow module supports evolutionary workflows through its conversation handler (see next subsection).

Linkages between MWMS and MCH

Conversations and plans are not the only substructures of the partial order representing the history of a cooperative process: the latter also contains linkages connecting communication and action events (and, therefore, conversations and plans). These linkages between heterogeneous objects reflect their dependency relations: sometimes a conversation is subordinated to a plan; sometimes a plan is subordinated to a conversation.

On the one hand, besides electronic documents such as spreadsheets and graphical pictures, the activity template is a special kind of enclosure that can be created in any conversation when the need arises to formalize an action to be performed. When its requester and performer agree on its content, the activity template becomes an object of the to do list (see the next subsection) of both: that is, regarding the execution aspects, it is handled by the MWMS. This feature of MILANO allows its users to agree on various subsequent activity templates within a conversation, relating them to one another. In this way, the idea of electronic circulation folders proposed in (Karbe et al., 1990) and successfully employed in (Prinz & Kolvenbach, 1996) is realized to support evolutionary workflows as well as any combination of them with plans and/or procedures.

On the other, the breakdowns occurring during the execution of a project and/or of a procedure are discussed within a conversation, eventually generating an agreement on an activity template to perform an authorized exceptional path (see previous section). Figure 4 summarizes how plans, conversations, cooperative processes, activity templates are mutually related.

Figure 4. The relations among MILANO objects

The MILANO Workspace

As we claimed above, the context of a cooperative process is mirrored by the partial order of communication and action events representing its history; the participants of a cooperative process are immersed in this history and need to refer to a representation of it in order to act effectively.

MILANO supports tailorable personal views (Malone et al., 1992; Trigg & Bødker, 1994) of the history of a cooperative process with some original features: for instance it avoids information overload selecting automatically from the historical context only those events in which the user is involved, in order to avoid information overload (for example it hides from her all conversations in which she neither is the sender/receiver nor belongs to the carbon copy list); whereas it allows the initiator of a plan instance to see its whole history in her personal view, it makes visible to the other participants only those activities in which they are performers or clients. In fact whereas those objects (conversations, activities, plans, etc.) whose a person is a direct user are recorded in her local workstation, the others are recorded in the community server in the Web. Finally, a user can always modify her view when she wants to do it: she can choose which objects to see in a particular moment (by the filtering mechanisms on the context objects) and in which way to see them (by choosing which information is relevant for her and in what order).

Besides making visible to its users the context of a cooperative process, the MILANO system also supports two operational views allowing them to be active in it: the mailbox and the to do list (see Figures 5 and 6), corresponding respectively to communicating and acting.

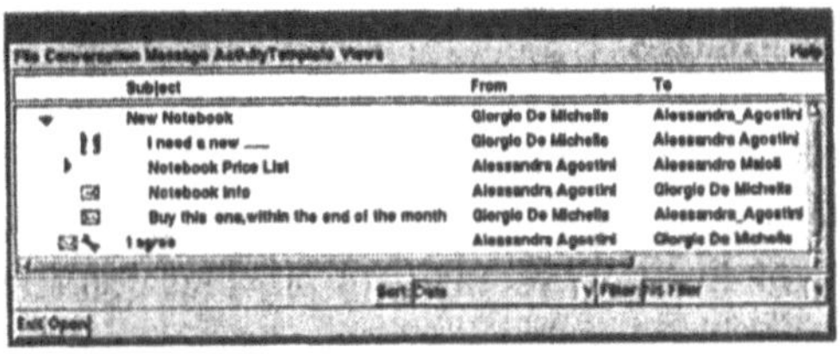

Figure 5. The mailbox presentation of the MILANO system

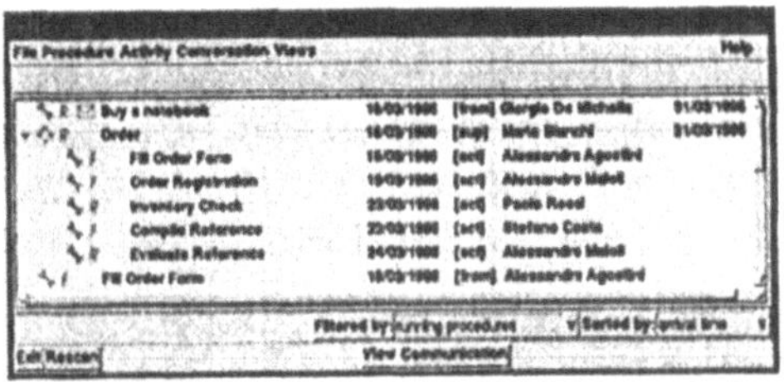

Figure 6. The to do list presentation of the MILANO system

To maintain multiple views of a single history MILANO must handle, as asserted in the MOR subsection, both the personal archives of each member on their workstations and the common archive of the whole community on a Web server.

Conclusion

Summarizing, the main innovative features of the MILANO system allowing it to satisfy the requirements proposed in the Introduction are the following:

- being based on the computational mail model, MILANO has an high degree of openness;
- since its conversations are unstructured, multipersons and multimedia, MILANO exhibits an high degree of continuity;
- since its conversations and workflows are mutually linked, MILANO integrates in a flexible and rich way the communication and action flows, offering a variety of representations of the history of a cooperative process.

It has to be underlined concluding this paper that the innovation proposed by MILANO is mainly architectural: with respect to some issues, in fact, it evolves from previous systems simplifying some features (conversations are *not* structured and *not* tailorizable; plans are *not* cyclic; etc.), while, with respect to other, it introduces new objects and mechanisms (conversations are multimedia; plans are based on a theoretical model allowing to compute run-time the exceptional paths; the users are always immersed in the context of the cooperative process in which they participate; etc.).

Acknowledgements

This paper presents a research that has been conducted with the financial support of the EC and of the Italian National Research Council (CNR). Special thanks to the anonymous referees of ECSCW'97 and of a previous conference, whose useful comments allowed us to improve the readability of the paper.

References

Abbott, K. R. and Sarin, S. K. (1994): Experiences with Workflow Management: Issues for the Next Generation. In *Proceedings of the Conference on Computer Supported Cooperative Work*, Chapel Hill, NC, October 22-26. ACM Press, New York, pp. 113-120.

Agostini, A., De Michelis, G., Patriarca, S. and Tinini, R. (1994): A Prototype of an Integrated Coordination Support System. *Computer Supported Cooperative Work. An International Journal*, vol. 2, no. 4, pp. 209-238.

Agostini, A., De Michelis, G., Grasso, M. A., Prinz, W. and Syri, A. (1996): Contexts, Work Processes and Workspaces. *Computer Supported Cooperative Work. The Journal of Collaborative Computing*, vol. 5, no. 2-3, pp. 223-250.

Beck, E. and Bellotti, V. M. E. (1993): Informed Opportunism as Strategy: Supporting Coordination in Distributed Collaborative Writing. In *Proceedings of the Third European Conference on Computer Supported Cooperative Work*, Milano, Italy, September 13-17. Kluwer Academic, Dordrecht, pp. 233-248.

Bentley, R., Horstmann, T., Sikkel, K. and Trevor, J. (1997): The World Wide Web as Enabling Technology for CSCW: The case of BSCW. In *Computer Supported Cooperative Work. The Journal of Collaborative Computing*, (to appear).

Bogia, D. P. and Kaplan, S. (1995): Flexibility and Control for Dynamic Workflows in the wOrlds Environment. In *Proceedings of the Conference on Organizational Computing Systems*, Milpitas, CA, August 13-16. ACM Press, New York, pp. 148-159.

Borenstein, N. S. (1992): Computational Mail as Network Infrastructure for Computer-Supported Cooperative Work. In *Proceedings of the Conference on Computer-Supported Cooperative Work*, Toronto, Canada, October 31-November 4. ACM Press, New York, pp. 67-74.

Borenstein, N. S. (1994): Email with a Mind of Its Own: The Safe-Tcl Language for Enabled Mail. In *Proceedings of the IFIP WG 6.5 Conference on Upper Layer Protocols, Applications, and Architectures*, Barcelona, Spain, June.

Bowers, J. (1994): The Work to Make a Network Work: Studying CSCW in Action. In *Proceedings of the Conference on Computer Supported Cooperative Work*, Chapel Hill, NC, October 22-26. ACM Press, New York, pp. 287-298.

Bowers, J., Button, G. and Sharrock, W. (1995): Workflow from Within and Without: Technology and Cooperative Work on the Print Industry Shopfloor. In *Proceedings of the Fourth European Conference on Computer Supported Cooperative Work*, Stockholm, Sweden, September 10-14. Kluwer Academic, Dordrecht, pp. 51-66.

Brown, J. S. and Duguid, P. (1991): Organizational Learning and Communities of Practice: a unified View of Working, Learning and Innovation. *Organization Science*, vol. 2, no. 1, pp. 40-56.

Bullen, C. V. and Bennett, J. L. (1990): Learning from User Experience with Groupware. In *Proceedings of the Conference on Computer-Supported Cooperative Work*, Los Angeles, CA, October 7-10. ACM Press, New York, pp. 291-302.

Ciborra, C. U. (edited by) (1996): *Groupware & Teamwork. Invisible Aid or Technical Hindrance.* John Wiley and Sons Ltd., Chichester.

De Cindio, F., De Michelis, G., Simone, C., Vassallo, R. and Zanaboni, A. M. (1986): CHAOS as a Coordination Technology. In *Proceedings of the Conference on Computer Supported Cooperative Work* , Austin, TX, December 3-5. MCC, Austin, pp. 325-342.

De Michelis, G. (1995): Computer Support for Cooperative Work: Computers between Users and Social Complexity. In C. Zucchermaglio, S. Bagnara and S. Stucky (eds.): *Organizational Learning and Technological Change*. Springer Verlag, Berlin, pp. 307-330.

De Michelis, G. (1997): Cooperation and Knowledge Creation. In I. Nonaka and T. Nishiguchi (eds.): *Comparative Study of Knowledge Creation.* Oxford University Press, Oxford (to appear).

De Michelis, G., Dubois, E., Jarke, M., Matthes, F., Mylopoulos, J., Pohl, K., Schmidt, J., Woo, C. and Yu, E. (1996): Cooperative Information Systems: A Manifesto. In M. Papazoglou and G. Schlageter (eds.): *Cooperative Information Systems*, Academic Press (to appear).

De Michelis, G. and Grasso, M. A. (1994): Situating conversations within the language/action perspective: the Milan Conversation Model. In *Proceedings of the Conference on Computer Supported Cooperative Work*, Chapel Hill, NC, October 22-26. ACM Press, New York, pp. 89-100.

Dourish, P., Holmes, J., MacLean, A., Marqvardsen, P. and Zbyslaw, A. (1996): Freeflow: Mediating Between Representation and Action in Workflow Systems. In *Proceedings of the Conference on Computer Supported Cooperative Work*, Boston, MA, November 16-20. ACM Press, New York, pp. 190-198.

Ellis, C. A., Keddara, K. and Rozenberg, G. (1995): Dynamic Change within Workflow Systems. In *Proceedings of the Conference on Organizational Computing Systems*, Milpitas, CA, August 13-16. ACM Press, New York, pp. 10-21.

Grudin, J. (1988): Why CSCW Applications Fail: Problems in the Design and Evaluation of Organizational Interfaces. In *Proceedings of the Conference on Computer Supported Cooperative Work*, Portland, OR, September 26-28. ACM, New York, pp. 85- 93.

Karbe, B., Ramsperger, N. and Weiss, P. (1990): Support of Cooperative Work by Electronic Circulation Folders. *ACM SIGOIS Bulletin*, vol. 11, no. 2-3, pp. 109-117.

Lave, J. and Wenger, E. (1991): *Situated learning. Legitimate peripheral participation.* Cambridge University Press, Cambridge.

Malone, T. W., Grant, K. R. and Turbak, F.A. (1986): The Information Lens: An Intelligent System for Information Sharing in Organizations. In *Proceedings of the Conference on Human Factors in Computing Systems*, Boston, MA, April. ACM, New York.

Malone, T. W., Lai, K.-Y. and Fry, C. (1992): Experiments with Oval: A Radically Tailorable Tool for Cooperative Work. In *Proceedings of the Conference on Computer-Supported Cooperative Work,* Toronto, Canada, October 31 - November 4. ACM Press, New York, pp. 289-297.

Nielsen, M., Rozenberg, G. and Thiagarajan, P. S. (1992): Elementary Transition Systems. *Theoretical Computer Science,* vol. 96, no. 1, pp. 3-33.

Orlikowski, W. J. (1992): Learning from Notes: Organizational Issues in Groupware Implementation. In *Proceedings of Conference on Computer Supported Cooperative Work,* Toronto, Canada, October 31 - November 4. ACM Press, New York, pp. 362-369.

Ousterhout, J. K. (1993): *TCL and the TK Toolkit.* Reading, Addison Wesley, MA.

Prinz, W. and Kolvenbach, S. (1996): Support for Workflows in a Ministerial Environment. In *Proceedings of the Conference on Computer Supported Cooperative Work,* Boston, MA, November 16-20. ACM Press, New York, pp. 199-208.

Reder, S. and Schwab, R. G. (1990): The Temporal Structure of Cooperative Activity. In *Proceedings of the Conference on Computer-Supported Cooperative Work,* Los Angeles, CA, October 7-10. ACM Press, New York, pp. 303-316.

Rodden, T. (1996): Populating the Application: A Model of Awareness for Cooperative Applications. In *Proceedings of the Conference on Computer Supported Cooperative Work,* Boston, MA, November 16-20. ACM Press, New York, pp. 87-96.

Rouncefield, M., Hughes, J. A., Rodden, T. and Viller, S. (1994): Working with "Constant Interruption": CSCW and the Small Office. In *Proceedings of the Conference on Computer Supported Cooperative Work,* Chapel Hill, NC, October 22-26. ACM Press, New York, pp. 275-286.

Shepherd, A., Mayer, N. and Kuchinsky, A. (1990): Strudel - An Extensible Electronic Conversation Toolkit. In *Proceedings of the Conference on Computer Supported Cooperative Work,* Los Angeles, CA, October 7-10. ACM Press, New York, pp. 93-104.

Suchman, L. A. (1987): *Plans and Situated Actions. The problem of human-machine communication.* Cambridge University Press, Cambridge.

Swenson, K. D., Maxwell, R. J., Matsumoto, T., Saghari, B. and Irwin, K. (1994): A Business Process Environment Supporting Collaborative Planning. *Collaborative Computing,* vol. 1, no. 1, pp. 15-34.

Trigg, R. H. and Bødker, S. (1994): From Implementation to design: Tailoring and the Emergence of Systematization in CSCW. In *Proceedings of the Conference on Computer Supported Cooperative Work,* Chapel Hill, NC, October 22-26. ACM Press, New York, pp. 45-54.

Wayner, P. (1996): Net Programming for the Masses. *Byte,* vol. 21, no. 2, pp. 101-104.

Whittaker, S. (1996): Talking to Strangers: An Evaluation of the Factors Affecting Electronic Collaboration. In *Proceedings of the Conference on Computer Supported Cooperative Work,* Boston, MA, November 16-20. ACM Press, New York, pp. 409-418.

Winograd, T. (edited by) (1996): *Bringing Design to Software.* Addison Wesley, New York.

Winograd, T. and Flores, F. (1986): *Understanding Computer and Cognition: A New Foundation for Design.* Ablex Publishing Corp., Norwood.

Wooldridge, M. and Jennings, N. R. (1995): Intelligents agents: theory and practice. *The Knowledge Engineering Review,* vol. 10, no. 2, pp. 115-152.

Effects of the amount of shared information on communication efficiency in side by side and remote help dialogues

Laurent KARSENTY
ARAMIIHS-CNRS, 31 av. des Cosmonautes, 31077 Toulouse Cedex, France
karsenty@anubis.tls.mms.fr

Abstract: If the sharing of context is now widely acknowledged as a condition for successful communication, existing studies do not allow to determine whether it is necessary to restore the maximum of shared information to obtain the best communicative performance. To address this issue, three help dialogue conditions distinguished by the amount of shared information, are compared. The analyses are focused on the comprehension problems raised by each condition. The results highlight that the quality of a help dialogue is not necessarily linked to the quantity of shared information. They also exhibit that the inability to share some specific information strongly affects communication efficiency. Implications for the design of computer-mediated communication systems are drawn from these results.

1. Problem and objectives

Given the current rapid growth of telephone companies providing support to customers (some call centers include more than 2000 agents and handle more than 200 000 calls per day, Rob Walters, 1996), there is a great interest in reducing the time of each communication. As Muller et al. (1995) claimed, « savings of even a tenth of a second per call are multiplied into significant corporate economies.»

One way to reduce communication time in remote settings could be to enhance the sharing of information between the caller -- I will call him the « novice » -- and the helper -- I will call her the « expert » (for convenience, I will use in the

49

J. Hughes et al. (eds.), Proceedings of the Fifth European Conference on Computer Supported Cooperative Work, 49-64.

following « she » to refer to the expert, and « he » to refer to the novice). Many researchers have pointed out that shared workspaces make collaboration easier (e.g., Dourish & Bellotti, 1992, Whittaker, Geelhoed, & Robinson, 1993). Moreover, some theoritical work on communication processes advocates the need for interlocutor to share not only a linguistic code, but also the *context* needed to interpret the literal content of any message (Clark & Marshall, 1981, Sperber & Wilson, 1986, Krauss & Fussell, 1990, Cahour & Karsenty, 1993). According to this trend, shared context is required to avoid misunderstanding. In this sense, improving the sharing of information in help dialogues should decrease the need for clarification sub-dialogues or erroneous interpretations, which both induce waste of time.

Unfortunately, no study provides precise directions on which information to include in the shared workspace. Existing studies (e.g., Tatar, Foster & Bobrow, 1991, Brown & Duguid, 1994, Heath & Luff, 1995) simply lead to state that communicative performances are dependent on the amount of shared information, which includes just as well computer screen, used documents, others' actions as proximity cues (body attitudes, eyes movements, facial expressions, etc.) However, since this statement is not precise enough, designers of computer-mediated communication (CMC) systems may deduce from it that the more the workspace is shared, the better the efficiency of the dialogue should be. It is then not surprising to note that most people currently involved in CMC system design projects believe that good communication performances in remote settings suppose the greatest possible number of communication channels: video, audio, synchronous written interactions, file sharing systems, etc.

Although this assumption seems reasonable, it neglects the *cooperative aspect of a communication process* (Grice, 1975). According to this view, speakers in a dialogue are assumed to be cooperative, which means that they are expected to adapt their speech acts to the hearers' cognitive environment (Sperber & Wilson, 1986). The hearer's cognitive environment consists of a set of beliefs easily accessible at a given time. This set of beliefs includes beliefs on the speaker's workspace and goals. Thus, when the interpretation of a speech act requires the use of contextual beliefs not immediately accessible (i.e., not evoked for interpreting the previous speech act, or not related to the closest perceptible environment), the speaker is expected to make these contextual beliefs explicit. In other words, the speaker is responsible for ensuring the sharing of the interpretative context. Previous studies on task-oriented dialogues without a shared vision (Grosz, 1978) or human-computer help dialogues[1] (Guindon, 1991) seem to support this theory: it was noticed that, under these circumstances, speakers refer to objects and events with very precise descriptions instead of pronouns, and produce very few ellipses and deictic expressions. Other related work on human explanatory dialogues (Karsenty

---

1 Note that these dialogues are in fact often simulated through a Wizard of Oz setting, where a human mimicks the computerized advisor. It is then a form of remote dialogue.

& Falzon, 1992, Karsenty & Brézillon, 1995) is also consistent with this theory: it was noticed that explanations, which may be conceived as speech acts aimed at changing the hearer's interpretative context, are most often volunteered in task-oriented dialogues and not provided after an explanation demand.

Therefore, we should expect novices in remote help dialogues to adapt the content of their requests depending upon the dialogue setting.

The study reported in this paper was aimed at testing the two hypotheses that have been formulated:

Hypothesis 1: The greater the amount of shared information is, the better communication efficiency is.

Hypothesis 2: A decrease in communication efficiency is limited by the novices' adaptive linguistic capacities when the amount of shared information is small.

To what extent and under which conditions a decrease in communication efficiency can be limited by the novices' adaptive power were also two central issues of our study. The answer to these questions is important because it should influence the design of CMC systems for help dialogues. Consider at an extreme that the novices' adpative power is proved to ensure mutual understanding in any case: this would highlight that good communication performances in remote settings does not require a mix of communication technologies; only one appropriate channel should be sufficient. At the other extreme, if this adaptive power is proved to be totally inefficient to limit misunderstandings in remote settings with a small amount of shared information, we should conclude that a mix of communication technologies is highly desirable.

Another objective of this study was to estimate to what extent one could expect remote help dialogues enhanced with information sharing tools to be confined to a single dialogue turn (one question-one answer). This question is especially important for user support office managers: if they believe single turn dialogues possible, they will expect (or impose) a certain operators' throughput. This expectation will then influence the way each operator will handle callers' requests. If single turn dialogues are not always possible, or even not always desirable, this managers' expectation will produce frustration and dissatisfaction from every sides: callers, operators and managers.

To tackle these issues, we have compared communicative performances of novice-expert couples placed in three help dialogue settings: (1) side by side by the same screen, (2) at a distance with the expert seeing the novice's screen, (3) at a distance with no shared environment. One may consider that the shared environment is maximal in condition 1, including screen information (buttons, menus, state of the displayed text, cursor, etc.), cues on novice's actions (typewriting, hand moves toward the screen), and proximity cues. The shared environment is intermediary in condition 3, composed only by screen information. And it is nil in condition 3.

2. Method

2.1 Data collection

2.1.1 Procedure

The task domain concerned by this study is text editing (with Microsoft Word™ on macintosh). This task domain was chosen for three reasons: first, it is familiar to most people working in our research area; second, the subjects were motivated to learn about editing tasks; and third, editing tasks require few prerequisites. The experiment consists of three phases:

1. *Phase of familiarization:* during the first phase, each subject is trained to use the computer and the main functions of its interface (mouse handling, understanding of the icon principles, menus, use of the cursor). This phase ensures that all the novices have the same level of experience at the beginning of the experiment.

2. *Phase of goal definition:* just after this first phase, the novice and a word processing expert examine the initial state of the text to be edited and the text to be obtained (target text), both texts being displayed on a separate sheet of paper. The comparison between these texts allows the novice and the expert to define the changes to be carried out (the novice's goals). This phase ends when all the changes have been defined. These changes represent elementary tasks related to a word processing task: replacing/inserting a word, changing the size of characters, creating spaces between lines, justifying lines, creating a footnote, and framing part of the text.

3. *Experimental phase:* just after the second phase, each novice is asked to modify the initial text in one of the three following conditions:

   Condition 1: Side by side. The expert and the novice are set side by side, in front of the same computer screen on which a text is displayed. The novice is asked to carry out a set of word processing tasks. The expert intervenes only when the novice requests help. The expert must not perform any of the novice's task, but is free to use any means judged necessary to provide help.

   Condition 2: Screen sharing. The expert and the novice are placed at a distance in the same room. Both have access to computers linked via a network. Timbuktu® software was used in the « Observe » mode only. This configuration permitted the expert to observe the novice's screen (including the cursor movements). No direct intervention was possible. Any assistance offered by the expert was conveyed verbally.

Condition 3: No shared environment. As in the previous setting, the expert and the novice are placed at a distance, in the same room. Direct access to the novice's screen was not permitted. Novice's requests and expert's assistance were conveyed verbally.

No constraint concerning the order of the tasks is imposed. In every experimental session, novices are videotaped so that the computer interface, the actions on the keyboard, and all the novices' hand gestures towards the screen (as well as the expert's gestures in the side-by-side condition) are all recorded.

2.1.2 Participants

Participants included 15 first year psychology students from a large university in the southwestern region of France. Three groups of 5 subjects were formed, one group per dialogue setting. No student was familiar with a computer. Their participation was doubly motivated: first, it was a chance for them to be initiated to word processing systems before their second year where such an initiation is mandatory; second, each subject was paid (100 francs).

Two experts were chosen for helping the novices. These experts were students from the same university but attending a master's degree in psychology. I call them « expert » because they were familiar users of the macintosh and the Microsoft Word™ software.

In order to guard against order effects, experts were randomly assigned to one of the 15 help dialogues.

2.2 Data coding

The dialogues between the novices and the experts were all extensively transcribed for the analysis, reporting every verbal interaction as precisely as possible (but without intonation), hand gestures, and actions on the system.

Six out of the 15 recorded dialogues were exploited for this paper. Data coding was done by two analysts, with all discrepancies reexamined in a combined session.

2.2.1 Help interactions

Only specific sequences, corresponding to « help interactions », were coded. An « help interaction » consists of any sequence of dialogue aimed at solving a novice's problem, initiated by a novice's help request, and ended by one of the following conditions: (1) the novice performs the appropriate action(s) with respect to the expert's answer, (2) the novice addresses another help request, either on a different topic, or aimed at clarifying the expert's answer. We identified 255 help interactions in our data.

Note that every help interaction is not initiated by a novice's request in the « side by side » and « screen sharing » conditions: these conditions allow the experts to anticipate some novice's problems, and consequently to volunteer help (see fragment 2, sequences 26 to 28). This type of help interaction has not been taken into account because this study is focused on problems of understanding raised by the novices' help requests.

Help interactions were all extensively transcribed for the analysis, reporting every verbal interaction as precisely as possible (but without intonation), hand moves, and actions on the system.

2.2.2 Communication efficiency and suboptimal communication

Communication efficiency has been measured using a single variable: the frequency of *suboptimal communication*. The notion of suboptimal communication refers in this study to any situation where the expert cannot immediately understand and/or adequately respond to a novice's help request, and asks him for further information. We consider suboptimal communication as an indicator of the situations where the context needed to understand and handle a novice's request is not shared.

2.2.3 Levels of contextual informativeness in help requests

According to relevance theory (Sperber & Wilson, 1986), a speaker should adapt her/his message to the hearer's cognitive environment. As a consequence, one can hypothesize that the level of contextual informativeness of help requests should be different with respect to the dialogue setting. We distinguish three levels of contextual informativeness:

- *I1: Requests with any reference to the novice's context.* Here are two examples: (1) « Do I need to select another menu ? », (2) « Do I do the same thing ? » Note that in the second example, a reference to the dialogue context exists: the asker refers to a procedure (« the same thing ») which has just been described by the expert. This type of contextual reference was not taken into account because any dialogue settings complicate the access to the dialogue context.
- *I2: Requests with a deictic reference* (« this », « here », etc.) A deictic reference does not convey contextual information per se, but helps the expert in finding the right context. In a sense, one may say that deictic references are « contextualization instructions ». In our data, the context indicated by the observed deictic expressions specifically corresponds to a piece of text or interface object displayed on the novice's screen. An example of this type of request is: « Do I shift my cursor here ? », where « here » refers to a location on the displayed text.
- *I3: Requests with elements of the context made explicit.* This type of request makes part of the novice's context explicit, often under the form of a justification of the help request. In the following example « *I want to write 'Toulouse', do I need to delete this now ?* », the first part of the request makes the novice's goal explicit. I3 requests are also identified when

the novice specifies a given mode of action in his request, as in the following example: « So, *with the mouse*, how do I do it ? ».

Note that in this study, only verbalizations *making explicit* some element composing the novices' context are treated. It is important to stress that information about the novices' context can also be conveyed implicitly, as it is illustrated in the following example:

N: That's not the right menu which has just unrolled

This statement implicitly conveys that another menu has just unrolled, one that was not desired. However, this implicit mode of communication will be neglected since the focus of this study is on cases where a novice feels that it is necessary to make her/his context explicit to the expert.

3. Results

3.1 Number of suboptimal communications for each dialogue setting

Across all dialogue settings and within all types of help requests, only 36 cases of sub-optimal communications were noticed out of 255 help interactions. The following analyses are mostly based on this sample of 36 cases. I am aware that this relatively small number reduces the significance of the conclusions drawn from this study. However I have found that the trends revealed by the following analyses lead to theoretical and practical considerations that are of value both for the study of cooperative work and the design of computer-supported cooperative work systems. The results may also serve as a basis for further investigations. A special emphasis will be put on these implications in the conclusion of this paper.

Some expectations have been formulated regarding the number of suboptimal communications for each dialogue setting: it should be the highest in the « no shared environment » condition, intermediate in the « screen sharing » condition, and the lowest in the « side by side » condition. Table 1 (below) shows that these expectations are partially met by our data. Specifically, we notice that suboptimal communications are significantly more frequent in the "no shared environment" condition than in both others ($\chi 2=12,03$, significant at $p<0.01$). But, surprisingly, we also notice that the number of suboptimal communications in the screen sharing condition, which is relatively small compared with the one obtained in the no shared environment condition, is virtually identical to the number of suboptimal communications in the side by side condition.

Table 1: Frequencies of suboptimal communication for each dialogue setting

Condition	Optimal communication (total number)	Suboptimal communication (total number)	Percentage of suboptimal communications
Side by side	78	7	8,2%
Screen sharing	62	5	7,5%
No shared env.	79	24	23,3%

Given the lack of difference between these conditions, how can we explain the occurrence of sub-optimal communications in the « no shared environment » condition ? In particular, does the lack of a shared environment make linguistic adaptations of the content of the help requests more difficult ? If it is the case, how to explain this failure ? We explore these issues in the following section.

3.2 Linguistic adaptations of the help requests according to the dialogue settings

If novices adapt their help requests to the dialogue setting, we should observe different distributions of types of help requests. More specifically, we expect to find:

1. More I2 requests (with a deictic reference) in both the « side by side » and « screen sharing » conditions;
2. More I3 requests (with part of the novice's context made explicit) in both of the remote dialogue settings, but more importantly in the « no shared environment » condition.

Table 2 exhibits results that confirm these hypotheses: there are more I2 requests in both the « side by side » and « screen sharing » conditions than in the « no shared environment » condition. There are more I3 requests in the « screen sharing » condition and still more in the « no shared environment » than in the « side by side » condition. These differences are statistically significant ($\chi^2 = 13,35$, $p \leq .01$).

Table 2: Number and percentages of help requests characterized by their level of contextual informativeness for each dialogue setting

	I1	I2	I3	I1	I2	I3
Side by side	49	19	17	57,6%	22,4%	20%
Screen sharing	30	17	20	44,8%	25,4%	29,9%
No shared env.	57	9	37	55,3%	8,7%	35,9%

Let us now consider to what extent these linguistic adaptations are appropriate and sufficient to ensure an immediate mutual understanding of a help request. The very fact that an important number of suboptimal communications have been noticed in the « no shared environment » condition tends to highlight that these linguistic adaptations are not sufficient. A more specific way to handle this issue consists in registering the number of help requests implying suboptimal communication, and observing how this number varies according to the dialogue setting (see table 3).

Table 3: Number and percentages of suboptimal communications/total number of each level of contextual informativeness for each dialogue setting

	I1	I2	I3	I1	I2	I3
Side by side	4/49	2/19	1/17	7,7%	7,7%	5,5%
Screen sharing	1/30	2/17	2/20	5,1%	5,3%	10%
No shared env.	9/57	3/9	12/37	15,8%	33,3%	32,4%

These results reveal that I2 and I3 requests imply, somewhat frequently, suboptimal communication, but specifically in the « no shared environment » condition (33,3% for I2, 32,4% for I3). The novices' linguistic adaptations are thus not sufficient to ensure an immediate mutual understanding of the help requests when experts and novices communicate only verbally.

3.3 Specific difficulties for communicating with no shared environment

In the following section, we explore several aspects that may explain why the novices' linguistic adaptations may be inadequate to ensure a shared context. The exploration of these aspects will help us to decide how to best support remote help dialogues. Four avenues are examined: (1) novice's misjudgments of the expert's cognitive environment, (2) expert's inability to recover communication errors, (3) discrepancies between experts' and novices' language, reasoning, and knowledge, (3) novice's inability to ensure the sharing of the context required to solve his problem.

3.3.1 Novice's misjudgments of the expert's cognitive environment

A certain amount of sub-optimal communications could be explained by the fact that novices make incorrect judgments about the expert's cognitive environment (i.e., the expert's mental representation of the novice's context). The following extract illustrates such a case, stemming from a « no shared environment » dialogue.

(N has just deleted a word, but because his cursor was incorrectly located, the last letter of the word remains)

11   N: And the « E » there ?

12   E: Which « E » ?

13   N: An « E » is remaining on the line.

14   E: Ah OK, put you again after it […]

When uttering « And the « e » there » ? », N seems to believe that E can see the « E ». The fact that he uses a definite reference (« the ») to refer to the object « E » supports this assumption: some experimental studies (Clark & Wilkes-Gibbs, 1986, Isaacs & Clark, 1987) demonstrated that the use of definite references is generally observed when a speaker refers to an object believed to be mutually shared. As a matter of fact, in the extract above, the referred object is not mutually shared, hence E's question in line 12.

The extract below illustrates another case when N seems to attribute to E the knowledge of his goal, when in fact this is not the case.

    88   N: Here too, I go down again ?

    89   E: What should you do now ?

    90   N: Well, put spaces before « monsieur »

    91   E: Oh yes, you need a blank line […]

When we examined the data, we observed 15 cases wherein N's help requests implying a suboptimal communication indicated that N wrongly believed that a given object was mutually shared. This number represents nearly 42% of the total number of help requests implying suboptimal communication. Furthermore, most of these cases (9 out of 15) were in the « no shared environment » condition. It thus seems that the occurrence of a novice's misjudgment is relatively more important when the dialogue setting does not allow the sharing of the novice's environment. But one must also note that this phenomenon is not totally absent from the two other experimental conditions.

We can hypothesize that these features arise from factors which are intrinsic to the achievement of editing tasks by a novice: this situation would be very demanding in itself, and limit the novice's communication abilities, whether the expert is near or at a distance. This could account for the fact that novice's misjudgements of the expert's cognitive environment are observed in every dialogue setting. But how to explain the higher frequency of suboptimal communications caused by novices' misjudgements? We believe this is due to the experts' inability to recover communication errors.

3.3.2 Expert's inability to recover communication errors

The sharing of a novice's environment, permitted in both the « side by side » and the « screen sharing » conditions, may allow experts to uncover the correct meaning of the help requests when their content is unsuited. As an example, let us examine the case where an expert would see the novice's interface at a distance, and receive the help request presented above: « And the « E » there ? » Even if the expert does not immediately understand which « E » is meant, she can look for it on the novice's screen, and in many cases find it. If she feels sure she has recognized the « E » identified by the novice, she will directly provide him with the appropriate answer, without any need of a clarification sub-dialogue, as in the original extract above. According to this view, it would not be so much the appropriateness of the novices' linguistics adaptation that would differ, depending on the dialogue settings, as the expert's ability to *recover* a novices' misjudgment.

This hypothesis is supported by observations made on remote dialogues between airplane pilots and air controllers. These observations (Hansman, Pritchett & Midkiff, 1995) reveal the importance of the « party line » effect on mutual understanding and safety. Within the aeronautical field, the words « party line » refers to the fact that all airplanes evolving inside the same air sector receive the same air trafic control messages. The party line allows pilots to augment their situational awareness (the number of airplanes flying through a given air sector, their relative positioning, etc.), which is then at least partly shared among them. Many pilot reports exhibit situations where the party line has been used to detect mistakes in an air trafic controllers' instructions or in a pilots' misunderstanding of the controllers' instructions. The shared environment provided by the party line then makes it possible to recover communication errors.

3.3.3 Discrepancies between experts and novices' language, reasoning and knowledge

According to Falzon (1991), work dialogues may be split into two categories: expert-expert and expert-novice dialogues. The invoked distinctive feature is the form of language used by the cooperative partners: expert-expert dialogues rely on specialized professional languages (restricted and domain-specific syntax and lexicon, with few ambiguities) while novice-expert dialogues essentially rely on a more flexible and semantically open language (Falzon used the words « natural language » to designate it), which is necessary to palliate discrepancies between partners' knowledge.

Our study confirms the relevance of the distinction between expert-expert and expert-novice dialogues, and allow a better understanding as to why the use of a domain-specific language is not possible with novices. Four reasons are pointed out below:

(1) *a novice does not necessarily follow a logical order across tasks*. This is due to his relative lack of knowledge with respect to the word processing software used. For instance, a novice may want to right justify a given text line, although he must right justify a whole paragraph which includes this line of text. In such a case, the expert may expect the novice to first correctly type all the lines composing the paragraph, and then right justify the whole paragraph. This is what we call here a « logical » order across tasks. This wrong expectation may lead the expert to experience difficulties in understanding the novice's question « Do I select the line? ».

(2) *a novice may employ inappropriate words to indicate his goals*. For instance, many novices uttered the question « Do I go down? » while their intention was to include blank lines between two paragraphs. Pilkington (1992) also reported the

same type of observation, and linked this characteristic of the novices' language to their lack of knowledge concerning the system functioning.

(3) *a novice's help request may be based on an erroneous goal representation.* For instance, a novice asked the expert if he had to select a piece of the text, his goal being to copy this piece of text and to paste it at the bottom of his sheet, as a footnote. The expert did not immediately understand this request because the selection of a piece of text is usually not required to create a footnote; the user must open a window called « footnotes », and types the piece of text directly inside.

(4) *novice's actions may result in intermediary goals, which the expert does not expect.* In particular, errors produced by a novice raise new goals aimed at recovering these errors. An expert placed at a distance, especially in a work setting without a shared environment, cannot observe the novice's erroneous actions. If the novice did not make them explicit in his request, the expert will contextualize the novice's request with a wrong representation of the novice's situation. Such a discrepancy between the expert's expected representation of the novice's situation and the novice's actual situation may cause difficulties in understanding.

In total, these four factors account for 12 cases of sub-optimal communication (which represents 33,3% of the total number of sub-optimal communications). We did not find that they occurred more frequently in either dialogue settings. After all, one can consider that this is normal, because all these factors are basically linked to the very fact of being a novice, and this does not change across the three dialogue settings.

3.3.4 Novice's inability to know all the relevant contextual information needed by the expert

Sometimes, the additional information requested for by the experts is not required to *understand* the novices' requests, but rather, it appears necessary to *solve* the novices' problems. In such a situation, it is somewhat normal that novices do not provide experts with all the relevant information. The following extract, stemming from a « no shared environment » dialogue, illustrates this latter case.

1. N: So, I delete « SOCIETE » ?
2. E: Yes
3. N: Damn ! It doesn't work ...
4. E: Is your cursor located where it should be ?
5. N: Ah no...Ok, so I'll move it up

In this extract, N attempts to delete a word, but does not succeed. He then expresses this inability (line 3). E does not directly provide him with the procedure that could allow N to reach his goal, because she lacks some information. In particular, she does not know where the cursor is. Given the novice's inability to delete the word, the expert assumes that the error stems an incorrect positioning of the cursor. The expert's information demand in 4 is the expression of a diagnosis activity: by invoking the cursor location, E expresses an hypothesis that could explain N's inability to reach his goal. Furthermore, this information demand is the expression of the fact that E has understood N's problem: she has understood that N was unable to delete the word « SOCIETE », and more specifically, that N had probably carried out some actions that failed to achieve the desired result. In brief, E has understood N's problem, but does not have all the required information to solve it.

This distinction between the information-needed-to-understand and the information-needed-to-solve is important for the following reason: one cannot expect a novice user to spontaneously make the latter type of information explicit since he is unaware of its significance on account of his being confronted with a problem. If he knew the significance of this information, he would know at the same time how to solve his problem. One could even say that there would be no problem at all.

In total, nine sub-optimal communications due to a lack of information needed to solve the novice's problem were noticed. All these cases were found in the « no shared environment » condition.

The information-needed-to-solve can be accessed by two means: (1) either the expert can infer it, (2) or she initiates a sub-dialogue aimed at making it explicit. The results of this study reveal that the expert, placed in work conditions without a shared environment, frequently opts for the latter strategy. This seems to highlight her difficulty in inferring the information-needed-to-solve under these circumstances.

On the other hand, it seems reasonable to assume that the need of sub-dialogues in remote cooperation could be reduced by a work environment providing a certain level of shared environment. We develop this proposal in the following section.

4. Conclusion

This study highlights that the quality of communication aimed at supporting users is not necessarily linked to the quantity of shared information. Considering comprehension problems raised by the handling of help requests, this study has revealed that remote help dialogues with a shared screen and audio communication are as efficient as side by side dialogues.

However, without a shared screen, remote communication efficiency becomes poorer when compared to side by side and « screen sharing » dialogue settings. Thus, good communicative performance at a distance may be obtained under certain conditions, and a shared screen, showing the state of the work in progress, appears as one of these conditions.

These results are important because they question an assumption often encountered in CMC system design projects: this assumption is that the more the workspace is shared, the better communication efficiency should be. Rather than looking for a mix of technologies ensuring a « maximum shared environment », decision-makers should provide participants in remote collaboration with a limited set of tools simply ensuring an « optimal shared environment ». Providing an « optimal shared environment » seems sufficient because the communicative system, composed by the caller and the expert, may adapt to its environmental resources: on the one hand, novices can adapt the literal content of their messages, to help an expert in considering the right interpretative content; on the other hand, the expert seems able to adapt his interpretative strategies, especially by exploiting differently her/his available environmental resources (recovering of dialogue errors without the need of further sub-dialogues). We can speculate that the fact that that *doubly adaptive human-human dialogue* can explains why a maximally shared work environment is not necessarily required to obtain better communicative performance.

This study also highlights that one should not expect help dialogues, whether at a distance with appropriate support tools or even face to face, to be confined to a single turn (one question-one answer). The reason explaining this conclusion if that novices, given the very fact of being novices, may pose questions which *cannot* be immediately understood by experts. In particular, their goals may be underspecified in their requests (see also Pollack, 1985, Aaronson & Carroll, 1987), and they cannot volunteer all the information needed to solve their problems.

Implications on the design of computerized support for remote help dialogues

This notion of « optimal shared context » has implications on the type of computerized support that could enhance remote help dialogues. It does not seem necessary to provide the helper and the helpee with the whole battery of available collaborative tools. In particular, this study suggests that a video link could be superfluous.

However, it also suggests that computer-mediated communication could make the help dialogue process easier. More specifically, this study leads to recommend a cooperative work environment exhibiting three main features[2]:

1. *The target system* (i.e. the system used by the user to achieve his tasks) *should be integrated with electronic communication facilities* (e.g., e-mail). This requirement is necessary to provide the communication system with a set of information that would be automatically recorded while the user uses the system and then transferred to the assistance service. Some other results of this study (not yet published) lead to expect the following pieces of information to be especially useful: (1) the current state of the interface, (2) previous user's actions (it should be sufficient to store only a limited amount of a user previous actions), (3) intermediary interface states

---

2 I do not claim that these features are new. Rather, I hope that readers will find in the results of this study new arguments for advocating their necessity.

associated to these user actions. Mechanisms for automatically capturing and transferring this information, for instance as attached files, should then be implemented. It would be more appropriate to let the user to choose to attach these files. One may anticipate that concerns over proprietary or security issues would preclude the viewing of sensitive material by a third party.

2. This study suggests that the novice's current goal is often too poorly specified to allow the expert to directly supply the appropriate help. As a result, we recommend providing a *structure to the user's messages* that are addressed to the assistance service around two text fields: the first one would be devoted to the *goal description*, the second to the *request description*. This structure should not force the user to fill in both text fields (one can figure out particular requests where the goal description could be avoided), but only encourage him to do so.

3. The results of this study do not lead us to consider that it is possible to confine every help dialogue to a single turn dialogue, even with the functionalities described above. These considerations conduct us to recommend *interaction-based solutions*. Interactivity can rely on electronic written communications. More simply, interactivity can rely on telephonic communications.

Acknowledgments

This study was carried on as part of the project GEDIC (Groupe d'Etude des Dialogues Coopératifs) funded by the PRC-Sciences Cognitives. I am grateful to all the participants of this project, and especially Claude Navarro and Alain Giboin who provided me with valuable comments on earlier versions of this paper. I also thank Philippe Aknine for his support in analyzing the data.

References

Aaronson A. & Carroll J.M. (1987) Intelligent Help in a One-Shot Dialog: A Protocol Study. *Proceedings of the CHI'87 + GI'87 Conference*, pp.163-168, Toronto, 5-9 April.

Brown J.S. & Duguid P. (1994). Borderline Issues: Social and Material Aspects of Design. *Human-Computer Interaction*, 9, 3-36.

Cahour B. & Karsenty L. (1993) Context of Dialogue: A Cognitive Point of View. *Proceedings of the IJCAI'93 Workshop on Context.*, Chambéry, France, August 29.

Clark H.H. & Marshall C.R. (1981) Definite reference and mutual knowledge. In: Joshi A.K., Sag I.A. & Webber B.L. (Eds.) *Elements of Discourse Understanding*. Cambridge Univ. Press.

Clark H.H. & Wilkes-Gibbs D. (1986) Referring as a Collaborative Process. *Cognition*, 22(1), 1-35.

Dourish P. & Bellotti V. (1992) Awareness and coordination in shared workspaces. *Proceedings of the ACM CSCW'92 Conference on Computer-Supported Cooperative Work* (pp.107-114).

Falzon P. (1991) Cooperative Dialogues. In: J. Rasmussen, B. Brehmer & Leplat J. (Eds.) *Distributed Decision Making: Cognitive Models for Cooperative Work* (pp. 145-189). Chichester, UK: Wiley.

Grice H.P. (1975) Logic and Conversation. In: Cole P. & Morgan J.L. *Syntax and Semantics*, vol.3. NY: Academic Press.

Grosz B.J. (1978) Discourse Analysis. In: Walker (Ed.) *Understanding Spoken Language.* (pp. 235-268).

Guindon A.R. (1991) Users Request Help from Advisory Systems with Simple and Restricted Language: Effects of Real-Time Constraints and Limited Shared Context. *Human-Computer Interaction*, 6(1), 47-75.

Hansman R.J., Pritchett A. & Midkiff A. (1995) 'Party Line' Information User Studies and Implications for ATC Datalink Communications. *Proceedings of HMI-AI-AS'95*, Toulouse, 27-29 Sept.

Heath C.C., Luff P. & Nicholls G.M. (1995) The Collaborative Production of the Document: Context, Genre and the Borderline in Design. *Proceedings of the International Conf. on the Design of Cooperative Systems* (COOP'95), pp. 203-218, Juan-Les-Pins, France, 25-27 Janvier.

Isaacs E.A & Clark H.H (1987) References in Conversation between Experts and Novices. *Journal of Experimental Psychology*, 116(1), 26-37.

Karsenty L. & Falzon P. (1992) Spontaneous explanations in cooperative validation dialogues. *Proceedings of the ECAI-92 Workshop on "Improving the use of knowledge-based systems with explanations"*, Vienna, August 4.

Karsenty L. & Brézillon P. (1995) Cooperative problem solving and explanation. *International Journal of Expert Systems with Applications*, 8(4), 445-462.

Krauss R.M. & Fussell S.R. (1990) Mutual Knowledge and Communicative Effectiveness.In: Galegher J., Kraut R.E. & Egido C. (Eds.) *Intellectual teamwork. Social and Technological Foundations of Cooperative Work*. Hillsdale, NJ: LEA.

Moore J. & Swartout W.R. (1989) A reactive approach to explanation. *Proceedings of the 11th IJCAI Conference*, 1504-1510.

Muller M. J., Carr R., Ashworth C., Diekmann B., Wharton C., Eickstaedt C., Clonts J. (1995) Telephone Operators as Knowledge Workers: Consultants Who Meet Customer Needs, *Proceedings of CHI'95*, Denver, Colorado, USA, May 7 - 11, ACM Press.

Pilkington R.M. (1992) Question-Answering for Intelligent On-Line Help: The Process of Intelligent Responding. *Cognitive Science*, 16, 455-489.

Pollack M.E. (1985) Information Sought and Information Provided: An Empirical Study of User/Expert Dialogues. *Proceedings of CHI'85* (pp. 155-159) San Francisco.

Sperber D. & Wilson D. (1986) *Relevance. Communication & Cognition*. Blackwell.

Tatar D.G., Foster G. & Bobrow D.G. (1991) Design for conversation: Lessons from Cognoter. *International Journal of Man-Machine Studies*, 34, 185-209.

Walter R. (1996) The integrated call centre defined. *Proceedings of Integrated Call Centre'96* (pp.13-20), Sept. 11-12, London, Unicom Seminars Ltd.

Whittaker S., Geelhoed E. & Robinson E. (1993) Shared workspaces: How do they work and when are they useful? *International Journal of Man-Machine Studies*, 39(5), 813-842.

MetaWeb: Bringing synchronous groupware to the World Wide Web

Jonathan Trevor, Thomas Koch and Gerd Woetzel
German National Research Centre for Computer Science (GMD FIT.CSCW)

Abstract: The World Wide Web is increasingly seen as an attractive technology for the deployment and evaluation of groupware. However the underlying architecture of the Web is inherently stateless - best supporting asynchronous types of cooperation. This paper presents a toolkit for application developers, MetaWeb, which augments the Web with basic features which provide new and legacy applications with better support for synchronous cooperation. Using three simple abstractions, User, Location and Session, MetaWeb allows applications to be coupled as tightly or as loosely to the Web as desired. The paper presents two distinct applications of MetaWeb, including the extension of an existing application, the BSCW shared workspace system, from which a number of observations are drawn.

1. Introduction

The World Wide Web (Berners-Lee et al., 1994) merges the concepts of hypertext and networked information to provide an easy but powerful global information system based on two public and simple standards: the HyperText Transfer Protocol (HTTP) and the HyperText Markup Language (HTML). The Web consists of many independent servers, which accept and service requests for information in the HTTP protocol from clients (Web browsers), such as Netscape.

This simple architecture has now become established as an important platform for developing, deploying and evaluating CSCW applications. Almost any new CSCW system has some type of Web interface, whether it is purpose built for the Web, such as BSCW (Bentley et al. 1997), or provides generic access to features in non-Web applications, as with POLIWEB (Freund, 1996). Even existing systems like LOTUS NOTES with DOMINO have been extended to present their interfaces as Web pages.

There are many reasons for the success of the Web, and its attractiveness for developers of CSCW applications. Dix (1997) provides an analysis of the advantages

J. Hughes et al. (eds.), Proceedings of the Fifth European Conference on Computer Supported Cooperative Work, 65-80.
© 1997 *Kluwer Academic Publishers.*

and problems of the Web for cooperative systems, highlighting a number of reasons behind its success: a core initial user community, the integration of existing information, the use of de facto standards, the spanning of organisational boundaries, and a software platform which is public domain, cross-platform and extensible. Perhaps the most important reason presented by Dix is that the Web has reached a critical mass, the point where the benefits outweigh the costs for the user - a traditional problem for CSCW systems (Grudin, 1988). These advantages have made the Web an important platform for CSCW development.

2. Limitations for Groupware on the World Wide Web

The basic client-server architecture of the Web (Figure 1) is sufficient for serving primarily static pages of information from fixed locations in the remote file system. However for applications which want to present information differently to different users, or where the information available changes frequently, the basic server needs to be extended. The most common method of doing this is through the Common Gateway Interface (CGI) (Figure 2). This interface describes how HTTP requests can be delegated by the server to some server-side application. The delegated request can then be processed by the application before returning a response (typically an HTML page) to the server, which returns it to the client.

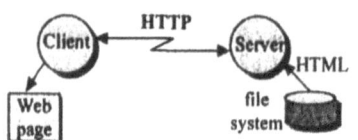 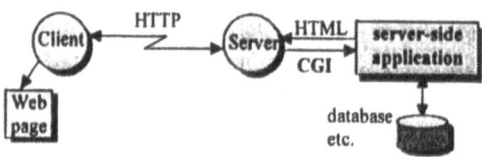

| Figure 1: The WWW architecture | Figure 2: Integrating applications in the WWW |

The problem for CSCW applications which adopt the Web as a platform for application development is that they inherit a key property of the Web - that the protocol it uses (HTTP) is inherently stateless. No information is stored between requests, and therefore the server (or application) has no idea what page the client is now browsing, how old that page is, and so on. The user could request a page from an entirely different server or application and the previous Web application would remain unaware of this change. The problem is bi-directional as the client invariably sees just a "snapshot" of the application's state. If something changes in the application, there is no way for the user to know this until he reloads the page (issues another HTTP request to the application).

This problem restricts those types of cooperative system supported by the Web to the "different time" half of the 2x2 classification of CSCW systems described by Ellis et al. (1991) - those supporting asynchronous local and distributed interaction. As such, cooperative tools and applications which require any significant degree of synchronous interaction between the users, and/or the application, such as chatting or shared whiteboards, cannot be supported by the current Web architecture.

A possible solution is to *modify the HTTP protocol* to incorporate more state information, to allow a stronger bi-directional coupling of the client to the server. Indeed, the NETSCAPE NAVIGATOR browser has introduced minor extensions to the HTTP protocol to satisfy some of these requirements (using "cookies" to maintain state and "Javascript" to move some computation from the server to the browser). An alternative approach to the problem, and often a consequence of the first, is to *modify the WWW client* to include specialised synchronous support. This may be building a complete replacement or embedding new functionality in an existing browser, using the Common Client Interface (CCI) or Java for example.

Unfortunately, in the context of the Web, these types of changes impact directly on the critical mass problem. For example, a specialised client means that effort required to use the Web application is drastically increased as a special piece of software must be located, downloaded and installed in addition a standard Web browser. *Any solution which affects the advantages the Web brings, such as changing the de facto standards or requiring a specialised software platform needs to be avoided* (Trevor et al., 1996). Therefore, we require some means of supporting synchronous groupware which does not change the way the Web currently works.

A solution to this dilemma is to provide some *additional* infrastructure which supplements the Web-based application with an architecture which allows information to flow both ways between the user and the application, supporting immediate feedback of the user's actions to the application and notifying changes of application state to the user. This additional infrastructure should not require any special client software or affect the standard protocols.

3. Addressing the shortcoming: Existing systems

A number of existing systems support applications requiring additional synchronous functionality, and may provide the additional infrastructure mentioned above. We separate these into general and Web-specific systems.

3.1. General support for synchronous collaboration

There are several non-Web oriented systems and toolkits which focus on addressing the general needs of synchronous CSCW application developers. These toolkits and systems include MMCONF (Crowley et al., 1990), RENDEZVOUS (Patterson et al., 1990), and GROUPKIT (Roseman and Greenberg, 1992). A number of concepts for synchronous collaboration development are common to these systems:

- **Session management;** Ellis et al. (1991) define a *cooperative session* as:

  "a period of synchronous interaction supported by a groupware system. Examples include formal meetings and informal work group discussions." (p.46).

  Most toolkits provide some mechanisms for applications to model and manage cooperative interaction between users, often grouping them into activities, rooms, conferences etc.

- **Mechanisms for accessing shared information**; mechanisms may be toolkit specific, such as who are the users in a session, or may be application-specific (provided by the application itself) to be shared between different instances of the application.
- **Support for application-specific message exchange;** Cooperative applications are often distributed across networks and require support for sending messages to each other.
- **Access control;** Necessary to control and restrict access to information and functionality available in the toolkit and application.

Unfortunately there is little support for the development or integration of these concepts into the Web itself. The emergence of the Web as a viable architecture for groupware, combined with its weaknesses, means that these existing (pre-Web) toolkits poorly address many new problems, such as how can the provided functionality be integrated with a Web page? How does the notion of a Web page relate to the concept of a cooperative session? and so on. In addition, the previously "desirable" quality of being platform independent is no longer merely desirable but critical within the context of the Web. Therefore, while the concepts are important for supporting synchronous applications, there is no simple or easy way to support Web-based applications in these toolkits.

3.2. Web-specific support for synchronous collaboration

The need for synchronous cooperation support on the Web is also addressed by a number of Web-oriented applications and toolkits, which attempt to couple their features more closely with the existing Web architecture and concepts. Some of the most notable of which include: YARNWEB (Woo and Rees, 1994) which supports chatting between users; VIRTUALPLACES (Ubique, 1996) where Web users can see and meet each other, GROUPWEB (Greenberg and Roseman, 1996) which supports collaborative navigation and allows groups to share pages in a relaxed WYSIWIS view; GROCO (Walther, 1996) which allows the development of Electronic Meeting Systems; and COWEB (Jacobs et al., 1996), which provides cooperative form-filling by dynamically transforming existing pages.

Unfortunately, there are problems with each of these toolkits. The most important is *restrictive cooperative session coupling to Web pages*. For example, in VIRTUALPLACES and GROCO a group always interacts within the boundaries of a single Web page, while YARNWEB only uses the Web as a launching point to a completely separate synchronous communication service. GROUPWEB and COWEB allow interaction over several pages in a group, but provide *no awareness of other users beyond the current page* - users must somehow navigate to the same page before they become aware of each other and interact. These limitations render them incapable of supporting applications whose sessions may span several pages, or conversely sessions where a single page acts as an access point to an application which supports distinct groups of users. Different applications require different ways of mapping their cooperation onto Web pages and cooperative session support on the

Web should support variations ranging from one session per page, to one session for a set of pages, to different sessions on the same page, to no coupling at all, where sessions exist without a corresponding page.

Another significant drawback of most of these systems is their *platform- and browser-dependence.* YARNWEB works with all browsers, but is restricted to the X-WINDOWS system. VIRTUALPLACES is a platform- and browser-dependant helper application. GROUPWEB is based on a specialised browser. GROCO and COWEB both rely on functionality only available in a now obsolete alpha release of Java and the HOTJAVA browser.

Finally, all these systems (except GROCO) provide *very specific solutions to specific problems,* or types of synchronous interaction, making them unsuitable as general toolkits to build and support CSCW applications on the Web. Although GROCO has a number of other problems, it demonstrates that through the use of mobile code (Java) and the provision of a generic infrastructure for synchronous groupware, the Web architecture *can* be extended to more fully support CSCW.

3.3. Goals for supporting Web-based synchronous applications

Section 1 highlighted reasons behind the success of the Web as an infrastructure for supporting CSCW applications, one of the most important being critical mass. Two aspects of this are the use of standard protocols and platform independence. Section 2 showed how the Web's support for applications requiring more synchronous interaction is flawed and argued that any solution should not affect the aspects which make the Web so successful. This Section has presented a number of existing systems, both general and Web-specific and has highlighted shortcomings in both.

From these studies of existing systems and their problems we argue that any system which attempts to support synchronous cooperative work on the Web should adopt the concepts commonly supported by general toolkits (session management, access control, accessing shared information and support for application specific message exchange) while addressing the additional needs of Web-based applications:

- variable coupling of application models of cooperation to the Web,
- platform and browser independence,
- generic support for a range of applications.

The remainder of this paper presents *MetaWeb,* a general architecture and toolkit for developers of synchronous Web-based cooperative applications which provides the common concepts of existing toolkits while accommodating the additional requirements of the Web itself.

4. The MetaWeb Toolkit: Model and implementation

The MetaWeb toolkit provides basic support for the flexible coupling of Web pages to synchronous activities using mechanisms to manage additional "meta" information about pages on the Web. This includes who is browsing the pages and which cooperative sessions are currently running in or around the pages.

MetaWeb provides three abstractions for supporting the cooperation of Web-based applications: user, location and session. A **user** is the representation in the application of the person interacting with the toolkit. Users *visit* **locations** which are places where group interaction can take place. A location may be a virtual representation of a physical room or correspond to a Web page. A location *hosts* zero or more **sessions**. Sessions are a medium through which communication can take place between users. A session may *contain* zero or more users (its membership), and may place restrictions on that membership. Figure 3 shows these concepts and their relationships.

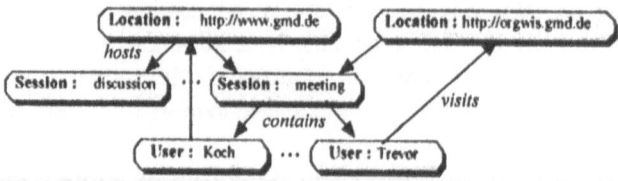

Figure 3. Example of Users, locations and sessions in MetaWeb

MetaWeb places no restrictions on how the notions of location and session are mapped to Web pages. Indeed, the concepts can be tightly coupled to the Web by assigning one location per page (as in Figure 3), and one session per location. In such a relationship, as a user loads different pages he "moves" between different locations in MetaWeb and on each page may see the users at that location/page. Different mappings between these concepts and the Web allow the various associations of the application's cooperative sessions to the Web listed in Section 3.2. In Figure 3 the "meeting" session is hosted by two locations (and Web pages in this mapping) while the "discussion" session can only be found in one. Indeed, Figure 3 shows users at different locations ("trevor" and "koch") in a common session ("meeting").

Although these relationships do not support the nesting capabilities of other session models, we believe that this simplified model *does* sufficiently support many Web-based cooperative applications in a straightforward and understandable manner. A much more complex model which may support every case is bound to be more difficult to understand, implement and use.

4.1. Object model

Each of the three concepts has a corresponding object type in MetaWeb. Applications make use of these concepts by creating instances of the object in MetaWeb. The MetaWeb toolkit maintains these objects and their relationships, which may be available to any application using the toolkit.

The user object is a representation of an application instance connected to the MetaWeb system. This application may present an interface to a real person, or may be an agent. The object is created when the application connects to the MetaWeb server (see below) and is used to identify the user in MetaWeb. Each user object has two default properties, a name, and a reference to its location.

Session objects maintain the current members of a session (as a list of user object references), an application-defined description of the session, and a list of potential members of the session (defined by the creator of a session). All remaining session behaviour and functionality, such as invitation, history maintenance and floor control, are responsibilities of the application itself.

Location objects have an associated list of zero or more session identifiers occurring at that location. This list may be changed to allow sessions to be attached or removed during the location's lifetime. Each location object also has a text identifier, which can be referenced to uniquely identify that location object in MetaWeb. For example, this identifier could be the URL of the page the location represents (as in Figure 3), or the number of a room.

In addition to the object-specific methods and values, instances of these objects can have any number of additional name-value pair attributes. This allows applications to add or remove application-specific named values from the objects during runtime. For example, an application may want to provide new user attributes, such as the user's phone number, or to add a description to its sessions.

4.2. Architecture and API

Figure 4 shows how MetaWeb extends the Web architecture through an additional client/server-system using its own protocol. This architecture can be split into four separate areas: application, API, client and server.

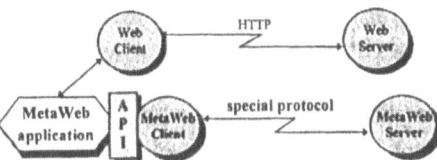

Figure 4. The MetaWeb architecture

The MetaWeb application is a part, or all, of the cooperative application that the developer builds. It is the developer's responsibility to present an interface to the user, take information from MetaWeb, display it in a suitable manner, translate user input into calls to MetaWeb and so on. This is where the application-specific semantics are supported and MetaWeb places no restrictions about what these are.

The application interacts with the MetaWeb toolkit through an API. This is a set of classes and methods which manipulate the object model (users, locations and sessions) and hide much of the underlying complexity from the developer.

The MetaWeb client provides two main services. Firstly, it acts as a representation of the user in MetaWeb. Whenever another application or the MetaWeb server needs to communicate with a certain user it is this client they refer to. Secondly, the client maintains local proxy representations of MetaWeb objects which are stored in the server. Whenever an application wants to use a particular object it is fetched locally, while a master copy of the object remains at the server. Changes to an object's state are first transmitted to the master, and then to any proxy representations.

The server itself is the heart of the toolkit, maintaining all the objects, enforcing access control, allowing interest registration and the propagation of events (see below). Any number of MetaWeb clients can be connected to the server at any time, supporting interaction across single or multiple applications.

4.3. Communication

Communication is based on the notion of events, which provide an abstraction of state changes in distributed applications. MetaWeb applications create their own events and send them to sessions, specific users or to the system in general (for anyone interested). Events are first created at the MetaWeb client, which sends them to the server, which propagates them to "interested" MetaWeb clients.

"Interest" may either be implicit or explicit. Implicit interest registration is derived from the concepts, where session members automatically subscribe to all events which are sent to the session. Explicit interest registration allows applications to specify various interest contexts (or templates), which describe the set of events an application wants to receive. Events that are sent to the member "anyone" are only received by applications which have registered an interest matching that event. The developer's application itself receives events from the MetaWeb client by registering callbacks with the API, and should define appropriate event handlers for them.

Events are defined as objects with four attributes: the originator (who sent the event), the target (where the event is going), a type (an application-defined text tag to identify the type of event), and a body containing the contents of the event itself. The toolkit defines several types of system event which are used to transport information about state changes in its objects, such as users joining or leaving sessions. Applications are left to define their own generic events which may be used to transport application-specific state changes or information, such as a line of text typed into a chat window.

4.4. Access control

Access control is implemented to restrict access to sessions or private information transported by events. Access to event information can be restricted by the sender of the event and access to sessions (including the events that are sent to sessions) can be restricted by the creator of each session. In both cases access control is specified through one or more user object templates. These limit access to the protected object to only those user objects which have a superset of the name-value pairs in the template. Access control is applied at the server, where access is granted if the user object matches one of the specified templates.

Additional attributes of a MetaWeb object (Section 4.1) can be specified as "hidden". This means that they can only be "seen" by the MetaWeb server. When the object is manipulated by a client these attributes are not available. These hidden attributes can be used in conjunction with access templates to provide authentication.

For example, a session may specify a list of user templates where each template has a single "authenticate" attribute (possibly encrypted using the UNIX "crypt" function). This attribute value contains the username and password of a user. If a MetaWeb client wants to access the session, it must provide a user object with a matching authentication attribute.

4.5. Implementation

The MetaWeb API, client and server are implemented as a set of Java library classes. The user, location and session objects are high-level objects served by the API. Connection management and event transportation from the MetaWeb client to the server is performed using a special "Connector" object. Incoming events are handled at the client by an *EventManager* while an *ObjectManager* supports the transparent synchronisation between the local object repository and objects in the server. All events are transported using a technique of object serialisation (they are written directly to the network stream) and therefore the body of all events in MetaWeb (an object) must support this. Events also contain a sequence number which provides simple message ordering and concurrency control.

Enhancement of the Web browser (Figure 4) to present and provide access to the new functionality offered by MetaWeb is provided through the integration of Java applets into a standard Web page. This functionality allows the application-specific code to be fetched transparently from a Web server and run when a Web page is loaded into the browser. Although our approach does conflict with the desire not to change the Web, requiring a browser which supports Java, by far the most commonly used Web-browsers, Netscape and Internet Explorer, *do* provide this support across all major operating systems (and future browsers, in order to be accepted, have to follow this de facto standard). Therefore the Java-based approach is preferable over other techniques for enhancing the Web client, such as separate applications which communicate with the browser (using OLE etc.), as these are platform specific and require an additional application to be installed by the user.

5. Examples of MetaWeb in use

In order to demonstrate the viability of MetaWeb for both new and existing applications, this Section presents a new application, CoNAVIGATOR, and the extension of an existing Web-based CSCW application, BSCW, which uses MetaWeb to augment its existing asynchronous support.

5.1. A new application: The CoNAVIGATOR

CoNAVIGATOR is an application built entirely on top of MetaWeb and runs side-by-side with an existing browser (in the current implementation Netscape). It provides presence awareness of other people who are browsing the Web at the same time and place (page), without requiring any changes to these pages - allowing add-hoc cooperation to take place whenever people meet.

The CONAVIGATOR is built as a single Java applet which connects to MetaWeb using the "connector" object. The applet uses a mapping of one MetaWeb location to one page. The applet obtains the current page a user is browsing through the use of Netscape's LiveConnect architecture, and when the applet observes the user navigating to a new page[1] it changes the user's MetaWeb location. At each new location the applet queries MetaWeb about any sessions on that location and presents these to the user in its interface. A MetaWeb event is triggered whenever a user moves to a new page (location) and joins any session at that page. Consequently, other CONAVIGATOR applets browsing the page implicitly receive notification of the new user directly from MetaWeb.

While the sessions at each location are maintained by MetaWeb (description, membership etc.), the applet applies its own application-specific semantics to the sessions. In the current implementation, the CONAVIGATOR uses MetaWeb sessions for coordinating chat, vote and shared whiteboard applications, and for sending application-specific events for these applications (such as the line of text a user has typed into a chat session).

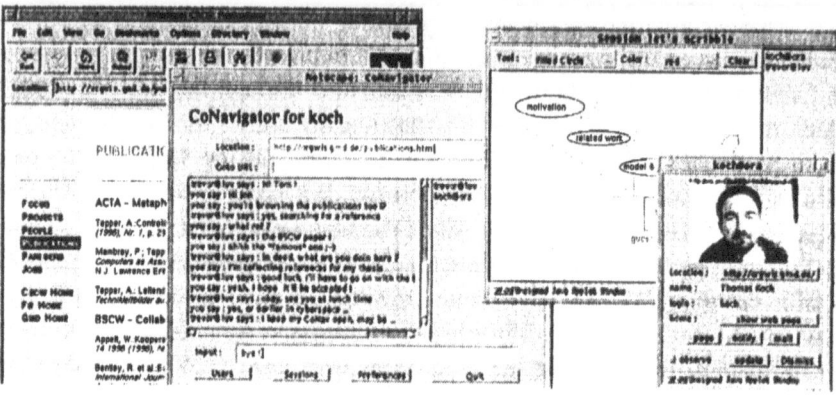

Figure 5. The CoNavigator

The CONAVIGATOR applet is started when a user submits a form from his browser. This form only requires a user name (no registration or authentication is performed) and users may add or remove additional information about themselves at any time later. Figure 5 shows the CONAVIGATOR in use and a number of cooperative sessions (chat and shared whiteboard) which have been started between the users "koch" and "trevor" on a page "orgwis.gmd.de/publications".

"Search" functionality which interrogates the underlying MetaWeb server extends the awareness between users beyond the single page being browsed, providing information (such as the location) of other CONAVIGATOR users. Once users become aware of the presence of others they can get detailed information about each other, similar to an electronic business card. The CONAVIGATOR supports the automatic establishment of communication between users using this information. For example,

---

[1] Due to security restrictions in Netscape a special "taint" flag must be set by the user prior to using the browser. This allows the applet to get the current location from the browser, but unfortunately causes Netscape to repeatedly issue warnings when this is done. This solution works, but is not ideal (see later for alternatives).

if a user enters his COOLTALK address in the CONAVIGATOR (which can be automatically filled in by the application), another user viewing this information simply clicks on the address and (providing he has set up his browser correctly) COOLTALK is launched and connects to that address automatically.

5.2. An existing application: MetaWeb and the BSCW system

The BSCW system (Bentley et al., 1997) is based on the idea of a "shared workspace" which the members of a group establish for organising and coordinating their work. A shared workspace as realised by BSCW is a repository for shared information, accessible to workgroup members using the normal user name/password authentication scheme. In general, a "BSCW server" (a standard Web server extended with the BSCW system through the CGI) manages a number of shared workspaces for different groups and users may be members of several workspaces, perhaps corresponding to the projects the users are currently involved in. These workspaces are accessible from any standard Web browser.

Figure 6. The BSCW system

A workspace can contain different kinds of information, represented as information objects arranged in a folder hierarchy. In Figure 6 the workspace "ECSCW97 paper" contains an article object which holds a simple text message ("important dates"), a folder containing postscript image files ("Screendump Figures"), a URL ("ECSCW97 home page") and a LaTeX document ("Submitted version"). The last "significant" operation performed on each object is described, and a list of clickable "event icons" give information on other recent changes. The operations which can be performed are given below each object and a description is also presented if one has been supplied (as with "Submitted paper"). Clicking one of the HTML anchors below an object requests operations on the object from the BSCW server (such as "rename"). After each operation the server returns a new HTML page showing the current state of the workspace.

BSCW provides little real-time awareness of the actions of other people co-using BSCW. In practice, a user would not realise that other members of the workspace are interacting with the system at the same time. The only indication a user receives that another user may also be working in a workspace is the event information which is presented about each object. If a user is working with a document, then any changes made to the document will be shown by an event icon in the workspace listing the next time the page is fetched from the server.

The goal of integrating MetaWeb is to extend the BSCW system with continuous feedback of the actions ("activity" awareness) and availability ("presence" awareness) of others. We expect that such awareness will promote a richer form of cooperation to occur, rather than the passive form supported now. There are several issues which need to be considered when extending BSCW with MetaWeb, which are also generally applicable to the extension of any Web-based application:

Relating BSCW concepts to MetaWeb: Workspaces and Sessions

Sessions in MetaWeb define a logical scope for event propagation through a scheme of simple implicit interest registration: an event that is sent to a specific session will automatically be sent to all session members by the MetaWeb server. The location concept allows sessions to be treated together. For BSCW, we want to provide awareness at the granularity of a workspace (which is the highest level at which BSCW provides awareness) for users collaborating within that workspace. Because MetaWeb locations do not have to have a physical or logical equivalent, we can choose to provide one MetaWeb location per workspace. Each of these workspace-locations contains one *BSCW awareness* session plus any additional application-defined sessions supporting synchronous collaboration (e.g. a chat session). The workspace-location and the BSCW awareness session are created and maintained by the BSCW event agent itself (see below), while any other sessions which may occur within that location can be created and managed by the MetaWeb clients themselves.

Integrating the MetaWeb Architecture

Figure 7 shows the BSCW architecture extended with MetaWeb. The underlying BSCW architecture remains unaltered, with the communication between the user's Web browser and the BSCW kernel still based around HTTP/HTML. The extended functionality is achieved by enhancing the Web browser with a MetaWeb client that connects to the MetaWeb event server at the workspace's corresponding MetaWeb location. Information about BSCW events is provided by the BSCW system to MetaWeb through a special *event agent*. Upon receiving a BSCW event from the BSCW kernel, the agent puts it into the body of a new MetaWeb event and delivers it to the MetaWeb event server, which is then addressed to the "BSCW awareness" session for the location representing the workspace in which the event occurred. The event is then distributed as normal and any MetaWeb clients (BSCW users) at the corresponding location (and session) will be notified of the new BSCW event.

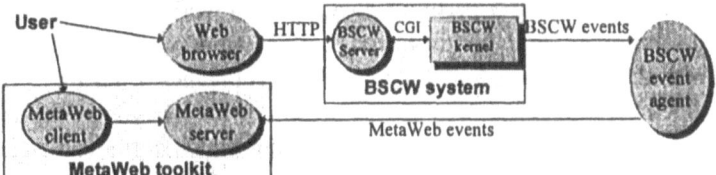

Figure 7. BSCW-MetaWeb integration

Duplicating access restrictions to application information: BSCW events

The BSCW system enforces access control over its objects and events which occur on those objects. In broad terms, the effect of this control is that users can only see events which have happened to objects in workspaces of which they are members. It is important that any provision of synchronous event notification through MetaWeb does not compromise this access control, which would allow viewing of events not otherwise possible. There are two implications of this requirement. Firstly, MetaWeb must restrict access to these events in the same way as BSCW. Secondly, and unlike the CONAVIGATOR, users of the BSCW-MetaWeb clients must be authenticated, i.e. they must be who they say they are.

There are two basic areas where access to events may be restricted: the events themselves (who can receive them) and in the MetaWeb objects (who can join a session). Although both methods are sufficient to mimic the access control provided by BSCW, we have chosen to use the second, session object, method for simplicity. If in the future the event access model in BSCW becomes more complex then the first method can easily be adopted instead.

The problem of authentication is solved using the "hidden" scheme of name-value pair matching (presented in Section 4.4). In BSCW, members authenticate using user names and passwords. Therefore, MetaWeb uses a combination of the user name and password to provide the hidden value to match.

Extending the interface: The BSCW-MetaWeb client

To make use of the synchronous awareness information provided by BSCW and MetaWeb, the workspace user must start a special BSCW-MetaWeb application that connects to the MetaWeb server. The application goes to the appropriate location which represents the workspace the user wants to be aware of, joins the BSCW awareness session at that location, and then receives and displays BSCW events as they occur. This application is built as a Java applet, Figure 8, launched when a user clicks on a special "Awareness" button which has been added to the standard BSCW interface (Figure 6). User details, maintained in a MetaWeb user object, are obtained from the BSCW system itself and encoded into the applet when it is started.

Figure 8 shows the BSCW-MetaWeb application interface. The "User" tab provides "presence" awareness, showing who else is "in" the workspace and using the MetaWeb client. If the user chooses not be "present" then they will not be seen by other MetaWeb users, but neither can the user see them. Clicking on a user's name brings up information concerning that user in the MetaWeb system. The "Events" tab gives "activity" awareness, presenting the BSCW events as they occur in the workspace. Whenever any user performs an action in a workspace, such as renaming a document, the event will be displayed in the window. The applet is tightly integrated with the browser and clicking on the object names or locations causes the browser to fetch the object from the BSCW system or the location to be visited. The "Session" tab shows the current cooperative sessions which a user can create or join (which have corresponding MetaWeb session objects), such as chat, whiteboard and voting sessions (see Section 5.1). These sessions and their semantics are managed by the BSCW-MetaWeb application and server rather than BSCW itself.

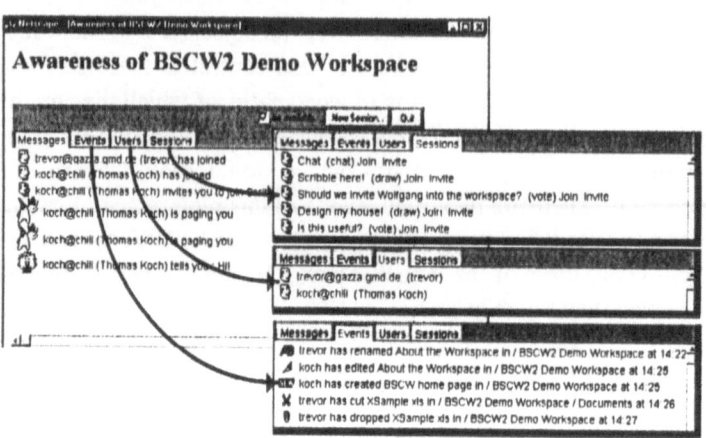

Figure 8. The BSCW-MetaWeb application.

A second tool is available which presents an "at a glance" overview of the presence and activities of users in all of the BSCW workspaces the member can access. Information about the changes in the workspaces can be unfolded to a greater level of detail and users can bring up a full MetaWeb awareness client for a workspace (above) simply by clicking on the workspace name.

6. Observations and discussion

The MetaWeb toolkit has been used to develop a variety of small applications on the Web, and two larger ones have been described in this paper. The different uses of Web pages to support cooperation in these applications demonstrates the need and importance of providing flexible cooperative session coupling to the Web, something novel offered only by MetaWeb. In CONAVIGATOR, cooperation takes place in single pages while in the BSCW integration the users' cooperative activities span many pages (which make up a workspace). However, our experiences with MetaWeb have highlighted a number of issues.

Firstly, Section 3.3. presented several goals for a toolkit which were addressed in the design and implementation of MetaWeb. This included the provision of mechanisms to support general access to shared information. In MetaWeb the only shared objects are those representing the core MetaWeb concepts of user, location and session. While it is possible for applications to define and maintain their own shared objects within the MetaWeb server using the event service, there is no fundamental support for this sharing within the toolkit itself.

Secondly, in Section 4 we explained our motivation to limit the relationship between sessions and locations to deliberately restrict session nesting. It remains to be seen if this simplification in both concept and implementation does not overly restrict other Web-based applications.

Thirdly, the use of a single centralised MetaWeb server may limit the scalability and performance of the current toolkit. For single applications, such as BSCW, this single server approach is not a problem, and Web-based applications tend to service all requests from a single HTTP server anyway (Figure 2). However, a single server approach does not promote inter-operation between different applications using the MetaWeb toolkit (unless they choose to use the same server). For applications which have no centralised coordinating server, such as the CONAVIGATOR, a multi-server approach (with local servers) should boost performance.

Fourthly, while the MetaWeb server guarantees a basic event message ordering, there is no support for such concurrency control in the MetaWeb applications themselves. Consequently, in the example of a chat session, ordering of messages is guaranteed by the client first sending a user's typed chat line to the MetaWeb server, and waiting for the event to be delivered back to itself before displaying the line in the main dialog window. Where more fine-grained or immediate feedback is required, such as with a synchronous shared authoring tool, the existing MetaWeb concurrency control scheme may be too limited.

Finally, this paper has focused on the technical issues and problems of supporting cooperation on the Web. Once that support is present, a number of interesting questions are raised. For example, users of the CONAVIGATOR cannot be sure that users they "meet" are who they say they are. People often ask strangers in the real-world for directions to a place without asking for identification first, and trust those directions they receive. Is it a problem therefore that users of CONAVIGATOR also lack that authentication? Future work with MetaWeb will explore some of the social implications of providing synchronous cooperation on the Web, as well as the more technical issues above.

7. Conclusions

The Web is an important platform for CSCW system development and deployment. Despite the many advantages which make the Web such an attractive platform, developers face a significant shortcoming in the Web's architecture for supporting synchronous cooperation. Changing the Web directly (either its clients or protocols) effects the very aspects which make the Web so useful. This paper has argued that the solution lies in an additional infrastructure which runs alongside the Web.

The MetaWeb toolkit attempts to provide this infrastructure by providing support for the common features found in more general toolkits, such as session management, access control, mechanisms for accessing shared information, and support for message exchange. Further, the MetaWeb toolkit also addresses the additional requirements which the Web brings: platform and browser independence, variable coupling of application models of cooperation to the Web, generic support for a range of applications, and the support for mutual awareness of others. By supporting both sets of requirements MetaWeb not only aids developers in building and representing a cooperative system on the Web, but also promotes the aspects of the Web which make it such a desirable platform for implementation.

Acknowledgements

The BSCW system reported in this paper is funded as part of the CoopWWW Project by the European Union under the Telematics Applications Programme (TE 2003). We thank Richard Bentley, Wolfgang Appelt, Klaas Sikkel, and David Kerr for their comments and contributions to the paper.

References

Bentley, R., Appelt, W., Busbach. U., Hinrichs, E., Kerr, D., Sikkel, S., Trevor, J. and Woetzel, G. (1997): "Basic Support for Cooperative Work on the World Wide Web". To appear in *International Journal of Human-Computer Studies: Special issue on Innovative Applications of the World Wide Web*. Academic Press. Available spring 1997.

Berners-Lee T., Cailliau R., Luotonen A., Nielsen H.F. and Secret A. (1994): "The World-Wide Web". *Communications of the ACM*, vol.37 no.8, August, 1994, pp. 76-82

Crowley, T., Milazzo, P., Baker, E., Forsdick, H. and Tomlinson, R. (1990): "MMConf: An Infrastructure for Building Shared Multimedia Applications", *CSCW'90*, October 7-10, Los Angeles, ACM Press, 1990, pp.329-342.

Dix, A. (1997): "Challenges for Cooperative Work on the Web: An analytic approach", *Computer Supported Cooperative Work: The Journal of Collaborative Computing: Special Issue on CSCW and the Web*, Kluwer, 6(2-3), in press.

Ellis C.A., Gibbs S.J. and Rein, G.L. (1991): "Groupware : Some issues and experiences". *Communications of the ACM*, vol.34, no.1, 1991, pp. 38-58.

Freund, R. (1996): "A Model to Access Groupware Systems via the World-Wide Web", Masters thesis, Bonn University, Informatik III., 1996. http://orgwis.gmd.de/projects/POLITeam/www/

Greenberg, S. and Roseman, M. (1996): "GroupWeb: A Web Browser as Real-Time Groupware", *CHI'96*, April 13-18, Vancouver, Canada, ACM Press, 1996, pp.271-272.

Grudin, J. (1988) "Why CSCW Applications fail: Problems in the Design and Evaluation of organizational Interfaces",*CSCW'88*, Sept.26-29, Portland, Oregon. ACM Press,1988, pp.85-93.

Jacobs, S., Gebhardt, M., Kethers, S. and Rzasa, W. (1996): "Filling HTML forms simultaneously: CoWeb - architecture and functionality", *5th International World Wide Web Conference WWW'96*, May 6-10, Paris, 1996, pp. 1385-1395.

Patterson, J.F., Hill, R.D. and Rohall, S.L. (1990): "Rendezvous: An Architecture for Synchronous Multi-User Applications", *CSCW'90*, October 7-10,Los Angeles, ACM Press, 1990, pp.317-328.

Roseman, M. and Greenberg, S. (1992): "GroupKit: A Groupware Toolkit for Building Real-Time Conferencing Applications",*CSCW'92*, Oct. 31-Nov 4, Toronto, ACM Press, 1992, pp. 43-50.

Trevor, J., Bentley, R. and Wildgruber, G. (1996): "Exorcising daemons: a modular and lightweight approach to deploying applications on the Web", *5th International World Wide Web Conference WWW'96*, May 6-10, Paris, 1996, pp. 1053-1062.

Ubique (1995): "Virtual Places", http://www.vplaces.com/vpnet/index.html

Walther, M. (1996): "Supporting Development of Synchronous Collaboration Tools on the Web with GroCo", *5th ERCIM/W4G Workshop*, GMD, Sankt Augustin, Germany. Arbeitspapiere der GMD Nr. 984, February, 1996, pp. 81-89.

Woo, T.K. and Rees, M.J. (1994): "A Synchronous Collaboration Tool for World-Wide Web", *2nd International World Wide Web Conference WWW'94*, Chicago, 1994.

Constructing Common Information Spaces

Liam Bannon and Susanne Bødker
Computer Science and Information Systems Department, University of Limerick,
IRELAND,
Department of Computer Science, University of Aarhus, DENMARK,
liam.bannon@ul.ie, bodker@daimi.aau.dk

This paper investigates an important, yet under-researched topic in CSCW, namely shared, or common, information spaces. Precisely what is meant by this term, however, is not always obvious. We provide some background to work in the area, and then proceed to examine features of such spaces through examples. The work involved in both putting information in common, and in interpreting it, has often not been sufficiently recognized. We show how, in various ways, it often requires added work to place items in common, and open up the question of how this might affect use of the WWW, often seen as the ultimate common information space. While there is still a need for further elaboration of many dimensions of the concept, and linkage to related ideas, we believe that the issues raised by this exploration are of importance to the CSCW field.

1. Introduction

One of the distinguishing features of the CSCW field over the years has been the continuing effort expended on understanding the nature of cooperative work, the sociality of work, with a view to assisting in the design of genuinely "supportive" computer-based information systems. In its attempts to achieve this goal, the field has embraced a variety of disciplines, conceptual frameworks and methodologies. Whilst not all members of the CSCW community share similar perspectives or approaches, the field as a whole has been shaped by a number of core ideas, e.g the

81

J. Hughes et al. (eds.), Proceedings of the Fifth European Conference on Computer Supported Cooperative Work, 81-96.
© *1997 Kluwer Academic Publishers.*

work of Strauss (1993) on actions/interactions in social worlds, and the importance of "articulation work", Suchman's work (1987) on "situated action", Flores and Winograd (1986) on "language as action", and the work of Schmidt and Simone (1995) on "coordination mechanisms" have become important frameworks for discussing key CSCW issues, irrespective of the position one takes on the efficacy or utility of these particular viewpoints.

In this paper, we analyse another key concept which we believe to be of central importance in CSCW, namely the construction, use and maintenance of what we call a *common information space* (CIS) among people performing cooperative work. Through the use of several examples, we examine features of this space, and attempt to construct an outline framework within which to discuss issues of collaboration and sharing of information among actors. Our efforts are aimed at pointing to interesting differences in the way in which people, artifacts and settings are brought together in order to accomplish work in different settings. Thus the concept of a CIS is not put forward as another loose abstraction, but rather as a potentially useful construct that may help in elucidating important aspects of cooperative work activity. Key features of our analysis of CISs include: the seemingly dialectical nature of these spaces, the frequent need for additional effort in order to put, or use, information "in common", the need for both closure and openness in representations, their simultaneous portability and immutability, etc.

The structure of the paper is as follows: In Section 2 we provide an outline of the CIS concept. In Section 3 we relate this conceptualisation to earlier discussions on aspects of this theme in the CSCW literature, and connect these discussions to a number of other important topics that have surfaced amongst researchers studying the boundaries between people, technology and work settings. In Section 4 we return to more extended examples of these information spaces, which align some of the apparently contradictory findings concerning the nature of shared information spaces by demonstrating the dialectical nature of these spaces, before concluding the paper.

2. Putting information in common

Ever since the founding of the CSCW field, there have been debates as to the fundamental nature of cooperative work. e.g., whether all work is not, ultimately, cooperative, or whether the term denotes a specific form of work (Bannon & Schmidt, 1991). While we do not wish to re-visit this debate here, we wish to note that in any cooperative work situation, there is a need for some form of communication or information sharing between actors, implicit or explicit, in order to ascertain what features of the work are of note in that specific situation. Exactly what constitutes this "information space" is not agreed. For some, it simply refers to information, events, or objects that are tangible, external, "out there" in the world, that can be described extensively. For others, the "space" necessarily involves an interpretative component - the meaning of the terms or objects are not simply "given", but require an effort of interpretation on the part of the human actors who inhabit this space. It is this latter view which we emphasize here. Thus, to the extent that multiple actors can construct and maintain a common information space, they are able to articulate their work, and thus perform cooperative work.

Common information spaces come in many forms. They are in some cases constituted for people that are co-present in time and space, whereas in other situations they are distributed across time and space boundaries, and the mechanisms used to support "holding in common" the information varies accordingly. The nature of these CISs vary depending on the work context. Thus, in the case of a physically shared workspace, due to the common work setting and exposure to the same work environment, actors are able to cooperate with each other, both in the production and reception of utterances and information, without having to resort to extended descriptions or elaborated codes, due to their understanding of the shared context within which they work. Thus in this setting, there is little additional effort required to construct and use the CIS. On the other hand, in distributed work settings, there is a much greater need for refining and "packaging" information into a meaningful context, in order to maximise the likelihood that the intent of the message is received appropriately, and the recipient is also required to expend some effort in order to "unpack" this information, and hopefully be able to re-create the context of its transmission. Note that we are not arguing for some notion of perfect information transmission here, as we do not believe such a concept makes sense within human activities, rather we wish to draw attention to the myriad of ways in which people struggle to make sense of each other, through drawing on cues from the work setting in order to understand each other. At this juncture, it is also important to point out that, while we are focusing on the need for CISs in this paper, there is also an equally important need to clarify the role of private and bounded spaces in cooperative work situations. In an important paper, Clement and Wagner (1995) provide an insightful overview of exactly this topic, developing "a conceptual framework which allows us to construct rich representations of "sharing and access" within and in between communities of practice". We will return to their work in several places in this text.

Most discussions of shared spaces in CSCW have tended to confine themselves to situations in 'real-time', or near real-time. Our conceptualization of CISs however extends to situations where information is entered into a database at one point in time and subsequently accessed by others, perhaps months or even years later. In what sense can we characterize this situation as a CIS? In our view, the reason is because both the producer and the receiver consciously make an effort to understand each other's context - of production and use, so that even though the efforts may be distributed over time and space, there is a form of communication, of "putting in common", going on in such activity. One major difference between such file use activities and those in the shared workspaces example mentioned earlier is that in the file example there is a more explicit attempt to "package" aspects of the context with the information, in an effort to ensure that in future use situations, the rationale for the original information is apparent. Of course, there is no way in which one can guarantee that this will be the case, but it does mean that the context of the production of information affects its form. Thus in cooperative work situations (defined as such even in the absence of a second actor "in the flesh", so to speak, but existing through the medium of their packaged information) we find situations where CISs are both open and closed - in a word, they have a dialectical nature. As we examine different settings, we will attempt to illustrate this dialectical nature of CISs, emphasizing on the one hand the open and malleable role of a CIS within a community of practice, as exemplified in the shared workspace concept, and, on the other, the role of CISs as boundary objects, packaged and being turned into immutables to allow for sharing across contexts and communities of practice, and over time, as in the filing system example. While this discussion may seem overly esoteric and, at first glance, of little relevance to ordinary CSCW system design, we hope to show through illustrative examples below how such ideas can assist us in understanding and constructing common information spaces. Let us first assess what aspects of CISs have been noted in the literature to date, before proceeding with our elaborations on the concept.

3. Dimensions of CISs - Links to earlier work

Perhaps one of the most detailed attempts to explicate the nature of this concept appears in Schmidt & Bannon (1992), following on from their earlier discussion of "shared information spaces"[1] in Bannon & Schmidt (1989, 1991), where they discuss common information spaces as an alternative mechanism to procedural or workflow-type arrangements that could support cooperative work:

> .. the construction and management of what we term a "common information space" has, in our view, been somewhat neglected, despite its critical importance for the accomplishment of many distributed work activities. Here the focus is on how people in a distributed setting can work cooperatively in a common information space - i.e. by maintaining a central archive of organizational information with some level of 'shared' agreement as to the meaning of this information (locally constructed), despite the marked differences concerning the origins and context of these information items. The space is constituted and maintained by different actors employing different conceptualizations and multiple decision making strategies, supported by technology. Schmidt & Bannon (1992)

Schmidt & Bannon note that this space does not simply consist of objects, events, e.g. in a shared database, but also crucially involves the joint interpretation of these objects and events by the actors involved :

> Cooperative work is not facilitated simply by the provision of a shared database, but requires the active construction by the participants of a common information space where the meanings

---

[1] While originally, in Bannon & Schmidt 1991, we referred to "shared information spaces", we subsequently shifted to talking of "common" spaces as it lessened the connotations associated with the word "sharing" - and indicates the transient and instrumental aspects of people having information "in common".

of the shared objects are debated and resolved, at least locally and temporarily. Objects must thus be interpreted and assigned meaning, meanings that are achieved by specific actors on specific occasions of use. Schmidt & Bannon (1992)

They discuss in more detail the issues surrounding the interpretation work that is required by the actors in order to construct common meanings. They indicate possible problems that may occur in the subsequent interpretation of information by others where the origins of the information, in terms of the person or system that constructed it, or aspects of the context within which the information was produced, may not be available to other actors in the space. In such situations, the intended meaning of the information may not be apparent to the new user, as the information objects typically do not record the originator of the information, nor the context of its creation. Examples of situations where this lack of contextual information can be important are also given. Crucially, the paper also distinguishes a variety of work settings, and shows how the work involved to make these information spaces cohere for the actors involved can be radically different in different settings. We will return to this point later in the paper.

The problems encountered when different groups of people are involved in the production and maintenance of an information space extending over time and space have surfaced in a number of quite disparate studies concerning the relation between people and technology, many of which have not been conducted by people in the CSCW field. Within the field of social studies of science and technology, the problems of "alignment" of human and technical actors has been noted, and the way artefacts both shape and are shaped by the actor networks within which they participate (Callon, 1991).[2] The work of Leigh Star and others on the concept of "boundary objects", and that of Latour and colleagues on the creation of "immutable mobiles", both can be viewed as being concerned with how communities develop means for sharing items in a common information space. For example, based on a study of a zoological museum, its creation, use and representations, Star & Griesemer (1989) introduce the concept of boundary objects characterising common intellectual tools, which play the role of containers and carriers:

> ...both plastic enough to adapt to local needs and constraints of the several parties employing them, yet robust enough to maintain a common identity across sites. They are weakly structured in common use, and become strongly structured in individual site-use. Like a blackboard, a boundary object 'sits in the middle' of a group of actors with divergent viewpoints (Star & Griesemer, 1989, p. 46).

The ordering and registration of the animals in the museum is one example of a boundary object, a map is another. They are both there to be used by all users of the museum, though these users use the boundary objects in very different ways. As we shall see, discussions of boundary objects can be a vehicle for further studies of common information spaces across organizational boundaries. Understanding how

---

[2] The validity of the actor-network framework is not our concern here, simply to note that some of the work done under its rubric is of relevance to our current concerns about the development of common information spaces.

people work together in networked communities is another area of investigation that has relevance for our discussions here. The concept of "community of practice" developed by Lave & Wenger (1991) to indicate the learning and working environment(s) in which most people work has important implications for the kinds of shared spaces that we might wish to develop for particular purposes. Whether we are moving information within or between communities of practice becomes of central concern. Robinson and Bannon (1991), within the CSCW field, explore some of the difficulties that can occur in sharing representations across different communities. While their paper discusses these issues in the context of systems development methodologies and practices, the problems noted pervade almost any distributed cooperative work setting where there is a requirement for the maintenance of some shared understanding of objects, events, information etc. within an information space peopled by actors from different communities of practice. Bücher et al. (in preparation), propose that whereas Lave and Wenger's concept of "community of practice" is useful in studying what in Bannon and Robinson's terms is called a semantic community, it may be helpful to seek inspiration from actor-network theory and Star's "boundary objects" concept when investigating situations where objects move across semantic boundaries. This is due to the fact that both the active construction by the participants of a common information space - where the meanings of the shared objects are debated and resolved - and boundary crossing of objects between semantic communities, often are very closely interlinked. As Bücher, Gill, Mogensen and Shapiro explain:

> We are therefore drawn to some parallels with the application of 'actor-network theory' to the study of science (..) There too, there is a concern with the way in which the resources of a process - people, machines, materials are mobilized; and with the way that the outcomes are sometimes simplified as 'punctuations' which realise a particular form of summation of a network's activity (...). This can often be as texts or what Latour (..) terms 'immutable mobiles' - artefacts which hold stable the intractable and heterogenous materials from which they were composed, and which can be conveyed, collated, compared. We consider that the intimate engagement of an ongoing work process is better understood as a community of practice, whereas an actor-network approach can be helpful in understanding the hand-offs and translations which are also a natural feature of the work. Crudely a punctuation can be a point of closure for a situated practice - albeit sometimes a local and temporary one, requiring maintenance and repair.

It is this tension between the need for openness and malleability of information on the one hand, and, on the other, the need for some form of closure, to allow for forms of translation and portability between communities, that we believe characterises the nature of common information spaces, and leads to difficulties in their characterisation. CISs are both open and closed - in a word, they have a dialectical nature. As an example, Bødker (in preparation a) discusses the development of "portable contexts" of representations for systems development (Brown & Duguid, 1994). The context of use is continuously changing, in a dialectical relationship with the practice emerging in the borderland between various communities of practice. These issues of translation, closure, contexts, portability, etc. relate directly to aspects of Latour's (1987,1990) analyses concerning the construction of "immutable mobiles". Again, we are dealing with the problem of maintaining and preserving some shared interpretation or representation, artefact, across divides of space, time and culture. The work of Clement and Wagner (1995) on fragmentation and regionalisation of communication spaces and their implications for the possibilities of shared communication is also quite pertinent, (although the concepts of CISs and communication spaces, while overlapping heavily, are not, in our view, identical). They also pay attention to the issue of boundaries - "greater attention must be paid to questions of boundary management - especially who is within (and outside) the space for particular types of communication." As a result, they recognize that "..there should be technical facilities for allowing participants to erect, shift, blur, harden, dissolve, and strengthen the boundaries to communication spaces."

Having now reviewed some of the literature relating to the CIS concept, we plunge ahead with our elaboration of the concept in the next Section.

4. Articulating dimensions of CISs

No representation ..... is either complete or permanent. Rather any description is a snapshot of historical processes in which differing viewpoints, local contingencies and multiple interests have been temporarily reconciled.

Gerson and Star (1986)

In this paper we describe how differing viewpoints, local contingencies and multiple interests are temporarily reconciled in the actual construction of a CIS; how information items may be supplied with some kind of portable context; how local contexts are re-established based on the unpacking of the information from other contexts of use; and how, as a consequence, information items can maintain their open and malleable character in local contexts. We propose that most common information spaces have two aspects: perceived as the working material of a community of practice, the CIS is open, malleable and interpretable, and a number of concerns, as exemplified by studies on centres of coordination, are highly relevant. At the same time, creating closures of various kinds - punctuations - is an equally valid perspective, suggesting a perspective on the common information space as boundary object (Star), border resource (Brown & Duguid), or immutable mobile (Latour). It is the interplay between these two perspectives that can help illuminate the nature of common information spaces.

We find further inspiration from Giddens (1990) who discusses organizations which have been delegated a certain area of societal competence which is not a part of the everyday competence of the rest of us. For such an organization it is extremely important not to reveal the complexity and ambiguity of phenomena/decisions "frontstage" -i.e. their operations and activities are accessible and visible to users. From the viewpoint of the organization, it is important that procedures are not only carried out correctly, but are clearly seen to be so, from the outside. This frontstage side of organizations in many cases puts an emphasis on closures and immutability whereas "backstage" the perspective of the CIS as open and malleable often makes more sense. In what follows we will use a number of examples to illustrate how common information spaces are constituted rather differently in different organizations, at the same time as there are interestingly similar patterns: In many cases, this is indeed a result of a trade-off between the concerns for openness and malleability on the one hand and for closure on the other. We will specifically look at the work required both to leave an information space malleable and open, and to create these necessary closures so as to transform the information into something that is immutable and ready to "travel" across boundaries of communities of practice.

4.1. Creating a CIS - within a shared workspace

In our first set of cases, work arrangements have evolved to produce complex centres of coordination (e.g. Suchman, 1993, Goodwin & Goodwin, 1996) where several people and artefacts are physically co-located, with shared reources, in real-time, and jointly handle the large number of complex interweaved tasks involved. In the airline operations room described by Goodwin & Goodwin, Suchman and others, the CIS is constituted by the representations of objects and events depicted on screens, charts, etc., spoken out loud in the room, etc. Many of the objects referred to are "out there" as planes, gates and such to be inspected through various more or less structured means. This is combined with complex sheets and other more specialized coordination devices. The common information space is shaped by reading out loud, by shared access to gate monitors etc. Goodwin & Goodwin (1996) emphasize how this common information space allows for different readings based on the purpose of the activity, and that the openness of access is important. In this example the common information space is open and situated, with the participants being able to make interpretations based on their shared physical context. Here, there is a need for as rich a common information space as possible, as the ever changing conditions may require modifications to established procedures, and any such changes require coordination across the set of activities being performed. In such situations, we find numerous examples of complex human coordination patterns, involving "looking over each other's shoulder", peripheral awareness, joint monitoring of status screens, broadcast announcements, etc., all intended to ensure that the group as a whole is aware of the current situation and monitoring the unfolding events. In such a situation, members of the team do not have the time to package their information in particular ways, but have to assume that others can interpret events correctly due to the massively shared context that exists in this work setting. This kind of work arrangement is one where the importance remains with an open and malleable CIS, and where parties outside the center of coordination has very limited access to, and interest in this CIS.

4.2 Constructing CISs when cooperating at a distance

In many situations, however, work is organized differently. There is a physical separation between workers, a rigid division of labour, more limited access to shared "material" and regulated procedures to package information and control its movement to selected people in the line. Such a work arrangement is characterized by the assumption that access to an open, malleable and shared information space is unnecessary because of the division of work, etc. Such organizational arrangements characterize, in Weberian terms, a bureaucracy, where the openness and malleability of the information have been minimised, and thus the information can pass to other groups working within the bureaucracy with a minimum of interpretative work (though work is still required, inevitably). In this situation, people are cooperating at "arm's length" (Schmidt & Bannon, 1992) and do not have the ability to clarify interpretations of information, as in situations such as air traffic control rooms or other coordination centres where people are co-located.

As an example, at the local branch of the Danish National Labour Inspection Service (AT), a centralized computer system (VIRK) is applied to record the interaction of AT with companies (see Bødker 1993). Visits to work sites as well as correspondence with companies are recorded, and various materials can be extracted, ranging from lists of specific types of companies within a geographical zone to lists of which recommendations and demands the AT has sent to a specific company. The underlying filing system is intended to support later retrival of information about particular companies for the organization as such. The files of interaction constitutes the organizational record of past cases and procedures, the retrieval of which is supported by VIRK. At the same time, there are limited possibilities, in the system, for the inspectors to maintain work material for the handling of a particular case, an issue that will be discussed in 4.3. However, whenever an inspector opens a case, he looks at the information that is available about previous encounters with the company: inspections made by himself, perhaps years earlier, or by somebody else. Whenever he closes a case he needs to be concerned with how the material may be used in later encounters with the particular company. At the same time he has no way of knowing what the purpose of this future case or encounter may be, and what information could potentially be vital at this later stage. Thus, a key concern here is with the active nature of the understanding process on the part of the participants. Without an understanding of the different contexts in which information is produced and potentially the different concerns of the originator, the receiver, as in this case a labour inspector, is liable to make incorrect inferences as to the meaning of the "shared" information. But the important point is to realize that one cannot just produce a common information space, that it does not automatically appear as the result of developing a common dictionary of terms and objects, as the meanings of these terms and objects must still be determined locally and temporally. In the labour inspection, what is considered serious offences and work hazards have changed dramatically over even relative short time spans. The common information space is negotiated and established by the actors involved. There is effort expended on the part of people who put information into the CIS, in terms of how they package the information or event so that it can be successfully be used by others, in some future use situation. There is also effort expended on the part of those people who lookup information in this common information space and attempt to make sense of what they find, when they may lack knowledge of the context in which the information was produced, or when this context has canged.

4.3 CISs - malleability for some yet closure for others

If one goes to the railway station and looks at the time table, one hardly cares who produced the time table. What matters is if the organization as such does not provide what they claim to provide: if there is no train, no announcement of its absence, etc. At the same time somebody, and most likely more than one person, provided the information, and knows about its ambiguities. In the AT case, the VIRK system is also used to provide statistics for the head office in Copenhagen. These figures (numbers of visits, demands, etc.) is the way in which central management has access to the doings of the branch office. The figures are provided by the inspectors though they have little need for them. Due to Danish legislation, citizens have access to all information kept in electronic files by public authorities. This makes VIRK interesting in that it is actually primarily meant to support internal division and delegation of work, i.e. backstage activity. However, because of the potential public access it is only possible to add things to the files that the labour inspectorate are willing to let the "customers" see. In the context of common information spaces, issues of how closures are created become important - what is inscribed in the record and what is left out. This makes internal notes and remarks highly problematic, and filing in VIRK can be seen as an unceasing transformation of material from backstage to frontstage, thus leaving a big hole as regards the maintenance of working material. Internal notes etc. are simply not able to be kept together with the case material. As described in Bødker (1993) the inspectors want to keep such notes and leave traces for later case work, but that is not possible in the current situation. From the perspective of providing as rich a context for interpretation of the information as possible, logic would indicate that working notes, comments etc. should be available on the system so that future users of the information could, if necessary try to re-construct the rationale. But as all of the information in these systems could legally be require to be produced in certain cases, in order to ensure proper procedures and provide a coherent frontstage view, it may be "logical" to refuse to allow these kinds of working notes to be inscribed in the record.

While bureaucracies may value anonymity for certain purposes, there are many situations where the interpretation of information in a CIS requires knowledge of the identity of the originator of the information. Due to the fact that people employ different problem-solving and decision-making strategies, people may need to allow for the different strategies used by people who are populating the information space. For example, as observed by Cicourel (1990) in medical practice, "the source of a medical opinion remains a powerful determinant of its influence." That is, "physicians typically assess the adequacy of medical information on the basis of the perceived credibility of the source, whether the source is the patient or another physician." Thus "advice from physicians who are perceived as 'good doctors' is highly valued, whereas advice from sources perceived as less credible may be discounted." As Schmidt and Bannon (1992) have noted, in cooperative work settings involving discretionary decision making, people may need to be able to mutually critique the decisions of their colleagues, thus requiring access to the identity of the originator of a given unit of information. So while in many situations organizations can efface the identity of the worker involved in specific tasks, there are many occasions of use of information where this anonymity places severe restrictions on the person who perhaps at some later date wishes to understand the meaning of a particular decision or directive.

4.4 Mediating CISs - evolving roles of human mediators

An important mechanism by which common information spaces can be supported is through the use of *human mediators* that help both producers and consumers to package and subsequently interpret information in the CIS. We take as an example a software company that develops computer support for, and planning of, public transportation (see Bødker, 1996). The company supports a number of object-oriented projects, with a technical platform that is based on Windows, C++ and Oracle. One of the major goals of the company has been to increase reuse of code and, the company has established a core library of 50-60 classes that are applied by all projects. This library is maintained by one person, the platform co-ordinator, who offers his service to the projects through active participation, in particular in the design of programs. The platform coordinator knows the platform well enough to be able to produce, for each project, a "parts list" of objects and classes that the project will need from the shared library. It is up to the platform co-ordinator to decide what is put in the shared classes. He does this through his close contacts with the projects, and at times upon direct requests. Bødker (1996) has illustrated how the role of platform coordinator is new and a result of the wish to share pieces of code, one of the much praised advantages of object-oriented technology. Based on this software development case and the experience of another case of shared standards in an office environment (in the AT case, Trigg & Bødker, 1994) we have noted how a variety of structures or mechanisms for sharing or distribution of the platform components are emerging, and how these are partly dependent on the skills of the platform coordinators, and partly on other conditions in the use/development environment. In both cases the efficiency and quality of sharing goes hand in hand with the additional work performed by the platform co-ordinators.

Thus, to assist in the process of developing a CIS, we find evidence of the emergence of a variety of human mediators whose purpose is to assist those producing items for the CIS, and also in packaging relevant information for those who might wish to use the information. What is interesting is that these new roles as mediators emerge because of the introduction of a common technical environment and develop hand in hand with this. Such mediation, thus, is an example of work that is added because of the introduction of the CIS, work that is there exactly because of the wish and need for sharing.

4.5. A Look at CISs on the WWW

The kinds of issues that we have been addressing take on new twists as we observe the ways in which information is produced and consumed on the World Wide Web. As an example, we will refer to a Danish case that we have been investigating. PlanteInfo is a Web site funded by the Danish Farmers' Associations containing a variety of sources of information about farming. The actual PlanteInfo web pages are provided by the Danish Institute of Plant and Soil Science. Through PlanteInfo the farmers and farming advisors are able to get daily updated information on the spreading of diseases, and access to data bases of agricultural providers, soil temperatures, and to various computer programs. Some of the pages are maintained by the Danish Agricultural Advisory Service. Other pages are maintained by the Meteorological office, pesticide manufacturers, and companies buying and selling fertilisers, etc. So here we have a number of different information providers, with different goals and objectives, providing information to a Web site that is used by a large number of people connected with the agricultural trade. Given this heterogeneity of user groups and possible uses, it is not surprising that a number of problems about the nature of the information space created by PlanteInfo have cropped up. The reliability of the information is vital to the farmer, raising a number of problems, the first one being the reliability of semi-automated updates based on figures entered across the country. Secondly, the farmers can make good use of information from the various commercial suppliers. The question is, however, to what extent this information is to be trusted? Both in terms of whether a web page can be guaranteed to be found, and in terms of substance: the companies of course promote their own products as remedies for particular pests. Provided that the farmer can see where the information comes from (that he is now on a web-page belonging to a commercial company) he is likely to understand this phenomenon, but how reliable are the offered calculations of doses etc.?. While the Danish Institute of Plant and Soil Science want to link to such information, they have no way of verifying it.

The situation is somewhat different with such agencies as the Meteorological office in that, in Denmark, they have no immediate commercial interest in the information they are providing. Also it is a State run agency who have their own official Web-pages and services. Independently, there is the problem that if the Danish

Institute of Plant and Soil Science does not want to process and verify all the information to be put on their web pages then they need to trust the information that they link to and the institutions or individuals who provide this information. And an important topic is how to create such trust, as it is obviously the case that there are many unreliable web pages "out there". A variety of potential contracts and rules for the maintenance of the pages that the Institute is connected to could be considered. The role of the Institute is in itself an instance rather similar to the platform coordinator. However, in order to do anything with the problem of validity of the information submitted by other organizations, there seems to be yet another level of articulation work needed, that of networking between platform coordinators in cases where information is not warranted by the organization, or by trusted individuals.

One perspective that has had relatively little relevance for the discussion of this case so far is that of an open and malleable common information space. Given the inherently open "substrate" of the common information space, the WWW, this is indeed a paradox. However, due to the large number of different kinds of users the information that is provided must be already packaged to an extent, thus making it more mobile while at the same time less flexible in its possible interpretations. Thus, in terms of our discussions of CISs, the Web may paradoxically be one of the most open - in the sense of accessible - electronic spaces that exists, while at the same time be one of the most closed - in the sense that due to the heterogeneity of users and possible use situations, the possible interpretations of the information that is presented is impossible to know. Thus, once one moves beyond very factual information it becomes very difficult to have any certainty as to how the information is being evaluated. While it is the case that one is never able to ensure just how information will be interpreted by others, in this situation the possible interpretations seem legion. One may see the WWW as a kind of substrate for common information spaces e.g. for farming counselling, and those developing such common information spaces may wish and need to set up their own rules and deal with them[3]. How such networking will eventually evolve remains speculation. Hopefully, however, it is possible to learn from the ways in which organizations have managed these problems under more conventional technology regimes, though we are convinced that some of the solutions need to take new forms.

5. Concluding Remarks: The dialectical nature of CISs

It frequently requires added work to place items in common, in order to package the material so that it may be understandable to others. It poses interesting challenges to CSCW research focusing on reducing the complexity of articulation work, when faced with CISs that introduce new kinds of articulation work that would not have

---

[3] On a technical level, progress is being made on suitable kinds of hypermedia/WWW integration to provide the functionality required. See Grønbæk et al (1997).

been there but for the CIS. Common information spaces come in many forms, and this paper has illustrated their dialectical nature, emphasizing on the one hand the open and malleable role of a CIS within a local community of practice, and, on the other, the role of CISs as boundary objects, packaged and being turned into immutables to allow for sharing across contexts and different communities of practice. We have discussed how the tension between "frontstage" and "backstage" needs is an important force in shaping the CIS. Common information spaces are in some cases constituted for collaborators that are co-present in time and space, whereas in other situations they are constituted across time and space boundaries, and the mechanisms used to support holding in common the information vary accordingly. This type of analysis may be elaborated on a variety of levels, emphasizing the variety of functions e.g. with an entry in the file of a public office, the entry is in itself situated in the community of practice of the office. It is often dealt with, and packaged by one person to be sent on to the next etc. At the same time, a similar analysis applies to the file as such - inside the organization, and as we have seen with VIRK, in relation to its surroundings.

As Bowker & Star (1994) note, in their study on the evolution of the international classification of diseases (ICD) framework, fairly large, and in some senses rigidly defined CISs benefit from an ongoing concern over the definition of the rules concerning how information is submitted. A common information space is not just a repository of information constituted once and for all, which raises interesting concerns for design: Designing a common information space entails concern for the possibilities of sharing, looking over shoulders, etc. on the one hand; for the rules of submission of information on the other; and on top of this for the possible roles of human mediators; it requires us to recognize frontstage/backstage concerns, and the potential reworking of rules. With the WWW example we have illustrated that just because the WWW provides a better substrate for a CIS, these problems still exist, and some are accentuated even more because of the vastly heterogeneous user base for Web applications.

In this paper we have discussed a number of dimensions of CISs and illustrated these with examples. While we are aware of the many unresolved issues in this account, we believe that we have managed to highlight a number of important issues concerning the bases for cooperative work, and we expect to revise our account as we deepen our analysis and test our concepts on a larger number of cases. We also hope to provide a more extensive discussion of related work which has not been covered here, such as the work of Weick on collective mind (Weick and Roberts, 1993) and Francophone studies on information spaces (e.g. Rognin, 1996) in the near future.

Acknowledgments

We wish to acknowledge funding support from the EU Human Capital & Mobility project ENACT, which allowed Susanne Bødker to visit and work at the University of Limerick for some months in 1996, and from the Irish Forbairt agency, through the Forbairt Programme for International Collaboration which allowed Liam Bannon visit Aarhus University for a short period in 1996. Thanks to Niels Oluf Bouvin, Ivor Perry, Laurence Rognin and the reviewers for useful comments.

References

Anderson, R. , G. Button, & W. Sharrock (1993). Supporting the design process within an organizational context. *Proceedings of CSCW'94*, pp. 243-252.

Bannon, L. & K. Schmidt, (1989). CSCW: Four Characters in Search of a Context. In Proc. *First European Conference on CSCW*, Gatwick, UK, September. (Reprinted in J. Bowers & S. Benford, Editors, (1991). *Studies in Computer Supported Cooperative Work: Theory, Practice and Design*. (Amsterdam: North-Holland). pp. 3-16.

Bowker, Geoffrey and Susan Leigh Star (1994) . Knowledge and infrastructure in international information management: Problems of classification and coding. In L. Bud (ed.). *Information Acumen: the Understanding and Use of Knowledge in Modern Business*, pp. 187-213. London: Routledge, 1994.

Bødker, S (1996). Mediating technical platforms to support the development of shared work practices, in *Proceedings of the 4th Software Cultures Workshop in Vienna*, TU Wien, pp. 91-102, 1996.

Bødker, S. (in preparation, a). Understanding representation in design, submitted for publication.

Bødker, S. (in preparation, b). Mature object oriented system development, submitted for publication.

Brown, J. S., & Duguid, P. (1994). Borderline issues: Social and material aspects of design. *Human-Computer Interaction, 9*(1), 3-36.

Button, G. (ed.) (1993). *Technology in Working Order*. London: Routledge.

Bücher, M., Gill, S., Mogensen, P. & Shapiro, D. (in preparation). Landscapes of practice, Lancaster University.

Callon, M. (1991). Techno-Economic Networks and Irreversibility. In J. Law (ed.) A Sociology of Monsters, pp.132-161. London: Routledge.

Cicourel, A. V. (1990). The Integration of Distributed Knowledge in Collaborative Medical Diagnosis. In J. Galegher, R. Kraut, and C. Egido (eds). *Intellectual Teamwork: Social and Technological Foundations of Cooperative Work*, pp. 221-242. Hillsdale, NJ: Lawrence Erlbaum Associates.Cicourel, A. (1990)

Clement, A. & Wagner, I. (1995) Fragmented Exchange: Disarticulation and the need for regionalized communication spaces. In *Proceedings of the Fourth European Conference on CSCW, ECSCW'95*, Stockholm Sweden. pp.33-49. Dordrecht: Kluwer.

Egger, E. & Wagner, I. (1993). Negotiating Temporal Orders - the case of collaborative time management in a surgery clinic. *CSCW Journal, 1*, 4, 1993, pp. 255 - 275.

Gerson, E. M., and Star, S. L. (1986). Analyzing Due Process in the Workplace. *ACM Transactions on Office Information Systems*, vol. 4, no. 3, July. Pages 257-270.

Giddens, A. (1990). *The consequences of Modernity*, Stanford CA:Stanford University Press.

Goodwin, C. & Goodwin, M. (1996). Seeing as a situated activity: Formulating planes. In D. Middleton & Y. Engeström (Eds.) *Cognition and communication at work*, Cambridge University Press, pp 61-95.

Grønbæk, K. , Bouvin, N.O., & Sloth, L. (1997) Designing Dexter-based hypermedia services for the World Wide Web, in Bernstein, M., Carr, L. & Østerbye, K. (Eds.), *Hypertext '97*, pp. 146-156.

Heath, C. & Luff, P. (1992) Collaboration and control: Crisis management and multimediatechnology in London underground control rooms. *CSCW Journal*, 1, nos. 1-2, pp.69-94.

Latour, B. (1987). *Science in Action*, Cambridge MA: Harward University Press.

Latour, B. (1990). Drawing Things Together, in Lynch, M. & Woolgar, S. *Representations in Scientific Practice*, MIT Press, pp. 19-68.

Lave, J., & Wenger, E. (1991). *Situated learning: Legitimate peripheral participation*. Cambridge: Cambridge University Press.

Robinson, M. & Bannon, L. (1991). Questioning Representations. In Bannon, L., M. Robinson, & K. Schmidt, (eds). *Proceedings of the Second European Conference on CSCW*. Dordrecht: Kluwer. pp. 219-233.

Rognin, L. (1996) Coopération et sûreté de fonctionnement des systèmes complexes. Ph.D. thesis, Université Paul Sabatier, Toulouse, France.

Schmidt, K. & Bannon, L. (1992). Taking CSCW Seriously: Supporting articulation work. *Computer Supported Cooperative Work*, vol. 1, nos 1-2. Pages 7-40.

Schmidt, K. & Simone, C. (1995) Mechanisms of Interaction: An approach to CSCW systems design. In COOP'95 - International Workshop on the design of cooperative systems, Juan-les-Pins, France.

Star, S.L. & Griesemer, J.R. (1989). Institutional Ecology,'Translations' and Boundary Objects: Amateurs and Professionals in Berkeley's Museum of Vertebrate Zoology, 1907-39. *Social Studies of Science* 19, 387-420.

Star, S.L. (1989). The structure of ill-structured solutions: boundary objects and heterogeneous distributed problem solving. In Gasser, L. & Huhns, M. (eds.) *Distributed artificial intelligence*, vol. 2, Pitman, London (pp. 37-54).

Strauss, A. (1993) *Continual Permutations of Action*. New York: A. de Gruyter.

Suchman, L. A. (1993). Centers of Coordination: A Case and Some Themes. Presented at the NATO Advanced Research Workshop on Discourse, Tools and Reasoning, Lucca, Italy, November 2-7.

Trigg, R.H., & Bødker, S. (1994). From Implementation to design: Tailoring and the emergence of systematization in CSCW, in Futura, R. & Neuwirth, C., *Proceedings of CSCW 94*, ACM press, pp. 45-54.

Weick, K. & Roberts, K.H. (1993) Collective Mind in Organizations: Heedful Interrelating on Flight Decks, *Administrative Science Quarterly*, vol. 38, pp.357-381.

Task Conflict and Language Differences: Opportunities for Videoconferencing?

Gayna Williams
Microsoft Corporation, USA
GaynaW@Microsoft.com

Abstract: Considerable research has found that adding audio to desktop conferencing improves problem-solving, but that there is no additional benefit from adding video. This paper describes an experiment that supports these earlier findings, while suggesting that video may provide significant benefit when used in tasks involving speakers with different priorities and different linguistic capabilities. The level of conflict in the experimental setting is consistent with that found in work settings, but is higher than that in most experimental situations. Tasks involving a mix of native and non-native English speakers are not universal but may be increasingly common. Thus, these findings provide encouragement to those working to improve videoconferencing technology.

Introduction

Studies contrasting audio, audio with video, and face to face problem-solving date back at least to Chapanis, Ochsman, Parrish, & Weeks (1972), who found no benefit in adding high-quality video to audio. In reviewing the history of research into the use of video to support communication and distributed work, Egido (1988) wrote "videoconferencing has been commercially available for over two decades, and despite consistently brilliant market forecasts, to date it has failed except in limited niche markets... Results (of systematic research) generally point to the dubious value of adding a visual channel... performance does not improve

97

J. Hughes et al. (eds.), Proceedings of the Fifth European Conference on Computer Supported Cooperative Work, 97-108.
© 1997 *Kluwer Academic Publishers.*

significantly... However, it can provide a sense of social presence and mutual knowledge (and) add to its desirability or appeal..."

The years since the first studies have seen tremendous technological innovation, ingenious attacks on identified weaknesses in video systems, attention focused on behavioral and social considerations, and much-improved interfaces. Despite this work and dramatic price-performance improvements, desktop videoconferencing has yet to spread appreciably. Studies have continued to find marginal or non-existent advantages in adding video to audio in supporting distributed groups. Examples include Sellen (1992), and Olson, Olson & Meader (1995), whose very careful study concluded "the average judged quality of the groups supported by audio plus video was *not* significantly higher than that for groups supported by audio only," and Doerry (1996), whose dissertation concluded that what he had found "bodes ill for the current crop of technologically-mediated environments." In a recent review, Whittaker (1995) echoed Egido's earlier remarks: "Evaluations of videoconferencing systems show that previous work has overestimated the importance of video at the expense of audio." This has been true even though many experimental systems have been of high quality (including computer controlled analog, which eliminates bandwidth constraints).

These reports and others do, however, include grounds for optimism. Video supports a sense of presence and mutual knowledge, which may be motivating, as reported by Egido (1988, quoted above) and Olson, Olson and Meader (1995) among others. Video can be useful for tasks in which the focus of the task (and the video) is on large objects (e.g., Magee, 1992). In addition, several research efforts have looked at video to provide opportunities for unplanned, informal contact (in contrast to substituting video for task-centered meetings), (e.g., Root, 1988; Fish et al., 1990; Olson & Bly, 1991; Dourish & Bly, 1992; Buxton, 1992; Mantei et al., 1991; Tang & Rua, 1994).

The experiment described below does not address this wide range of possible video use. This study focuses on the use of video to support distributed workgroups carrying out assigned tasks in concert, which remains a major concern. It was motivated as part of a RACE (Research and development on Advanced Communications in Europe) project to support concurrent engineering within the European automotive industry.

Support for multinational efforts brings distributed work to the fore and raises unexplored issues. These issues are particularly pertinent considering the development of computer networked global communities, which are leading to an increase in international business partnerships. The participation by non-native speakers of the language being used could affect the use and usefulness of video. With reduced linguistic competence, nonverbal cues to meaning or intent may be sought. Nonverbal communication skills are culturally based (Argyle, 1969), so we cannot assume they will be useful in all such situations. However, cues may be more readily understood across cultures with relatively high levels of contact, such as among Europeans. This study, although carried out in a laboratory, contrasts groups of native English speakers with groups of Europeans whose first language is not English (i.e., non-native English speakers), and groups that mix native English speakers with non-native speakers. (Because this work was motivated by research into the communication requirements of Europeans in the automotive industry, participants from countries outside Europe were excluded from this particular study.)

Another issue addressed in this study is that of goal conflict or differing priorities within workgroups. In many laboratory situations, participants may generate and then promote or defend their ideas, but have less stake in the outcome than in many work situations. Laboratory studies of non-contentious tasks have generally shown no benefit of adding video to audio in problem solving (e.g., Weeks & Chapanis, 1976; Olson, Olson & Meader, 1995; Doerry, 1996). Contention in work pairs was investigated by Weeks and Chapanis (1976), who found no differences in performance between audio and video communication media. However, contention could direct participants to nonverbal cues in situations involving more than two people, where group dynamics and social cues may be more variable. In my within-subjects study, a non-contentious design task is followed by a task in which group members were randomly assigned the roles of ergonomist (human factors engineer), accountant (with fiscal responsibility), and designer. The resulting level of contention, although typical of development projects, did affect the use of video, especially in the presence of language differences. The experiment, results and discussion are reported in the following sections.

Experimental Method

Design

Table I identifies the three factors that were varied in the experiment. All tasks were completed by groups of 3 participants working in separate rooms with earphones and desktop conferencing software (Timbuktu).

Teleconferencing conditions	1. Audio (A)
	2. Audio and video (AV)
Design task conditions	1. Non-contentious (NC)
	2. Contentious (C)
Language conditions	1. Native speakers (NS)
	2. Non-native speakers (NNS)
	3. Mixed speakers (MIX)

Table I. Experimental conditions

1. In half of the tasks, participants were linked only by audio. In the other half, participants also had a video link, consisting of two monitors to the right of the computer display. The order of the communication media was counterbalanced across the groups.
2. As detailed below, each group carried out one non-contentious and one contentious design task. Each individual then completed a questionnaire.
3. Each group consisted of 3 subjects. One-third of the groups consisted of native English speakers (NS), one-third consisted of non-native English speakers (NNS), and one-third consisted of one native and two non-native English speakers. No group had non-native speakers from the same country. Group members had not previously worked together.

Subjects

All subjects in the experiment were students at Loughborough University of Technology. Each was paid £7.50 for participating in the two-hour experiment. Sixteen were native English speakers (8 male, 8 female); the other 20 were from seven different European countries (11 female, 9 male). (Gender was noted but not a factor in the study.)

Apparatus

Each participant worked in a room with a Macintosh computer running MacDraw and Timbuktu software, a headphone for 3-way audio communication, a Sony CCDGIE video camera, and two video monitors for video support in one of the two tasks. In addition, a camera was focused on the video monitors to record the actions of each participant, and audio communication was recorded.

Figure 1. A diagram of the apparatus used in the study. Each room contained the same setup.

Analog video was displayed on video monitors to the right of the computer display (Figure 1). This approach, used in CRUISER (Root, 1988) and other systems, creates a "seam" but allows the number and duration of glances at the video monitors to be determined from the video recordings of the participants.

Task

The task was based on a design exercise devised by Brian Shackel to train people in skills such as negotiation, compromise, and team work, all skills which are required in industrial design settings. Participants in this particular exercise are given the task of individually designing a control panel for a stereo sound system from a set of component requirements. After completing this task the students are required to design the control panel in groups; this can lead to discussion, disagreement, and compromise of their individual designs in order to achieve a group design.

The task was modified to accommodate the time constraints of the study session and the skill set of the subject population (i.e., they were not trained designers and perhaps wouldn't be as sufficiently passionate about their design to cause conflict). The subjects were provided with an on-line catalog of 60 components, grouped by type of component (e.g., volume controls), and an outline of a control panel. The MacDraw windows were arranged so the catalog occupied one half of the screen and the control panel the other half. The components could be copied from the catalog and pasted in the control panel. For the non-contentious task, subjects were provided with a list of essential components that needed to be used in the design (e.g., power control, volume control). When working in a group, the Timbuktu software was used to enable subjects to see a common version of MacDraw and to share control of the cursor. For the contentious task, subjects were assigned roles which are commonly found in industrial situations: an ergonomist, a designer, and an accountant. Each role had 5 design principles to use in the design of the control panel. Essentially the roles encouraged the ergonomist to consider usability, the designer to consider style, and the accountant to consider cost.

Procedure

At the start of the study the subjects were introduced to each other. An overview of the controls required to complete the design tasks in MacDraw was given. Subjects were then assigned to individual rooms.

Subjects spent a few minutes examining the communication tools. They could adjust the cameras, microphones and volume controls until they were comfortable with the quality of each other's video image and could hear each other. The operation of the shared mouse, which is available with Timbuktu software, was explained to the subjects and they experimented with it. The communication tools were then switched off until required.

Subjects were given 10 minutes to design the control panel for a stereo. This individual task was provided to allow the subject to become familiar with the design requirements for the control panel. Before proceeding with the group task the subjects read the group task instructions. In addition to designing the control panel, and to encourage discussion, the instructions told them they would need to justify their choice of component type and the location of the component on the control panel. When they were comfortable with the group task instructions, the communication medium was switched on; when communication was established, a 20 minute timer was started. Occasionally, additional elaboration of the task instructions was required for non-native English speakers.

Subjects were randomly assigned a role for the second individual task. Again, a 10 minute individual task allowed subjects to become familiar with the task and their design principles for their role. Prior to switching on the communication medium for the second 20 minute group task, subjects confirmed that they understood the goals of the task. In addition to the design principles for the role, the group task included the identification of the roles of the other two members of the group and some suggestions as to why they might not be in agreement with their principles (e.g., "The designer and ergonomist are not aware of the financial problems of the company").

Following the completion of the group task a questionnaire was completed that asked for ratings on the communication media and some personal background information.

Measures

The measures provided a means to understand how the language and design task affected the use of the video link, and how subjects with varying language abilities compared video to audio communication.

Video data collection

To evaluate the use of the video communication link two types of data were collected from reviewing the video tapes: the amount of time spent looking into the video monitors and the number of glances toward the monitor.

The video tapes were reviewed in order to record the number of glances toward the monitors and the total time spent looking at the monitors. These were then broken down into the number of glances and time spent looking at the monitors while talking and while simply observing.

All groups took at least 15 of the 20 available minutes to complete the group design tasks; therefore, to allow comparisons across conditions, data collected from the first 15 minutes of each design session were used.

Questionnaire data

A questionnaire was used to assess subjects' opinions of the communication media. The questionnaire required ratings for 20 statements for both the audio and video communication conditions. (Each statement was rated on a 5 point scale.) The questionnaire covered 10 communication factors including the following problematic communication types: miscommunication, conversation repair, turn-taking, non-communication, and communication breakoff (Gass & Varonis, 1990).

Results and Discussion

Video results

Table II presents the group means for both the time and the number of glances. A main effect was found for the design task condition—non-contentious (NC) and contentious (C)—for all the video data sets. The subjects used the monitors significantly more in the contentious condition than in the non-contentious condition. Results between language groups showed significant differences with a greater tendency to face the monitors in the non-native speaker (NNS) and mixed (MIX) groups.

(Time in seconds)	NS		NNS		MIX	
	NC	C	NC	C	NC	C
Total time spent facing video monitor	61	155	62	242	112	274
Time spent talking to monitor	17	77	20	78	48	102
Time spent observing to monitor	45	77	42	163	65	172
Total number of glances	40	86	41	80	71	94
Total number of glances to talk	9	36	12	23	16	36
Total number of glances to observe	31	50	29	57	55	58

Table II: Means for amount of time spent facing the video monitors, and the number of glances towards the video monitors.

Figure 2 shows a strong difference in the use of the monitors across design tasks (f = 45.26, p < 0.001) and language groups (f = 5.25, p < 0.01).

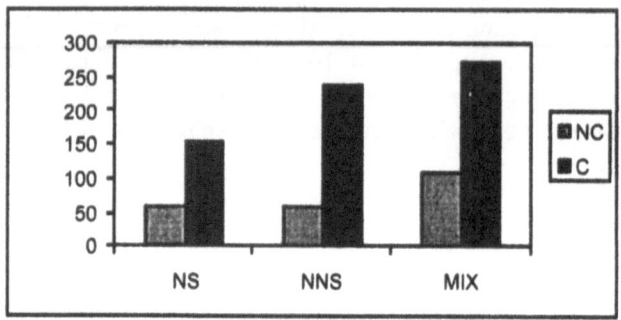

Figure 2: Total time spent facing the monitors

In considering the time spent observing the video there were main effects of design task (f= 39.44; p < 0.001) and language group (f= 6.13; p < 0.01). This was not the case for talking to the monitors. The subjects talked to the monitors more in the contentious than in the non-contentious design task (f = 20.94, p < 0.001), but there was no difference among language groups. A possible explanation could be that the NNS subjects find they need more information to interpret what they are listening to, but do not feel a greater need to speak toward other group members.

An interaction was present in the observing video data. The MIX group used the video significantly more in the contentious condition (f = 3.94, p < 0.05). This trend was also observed in the talking to video data, although it did not reach significance. The overall pattern is shown in Figure 2.

Similar effects in the time data are shown in Figure 3. The number of glances to the video monitors increase in the contentious design task condition. This was true for the summed glance data, and for the component elements of glancing to talk (f = 22.75, p < 0.001) and glancing to observe (f = 8.20, p < 0.01).

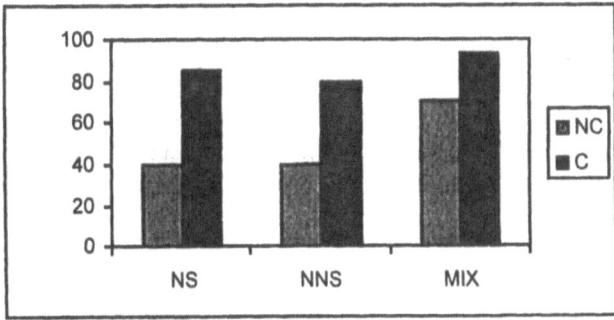

Figure 3: Total number of glances towards the monitors.

When considering the change in the use of video in accordance with the design task, the time spent facing the monitors in the contentious situation is almost 3 times that of the non-contentious condition. However, the increase in the number of glances in the contentious condition is less than twice that of the non-contentious condition. Therefore because the use of video monitors increases more than the number of glances, the average glance time increases. The duration of the glance to observe the monitors is higher in the contentious task than in the non-contentious design task for both NNS and MIX groups.

Questionnaire results

Consistent with other studies (e.g., Olson et al., 1995; Egido, 1988), subjects rated social presence and team spirit higher in the video than the audio only condition. For three out of five problematic communication types, subjects had greater problems in the audio-only condition: miscommunication (i.e., subject felt others did not understand what subject had said), $z = -2.56$, $p < 0.01$; turn-taking (i.e., subject was interrupted), $z = -2.17$, $p < 0.05$; communication breakoff (i.e., subject gave up communicating as it was too difficult to explain ideas), $z = -2.17$, $p = 0.05$. The MIX group rated audio lower than video for all the problematic communication types: miscommunication ($z = -2.31$, $p = 0.05$); communication breakoff ($z = -1.96$, $p = 0.05$); turn-taking; conversation repair (i.e., the ease with which conversation could be repaired after a misunderstanding was noticed); and non-communication (i.e., subject not bothering too communicate as it was too difficult). (The last three showed non-significant trends).

Discussion

The video data make it clear that video is relied upon by all language groups when communicating in the contentious situation. It is most profitable to the groups who don't consist of speakers of the same native language. Although there is some increase in the use of the video link to talk directly to others, it is of most use in gathering additional non-verbal cues to better understand the dialog, especially in situations where conversation may be less predictable, such as when new information is presented, as in the confrontational situation.

The questionnaire data suggest that video provides positive benefits over audio in terms of the social aspect of communication and reduces the problematic communication situation, clearing the way to appreciating the content of the communication.

The MIX groups were observed to have communication problems in the design tasks with video communication, and they also self-reported that they had significant problems communicating in the audio condition. These results show the MIX group having the most difficulty in communicating regardless of the medium. Because they report having significant problems in the audio condition, it seems almost predictable that they would make the most of any enhanced channel of communication, accounting for the greater use of the video monitors. The particularly large increase in the use of the video monitors by the MIX group in the contentious task may be explained by the fact that even the NS group used the monitors significantly more in the contentious design task, whereas for the MIX group the increase in task complexity caused by the contentious task was further compounded by language communication problems.

It should be remembered that the MIX group consisted of one third native English speakers. This suggests that in mixed groups, fluency in the language being used may offer advantages, but the quality of the communication is dependent upon a joint understanding by the group. Further analyses examined differences between the behavior of the NNS subjects and the NS subjects in the MIX group. No differences were found in the non-contentious condition, but the NS subjects were found to use the video more in the contentious design task. I speculate that the difference may be related to the fact that the number of NS to NNS subjects was 1:2. The NS subject may have less experience in communicating with people speaking his/her native language as a second language and was thus experiencing communication problems not previously encountered. However, the sample size of this group is small, and further research is required to expand upon individual differences in mixed language ability groups.

A post hoc test showed a communication medium order effect for communication breakoff. The groups which received the audio condition for the non-contentious task and video for the contentious task did not report a difference in communication breakoff. However, groups that received the communication media in the order video first, then audio, report having more problems with communication breakoff in the contentious task with audio. This suggests the subjects who had received the richer communication medium for the friendly task felt a reduction in the ability to communicate ideas when the communication medium was reduced for a more complex social task, whereas the subjects who went from the poorer to the richer communication medium for the more complex task perhaps didn't appreciate the benefits the video communication was bringing them.

This study focused on the use of the video monitors and did not measure computer screen based interactions, but a crude measure of computer use was provided by the number of components the groups had positioned in their design at the end of the experimental period. A trend suggested that with more components present on the computer screen, subjects used the video monitors less during the final 5 minutes of the experimental period. Further studies are required to explore this finding.

Conclusion

This study addresses two aspects of video use: task contention and language ability. Although a laboratory study, it demonstrates that under certain conditions people will make significantly heavier use of a video channel. It is plausible that in workgroups showing the same characteristics, video would be more heavily relied upon. With a growing emphasis on multi-national activity, the conditions modeled in the study become more prevalent and should be investigated further.

Understanding appropriate tasks and settings for video may lead to video communication achieving some of its potential. It is hoped that this work will complement and help motivate further work on improving desktop videoconferencing quality, such as interfaces that promote a seamless transition across workspaces and maintain eye contact and awareness of gaze direction (Ishii et al., 1993; Okada et al., 1994; Ichikawa et al., 1995), and approaches that vary camera views to increase interest and awareness (Inoue et al., 1995).

Further research, including studies of longer duration and in natural work settings, is needed to confirm the findings that video is particularly helpful for groups with different priorities and linguistic backgrounds. Eventually video may find broader use; we will benefit from identifying the most promising conditions for testing and introducing the technology.

Acknowledgments

This study was completed at Human Science Department, Loughborough University of Technology. I would like to thank Caroline Parker, Sue Joyner, and Murray Sinclair from HUSAT (Human Science in Advanced Technology) for their support and discussions on this project. Initial findings appeared in Parker, C. & Williams, G. (1994), Do you speak English? The use of telecommunications media in mixed language CSCW. *Proceedings of the 12th Triennial Congress of the International Ergonomics Association*, 1994, Vol. 4, pp. 375 - 377. I also thank Jonathan Grudin for comments and feedback on earlier drafts.

References

Argyle, M. (1969). *Social interaction*. Methuen.

Buxton, W. (1992). Telepresence: Integrating Shared Task and Person Spaces. Reprinted in R. M. Baecker (Ed.), *Readings in Groupware and Computer-Supported Cooperative Work*. Morgan Kaufmann, 1993, pp. 816–822.

Chapanis, A., Ochsman, R., Parrish, R., & Weeks, G. (1972). Studies in interactive communication: I. The effects of four communication modes on the behavior of teams during cooperative problem solving. *Human Factors, 14*, pp. 487-509.

Doerry, E. (1996). An empirical comparison of copresent and technologically-mediated interaction based on communicative breakdown. Doctoral dissertation. Available as CIS-TR-96-01, Department of Computer and Information Science, University of Oregon, Eugene, OR.

Dourish, P., & Bly, S. (1992). Portholes: Supporting awareness in a distributed work group. *Proc. CHI'92*, pp. 541-547.

Egido, C. (1988). Videoconferencing as a technology to support group work: A review of its failure. *Proc. CSCW'88*, pp.13-24.

Fish, R. S., Kraut, R. E., & Chalfonte, B. L. (1990). The VideoWindow System in informal communication. *Proc. CSCW'90*, pp.1-11.

Ichikawa, Y., Okada, K., Jeong, G., Tanaka, S., & Matsushita, Y. (1995). MAJIC videoconferencing system: Experiments, evaluation and improvement. *Proc. ECSCW'95*, pp. 279-292.

Inoue, T., Kobayashi, T., Okada, K., & Matsushita, Y. (1995). Learning from TV programs: Application of TV presentation to a videoconferencing system. *Proc. UIST'95*, pp. 147-154.

Ishii, H., Kobayashi, M., & Arita, K. (1994). Iterative design of seamless collaboration media: From TeamWorkStation to ClearBoard. *Communications of the ACM, 37*, 8, pp. 83–97.

Mantei, M., Baecker, R., Sellen, A., Buxton, W., Milligan, T., and Wellman, B. (1991). Experiences in the use of a media space. *Proc. CHI '91*, pp. 203–208.

Magee, B. R. (1992). Enhanced factory communications (video). In CSCW'92 Video Program, SIGGRAPH Video Review Issue 87.

Okada, K., Maeda, F., Ichikawaa, Y., & Matsushita, Y. (1994). Multiparty videoconferencing in virtual social distance: MAJIC design. *Proc. CSCW'94*, pp. 279-291.

Olson, M., & Bly, S. (1991). The Portland Experience: A report on a distributed research group. In S. Greenburg (Ed.), *Computer supported cooperative work and groupware*. London: Academic Press, pp. 81–98.

Olson, J.S., Olson, G. M., & Meader, D. K. (1995). What mix of audio and video is useful for doing remote real-time design work. *Proc. CHI'95*, pp. 362–368.

Root, R.W. (1988). Design of a multi-media vehicle for social browsing. *Proc. CSCW'88*, pp. 25-38.

Sellen, A. (1992). Speech patterns in video-mediated communication. *Proc. CHI'92*, pp. 49-59.

Tang, J.C., & Rua, M. (1994). Montage: Providing teleproximity for distributed groups. *Proc. CHI'94*, pp. 37-43.

Varonis, E.M., & Gass, S.M (1990). Miscommunication in non-native discourse. In N. Coupland, H. Giles, & J. M. Wiemann (Eds.), *Miscommunication and Problematic Talk*. SAGE publications.

Weeks, G.D., & Chapanis, A. (1976). Cooperative versus conflictive problem-solving in three telecommunication modes. *Perceptual and Motor Skills, 42*, pp. 879-917.

Whittaker, S. (1995). Video as a technology for interpersonal communications: A new perspective. *SPIE, 2417*, pp. 294-304.

The Social Construction and Visualisation of a New Norwegian Offshore Installation

Vidar Hepsø
Statoil Research Centre, Trondheim, Norway
vihe@statoil.no

Abstract: This paper exemplifies how to make aggregated descriptions or requirements of work processes to serve as references or resources for future situated actions in the operations of a new oil installation. It describes a joint organisational and IT-development process of a CSCW-application that supports personel in their daily preparations for operations. The paper discusses how the organisational members themselves were empowered to describe the proper format of representation, with activities, products, roles, responsibilities and co-ordination mechanisms in general.

Introduction

An important research issue in CSCW has been to study how collaborative systems can be instrumental in reducing the complexity of co-ordinating co-operative activities often individually conducted but yet interdependent (Schmidt, 1996). CSCW as a field has also been devoted to exploring how computer based systems can improve the ability of co-operating actors in articulating their activities (Winograd 1994, Malone 1995). To develop and implement reasonable conceptual and structural units to express activities, tasks, interdependence and responsibilities in a flexible and well-integrated manner has been a challenge. The problem has often been that the underlying protocol has been too rigid, not accessible or not modifiable. These protocols have therefore not been able to handle situated actions (Suchman 1987; 1994, Randall 1995b) and the flexibility and unpredictability of real life practice.

J. Hughes et al. (eds.), Proceedings of the Fifth European Conference on Computer Supported Cooperative Work, 109-124.
© 1997 *Kluwer Academic Publishers.*

Norne is a new oil production ship being put into operations by Statoil[1] in mid 1997. This new installation is different from former permanent concrete and steel constructed giants that up to now mainly have inhabited the Norwegian Continental Shelf. Norne has a very lean organisation, about 1/3 compared to its older counterparts. Still, it is the same functions (production of oil) and these must be more efficient in Norne. The Norne onshore support organisation is placed in Northern Norway, Harstad. In addition, Norne needs technical support from centralised Statoil units in Stavanger, Trondheim and Bergen (500-1100 km away), and external vendor support on production and maintenance from both inside and outside of Norway. In order to achieve their goals Norne will have to challenge present work practice and develop new ways of working, not only on the boat itself, but also with regard to onshore-offshore co-operation inside Statoil and through vendor co-operation outside Statoil. The newly employed Norne people have diverse operational backgrounds from other parts of the company and are bringing their old experience and expertise with them into the new installation. This past experience is vital. However, it is important to reflect upon how Norne can improve present practice, and there must be developed contexts where new communities of practice in Norne can discuss a potentially new practice. In essence, Norne will have to create a new operational reality based on the potential and restraints in their business context. The new "Norne reality" will cover more formal aspects as procedures, structures and more informal aspects like informal work patterns, culture and attitudes.

In this paper we try to show how it is possible to make formal aggregated descriptions or requirements to serve as references or resources for future situated actions in operations. A flowchart method is used for the purpose of planning the operational phase of the Norne installation, enabling the organisational members themselves to describe the proper format of representation, activities, products, roles, responsibilities and co-ordination mechanisms in general. In viewing the development of "structure" as an organisational development or empowerment process, we try to avoid falling into the many traps of formal and rigid representations of work-flow. We will focus on the social construction of the new work processes. Further, how this organisational development process was combined with the design and implementation of a CSCW-application that supports Norne personel in their daily preparations for operations. This integrated approach can be seen as the process of change of an organisation, in which organisation and technology are designed and developed jointly in a task- and need- oriented way by the members affected: e.g. the organisational members affected consider the existing problems, search and evaluate the problems' causes, and consider measures to solve the problems (Hartmann, 1994 in Wulf, 1995). Some features of the application will be presented including some preliminary conclusions on how this work has helped Norne in achieving their business objectives.

---

[1] Statoil is the state oil company of Norway. Primary activities are exploration of new oil and gas fields, operation and maintenance of a number of offshore oil and gas production installations, operation and maintenance of refineries, transportation, marketing and distribution of intermediate and end products.

The Construction of Norne Work Processes

This R&D-project that started in December 1995 had the following scope:

- To help Norne develop their most important work processes in operations, by acting as facilitators in the Norne organisation, i.e. providing a method for describing work processes and perform process support during an organisational development process

- Develop a groupware application that would be used as an operative enterprise model, including an overall description of Nornes main work processes and products and, down to the daily checklists in operations, in order to develop some shared representations of Nornes operating philosophy

As a consequence of the scope, we were to help Norne develop scenarios for how to use CSCW-applications in operations (groupware and desk top conferencing systems). For the Norne personel the challenge have been how the development of a future operational structure or practice can be an organisational development process where the organisational members themselves describe the ideal "to be"-situation in operations. In February 1996 we arranged a workshop with Norne personnel, both managers and operators/technicians. The idea was to make them reflect on their work processes, start discussing what had been already described so far in an operating philosophy document, and identify their most important work processes. We used considerable time to discuss what a work process was. Here we followed a pragmatic BPR-definition (Hammer and Champy, 1993) and defined work processes as: a collection of activities that takes one or more kinds of input and creates an output that is of value to a customer. The main challenge was to discuss which of the processes did not have any proper products and customers and question if Norne had to do these activities at all. This discussion went on beyond that meeting, through the winter of 1996 at all levels in the Norne organisation, and the end result was an overall enterprise model[2] with the following processes:

Norne has three main physical processes, with defined products: There is an oil reservoir, with special characteristics that contains oil with specific properties. Norne has a production and injection system that offer you possibilities and restraints based on its technical construction. There is also a product shipment process since Norne must export the oil that has been processed onboard to a market. These three main physical processes are the main conditions the Norne organisation must operate under and comprises their value chain. In order to

---

2   An enterprise model is defined as a model of what the enterprise intends to accomplish and how, and is a way of understanding complex social organisation by constructing models (Rumbaugh 1993). Norne defined an enterprise model as a model of what they want to accomplish and how to function when in operations. It contains basic elements and necessary decomposition of activities, roles and specifies information requirements to activities.

operate the physical processes in the most effective manner, Norne personnel developed 16 main work processes. These processes are: operations, maintenance, modifications, technical support, accomodation (on board), logistics, marine operations, emergency preparedness, human resource, finance, quality, reservoir management, health, environment and safety (HES) and procurement, to mention the most important. This model had its weaknesses which we will return to later, but it enabled the organisation to consolidate on the most important business objectives.

For each of these work processes Norne personel were chosen as process owners. The role of a Norne process owner was to involve other people in the Norne organisation in order to describe the defined process. The people that were chosen came from different levels in the organisation, from supervisors to operators and technicians. However, some supervisors were not "ripe enough" for the idea. When picking out people we wanted the process owner to be a person that would be working with the process in operations, who would know the process and who had basic communication and facilitator skills. When these persons were chosen we helped them in the process of establishing a facilitator role for their process. We taught them some basic facilitator skills, how to create involvement, how to use problem solving techniques and gave them a basic introduction to our methodology.

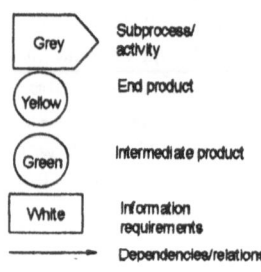

Figure 1. Description of flowchart symbols

The methodology is very simple, based on simplified flowchart symbols and has been used in Norwegian work research in different versions since the late 1960's (Thorsrud, 1969). They grey box (figure 1) signifies the activities within a process (e.g. within maintenance to create a work order). There are products associated with the processes. For maintenance the end product is technical condition re-established, while an intermediate product can be a created work order. Linked to products and processes you have information requirements, e.g. to the sub process create work order one information requirement is access to the plant management system. Finally, there are also dependencies between processes and products on different scales that can be addressed by using arrows between the objects. Some small changes were done compared to old flowchart symbols to indicate that we did not deal with technical systems here.

These symbols were then combined in order to create the Norne work processes. An example from maintenance shows this more in detail. The first sketches were made on paper in groups. The typical situation like e.g, maintenance, was that the process owner gathered 5-6 of his or her people in a full day workshop to design the overall maintenance process. Here they would discuss activities, roles, products and dependencies using the above methodology. Researchers participated as facilitators and assisted when needed. Our job was to follow up the defined processowners, check if they did the work that they committed themselves to, and help them in their own processes and workshops.

We also reviewed the maps to make sure that the processes were not duplicated, and that dependencies between different processes were taken care of.

Some guiding principles were developed. The Statoil division which Norne belongs to is ISO-certified and the quality system that Norne is part of will in most cases describe work processes good enough for Norne's purpose. In cases where Norne will have to work differently or deviate from the ISO-standard, this will have to be described in more detail. This meant that Norne should use flowcharts in cases where they felt that going through the work process roles and responsibilities could give them substantial improvements in performance. Norne personel decided to describe tasks that they knew they would have problems with based on earlier experiences, e.g. communication onshore-offshore. The constructed maintenance process (figure 2) shows some of the features described.

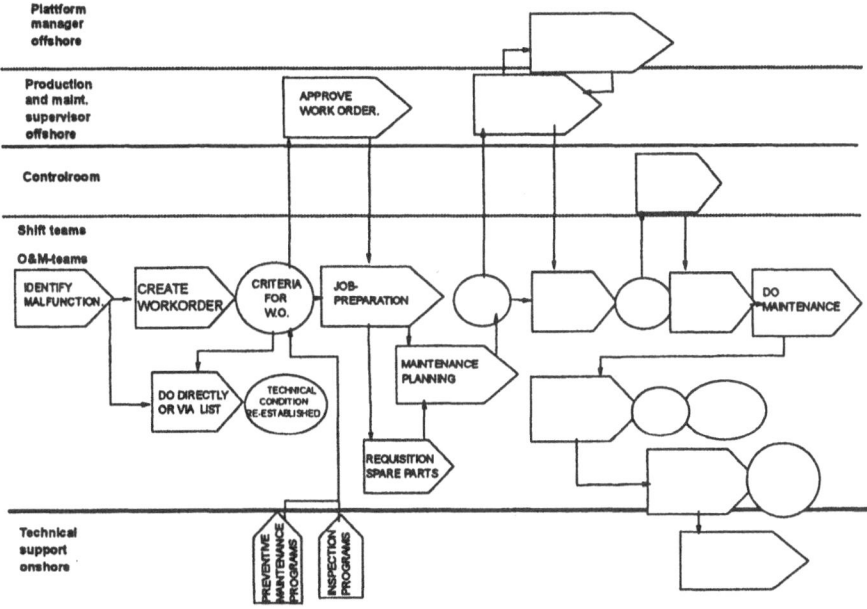

Figure 2. Flowchart of Norne maintenance work process (principal sketch, simplified)

We will not elaborate this process chart in detail, but describe some important aspects of it, to illustrate our approach as an organisational development process. The traditional way of describing maintenance in the oil industry is to write a procedure that regulates activities, and many of these activities must be based on strict procedures because accidents can have disastrous effects on people onboard the installation and on the environment. Described here are different roles in the Norne organisation that take part in the maintenance process, from the different levels offshore to technical support onshore. The more the arrows and the sub processes passes over the lines, the more bureacratic the process becomes. In order to avoid bureaucracy in the maintenance process, Norne decided that most of the maintenance should de done by the shift teams and operations and maintenance teams, with minimum interference from others. In the maintenance process, to write, wait and approve work orders requires considerable time. This has to do with the health hazard, since you must control what kinds of work is conducted at different locations on the installation. However, Norne has taken measures to reduce their maintenance work orders by 75%, by differentiating between different kinds of work orders. Much of the maintenance work is rather simple (with no potential hazard) and can be done by the teams without work orders. To be able to do so they had to design teams based on system responsibilities that can self-organise, instead of having a traditional disciplinary responsibility. Specific technicians are given the responsibility to both operate and maintain their defined technical systems and within that area they have large autonomy. The rest 25% of work orders that is hazardous or requires more skilled expertise must follow an approval process and involve the control room on the installation and platform management. It took several discussions and iterations before the process found its final form.

The first process maps were written on paper, but as the charts became more and more described as "finished" by the Norne people, the map was re-drawn in LOTUS FREELANCE GRAPHICS (graphical slide presentation tool) and incorporated in a LOTUS NOTES release 3 discussion database (either by us or by process owners). A simple graphical editor was chosen to avoid creating too detailed maps. All maps should be confined within one presentation slide (see figure 2) and cover the overall description of the process. The further discussion would continue in the group informally. When the maps became digitalised it was possible to create improvement proposals in the NOTES database to every process. Now, process owners could follow up each others work more simply, and it became easier to see duplicated work and dependencies that were created. Most Norne personnel had used NOTES before in their former jobs and engineers and technicians were relatively eager to use the discussion database. The use of discussion databases was also a strategic decision in order to let Norne personnel become familiar with electronic work, something they expected they would benefit from when in operations.

The Groupware Application

A basic premise for the project was to be able to help Norne personel visualise what a potentially new organisation could look like, and help them to develop shared representations of such a new organisation. They wanted a Norne overall enterprise model, a Norne workspace with an intuitive interface to enable Norne people not only to find the information they need in their daily work, but also to develop a coherent understanding of what Norne is and its basic work processes. The intention was that the organisation should co-evolve together with the groupware application. Processowners and helpers felt that the old release 3 Notes database could not do this properly. The representations that we called work process charts or maps (figure 2) were incorporated in a LOTUS NOTES release 4 database. Through the use of hypertext/media and "hotspots" we made links to information and additional computer systems needed in the work processes (since Norne personnel themselves defined information requirements connected to activities in their development of the process charts). The point of entry of the application is a graphical presentation of the overall Norne enterprise model, from there you can click further down to the different work processes like maintenance (previously seen in figure 2). The representation of the maintenance process has a number of "hot spots" with hyperlinks (figure 3). The flowchart itself may not always give enough information regarding the process. You can see what is hidden behind the boxes by clicking further down to a more detailed textual description of the box, start up the plant maintenance computer system, access Statoil ISO-procedures that regulate maintenance and read electronic copies of operational manuals, access vendor information on WWW, select small unfinished maintenance jobs, and write improvement proposals to any of the work processes.

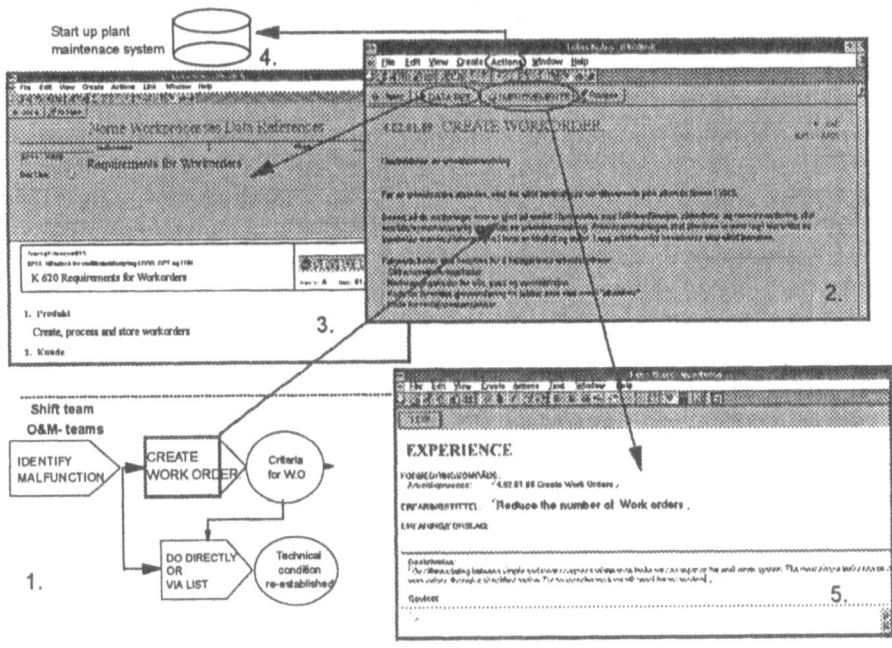

Figure 3. A detail of the maintenance work process, where you can open more detailed information about work orders in Norne, read Statoil ISO-procedures on work orders, open the plant management system and write improvement proposals related to work orders.

The CSCW-design and Implementation Process

Our design strategy was to start with an existing system like LOTUS NOTES, to be able to evaluate the use of the system under real working conditions and see how the system could improve Norne's work processes along the way, and train for operations. We decided to use Statoil's existing computer network infrastructure to minimise technical support during the prototyping process. NOTES is the groupware standard of the corporation and is widely used in Statoil, we therefore chose NOTES as the platform. NOTES Release 4 had the necessary technical flexibility we needed. Norne was appointed a pilot by Statoil general management and Statoil Data (Statoil's IT-division) made available the necessary technical infrastructure (NOTES release 4, test servers), NOTES R 4 programming or coding skills and technical support along the way.

The design process closely coincides with a co-operative and constructive design philosophy (Klöckner, 1995) and participatory design (Schuler, 1993). Evolutionary prototyping approaches presume close connections to participant situations of use (Schuler 1993, Klöckner 1995). A preliminary groupware prototype in release 3 of NOTES was used from the start by the process owners and a core of their helpers. NOTES release 4 was installed in May 1996 and as much as possible of the activities in preparations for operations were done via the application, even though it was run in a test environment. Since we were using standardised software we felt it was our responsibility to tell the users about the potential of the technology by developing user scenarios. In what possible directions could the new development move? It was the strategy to view the groupware application as an "actor" or "actant" with specific values and perspectives in the process (Latour 1987). Reflection is important when dealing with standardised groupware, since LOTUS NOTES must be regarded as a socially shaped technology. Both database structure and the metaphors of paper based work flow gives NOTES both potentials and restraints in use. Reflection on these issues was necessary for Norne in order to avoid seeing LOTUS NOTES as objective and fixed. Any software technology will have embedded categories whether implicit or explicit, and the aim was to discover, discuss and even accept the limits of these categories. In order to reduce the importance of the embedded NOTES categories, we tried to design new categories together with the Norne organisation, using flowchart symbols that they were familiar with. These are also categories but are understood by technicians/engineers and make a chaotic social world understandable for them. This is an issue we will re-visit later in the paper.

In the Norne case we spent considerable time on fieldwork, to become acquainted with the Norne people in their own environment. Here we used short ethnographic fieldworks (Hughes 1995, Randall 1995a; 1995b), workshops with users, debriefings and prototyping as methods. However, as a contrast to traditional descriptive ethnography, this was also an interventionist project, because in Norne we worked as mediators (Okamura et al., 1994).

In May 1996 with the introduction of NOTES release 4 Norne had the overall structure of the application, with the main work processes. We gradually increased the number of users as Norne recruited new personnel. Changes and improvements in the application were handled during our weekly fieldworks in the Norne organisation. Larger changes in the functionality were discussed with the process owners in summit meetings. Daily support and small changes were handled informally either via our fieldwork or via the "hot" telephone line directly to our programmer. The process owners continued to design the flowcharts in LOTUS FREELANCE GRAPHICS. The old release 3 database was incorporated as a module in the release 4 NOTES application. Process owners could detail their maps as they were used to do. When they were finished, they flagged them ready for transfer. They were imported as bitmaps in the presentation module as a part of the enterprise model. When this was done the processowner or a helper could write textual descriptions and link up ISO-procedures to each "hot spot" (or box defined in the process chart).

From any work process it was possible to create improvement proposals, via a button at each process chart. Anybody in Norne could give comments to any process or sub-process. It became the responsibility of each process owner to enter the improvement proposal module to track proposals regarding his/her process, and on a regular basis discuss these proposals together with helpers or other people in the Norne organisation that it might be of interest to. The process owner could dismiss the proposal or implement it directly if it was a small change, e.g. change in text. If the proposal was complicated and had consequences for other processes, as the work order example mentioned earlier, it had to be discussed by management or with other process owners before it could be implemented. When the process maps had to be changed, the process owner made the changes in the discussion database module and the programmer re-imported a new revised bitmap into the presentation module. Improvement proposals became the first attempt to create a system for continuous improvement in Norne.

In the fall of 1996, Norne gradually took over more and more of the responsibility, both for the development and improvement of the work processes and the maintenance or development of the CSCW-application. A group of super-users in Norne operations were coached to perform simple maintenance and improvements on the application. At the end of December 1996 the research project came to an end and we withdrew, enabling Norne to take full responsibility of the further development themselves, together with Statoil Data.

A critical reflection on the CSCW-design and implementation process

In the world of engineers and technicians flowcharts are a well-known technique to describe "system" phenomena and dependencies. Over the years this has been a fruitful method to understand the composition and decomposition of technical systems. There are a number of problems associated with using this machine like metaphor to understand organisational phenomena. Lucy Suchman (1994; 188) claims that the inscriptions of formal representations of action in technical systems transforms the debate more clearly into a contest in how our relations to each other are ordered and by whom, and that those who are committed to an reproduction of an established institutional order might try to replace the contested moral ground of organisational commitment and accountability with a scheme of standardised, universalistic categories, administered through technologies implemented on the desktop. In his answer to Suchman, Terry Winograd (Winograd, 1994) regarding the critique of speech act theory and THE COORDINATOR, says that no systematic account can fully capture the richness of mental life, social interaction, and he claims that the guiding question is not if you have taken account of all human behaviour, but if you can design to augment peoples capacity to act.

We share Winograds pragmatic position, since the main objective was to enable a flexible structure that was effective for co-ordination within Norne. However, the following structure became as Winograd states (Winograd 1994; 195): not an imposition of control for authoritarian motives but a necessity for continued operation, and the question was not whether to impose standardised regimes, but how to do it appropriately. In a potentially hazardous environment like an oil installation this structure is necessary for continued operation. We also argue that using or imposing one system of categorisation does not necessarily displace other possible constructions of the situation. Flowchart representations can be used to pinpoint important issues in the preparation for operations in Norne, but other aspects must be brought forward in the process of reflection and fieldwork to cover other issues that this rationale does not envision. The post-modern stance of Gareth Morgan (Morgan, 1986) is important here, that seeing the phenomena from different perspectives will improve the understanding of the whole. A structural and rationalistic perspective will give a partial but important picture, and human resource, political and cultural perspectives makes it possible to understand the setting as a social system, with communities of practice, local knowledge and inevitable power struggles. We need to do as Thomas Malone (Malone, 1995) argues, learn the art of applying categories well, avoid rigid devotion to a particular set of categories, and find and support useful patterns of interaction.

Both Winograd and Suchman agree in their discussion on the fact that organisational design succeeds when it is grounded in the context and experience of those who live in the situation. Most engineers and technicians do not have sophisticated knowledge and vocabulary to address organisational phenomena in sociological or anthropological terms. If the people themselves should create the workplace in which they will be working in the future, as is the case in Norne, they need a "practical" method that makes sense based on their prior understanding of the world. The flowchart with its weaknesses at least enables them to talk about organisational problems, roles, responsibilities, apparently irrational phenomena, relations between phenomena and discuss what measures can be taken to improve the situation. This use of "black boxes" becomes useful as what Gregory Bateson (Bateson, 1972) called "heuristic devices". It is not necessary to know the exact content of a black box to have a pragmatic discussion of relations of "black boxes" at a more aggregated level. Even though people interpret the "black boxes" differently this is less of a problem when people come from a relatively joint Statoil culture and have been working with the same things in operations for years. To describe, discuss the boxes and their content in new communities of practice enables a better understanding of a new potential operational practice.

As an industrial anthropologist I see the apparent easiness in the use of "black boxes". It takes for granted the notion of a systematic world with formal, rational and structural perspectives of enterprises as techno-economic systems per se. Organisations not only consist of identifiable system relations, objects that can be decomposed or substituted, logistic systems and workflow. There is a possibility that too much focus on these issues will set frames for a "machine"-like perspective on the world, where the latest fashion depicts the enterprise as a computer like construction. A major problem of such an understanding of the organisation is that the social system tends to become a "remaining factor". It views the social aspects as "what is left", that could be put on top of the rational process in terms of "criterias for success", when all the formal objectives, roles and responsibilities have been settled.

A rational perspective does not address how people in the organisation adjust, interpret and behave in daily working situations, what Erving Goffman (Goffman, 1961) titled "secondary adjustments" as a response to the formal requirements of officials and supervisors. This rational approach is useless to describe the development of local knowledge and the importance of communities of practice. As a consequence, it does not show vital social processes in the organisation like; informal networks, team building processes, intuition, learning and motivational processes. It therefore ignores tacit knowledge and work as a social activity, with its focus on workflow instead of "the flow of work". To understand the work context then becomes of decicive importance, and deals with aspects complementary to the process perspective (Randall, 1995a; 1995b).

Since the Norne organisation was in preparations for operations it was very difficult to do a traditional workplace study and study Norne people in their real setting in operations. However, we have conducted several shorter ethnographic studies before on older oil installations (Borstad 1993, Hepsø 1997) so we have a rather clear picture of the "flow of work". The fieldwork that was conducted in the Norne organisation one or two days every week from February to December 1996, could only indicate how Norne functioned in its present preparations for operations.

In order to start the discussion on the future organisation of Norne in operations we chose to use flowchart symbols to describe social phenomena since this was a way of representing organisational issues that the people in the Norne organisation both understood and found constructive. Before the project started we discussed some overall requirements with Norne management and operators/technicians. We agreed to stick to the following premises and address these issues continually throughout the process if and when they were broken:

- Norne wants to remove as many of the detailed procedures as possible that regulate work offshore, standard Statoil ISO-procedures that only give minimal requirements will be enough

- Norne have competent personnel on all levels that are eager to take responsibility, supervision is not an issue

- We will not tell competent people how to do the work they are skilled to do. As a consequence, we make aggregated descriptions of work flow, and do not go into details

- Automation no, quality of working life yes....

To summarise, the aim was to make aggregated descriptions or requirements, and the flowcharts were looked upon as resources for future situated actions in operations, a general reference for orientation purposes and self organisation. In order to open the "black boxes", we stressed the other aspects through our participation as mediators in the process description workshops, via informal discussions with groups and members during our fieldwork days in the Norne organisation. An example of this can be that one of us asks what does this box contain, like the box "create work order" on figure 2 and 3. The context is an informal discussion with a Norne process owner and four of his helpers. The start of a dialogue on this issue went like this:

Anthropologist:	"Take a look at the "create work order" sub-process. I know from past fieldworks I have conducted that the "bureaucracy" with work orders take considerable time. You have said that Norne will try to reduce the number of work orders with 75% How do you plan to do this when you are in operation, since both you and me know that it is easy to fall back on old practice ?"
Process owner:	"You have seen our criterias to differentiate between work orders, they are fairly clear. However, I do agree that we have to do something more than just define these criterias, these things will not happen by themselves."
Anthropologist:	"How do you plan to do this?"
Process owner:	"Good question ! We have already taken measures to present this way of thinking during our presentation to new recruited Norne people. Another idea is to live by and learn from the usage of these principles during our commissioning phase. I think this is the only way we can make Norne personnel understand what this really is about."
Process owner:	(Addressing his four colleagues) "I want you to help me plan how we can take steps to live by these principles before we come into operations."

In similar situations the dialogue that developed by discussing the content of the boxes, enabled them to discuss roles and responsibilities. In essence, it helped the groups to reflect upon their culture and what should be Norne's "rules of the game" but not to describe in detail how the work should be done. Our combined focus on formalism and dialogue uses a double level language (Robinson, 1991). There was a restrictive formalism in flowcharts and computer representations. Understanding, interpretations and changing items at the formal level were mediated by conversations on a cultural level, giving power and meaning to the formal representations. We agree with Mike Robinson (Robinson, 1991) that computer support is valuable in so far as it facilitates the separation between the formal and the cultural.

It becomes very difficult to describe the methodology that has been employed here. If we are to take Davenports (Davenport, 1993) definition of process design it will match our work fairly well. A holistic approach that looks at most dimensions of an organisation's activities, take steps to design the future, envision new work strategies, do the actual process design activity and lastly take part in the implementation of the change with all its complex, technological, human and organisational consequences. However, our approach also deviates from that of BPR. We use the concepts of BPR when we talk about defining the value adding processes of the Norne organisation. Processes, value chains, products and work flow are definitely terms associated with BPR. In order to problematise BPR as a systematic solution to business problems we have coupled it with ethnographic descriptions and a constructive evolutionary design. Through dialogue and via the reflective process we have opened the "black boxes" and tried to address the issues that in most BPR-methodology is considered a remaining factor. To delineate and say what is a value adding process is not a simple issue as we have discussed. We have not focused on measurement in itself, since we believe that this would restrict the internal process in Norne. The interventionist perspective employed here is not special for BPR, but has a long tradition in the action research schools of organisational theory (Argyris 1978, Schein 1987, Whyte 1991).

What Has Norne Learned so Far: the Use of the Work Processes and the CSCW-application?

Norne has up to March 1997 had almost a years' experience with the design of work processes and the incorporated versions of the flowcharts in the NOTES application. Norne is not in production yet and we can only speculate on future usage in operations. However, some preliminary conclusions can be made on how the use of this application changed their ideas on how they plan to operate the installation and how it has eased their work in preparations for operations. Around 90 of totally 110 in the Norne organisation have up to now been defined as users.

One important observation is that it is the people in operations offshore that has found most use of the application, and less the staff support units onshore. This is mainly because of a need for detailed asyncronous communication offshore. Status information must be shared between weekly arriving and departing personnel as well as between day and night shifts.

The timing was perfect since they needed a systematic approach to co-ordinate many ongoing activities that had just started. Managers and process owners in operations/maintenance discovered benefits in using the application in their preparations. This does not only cover the flow charts themselves, but very much how you can link up information to the process maps. The operation manuals of starting and shutting down the technical systems have been incorporated into the application, these have always been paper based up to now. Another problem has been the version handling of these and other procedures, now there are only one electronic copy that is always updated. Other procedures related to operations that used to be in different NOTES databases are linked up, which indicates that the workers do not need to spend time finding this information. Finding the right information has become an increasing problem in Statoil, with over 3000 NOTES databases. The idea implemented here has been to describe the formal process and then link up the information needed to perform that job and let the process owner have the responsibility of updating and improving the links. As a consequence other computer systems (the plant maintenance system, the technical information system and vendor information on WWW) are linked up via the Norne NOTES application.

On the lowest level in the organisation, checklists for the maintenance of the technical systems are also incorporated in the application. These weekly check lists that regulate what technical systems should be maintained, by whom, at what time interval, and with a short description of the work itself, was not intended to be a part of the application in the first place. When using the application the Norne personnel found new potential functionality that created larger dependency.

We have discovered that the application is highly important for training the newly employed personnel. The simple symbols in the enterprise model from bottom to top enable the newcomers to understand more of the ideal Norne model of operations. The alternative would have been an operational philosophy document or a set of procedures. Although the graphics is fancy for a newcomer, the super user finds them increasingly boring to use. He or she wants to go directly into the sub-process they need in their daily work. To be able to do this we have developed a separate collapsible view without graphics. However, the superuser also uses the graphics when he/she enters a process not known in detail. The technician would use the graphic navigator to go to the financing process and the budgeting sub-process.

This CSCW-application is therefore conceived by Norne as a navigation device, a superstructure or an information and communication backbone that Norne people can use in their daily work and for orienting themselves in relations to a number of another computer systems and NOTES databases. Norne personnel do not interpret the application to be a work flow system, even though some flowchart symbols have been used. They see it as a structured way of representing work processes, representations or resources made available that up to now have been hidden in paper based strategies and procedures. In our case we tried to align interested people in the organisation from the very start, via strong and committed management support, and devoted process owners. Finally, the Norne personnel themselves designed their processes. The evolutionary development of the application created dependencies in the Norne organisation, since it became their preparations for operations project. With respect to ISO and Norwegian petroleum authorities inspections they are dependent on this application to show how they will operate. A preliminary conclusion is that Norne has gradually taken over the application and Norne operations offshore will not function without the application. Norne has also incorporated the application in their process for continous improvement.

In Statoil we have been trying to build rigorous enterprise models for years, with complicated modelling tools. Very few have been used by the organisational members themselves (Christensen, 1995). What has made Norne different is that we have used simple standardised technology already in use in Norne operations. We have tried to build a collective representation of Norne's operational model based on input from the Norne organisation, a model of their own construction. Hopefully this will enable Norne to develop some shared representations of their future operational practice, and that the use of the application perhaps will be less important when they have internalised these representations in operations. This is not because of the application alone, but would be the consequence of a larger organisational development process.

Acknowledgements

I am indebted to my colleagues at the Co-ordination Technology Department at Statoil R&D who have through years of fieldwork developed the methodology that made this work possible. In this project I thank Lars Thuestad, Arnstein J. Borstad, Jan Onarheim, Geir Jarle Strøm, John Olav Midtlyng and Johnny Litzheim in particular. Thanks to the visions and persistence of Norne operators/technicians and managers: Tor Hoås, Terje Tellefsen, Wiggo Lønøy, Knut Ystgård, Steinar Helle, Leif Belaska, Marta Vabø and others. Finally, thanks also to Statoil Data who set up the necessary LOTUS NOTES R4-infrastructure and made this project possible.

References

Argyris, C. and Schön, D. (1978): *Organizational Learning: A Theory of Action Perspective*, Reading, Mass.

Bateson, G. (1973): *Steps to an Ecology of Mind*, Ballantine Books, New York.

Borstad, A.J., Hepsø, V., Onarheim, J., Tvedte, B. Aune, A..B. and Engelsen, K. (1993): "Experience Transfer in Statoil", *Proceedings of IPCC'93-IEEE International Professional Communication Conference, October 1993*, Philadelphia PA., IEEE .

Christensen, L. C., Johansen, B. W., Midjo, N., Onarheim, J., Syvertsen, T. G., and Totland, T., (1995): "Enterprise Modeling - Practices and Perspectives", *Proceedings of the Ninth Annual ASME Engineering Database Symposium*, Boston, Mass.

Davenport, T. H. (1993): *Process Innovation: Reengineering Work Through Information Tecnology*, Harvard Business Press, Boston, Mass.

Goffman, E. (1961): *Asylums*, Anchor Books, New York.

Hammer, M. and Champy, J. (1993): *Re-engineering the Corporation: A Manifesto for Business Revolutions*, Nicholas Bealey Publishing, New Work.

124

Hepsø, V. (1997): "CSCW-Design and Implementation of Experience Transfer in Organisational Networks", in: Mambrey, P., Paetau, M., Prinz, W., Wulf, V., *Self Organization: A Challenge to CSCW*, forthcoming.

Hughes, J., King, V., Rodden, T. and Anderson, H. (1995): "The Role of Ethnography in Interactive Systems Design", *Interactions*, Vol 11.2, April.

Klöckner, K., Mambrey, P., Sohlenkamp, M., Prinz W., Fuchs, L., Kolvenbach, S.,Pankoke-Babatz, U. and Syri, A. (1995): "POLITeam: Bridging the Gap between Bonn and Berlin for and with the Users", *Proceedings of the ECSCW 95*, Kluwer Academic Publishers.

Latour, B. (1987): *Science in Action: How to Follow Scientists and Engineers Through Society*, Harvard University Press, Cambridge.

Malone, T.W. (1995): "Commentary on Suchman Article and Winograd Response", in *CSCW*, vol. 3, No 1.

Morgan, G. (1986): *Images of Organisations*, Sage, Beverly Hills

Okamura, K., Fujimoto, M., Orlikowski W.,J. and Yates J., (1994): "Helping CSCW Applications Succeed: The Role of Mediators in the Context of Use", *Proceedings of CSCW 94*, ACM Press, NewYork.

Randall, D.W. (1995a): "A Comment on Lucy Suchman's: Do Categories Have Politics", *CSCW*, vol 3, No. 1.

Randall, D.W., Rouncefield, M. and Hughes, J. A. (1995b): "Chalk and Cheese: BPR and ethnomethodologically informed ethnography in CSCW", in *Proceedings of the ECSCW 95*, Kluwer Academic Publishers.

Robinson, M. (1991) "Double-Level Languages and Co-operative Working." *AI & Society* 5: 34-60.

Rumbaugh, J. (1993): "Objects in the Constitution- Enterprise Modeling", *Journal on Object-Oriented Programming*, pp 18-24, January.

Schmidt, K. and Simone, C. (1996): "Coordination Mechanisms: Towards a Conceptual Foundation of CSCW System Design", *CSCW*, vol 5, No 2/3.

Schein, E.H. (1987): *The Clinical Perspective in Fieldwork*, Sage Qualitative Research Methods Series No 5 Sage, Ca.

Schuler, D. and Namioka, A. (eds) (1993): *Participatory Design: principles and practice*, Hillsdale New Jersey NJ.

Suchman, L. (1987): *Plans and Situated Actions. The Problem of Human-machine Communication*, Cambridge University Press Cambridge.

Suchman, L., (1994): Do Cathegories have Politics, *CSCW*, vol 2, No 3.

Thorsrud, E. and Emery, F. (1969): *Form and Content in Industrial Democracy*, Tavistock, London,

Whyte, W. F. (ed) (1991): *Participatory Action Research*, Sage Ca.

Winograd, T. (1994): "Categories, Disciplins and Social Coordination", *CSCW*, vol 2, No 3.

Wulf V. and Rohde M. (1995): "Towards an Integrated Organization and Technology Development", in *Proceedings of the Symposium on Designing Interactive Systems*, ACM-Press, New York.

Staging a Public Poetry Performance in a Collaborative Virtual Environment

Steve Benford, Chris Greenhalgh, Dave Snowdon and Adrian Bullock
Department of Computer Science, The University of Nottingham, UK

We discuss the design of a CVE poetry performance and experiences arising from staging it to two hundred members of the public. The design, a collaborative effort between computer scientists, artists, poets and producers, addresses issues of: virtual world structure; embodiment of performers and audience; navigation interfaces; temporal structure of the event; and mixed reality presentation. Experiences include virtual audience members often ignoring the poets and conflicting attitudes towards embodiment. New CVE design possibilities are proposed, including object centred interaction, context sensitive interaction and tools to define and manage the spatial and temporal structure of events.

1. Introduction

In this paper, we present the design of a poetry performance in a collaborative virtual environment (CVE) and discuss the experience of staging this performance to an audience of two hundred members of the general public.The performance took place in Nottingham on 11th November 1996 as part of the NOWninety6 arts festival and involved an extensive collaboration between computer scientists, poets, a graphic artist and an event production team. This paper explores a range of CSCW issues arising from this experience, including:

- developing rich and engaging forms of content for CVEs;
- exploring the tension between autonomy of action for audience members and the management of a performance so as to encourage appropriate behaviours at relevant times and places;
- considering the role of 'virtual architecture' in enabling different modes of awareness and communication between participants as an event unfolds;
- developing appropriate embodiments for performers and audience;

J. Hughes et al. (eds.), Proceedings of the Fifth European Conference on Computer Supported Cooperative Work, 125-140.
© 1997 *Kluwer Academic Publishers.*

- developing appropriate navigation interfaces for different participants (e.g. for members of the public with no previous experience of VR as compared to the performers and 'camera-people');
- exploring different ways of situating interfaces to the virtual environment within different physical spaces based on notions of mixed reality as proposed in (Benford, 1996);
- understanding the issues involved in designing and managing such an event and how these might influence world construction tools for CVEs.

The exploration of these issues is particularly relevant at the present time for several reasons. First, we believe that so-called 'citizen' applications of CVEs, such as performance, art and entertainment, represent a significant future application area for this technology. Recent months have seen a rapid growth of interest in publicly accessible virtual worlds on the Internet as discussed at the closing panel at CSCW'96 (Damer, 1996). Furthermore, in addition to the considerable interest of artists in VR technology as a medium for generating interactive artistic works, several people have begun experimenting with VR as a medium for performance and social interaction. Recent examples include the Membrane series of performances staged by Fahlén and Bowers (Fahlén, 1995) and 'The Mirror', a UK based public trial of a graphical and textual CVE running over the Internet and alongside the BBC Television series The Net. As the underlying technology matures, so the issue of providing appropriate content will become increasingly important. Second, this work involves a combination of artistic and technical perspectives on the design of a CSCW application. Just as the multi-disciplinary combination of social science and computer science has been at the heart of CSCW, so a synergy between art and technology might stimulate new innovations in systems design, especially in terms of user interfaces and new forms of content targetted at citizen users. Third, we believe that it is important to take CSCW technologies out of the laboratory and to demonstrate them and experiment with them publicly.

Section 2 offers a brief summary of the event. Section 3 then discusses key design issues in detail. Following this, section 4 reflects upon the experience of staging the event and key lessons learned. Finally, section 5 proposes a number of new design possibilities for general CVEs based on these lessons.

2. A brief overview of the event

Our poetry performance involved four hip-hop poets, Remi Abbas, Roger Robinson, Akure Wall and Dave "Stickman" Higgins, performing in turn in a collaborative virtual environment designed by the artist Sean Varney and supported by our own MASSIVE-2 CVE software. In addition to the performers, the environment was populated by ten virtual audience members at a time, where each audience member was an autonomous, mobile and embodied participant who could explore the environment and could interact with the other participants over live audio links (active participation and social interaction by audience members was one of our principal goals). The virtual environment was structured as a central stage area in which the virtual poets appeared, surrounded by four outlying worlds containing different graphical designs and embedded text from the poems. The audience members were encouraged to explore these outer worlds during breaks in the performance, thereby adding an exhibition aspect to the event. The virtual poet embodiments featured a moving head and hands driven by Polhemus motion trackers attached to the head and hands of the physical poet. The audience members were embodied as "angels" and used a conventional workstation.

The performance was located in two quite different physical spaces. The ten workstations used by the audience members were located in a crowded café-bar. In contrast, the poets performed in an adjacent cinema which was structured as a more traditional performance space with a stage and seated audience. The use of projected graphics and audio links provided a limited form of mixed reality between the two physical spaces and the virtual one. In particular, the seated audience members in the cinema were given a view into the virtual environment so that they could see the virtual poet embodiment moving alongside the real poet and could also see and sometimes hear the virtual audience members.

The event lasted for four hours and was attended by a total of 200 paying members of the public. Given a cyclic performance schedule, 60 of these managed to experience some poetry as an audience member in the virtual world. The others were able to wander between the two physical spaces, watching a mixture of live performance and the virtual audience members using the system.

The software used was our own MASSIVE-2 system (Benford, 1997), a successor to MASSIVE as reported at ECSCW'95 (Greenhalgh, 1995). Like its predecessor, MASSIVE-2 supports communication in shared virtual worlds using graphical, audio and textual media. In addition, it supports an extended version of the spatial model of interaction which allows for greater scaleability and also the implementation of different structural effects on awareness such as nested bounded regions and dynamic crowds. This is mapped onto an underlying network architecture based on a dynamic hierarchy of multicast groups. This software was run over a purpose built Ethernet connecting a mixture of Silicon Graphics computers (Onyx, Impact, O2 and Indy) connected to various video projectors and Polhemus trackers. The default machine for audience members was an O2.

3. The design of the event in more detail

In this section we focus on several key aspects of the design in the event in greater detail. These include: the structure of the virtual world; the embodiment of the different participants; the temporal structure of the event; the presentation of the virtual world within the physical world; and navigation interfaces. However, before progressing further, we should briefly mention the design process itself. The concept of the event was first formulated by a combination of Computer Scientists and the NOWninety6 festival producers in March 1996. The poets and VR artist were then invited into the team and the concept evolved considerably over the following nine months. The VR artist was given the task of designing the virtual world and embodiment graphics, subject to some fairly severe constraints on complexity. These designs were provided in VRML format and a series of meetings over a period of several months were needed to refine them and integrate them into the MASSIVE-2 platform. A few of these meetings involved the poets who consequently had a limited opportunity to participate in the world and embodiment design (the major constraint being travel). Finally, there were several in-laboratory rehearsals followed by a full two day period just before the performance where the whole system was built from scratch in an isolated environment for final rehearsals.

3.1. The structure of the virtual world

The virtual world was designed to house a combination of performance and exhibition activities and consisted of a central stage area surrounded by four outlying worlds (one per poet). The screen-shot in figure 1 gives an overview of this structure, with the four outer worlds shown in collapsed form as seen from outside, i.e. as simple coloured cones (see below). The content of these outer worlds was designed by the VR artist so as to offer a visually engaging experience to an observer and to naturally lead them to some textual fragments of poetry located at their centres. Figure 2 shows the contents of each of the outer worlds in detail. The stage area consisted of a central raised platform on which a virtual poet embodiment would appear, surrounded by ten marked locations which acted as virtual seats for the audience members and which defined their individual home positions (see the discussion of navigation below and figure 4).

This structure was also designed to have a number of effects on the mutual awareness of its inhabitants. In particular, it used MASSIVE-2's notion of third party objects (an extension to the spatial model of interaction described in (Benford, 1997) to define the outer worlds as separate bounded spatial regions. Each of these outer worlds was defined as a region with the following properties:

- When viewed from the outside, its internal structure would be hidden away and replaced with a simple external view (a coloured cone). This extended to the region's inhabitants who would be invisible to those on the outside.
- On entering a region, it would be unfolded to reveal its contents (graphical structure and other inhabitants) in detail. In addition, those people located inside the region would still be able to see the structure of the outside world (i.e. stage area) and its inhabitants in normal detail.
- The audio medium was treated in the same way as the graphical one; all conversation occurring inside the region would not be heard by those outside, but any audio from the central space (e.g. the poetry) would still be heard by those on the inside.

Figure 1: Overview of the virtual world as seen from the stage area

Figure 2a: Stickman's world

Figure 2b: Roger's world

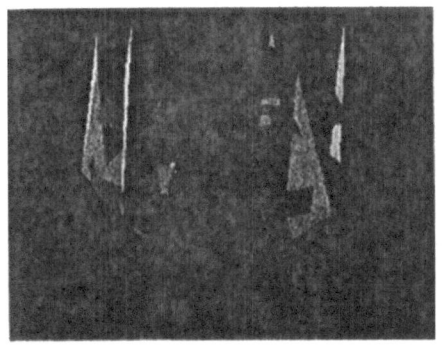

Figure 2c: Akure's world

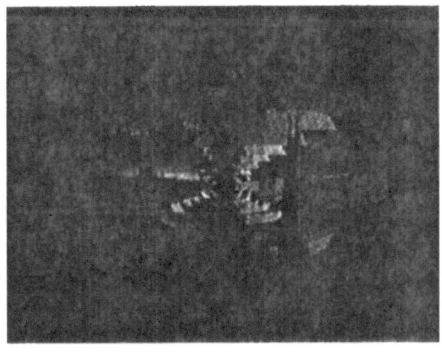

Figure 2d: Remi's world

In other words, the boundaries of the four outer regions were defined to have an asymmetric effect on awareness. From the outside, they were opaque (both visually and aurally), but from the inside they were transparent. There were two motivations for this design. First, the regions were designed to offer private zones for social interaction, such that conversations within the regions would not interfere with the poetry in the stage area or the conversations in other regions and yet the poetry (and interactions of those near the stage) would still be visible and audible within the regions. Second, the regional structure aided network and computational scaleability; the detailed structure of each region would only be rendered by its occupants and there would be no transmission of audio or movement data from those inside a region to those outside. In this way, the artist could be given freedom to design more complex graphical structures than would otherwise have been possible.

3.2. Embodiment of the different participants

The two different classes of participant in the virtual world, poets and audience members, were embodied in different ways.

The poets' embodiments needed to be visually interesting. In particular, we felt that they should be capable of gesturing. Thus, they were provided with relatively expressive embodiments, uniquely designed for the individual poets (see figure 3). Each poet embodiment consisted of a graphical object for a head, a separate body and two separate hands (in one case, one of the "hands" was actually a staff). The body section showed the poet's position within the virtual world. The movements of the graphical head and hands were driven by the movements of the physical poet through the use of Polhemus magnetic position trackers which were attached to some light-weight elastic loops that could easily be put on by the different poets. Consequently, the physical poet's head orientation and hand movements were mimicked by its virtual embodiment, allowing a range of gestures to be performed (although it took several rehearsals for the poets to adapt themselves to the exaggerated gestures that were required to produce something visually interesting on their graphical embodiment). A simple graphical mouth was also provided which would change shape whenever the poet was speaking.

Following early rehearsals, it was decided to locate two virtual poet embodiments back to back in the virtual world. This allowed for a circular stage design with each audience member getting a front-on view of the poet. It also supported the development of a 'camera control' interface for the projected display in the cinema (see below) which could keep both a frontal poet view and several audience members in shot from any position around the stage.

The audience members were provided with somewhat simpler embodiments (given that ten of them would be in the world at a time), being represented as graphical angels. Each angel was given a different colour and number, a name label above its head and a graphical mouth that would appear whenever its occupant was speaking. Unlike the poets' embodiments, the angels weren't articulated, and only served

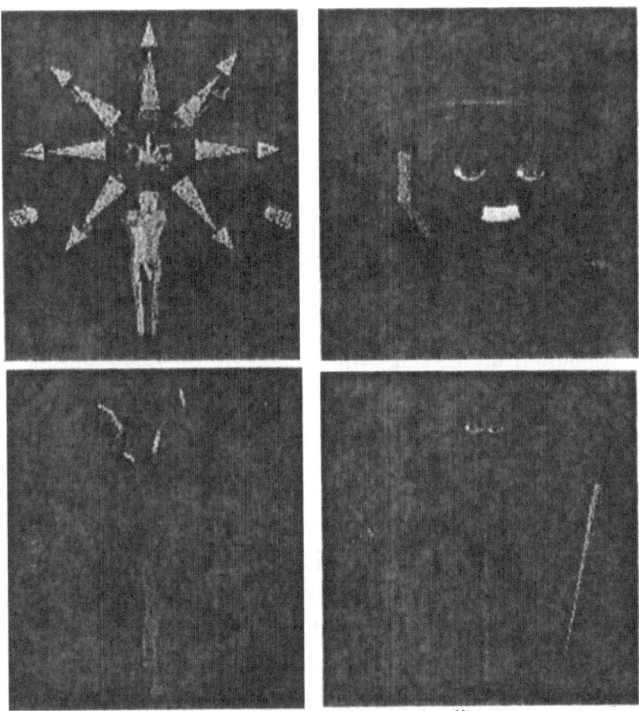

Figure 3: The Poet's embodiments

Figure 4: Angel embodiments within the virtual world

to indicate 3-D position and orientation within the virtual world. Figure 4 shows several angels within the virtual world alongside one of the poets.

The design of the embodiments included the definition of foci and nimbi for the management of awareness and particularly for the spatial control of audio communication. All participants (poets and angels) were given a constant valued nimbus across the whole world, effectively providing an unconstrained opportunity for overhearing them. The audio focus of each participant was a multi-valued field with a peak of maximum focus within a range of five (virtual) metres, gradually dropping off to a zero at a range of three hundred metres (from the centre of the stage to the centre of one of the outer worlds was two hundred metres). Thus, the volume at which people were heard would decrease with distance, although it would still be possible to hear audio from the stage while in one of the outer worlds.

3.3. The presentation of the virtual world within the real world

An important aspect of our design was the ways in which interfaces to the virtual world were situated within different physical spaces and also the ways in which occupants of these various spaces were provided with some degree of mutual awareness to create a form of mixed reality as initially proposed in (Benford, 1996).

The event was distributed across two distinct physical spaces. The first was a fairly traditional performance space created in a cinema. This involved a seated audience facing a stage on which the physical poets performed. The second was a "cyber café" created in an adjacent café bar. Here, people could sit down at workstations in order to control an angel in the virtual world.

Our aim was to create two quite different environments, with people wandering between the two. The cinema was intended to provide a well managed and disciplined environment within which the poets could perform. The café bar, on the other hand, was intended to be a noisy and relatively unstructured environment. Several further linkages were made between these two physical spaces and the virtual world:

- A view of the virtual world was projected in the cinema alongside the stage so that the cinema audience could see the virtual poet embodiment moving alongside the physical poet and could also witness the behaviour of the angels. This view was controlled by a dedicated "camera person" using a specially created interface (see below). In addition, audio from the virtual world (i.e. conversations between the angels) could be mixed into the house PA in the Cinema.

- A view as seen by one of the angels was projected onto the wall of the café-bar so that all of its occupants (up to a hundred people) could keep track of events in the virtual world. The audio from the poets was also broadcast into this space.

To complete the mixed reality, it was initially intended to provide video views into the two physical spaces to the angels within the virtual world similar to those used in the Internet Foyer application described in (Benford, 1996). However, this idea had to be dropped due to lack of time, concern about the impact on the network and the lack of suitable available hardware.

3.4. The temporal structure of the event

Given budgetary constraints and hence the limited availability of workstations, one of our biggest problems was how to give an exciting experience to as many people as possible. We also needed to balance the needs of the audience in the cinema, who would be experiencing a fairly conventional style of performance, against those of the virtual audience members who needed to mix attending a performance with exploring the outer worlds. These issues all related to the temporal structure and rhythm of the event.

Our solution to this problem involved a cycle of performances. In the cinema, each cycle was an hour long: fifteen minutes change over; fifteen minutes performance from a poet; a short change followed by fifteen minutes from a second poet; and finally fifteen minutes "touring" where the cinema audience would be taken on a tour of the virtual world and would observe the angels exploring and interacting with one another. The cycle was quicker in the café bar involving a half-hourly change over. Each batch of ten angels would either explore for fifteen minutes and then experience fifteen minutes poetry (corresponding to the first half of a cinema cycle) or vice versa (corresponding to the second half). The whole event involved three cinema cycles, allowing sixty people to experience the virtual world. These were preceded by an introductory talk and followed by a discussion session.

In order to manage smooth change overs within the Cinema and Café Bar, additional workstations dedicated solely to management tasks were located in each space. These were used to start up and shut down different processes (e.g. user clients, poets embodiments and the world itself) and to control the display of change over notifactions on different workstations. Extensive use was made of UNIX talk between these two machines in order to coordinate the overall event. These machines were continually manned by technicans. Other technicians were provided to help with the tracking equipment at the stage and each angel workstation was also assigned its own assistant.

3.5. Navigation interfaces

Given that our system had to be used by members of the public with no previous experience and given some of our previous observations concerning the difficulties of navigating CVEs (Greenhalgh, 1995), the design of the user interface was assigned great importance. In fact, we designed and implemented two quite different navigation interfaces for the event, intended for use by different kinds of participants: an angel interface for members of the public and a camera interface to be used to drive the projected view in the cinema.

We begin with the angel interface. We decided to allow the angels to be able to fly up and down off of the ground plane and to rotate forwards and backwards, even though the whole event could quite easily have been experienced from ground level in the virtual world. However, we took several steps to minimise the risk of getting lost and disorientated. First, we separated all controls for movement off of the ground plane into separate areas of the interface. We provided buttons to reset position to ground level and orientation to straight ahead and we also retained the idea from MASSIVE of providing different camera angles, giving both in and out of body views (straight ahead, over the shoulder, mirror and birds-eye were provided).

A particular concern was how to encourage people to move about the virtual world at appropriate times (e.g. how to easily get them to the outer worlds for exploring and back to the stage in time for a performance).We introduced two mechanisms to support this. First, we defined a number of travelators from the stage to the outer worlds (visible as grey pathways in figure 1). People moving onto one of these would gently drift towards an outer world unless they deliberately moved otherwise. Second, we provided a "back to seat" button which, when continuously held down, would turn its angel to face the stage, move them back to their seat and then turn them to face the centre of the stage in a smooth animated movement. In this way, we hoped to make it easy for people to move to appropriate places without taking away their autonomy of control.

We also implemented two further general navigational aids: a 2-D plan view of the world with a zoom function and with labelled positions of the other angels; and stereo panning of audio so that people to one's left would be heard on the left hand side of the stereo mix and vice versa. We did consider the use of "solid" objects as another way of avoiding disorientation, similar to the approach of games such as Doom where one is constrained by solid boundaries to move through corridors and other enclosing spaces. However, given the relatively open structure of our world combined with the irregular design of the outer worlds and the relatively high computational cost of collision detection, we decided that this would not be an appropriate or cost effective solution for this particular event.

The camera-control interface was quite different. First, it was defined so that all movements were about a single point of focus - the stage area. Thus, the camera always pointed towards the performers and the only available movements were various rotations and zooms about a central point. The camera person could navigate by specifying a destination for the camera and then requesting a smooth animated transition to this new location. They could also create a list of stored positions and could animate transitions to these. In this way, we ensured that the projection interface in the Cinema always kept the performer in view and also that it offered smooth transitions between attractive viewpoints (e.g. sweeps around the performer, zoom into a poets face, move to a birds-eye view and so on).

This concludes our discussion of the design of the poetry event and the various features that were introduced in order to help manage participation and navigation. In the following section we reflect upon what actually happened at the event.

4. Experience

The following observations have been derived from a variety of sources including video recordings of the event; informal interviews with participants during the event; a final public discussion session involving the performers, artists, technicians, producers and members of the audience; and our own reflections. In many ways we consider the event to have been a great success, especially given its innovative and experimental nature. The virtual audience members clearly enjoyed themselves, there was plenty of social interaction between them (perhaps too much, as we shall see below!), they seemed to learn to navigate reasonably well, the software and hardware performed to our expectations and the management of the event and change overs progressed fairly smoothly. However, we did experience a number of unforeseen problems which suggest new design possibilities. It is these problems that we focus upon in this section.

4.1. The angels ignoring the poets

The most obvious and major problem with the event was that the angels tended to ignore the virtual poets. They often moved away from their seats within seconds of a performance beginning; they constantly spoke to one another over the poetry; and they sometimes even wandered into the centre of the stage during a performance. We suspect that there were a number of causes for this behaviour, spanning social, production and technical issues.

A key technical problem was that the poets were simply not loud enough in the virtual world. First, there were some problems with getting a clear audio feed from the house PA system into the virtual environment. Second, giving the angels the same foci and nimbi as the poets may have over-empowered them. Giving them smaller nimbi would have reduced their ability to interrupt the poetry. However, this step might also have reduced the potential for encounters and social interaction between angels during the exploration phases of the event (our initial design was based on the assumption that relatively large foci and nimbi were needed to ensure adequate levels of awareness for encounters to occur between only ten participants distributed across four outer worlds). Ideally, we would have needed to dynamically adjust the size of the angels' foci and nimbi at different stages of the event or at different locations, contracting them during the poetry and expanding them during exploration.

A second technical problem concerned the navigation interface. It was very easy for the angels to leave their seats - much easier than it would be in a conventional physical performance space. A physical theatre seat constrains one's view and movements to a much greater degree than our virtual seats which basically just marked a home position. On reflection, it may have been better to have given the angels a more performer centred navigation control during the performance, similar to that used to control the projected display, effectively forcing them to keep the poet in view as they moved about. We could also have made it more difficult for them to leave their seats or perhaps could have introduced a gravitational pull back to their seats during the performance based on the travelator mechanism used to transport them to the outer worlds. However, like the reduction in nimbi discussed above, these changes would probably have been inappropriate for the exploration phases of the event. From a social perspective, it may be that, given the novelty of the multi-user VR experience for our audience members, the temptation to fly around and talk to other people was just too great. In many ways, the problem might even be seen as indicative of the attractiveness of the idea of social interaction within CVEs. This may have been exacerbated by the temporal structure of the event - half of our virtual audiences were expected to sit still for the first fifteen minutes of their experience.

Finally, there was clearly a lack of feedback from the poets to the audience members as we shall discuss in the section below.

It is interesting to note that we did not experience this problem when rehearsing with the system in the laboratory. Of course, our audience members for rehearsals tended to be more experienced users, were more personally involved in staging the event, were possibly more familiar with their expected behaviour, were in a different social setting and had consumed less alcohol. There were also fewer angels present in rehearsals. However, whatever the causes, the behaviour of the angels on the night would have been difficult to predict in advance and may also have operated in a vicious circle; once some people started to talk over the poets so it became harder for others to pay attention. Again, this points towards a requirement to be able to dynamically influence social interaction, perhaps through dynamic manipulation of spatial model mechanisms such as focus and nimbus, as an event unfolds.

4.2. The poets ignoring the angels

A contributing factor to the above problem was undoubtedly that the virtual poets were clearly not addressing the angels. Although the virtual poets appeared in the performance space, gestured and spoke, they were driven by the physical poets who were performing to the physical audience in the cinema. Consequently the poets did not, and indeed could not, directly engage individual angels using gesture or gaze. Given their limited awareness of what was going on in the virtual world (the projected view could be seen to the side of them, but only with difficulty), the poets could not even refer to events in the virtual world. Thus, there was no reaction from the virtual poets when the virtual audience talked over them or otherwise behaved "badly". In short, it was too easy to ignore them without appearing to cause offence.

In some ways, this problem stemmed from a deliberate design decision. We had decided that, given their lack of experience with the system, it would be safest for the poets if they could perform to a live audience. As an alternative, we could have structured the event so that they performed to the virtual audience and were only observed by the physical one. The inclusion of video views of the physical poets and audience in the virtual world as originally aimed for might also have helped with this problem. Either way, the result of our strategy was that both the physical performance space and the virtual world worked well as spaces in their own right, but not really in a properly integrated way. To put it more formally, an integrated mixed reality was not successfully created. One of the causes behind this problem may have been the lack of a stable and consistent spatial frame of reference that spanned both the physical and virtual spaces. In particular, the use of the camera interface in the Cinema with its changing viewpoint, although aesthetically pleasing, made it difficult to establish any consistent reference between the two spaces.

4.3. Embodiment and symbolism

One of the key issues raised in the post event discussion was the symbolism of the embodiments and of the virtual world design. As black poets, much of whose work dealt with issues of race, the performers were obviously highly interested in the symbolism of their embodiments. So was the artist (who incidentally was white), but with a different perspective; he was clearly interested in the aesthetics of the environment and also in reflecting a specific design concept. In this case, he designed the world around a religious theme of angels (audience members) and devils (the poets). This clearly raised some concern with the performers! Much of this had completely passed by the computer scientists (also all white) who judged the poets embodiments on their aesthetic value, with little consideration of their symbolism. Some broader observations arise from this. First, as we have seen before with CSCW, inter-disciplinary working raises new problems. In this case, we were seeing quite different perspectives on a design issue from performers, artists and technologists, all of whom were essential to the event. Although there had been some discussion between all of these parties on the design of the embodiments, resulting in several changes, the issues of their symbolism had not been raised! Second, this problem raises yet another issue to be considered by embodiment designers in addition to those discussed in previous papers (Benford, 1995; Bowers, 1996).

4.4. Problems with starting-up

Our final problem involved starting up the system simultaneously for our ten audience members. Due to concerns about the stability of the software if run uninterrupted for several hours, we decided to restart the system at every audience change over. Although we had run with this many users before, we had never started them all simultaneously. The result of so doing was severe delays in initialising processes, time-outs and system crashes. The short term solution to this was to stagger the start-up for the audience members. This would have been much more difficult over a wider area network due to the large amount of coordination involved. Although some of the problem was down to specific software problems with MASSIVE-2, we suspect that initialisation for large numbers of users is going to be a problem area for many CVE systems.

5. Towards new design possibilities

Although interesting in themselves, the problems described above are of particular relevance because they offer general insights into the development of CVEs. In this section, we explore some of the resulting design possibilities.

5.1. Object centred interaction

One way of focusing an angel's attention on the poets might have been to provide them with a similar navigation interface to that used with the projected display, where all movements are relative to a common point of focus. We might generalise this to a notion of "object centred navigation" - a new way of navigating in CVEs which involves designating objects as a focal point and then moving about them. Such objects might be elements of the world structure (e.g. a stage), data objects in an information visualisation, elements of a 3-D design or even other participants. We have recently extended MASSIVE-2 to include such a navigation interface. Our interface allows a user to dynamically designate an object in the virtual world to be their current navigation focus. They can then move towards this object, away from it or around it. At any time they can select another object and make this their navigation focus. Other aspects of interaction might also be dealt with in an object centred way. For example, "object centred awareness" would involve several people who were locked onto a common focus experiencing heightened mutual awareness (e.g. two people focusing on the same element in a 3-D information visualisation might automatically get an audio channel allocated to them). In fact, the mechanism of third party objects from the extended spatial model already provides lower level support for this idea; a third party object is able to adapt (amplify or attenuate) existing awareness relationships according to how aware it is of the other objects or vice versa (Benford, 1997). Thus, a third party could amplify the mutual awareness of objects that were highly aware of it (i.e. were focused upon it).

Consistency might also be dealt with in this way; objects dealing with a common focus might experience a more consistent world view than those with different foci. In general, what we are proposing is a general consideration of how common objects of interest might be used as the basis for mediating different aspects of interaction in CVEs, including navigation, awareness, consistency and perhaps others. In its most general form, we might refer to this idea as "object centred interaction".

5.2. Context driven interaction

The poetry event involved the angels in two distinct activities: attending the performance and exploration. Each of these has different interaction requirements. For example, the performance requires smaller foci and nimbi for the angels and performer centred navigation whereas exploration may require larger foci and nimbi (to enable communication among a more widely dispersed population) and a more traditional 3-D style of navigation. To generalise, aspects of interaction such as awareness, navigation, consistency and so forth might best be dealt with in a context or activity sensitive way. Two especially interesting aspects of context are: spatial context (i.e. where people are) and temporal context (i.e. what stage is an event at). In other words, it should be possible to trigger changes in the interface and system functionality according to both spatial location and temporal events. As noted above, aspects of adapting focus and nimbus according to spatial context have already been addressed through the third party extension to the spatial model (Benford, 1997). Our experiences with the poetry event suggest that third parties might be extended to influence other aspects of interaction such as navigation. We also need to develop models of the temporal structure and flow of events which can be used to manage interaction. Given such models, we can consider extending virtual world modelling tools such as (Colebourne, 1996) to include systems support for both temporal and spatial structuring of events in CVEs and the management of transitions between them. Finally, dynamic management of such facilities is required so that event producers can react to evolving circumstances and behaviours.

6. Summary

This paper has discussed the design of a public poetry performance in a CVE. At the heart of this design was the objective of enabling the virtual audience members to be autonomous and socially active participants in the event. Our design addressed a broad range of issues including developing a virtual world structure that would support a combination of performance and exploration; developing appropriate embodiments for both the performers (a semi-immersive interface to support gesturing) and the audience members; adapting mixed reality concepts for the display of the virtual world within two quite different physical spaces; determining an appropriate temporal structure for the event; and developing different navigation interfaces for the audience members and for projection interfaces.

A number of interesting issues were raised by the actual staging of the event. First, for a combination of technical, social and production reasons, it transpired that the virtual audience and performers practically ignored one another. Second, the post-event discussion revealed that the design of the various embodiments, especially their symbolism, was an important and controversial issue. Finally, a number of specific technical problems were revealed such as those caused by simultaneously starting the virtual environment for ten audience members.

Several more general conclusions can be drawn from this work. The design of this kind of event requires that many different issues are addressed against a backdrop of very specific technical constraints (networking, performance of computers etc.). The staging of this kind of event in a public forum provides a powerful focus for defining and dealing with such issues. It is also possible to generalise the lessons learned from such experiences. In this case, section five raised to possibility of new approaches to managing interaction in CVEs, "object centred interaction" and "context centred interaction".

Finally, the staging of this event has required extensive collaboration between computer scientists, artists, performers and producers. Although not without its problems, this has been an extremely positive experience. Furthermore, as the technology of CVEs matures and is directly taken up by the public (as we believe it will be within the next few years), so bringing artistic and production expertise into the development of CVE applications will become increasingly important. Thus, "content will be king", and events such as the one described in this paper will become an increasingly important aspect of research into CVEs.

Acknowledgements

We would like to thank the EPSRC and the European Commission (ACTS programme) for funding the development of the underlying technologies and The University of Nottingham and Nottingham City Council for funding for the event itself. We would like to thank artist Sean Varney; poets Dave "Stickman" Higgins, Akure Wall, Roger Goodwin and Remi Abbas; producer Andrew Chetty and all of the NOW'96 team for working with us on creating and staging this performance. We would like to thank Jolanda Tromp and Mike Fraser and other colleagues at Nottingham for helping out during the event and for their input into its design.

References

Benford, S. D., Bowers, J. M., Fahlén, L. E., Greenhalgh, C. M. and Snowdon, D. N., User Embodiment in Collaborative Virtual Environments, Proc. CHI'95, May 7-11, Denver, Colorado, USA, ACM Press.

Benford, S. D., Brown, C. C., Reynard, G. T. and Greenhalgh, C. M, Shared Spaces: Transportation, Artificiality and Spatiality, Proc. CSCW'96, Boston, pp. 77-86, ACM Press.

Bowers, J., Pycock, J. and O'Brien, J., Talk and Embodiment in Collaborative Virtual Environments, Proc. CHI'96, ACM Press, 1996.

Benford, S. D., Greenhalgh, C. M. and Lloyd, D, Crowded Collaborative Virtual Environments, Proc. CHI'97, Atlanta, Georgia, US, March 22-27, 1997 (in press).

Colebourne, A., Rodden, T. and Palfreyman, K., VR-MOG: A toolkit for building shared virtual worlds, Conf. FIVE Working Group, London, 1995, 109-122, M. Slater (ed).

Damer, B and Bruckman, A (moderators), Peopled Online Virtual Worlds: A New Home for Cooperating Communities, A New Frontier for Interaction Design (panel), Proc. CSCW'96, Boston, USA, Nov 16-20, 1996, pp 441-442, ACM Press.

Fahlén, L. E., The Synthetic Hyper Theatre: The Conceptual Symbiosis of VR, Art and Aesthetics, Invited paper Conf. FIVE Working Group, London, 1995, 109-122, M. Slater (ed).

Greenhalgh, C. M. and Benford, S. D., Virtual Reality Tele-conferencing: Implementation and Experience, Proc. ECSCW'95, Stockholm, September, 1995, North-Holland.

On Distribution, Drift and the Electronic Medical Record

Some Tools for a Sociology of the Formal

Marc Berg
Maastricht University, the Netherlands
Marc.Berg@GW.UniMaas.NL

Abstract: Formal tools (i.e., tools that operate on circumscribed input using rules, and that contain a model of the workplace in which are to function) are attributed central roles in organizing work within many modern workplaces. How to comprehend the power of these tools? Taking the (electronic) medical record as an example, this paper builds upon recent calls to overcome the dichotomy between the Formal and the Informal and proposes an understanding of the generative power of such tools which does not attribute mythical capacities to either tool or human work. The concrete, real-time use of formal tools is the starting point. These steps towards a sociology of the formal are crucial for a more comprehensive understanding and evaluation of such systems.

Introduction

Through offering abstracted models of the work, and/or through the processing of input into output, formal tools are attributed central roles in organizing work within just about any modern workplace. What is it that these tools do in practice? How do they add to or interfere in the work performed? Answers to these questions are highly relevant for all those who believe that technology design might be improved through theoretical insight into the processes of everyday work. Yet any answer has to sail a risky course between either granting too much power and self-sufficiency to the tool at the expense of the workers (and thus replicating the rationalist discourses of 'naïve formalists' (Star, 1995)) or overly stressing the versatile and creative skill of the human workers versus the 'rigidity' of the formal tool. Both alternatives overlook how it is in the *interrelation* of the tool's functioning with the

J. Hughes et al. (eds.), Proceedings of the Fifth European Conference on Computer Supported Cooperative Work, 141-156.
© 1997 *Kluwer Academic Publishers.*

human workers' work that new potentialities emerge. Through this interlocking, for example, new competences for workers can be achieved, higher levels of complexity in work tasks can be reached, and activities can be coordinated over time and place (Bowers, 1992; Suchman, 1993; Robinson, 1994; Berg, 1997).

Yet what does this interrelation look like? How does it yield new workplaces? The danger of speaking of 'interrelation' is that one may be seen to end up in some middle ground, taking over too many assumptions from the naïve formalist's position and its 'naïve informalists'' sibling. In fact, this is what often occurs in much recent work on the interrelation of formal tools and work practices. Yet how can we grasp the generative power of these techniques without having to assume the superiority of their models, or the purity of their logic? Likewise, how can we account for functioning tools without having to fall back on the interpretative skills or superior flexibility of human workers as the bottom-line explanation? Either of these two options would re-invoke the grand categories of the Formal or the Informal, and would draw on *a priori's* questioned in recent science and technology studies (e.g. Haraway, 1991; Latour, 1994). This would constrain our analytical understanding of such workplaces, and woud ultimately limit the innovative contributions that can be made to technology design. Building upon recent work in science and technology studies and related fields, then, I will propose a more mundane understanding, and touch - in the limited space available - upon the differences such an understanding could make.

The route into this analysis investigates the real-time work of and with formal tools in current practice.[1] The materials presented here are taken from an ongoing study of the construction, implementation and use of an electronic medical record system in an intensive care unit (ICU) in a research hospital in the Netherlands. This system was thoroughly adapted from the generic, commercial version by two nurses and an anesthesiologist, all working on the ICU. At this moment it has all but completely replaced the 'paper' record, functioning as *the* patient record for both nurses and physicians: a rather unique situation.

Distribution

Only as part of a concrete work practice does a formal tool come to life. By itself it does not do anything: people must turn on the computer to use the record. Organizational routines, instruments, specific forms: all will have to be in circulation, interlocking with the tool for it 'to work'. This is not a deep metaphysical point: it is like saying that a bicycle doesn't work unless someone sits on it, and you have a road, a pump for your tires, gravity, an urge to cycle, and so

---

[1] . This paper is adapted from a larger paper (forthcoming in *Science, Technology and Human Values*), in which I also explore a historical route, asking how the current map and terrain have been co-produced through time.

forth. And just as the activity of 'biking' is then produced by this assembly of sorts, the generative power of the record is produced by this hybrid.

Yet this point does lead to a reconsideration of the way tool and practice are related. Let us look at a section of the record crucial for nursing work: the 'fluid balance'. This section maps the total daily difference between all the fluid that has 'gone in' (i.e., infusions, drinks) and all that has gone out (i.e., urine, saliva, blood loss, fluid from a drain). The number in the record is the result of a series of procedures. In the paper record, the nurse adds the numbers that are listed on the 'intensive care list' (Figure 1). These numbers (itemizing the amounts and types of fluid gone in and out within a 24 hour period) are themselves the result of meticulously structured work routines: all infusions that are given need to be written down, and care should be taken, for example, to write down at the end and beginning of a 24 hour period how much still remains in the infusion bag. All drinks should be registered, and the amount of urine, feces and drain fluid should be monitored and divided into 24 hour segments.

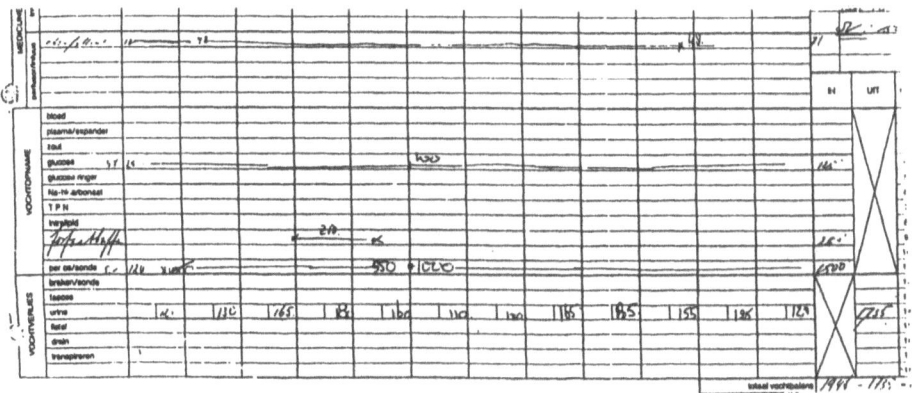

Figure 1. Fragment of the paper record's 'intensive care list'. This form covers one day, the columns marking two-hour periods. Not shown are the temperature, blood pressure and pulse graphs, the respiration parameters and the medication list. These are all on the same page, in the same temporal format, so that interrelated changes are rendered visible. The fluid balance is produced through the two sections shown here: 'vochtopname' (fluid intake) and 'vochtverlies' (fluid loss). The separate rows indicate forms of intake and loss, which are to be added, at the end of the day, in the last two columns: IN and OUT. Adding these columns, and subtracting the difference, yields the 'totaal vochtbalans' (total fluid balance).

In the electronic version of the fluid balance the lay out of the form was kept intact, but it was designed as a spreadsheet: the program automatically gave the totals of the data input in the columns and rows, for example, and it updated the fluid balance when infusions were entered in the 'medication list'. (As in the paper form, the medication list is just above the fluid balance - it is partly visible in Figure 1).

The fluid balance is the ultimately formal: the rendering of a range of sufferings and activities into a single number, ready for further manipulation. How is this formal rendering produced? It is not simply 'inferred' from the practice by the formal tools that are in place: intricate nursing routines are required to get the right numbers in their right places. Is it, then, humans performing the active translation, producing a number out of a dense ensemble of bodies, tubes, containers and paperwork? Yes, in a way: if the nurses didn't do their work, nothing could be written in the record. Yet the gap between the formal representation (the *map*) and the actual sphere of work (the *terrain*) is not crossed in one step. Rather, we see a *chain of re-representations* (Star, 1989; Bowers, 1992): a series of intermediate, representational activities performed by *materially heterogeneous entities*. At each step, input from the territory is condensed, elaborated and transformed until it matches the abstract level of detail of the map.

First, the nurses' work already *begins* with many numbers. The first step from the 'empirical' to the 'formal' is performed, for instance, by using precisely dosed infusion bags, by letting the patient drink from cups and glasses whose contents (in milliliters) are known, and by collecting the urine, through a catheter, in a container which indicates the produced quantity. The cup, bag and container each perform parts of the miraculous jump across the gap, from 'informal' to 'formal': these artifacts themselves already transform the unmediated, empirical realm into a number - into an element of the calculation that will produce the day's fluid balance. The drips of fluid are transformed, through the shape and transparency of the container, into an indicator. The fluid becomes a pointer on a dial: a fine line moving up and down a series of other fine lines indicating quantities. The task of producing a formal representation is partially *delegated* to mundane artifacts which perform, in Latour's terms, 'the practical task of abstraction' (1994). Moving from the empirical to the formal, here, is not a step wholly provided for by the formal tool. Nor, however, is it a human act of interpretation: providing meaning to the world is not the sole task of humans. We leave, here, the question of how language can be said to speak for the world and turn to its forgotten other half: how the *world* is stirred and thus *becomes* discourse itself (ibid.). These artifacts perform the first re-representation. The nurses' task is to perform the second: to transport the numbers produced by the artifacts to the appropriate fields in the record - meanwhile checking whether the current reading is possible in the light of the previous one, and whether the urine container has not been emptied by accident.

In the paper record, the tabular form of the recorded numbers performs yet another small crossing (see Figure 1). Here as well, a simple artifact actively participates in the production of a formal representation. Horizontally, these forms map the passing of time, and vertically, they list the different means fluid can enter or leave the body. Because of this spatial layout, the numbers end up in rows and columns which now merely need to be added. Moreover, the special configuration of the form (see the IN and UIT [out] columns) constrains the placing of the calculated results, and affords the production of a total fluid balance much like an accountant keeps track of the in- and out-going flow of money.

Crossing the gap, then, is an intricate achievement - but it is not an achievement of the formal tool, nor is it a task of human interpretation or abstraction. Rather, the ensemble of heterogeneous entities performing the chain of re-representations *as a whole* crosses the gap. In the historical production of this work practice, the nurses' task has been transformed and displaced to the much smaller subtask of re-representing the data on the form or into the computer (Hutchins, 1995).

To take this point further, the capacities and characteristics that formalists and their opponents attribute to the formal tool or to a human agent appear to be highly distributed.[2] One may point to the electronic medical record and state that that is the formal tool we are discussing, but one should not forget the simple, low-tech urine container hanging at the bedside which also enters into the production of the formal representation. The work that is performed in this way, then, is highly distributed. Calculating, decision making, controlling - are these done by the formal tool (the record, the spreadsheet)? Or is it in fact the human agent who ends up in control, who does the skilled, 'cultural' part of calculation while delegating the 'mechanical' part of it to a machine (see e.g. Collins, 1990)?

Neither position holds much ground. The 'calculation' of the fluid balance is the *total net effect* performed by this hybrid. If one enters the network itself, however, one sees a chain of small re-representational tasks being performed by a series of heterogeneous entities none of which resembles anything like 'doing a fluid balance'. This is an activity that only occurs at the level of the whole hybrid.[3] The particular position of the formal tool is not that it is in control, doing the calculation while the other elements in the network merely bring it some input, and process its output. Neither should we say that these technologies make it 'easier' for humans to do this task. Both formulations overlook that the urine container and the form already do some of the calculations. Not only does the container transform the urine produced by the patient into the required numerical datum: through its intricate design, it also rounds off the measurement appropriately. Slight urine production is measured in 2 milliliter steps, while more profuse production is rounded off to steps of 10 to even 50 milliliters. Similarly, the paper form first establishes the formal equivalences of such variable substances as blood, glucose solution, feces, and sweat - and it subsequently materially *contains* the required relations between the isolated observations.

---

[2] . See also e.g. Lave (1988) on the social, non-individual nature of cognition. Hutchins' work is exemplary in focusing on the role of non-human actants in distributed cognition.

[3] . This formulation is reminiscent of Activity Theory, which argues that the unit of analysis in studies of work should be the complex of humans, tools, the organization of work, and so forth which constitute the Activity System (see e.g. Engeström, 1990). From the perspective of this paper, however, Activity Theory's explicit underwriting of the a priori asymmetry between humans and non-humans is problematic.

The nurses or physicians, in their turn, transfer numbers from displays to the form, compare them, and add up rows. They perform small tasks, interlocking with the other small tasks performed by the container and the form. They do not *use* these artifacts to calculate the fluid balance. A phrase like that assumes that the essence of the calculating activity remains in the hands (or heads) of the human; as if nurses and physicians can simply choose whether to use an artifact. But the very task they perform has been transformed and displaced by the artifacts mentioned. These are a crucial part of the network, not just 'tools' which the nurses can draw upon as they see fit. As Hutchins phrases it in his study of Navy navigation, these 'mediating technologies do not stand between the user and the task. Rather, they stand with the user as resources used in the regulation of behavior' so that the chain of small tasks performed interlock and together produce the calculation (1995). The tools' re-representation work sets constraints on the nurses' subsequent task - constraints which render their subtask do-able, but which also render it a component of the overall process. Likewise, the computer based record performs fragments of the total calculation: it adds up the entered figures. But the whole calculation is done by the network as a whole. All the small subtasks requires in- and output - and the chaining together of these steps (i.e., the organization of the hybrid) produces the net effect: the fluid balance.

This also implies that no one or no thing is 'in control'. Nurses, physicians, the formal tool - all have only partial knowledge of the intricacies of the work of other entities. In Hutchins' terms, 'an interlocking set of partial procedures can produce the overall [task] without there being a representation of that overall [task] anywhere in the system' (1995). They react upon what they receive as input, and work from there. No single element is master: the configuration is neither subjected to humans fulfilling their task, nor to the formal tool. The electronic record controls the nurse: as soon as s/he tries to enter an infusion dosage the computer considers 'too high', the computer emits a red warning signal. Likewise, it checks the input: one cannot enter non-numerical characters when entering the blood pressure, and one can only pick from a list of some eight options to describe the heart rhythm. Moreover, the entry fields have circumscribed lengths, and they remain visibly empty when not filled in. Yet the staff members control the computer: nurses have to validate every piece of data the computer draws from the monitor, and nurses and doctors can add remarks to all the computer data. Yet in its turn, the computer again controls the nurse whether indeed s/he has validated the data: if not, the numbers remain in italic font. And the computer controls all modifications made by automatically registering who changed what and when. Now who controls what? These relations cannot be captured hierarchically: they are *non-transitive*. There *is* no one center of control, not one core figure (whether formal tool or human) around who or what the whole activity is organized.

One point requires clarification here. Crossing the gap is often seen to be about (the possibility of) producing or applying an *accurate representation*. However, 'accuracy' is not the point - if with that is meant 'closeness' to some reality residing outside the ongoing interlocking of subtasks. For the agents performing these tasks, the goal is to maintain the flow through the chains of re-representations; to perform the subtasks in response to and required by other subtasks. Only on the level of the whole hybrid can 'accuracy' become a meaningful notion. But then it can no longer be seen as referring to some inherent quality of the tool's representation: it can only reflect the *achieved* fit of the map with the historically re-written work practice.

The formal tool, then, is an active element within the practice, and it performs subtasks in the production of, for example, the fluid balance. Yet whether we are referring to the production of a numerical representation of a state of the body or to the act of calculation, the powerful net effect a formal tool can produce is not due solely to this isolated element. But neither is this effect 'in the end' due to skillful humans. By zooming in on the way tool and work practice are interwoven, the distributed nature of the tasks comes into view - and thereby the way control and responsibility are transformed and dispersed over the heterogeneous assembly. We witness a myriad of little powers, together exhibiting capacities which the formalists would want to grant to the Formal tool, and their opponents would like to keep apart for the Human. The formal tools themselves are infinitely less powerful than the former would argue - but infinitely more than the latter claim.

Drift

Speaking about distribution in the way I have done so far, however, leaves some important questions unaddressed. How can the individual subtasks and their interlockings be characterized? Does the whole practice now function as a large formal Machine, with subtasks efficiently being performed according to pre-set rules? Does speaking about a territory re-written in the light of the map imply that the whole practice has been captured in the iron, instrumental rationality of Taylorism?

This interpretation would be a misunderstanding: there is nothing 'formal' about the way these networks actually operate. Before elaborating on this, however, it is interesting to note that several central traditions within the field of science and technology studies actually seem to collude with this image. Studies within the framework of SCOT or actor-network theory generally demonstrate the social nature of a technology through a study of its production: focusing on technologies-in-the-making allows one to highlight the negotiated and contingent history of their emergence. Yet in the operation of this focus, all too often the *ready-made* technology is reified, 'black-boxed'. In the argumentative move to demonstrate how Efficiency is an *effect*, not an a priori asset of Technology, the smooth functioning of the produced technology is taken for granted. It has become a Machine, in Latour's terms; 'where borrowed forces keep one another in check so that none can fly apart from the group' (1987). The Machine, the heterogeneous network that is put and kept in place, produces the effect of Efficiency; it is the illusion of instrumental reason *made* true (Bowker, 1994). In creating this new opposition ('in production' - 'ready made'), however, the illusion of Efficiency now recurs at the level of the 'ready-made' technology, the technology-in-use: it has only been displaced. This rhetorical move thereby glosses over the fundamental issues at stake in the real-time functioning of the hybrid. I want to argue that *in studying technologies-in-use we should not grant them qualities that we would withhold while studying their production*. Actual machines-in-use are not Machines, and instrumental reason is not what makes these hybrids tick.

The notions of 'heterogeneous elements keeping each other in check', or of a network of smoothly and efficiently interlocking subtasks, are ideal images, indeed colluding with the formalist dream of total order. They downplay the processes of internal corrosion, of drift, which characterize the dynamics of these hybrids. As Jordan and Lynch point out, speaking about 'technologies' as 'black boxes' 'does not attend to the continual genesis of incoherence and fragmentation within the relatively settled development of an established technology' (1992). This point is not limited to formal technologies. A focus on such tools, however, is an interesting, hard case to start with - if any technologies-in-use could be characterized by instrumental rationality and efficiency it would surely be these. Yet this is not the case.

First, the different 'points' in the network, the different intermediaries aligned, *themselves* tend to drift apart from each other (Dodier, 1995). Each actant does more than its specific position in the network calls for: since it is always also tied up into other, cross-secting networks, its concrete form will always *overflow* its definition in the particular network under study. For the electronic medical record, for example, so-called electronic data exchange procedures are crucial for the record to function: they allow the laboratory results to be imported directly from the Hospital Information System. They were developed by the vendor's representative as part of another project, and have been incorporated into this record system. They translate the data unhesitatingly - in that sense they are fully docile actants. Yet the combined effect of the hundreds of laboratory results processed each morning leads to the - unexpected - result of irritating waiting times, and moments the record system seems 'locked'. That the exchange procedures take their time exchanging had never been a problem in the other networks in which they functioned. Yet here, given the unforeseen peak of laboratory results coming in at the same time, they turned into important obstructers of the network's smooth functioning.

Likewise, multiplying the number of cups and glasses drunk by their measured capacity is a practical way to measure the fluid taken in 'orally'. Yet cups and glasses are familiar objects to patients and family members, who refill half-emptied cups, throw away stale drinks - as they are used to doing. Overflowing their definition as 'standardized input measurement', the way family members and patients deal with them tends to render the fluid intake measurement imprecise.

As a final example, the record could not function without the physicians working with it and entering their data. Yet to them, the electronic medical record is only one of a whole array of exigencies they have to cater to. Residents have to 'do' each patient before the daily grand round at 11:30 am[4], they have to coordinate the activities of the different specialists involved in a case, and they have to talk to patients' families. Often, they skip entries, do not fill in forms, or work from a small piece of paper they carry around rather than deal with the computer. Similarly, consultants often do not work in the intensive care unit, but are just called in to give an advice on a specific patient. They have many other priorities than 'learning to type', as one anesthesiologist ironically put it. Many just continue to write down their remarks on the traditional, paper consultation forms. Physicians, then, have to be made part of the network for the record to become a reality - yet in taking them aboard, a tendency of the network to erode itself from within is introduced as well.

This phenomenon holds whether we are talking about the individual components that constitute the electronic medical record *as artifact* (its wiring, its screens, its software), or whether we are talking about the heterogeneous network within which this artifact comes to life. In both cases, the individual elements that constitute the larger whole have additional tendencies, desires, urges, which together create a centrifugal pull. A computer program may be meticulously designed - yet it inevitably contains features that nobody has foreseen, or that end up working against its functioning. The electronic record made log files of all the operations it performed. Since the way the program was implemented in this hospital yielded a very large number of operations, it created huge log files that slowed overall performance considerably. Moreover, a program as complex as a computer medical record is the result of a collaborative effort, where specifications are stipulated which must be met by the different programming groups that construe the program's subparts. These groups have different goals, may be in conflict or competition with each other, have only a limited amount of resources to work with, and have to fulfill criteria that to them might be opaque. These processes, which iterate through time (through different upgrades, new versions, debugging, and so forth), result in a program whose detailed functioning can never be fully predicted (Weizenbaum, 1976; Berg, 1997).

Every network, then, has the tendency to fall apart, to contain glitches, and to behave unexpectedly. We do not witness the polished, smooth functioning that would characterize a practice or tool where instrumental rationality reigns. The 'borrowed forces that keep each other in check' are *themselves* in constant motion.

Having dispelled this misunderstanding, however, another problem arises. If these configurations tend to fall apart, what keeps them going, if they do? Recent ethnographies of (formal) technologies-in-use (e.g. Button, 1993), demonstrating the fragility of these configurations, give us clues to start from. The following

---

[4]. I.e., they have to update the record, get an impression of the current state of the patient, and order tests and changes in policy.

vignettes can illustrate these insights, as well as an important danger we encounter here:

John, a nurse, is entering a new patient in the computer: the doctor's orders, the medication for today, and so forth. When entering the vital signs he says: 'This takes so much time. I have to validate every data item I enter. When a patient is unstable, when the vital signs differ from one moment to the next, you're constantly typing in your code... it drives you crazy. So I just scribble it all down on a little paper, and fill in some of these data afterwards. You have to re-set the time when you do that, because you're feeding data in retrospectively'. He goes further, and gets irritated by the fact that he has to open different windows to find information he needs. The system only supports one open window at the time: to get the doctor's policy in the nursing work-list, John has to quit that worklist, open the physician's progress form, write down the policy, quit the progress form, open the work-list again, move to the field where he had left off, and enter the policy. After he has done this twice, he grabs the terminal standing near the next bed and opens the physician's progress form there. 'Now I no longer have to jump back and forth all the time', he mutters.

Agnes, a resident, is filling in the physician's progress form. This form is implemented so that the progress notes are entered in the *same* fields, every day: to enter new data, old data first have to be removed. The progress form is printed every night ('to keep a record'), and the residents change daily whatever they feel needs to be changed to 'update' it. Agnes does not change the X-ray reading which was jotted down yesterday: since she hasn't heard about another X-ray, that reading still stands. The working diagnosis, the cardiac findings: all that she leaves unchanged. And although the blood pressure monitor says '125/65' she does not change the reading in the progress form, which is '136/72'. Under 'remarks' it is written 'tracheotomy yesterday'. She sighs. 'Well, that's confusing. That is the day before yesterday, now. And that... [she points to a remark saying 'attempt detubation tomorrow'] should be today..'. She changes the references to dates ('yesterday' becoming 25/9, 'today' becoming 26/9). Filling in the current date she runs into trouble: the computer accepts only a standard format (it accepts '25sep95', and not '25/9'). The progress form cannot be stored until this field is filled in properly.

The first vignette depicts what might be called a classic example in these ethnographies: a nurse *works around* the limitations of the formal tool (Gasser, 1986; Button and Harper, 1993). Following the exigencies of the tool would stand in the way of his primary task - dealing with an acute patient. So he performs a detour, satisfying both this acute need and (albeit post-hoc and cursory) the record's demands. The nurse re-establishes 'compatibility' between the different exigencies of the different networks he is a part of (Dodier 1995). It is this type of example Star (1989) and Bowers (1992) focus on when they argue that in moving out of the self-contained sphere of the formal, the effect of 'deletion' is inevitably felt. Tension arises between the tool's model and what it models: since the record embodies an impoverished version of what nursing work is like, humans working with the tool need to re-add detail, or to repair the tools' functioning when it is used in practice (Collins, 1990).

Working around, tinkering with the tool, are omnipresent features of these hybrids. However, selectively focusing on these, and showing how humans 'save' the faltering formal tools and keep these configurations going runs the danger to again pit the former against the latter. We hover dangerously close to the informalists' discourse here: reinstalling the informal in its privileged position to overcome the limitations of the formal. Yet we do not have to interpret these moments as instances where the formal is 'rescued' by the informal. We can also understand the persistence of these configurations in a different way. When John grabs a second terminal to facilitate his work, he is indeed working around the system's limitations. But the fact that the system can only have one window open at the time has nothing to do with specific characteristics of 'the formal': we see, rather, a nurse making do with what everybody involved sees as an idiosyncratic, stupid limitation of the program. Moreover, in the second example Agnes is not repairing the system - she is repairing what she calls 'unthoughtful' work of her colleagues. Relative temporal references such as 'yesterday' or 'today' are confusing in a form which is re-used the next day.

This is not, then, an argument about humans 're-appropriating' or 'saving' the technology. Humans are not pitted against the formal: the tinkering activity is directed at mending the drift in *all* juxtaposed elements. In addition, speaking about humans 'saving' or 'repairing' the formal tool re-installs the human in a position of control and oversight, and that is not what we encounter here. Nurses and physicians' perform their subtasks, and tinker with upcoming problems and glitches as they present themselves in the performance of their subtasks (see e.g. Hughes and King, 1992). John is not 'taking control' over the system when he pulls a second terminal towards him: he is simply tinkering to get his job done. Within the work, the 'oversight' that would be required for staff-members to 'appropriate' formal tools, to 'use' them at will, is nonexistent. As Hutchins would argue, it is *because* of the very shallow insight into the 'inner details' of the other elements' functioning that the performance of their subtasks remains do-able (1995).

To speak about 'repair' or 'appropriation', moreover, suggests a return to some original state: to the technology's 'proper' functioning, or, more often, to the original aims and ways of the practice. Yet this disregards the *transformation* of these 'original states'. When John has a new, unstable patient, his routine is to scribble data on a piece of paper, and enter these into the record afterwards. This detour fulfills the conflicting demands of the record system and of his acute need to care for the patient. Yet his activity is not so much a repair but a *balancing act* between two cross-secting networks - which are changed in the process. He does not tinker with the record to restore some 'informal', prior-to-the-tool practice: as argued, the tool is part and parcel of this practice, and has fundamentally changed its working patterns. John does not 'undo' this. But neither does he 'save' the tool's pre-determined mode of functioning: he fills in the data afterwards, and makes a rough selection of the monitor readings to create an indication of the unstable period. In this filtering and post hoc entry of the data, the record's original

152

functioning is altered as well: what was meant to be complete, direct input, only checked upon by the nurse, now becomes an abbreviated set of data, filled in by the nurse as a summarized, second order entry.[5]

The same can be said for Agnes' intervention. In her dealing with the computerized progress notes she is *learning* how to deal with a novel means of writing. She is no longer filling in an empty, unstructured sheet of paper, but a pre-structured form which is already completed - with yesterday's notes. In selectively leaving pieces of text on the form and deleting and adding fragments, residents change their own progress note writing habits, learning that terms like 'yesterday' are not very practical on such forms. Yet they thereby also transform the ideals of this electronic medical record. By just editing the filled form, data and information are accepted which were accurate yesterday but may be just 'approximately' so today (Agnes, for example, does not change the now-different blood pressure reading) - curbing the record designer's hopes for 'exact' and 'complete' data.

The consultant's paper forms, finally, are stored in a paper, 'shadow' record, together with the printed progress notes. The residents enter summaries of the consultant's findings into the computerized progress notes. Doing so, they may be said to 'repair' the specialists' hesitancy about typing - but they thereby also take over the responsibility to convey this information from the record, and thus erode the record's position as source of all 'primary' data.

The persistence of these fragile configurations, then, is not due to skillful humans mending the formal tools' shortcomings: such a description overestimates the mastery human worker, and overlooks the drift in all other elements. It further overlooks how artifacts situated at the crossroads between networks also perform balancing acts. To balance the busy day-to-day demands of nursing work with the unstructured, large number of printing options the program offers, a written protocol exactly prescribes what to print when a patient is transferred to a different ward; what to print every Friday; and what to print every day. Similarly, notes (listing observation categories) are taped to the computer screens to aid nurses fill in their observation forms.

If the network persists, it is because the exigencies of the other, cross-cutting networks balance out against the exigencies of the network in question. This is not some mechanistic play of static forces: the network itself is in constant transformation due to these ongoing balancing acts. At the intersection of two cross-secting networks, the conflicting exigencies transform *both* the operation of the tool-in-use, and the primary work tasks of nurses, residents and consultants.

To round off this discussion on drift it is important to return to Hutchins' marvelous study of navigation, in which he (amongst other things) demonstrates the phenomenon of distribution discussed above. Hutchins' networks are depicted as smoothly operating and as pre-designed by Navy-officials. The subtasks are

[5]. This is what I have elsewhere called the process of *localization* of a formal tool (Berg 1997).

meticulously aligned, and the way they are to interrelate laid down in extensive protocols. Doing so, Hutchins denies the existence of central, planning and controlling agencies at the level of the actual work of navigation. However, he implicitly re-invokes this agency at the next higher level of aggregation: the overall task seems to be organized, designed, set up by just the centralized Agency that he is at pain to dispel elsewhere. In this paper, however, there is no such Agency either designing these networks from above - nor 'saving' them from below. Rather, we witness a fragile, never static equilibrium, characterized by never ending frictions, loose ends, and unforeseen consequences. Tricks, devices or routines may be created to 'fix' recurrent tensions - but these will also produce new problems. New intermediaries will inevitably yield new diffractions: every time, every new actant does more than it was called upon to do. Moreover, it is important to recall that there are multiple actants performing these balancing acts. This it is yet another reason for the persistence of the drift described - for the continuation of a phenomenon these interventions at the same time attempt to counter. Nurses, protocols, but also the record's vendor and the programming nurses are constantly working to balance the differently pulling exigencies and desires. But the vendor is also constantly tinkering with the system: to deal with complaints, or to implement improvements. Given the history of protracted negotiations between multiple, hetero-geneous elements (wires, people, hospital boards, computer vendors...), given the distributed nature of the tasks performed, and given the multiple goals that went and go into the construction and functioning of this hybrid, it would be an illusion to believe that 'control' or 'redesign' would or even could be done from one, central position.

Conclusions

The generative power of formal tools, then, lies in the very existence of the gap between the workpractice and its formal representation. Through deleting detail the map is functional in tracking a route between distant sites: the record feeds into the separating and linking of different organ systems, and into the planning of complex treatments (Wood, 1992; Robinson, 1994, Berg, 1996). The electronic fluid balance's manipulation of the input data affords a more continuous and more precise monitoring, while taking some chores out of the hands of personnel. Yet the consequential role such formal tools may play is not due to some inherent superiority of the formal, nor to the repair and interpretative work of humans. A formal tool performs a crucial role in many work practices, yet to understand its functioning we do not have to leave the domain of the ordinary: it selects, deletes, summarizes; it adds, subtracts, multiplies. These simple subtasks have become so consequential because they interlock with a historically evolved, increasingly elaborate network of other subtasks: nurses filling in the data in the balance sheet, complex fluid containers, organizational routines, and so forth. This description does not imply that the number representing the fluid balance and the computerized progress notes are produced through the fully disciplined behavior of actants captured in some iron logic. Nor does it imply that the elaborate whole of interlocking subtasks is centrally (re-)designed. The networks develop in piece-meal fashion, through a complex interplay of driving forces, and partly through the ongoing balancing acts that occur wherever cross-cutting networks intersect.

The work performed and its formal rendering, then, are the *outcome* of historical and real-time processes. In real time, the difference between the drunk, spilled and expelled fluids and the single number blinking on the screen is produced by the articulation of subtasks and balancing acts: these processes bring the map to life, and allow it to function as a representation of the terrain. These very same processes also *bridge* the gap: they produce the ongoing flow of re-representations which link the map to the terrain, and which allow the generative power of these tools to exert itself.

This focus allows one to study the transformations of work practices that occur as the intertwinement between tool and practice evolves (Simone and Schmidt, 1993; Star, 1995; Berg, 1997). Will the final record be more congenial to the nurses' demand for practicality and simplicity of use or to the specialists' desire for research data? What type of body is produced when we shift from a paper-kept fluid balance to an electronic one, where the balance is now 'continuous'? How is the hierarchy between junior and senior doctors affected when the progress notes become increasingly pre-specified and accessible to all? How is the decision-responsibility distributed over the different elements that perform the overall task? To address these questions in the formalists' or informalists' vocabularies (or in a combination of these) restricts our understanding of these processes since so much explanatory power is invested in the capabilities of either the tool or the worker - or both. This is crucial, since a finetuned appropriation of the generative power of formal tools can only evolve from an equally finetuned understanding of how this power emerges and operates!

The conceptual tools developed here, then, might contribute to a better analytical grasp on the workings (and failings) of formal tools in workplaces. The relationships between junior and senior doctors, for example, will surely change through the implementation of the electronic medical record - but the concepts introduced here make clear that a simple increase or decrease in hierarchy or efficiency will be the exception rather than the rule. And rather than getting 'more' or 'less', it could be the very *meaning* of 'hierarchy' or 'efficiency' in this setting that might change.

Moreover, the analytical tools developed here offer the opportunity to address these questions while avoiding the pre-set evaluative axes that accompany the vocabularies mentioned (Berg, forthcoming). Speaking about the generative power of formal tools, of distribution and drift opens up the possibility of scrutinizing

configurations of artifacts and personnel without im- or explicitly projecting the
direction of these changes in terms of either efficiency and accuracy, or
(de)humanization and (de)skilling. These axes too often still structure the debates
around formal tools, even if the caricatured discourses themselves are said to be left
behind. This does not mean abandoning a political stance - rather, it allows new
issues for debate and design (such as the shape of the heterogeneous distribution of
responsibility, the different meanings of 'efficiency', or the patient's body that is
implied in these configurations).

References

Berg, M. (1996): "Practices of Reading and Writing. The Constitutive Role of the Patient Record in Medical Work", *Sociology of Health and Illness*, vol. 18, pp. 499-524.

Berg, M. (1997): *Rationalizing Medical Work. Decision Support Techniques and Medical Practices*, MIT Press, Cambridge.

Berg, M. (forthcoming): "Heidegger® Inc. and the Garfinkel™ Copier: What Use for Social Theory in Designing Technology?, in review.

Bowers, J. (1992): "The Politics of Formalism", in M. Lea (ed.) *Contexts of Computer Mediated Communication*, Harvester, Hassocks.

Bowker, G. (1994): *Science on the run. Information management and industrial geophysics at Schlumberger, 1920-1940*, MIT Press, Cambridge, MA.

Button, G. (ed.) (1993): *Technology in working order. Studies of work, interaction, and technology*, Routledge, London.

Button, G. and Harper, R.H.R. (1993): "Taking the organisation into accounts", in G. Button (ed.) *Technology in working order*, pp. 98-107.

Collins, H.M. (1990): *Artificial experts. Social knowledge and intelligent machines*, MIT Press, Cambridge.

Dodier, N. (1995): *Les hommes et les machines*, Métailié, Paris.

Engeström, Y. (1990): "When is a tool? Multiple meanings of artifacts in human activity", in Y. Engeström (ed.) *Learning, Working and Imagining*, Orienta-Konsultit Oy, Helsinki.

Gasser, L. (1986): "The Integration of Computing and Routine Work", *ACM Transactions on Office Information Systems*, vol. 4, no. 3, pp. 205-25.

Haraway, D.J. (1991): *Simians, Cyborgs, and Women: The Reinvention of Nature*, Routledge, New York.

Hughes, J.A. and King (1992): "Paperwork", *CSCW*: COMIC-LANCS-4-1.

Hutchins, E. (1995): *Cognition in the wild*, MIT Press, Cambridge.

Jordan, K. and Lynch, M. (1992): "The sociology of a genetic engineering technique: ritual and rationality in the performance of the 'plasmid prep'", in A. E. Clarke and J. H. Fujimura (eds.) *The right tools for the job. At work in twentieth-century life sciences*, Princeton University Press, Princeton, N. J.

Latour, B. (1987): *Science in action*, Open University Press, Milton Keynes.

Latour, B. (1994): "The 'pédofil' of Boa Vista. A photo-philosophical montage", *Common Knowledge*, vol. 4, no. 1, pp. 144-87.

Lave, J. (1988): *Cognition in practice*, Cambridge University Press, Cambridge.

Robinson, M. (1994): "Intimacy & abstraction & maps & terrains", Conference on *Locating Design, Development and Use*, Oksnoen, May 13-18.

Simone, C. and Schmidt, K. (1993): 'Computational Mechanisms of Interaction for CSCW', ESPRIT Report, COMIC Deliverable 3.1.

Star, S.L. (1989): "Layered space, formal representations and long-distance control: the politics of information", *Fundamenta Scientiae*, vol. 10, , pp. 125-54.

Star, S.L. (ed.) (1995): *Ecologies of Knowledge: Work and Politics in Science and Technology*, State University of New York Press, New York.

Suchman, L. (1993): "Technologies of accountability. Of lizards and aeroplanes", in G. Button (ed.) *Technology in working order*, pp. 113-126.

Weizenbaum, J. (1976): *Computer power and human reason. From judgment to calculation*, W. H. Freeman and Company, San Francisco.

Wood, D. (1992): *The power of maps*, Guilford Press, New York.

Tailoring Cooperation Support through Mediators

Anja Syri

GMD-FIT, German National Research Center for Information Technology

syri@gmd.de

Abstract: Cooperative processes are strongly influenced by their context. Individual and group experience, work practices, and the organisational setting are variable factors that help shape a cooperative work context. In an electronic environment the variability and dynamic nature of cooperative processes has to be taken into account. This suggests a requirement for configurability of basic cooperative functionality. In this paper, a concept for the development of a generic CSCW platform is proposed, which offers the possibility to configure its basic cooperation support functionality. Mediating objects are the key feature which enables the tailorability of functionality to the cooperative setting at run-time.

Introduction

Cooperative processes among human beings are very complex and strongly dependent on their environment; different organisational cultures as well as different teams develop individual forms of cooperation. Here distinctions can be made related to the structure of the cooperative process, the interdependence of the activities, or the transparency of the process. In order to develop a generic CSCW system, we need a framework offering basic cooperation support functionality without being limited to specific forms of cooperation. A suitable framework has to allow configuration on different levels—for the system designer, the system administrator as well as for the end-user—to adapt the system to the working environment.

J. Hughes et al. (eds.), Proceedings of the Fifth European Conference on Computer Supported Cooperative Work, 157-172.
© *1997 Kluwer Academic Publishers.*

We can distinguish two classes of CSCW systems which differ in the bandwidth of cooperation support they provide to their users. On the one hand, there are *CSCW applications* focusing on certain forms of cooperation. This group includes video and audio conferencing tools supporting communication, workflow systems focusing on coordination and shared workspace systems allowing the shared usage of information. On the other hand, efforts in developing *CSCW platforms* (e.g. LOTUS NOTES) have been undertaken, offering a cooperation environment with support for a range of cooperation activities.

Existing CSCW systems (CSCW applications as well as platforms) do not meet the requirements of generic cooperation support. Whereas applications are often closed, most platforms provide a programming interface and allow the integration of new tools. Nevertheless, these platforms neither support configuration of embedded basic cooperation support functionality (e.g. access control mechanisms, event services, or locking mechanisms) nor do they allow the integration of new cooperative functionality. Both features are necessary to adapt the system to a specific form of cooperation and the needs of the users.

This paper proposes a concept for the design of a lightweight CSCW platform. This platform provides a framework that allows the integration of basic cooperation support services by a developer or system administrator. Parts of this functionality are made visible to the users allowing them to become aware of how the chosen form of cooperation is supported by the system. The user has the possibility to do the fine-tuning: basic cooperation support can be complemented by additional services, for example services supporting norms that have been developed in the specific cooperation context.

The paper starts with the presentation of the requirements that a generic platform has to fulfil. The next section introduces our concept for the development of a generic CSCW platform and the configuration features it offers. This is followed by a presentation of related work and a comparison of the different approaches. The conclusion summarizes the results and explains the benefits of our concept.

Requirements

In developing a generic CSCW platform several aspects must be considered. This section presents requirements based on the experiences which we have made in the POLITeam project (Klöckner et al., 1995). The project aims to develop a CSCW platform that supports cooperative processes within large organisations. The development is done with special regard to the problems that are caused by the gradual movement of the German government, which will result in a distribution of labour between Bonn and Berlin. We follow a participatory design approach involving end-users from Ministerial sites (Mambrey et al., 1996).

The following list identifies some requirements for a generic CSCW platform.

Modelling the cooperative process. The basis of a CSCW platform is a model representing the entities of the cooperative process as well as the relationships among them. Much attention has to be paid to capture the dynamic aspects of the cooperative process within the model. How to represent activities, the progress of activities, the history? The model has to reflect rules and conventions that determine the cooperative process. Further issues that have to be considered here can be summarised by the keyword "awareness". Our users' demand for a visible cooperation process is described in (Sohlenkamp et al., 1997).

Supporting the transition between different forms of cooperation. Many CSCW applications have been developed, which focus either on well-structured or on less structured work processes. Whereas workflow systems impose a certain level of control on their users, shared workspace systems offer a high degree of freedom. Considering a concrete cooperative process, it is difficult to predict the "right" level of coordination support. A process that seems to be well-structured at the beginning and therefore best supported by a workflow system may require a broader scope of action for the persons involved at a later stage, which suggests the usage of a shared workspaces (and vice versa). Dourish and Bellotti (1992) show how the provision of awareness information can help members of a shared workspace to move smoothly between close and loose cooperation. Prinz and Syri (1996) describe a typical process in a department of a German Federal Ministry that underlines the need for an inter-linked usage of electronic circulation folders and shared workspaces. Learning from these experiences, a generic CSCW platform has to provide configurable cooperation support in order to support the dynamic character of real cooperative processes as well as the transition between different forms of cooperation.

Supporting context-specific norms. Cole and Nast-Cole (1992) stress the importance of group dynamics concepts for the development of CSCW systems. They identify the following stages in a group's development: "forming, storming, norming, performing, adjourning". Before cooperating effectively ("performing"), groups have developed a set of norms or group conventions. This shows the importance of supporting norms and conventions by a CSCW platform. One POLITeam user stated (Mark and Prinz, 1997):

> "There must be ground rules established for working together and dealing with groupware. The culture is lacking with the new technical possibilities to be able to get around this problem. The stronger the technical flexibility, the more rules must exist for how we can get around this."

Whether this results in just making visible these rules or forcing the user to keep to them depends on the cooperation context.

Tailorability of the system. A generic CSCW platform that can be applied to support various cooperative processes characterized by different forms of cooperation has to provide a broad range of basic cooperation support services. Since these services and their realization greatly affect the cooperative process they support, they have to be tailorable. Instead of hardcoding policies into the

160

services, they have to be realized in a modular way and kept separate from the services.

This list has introduced the most important factors that have to be taken into account when designing a generic CSCW platform. The next section introduces our concept for describing the design of a generic CSCW platform.

The Design Concept

The basis of a CSCW platform forms a data model representing the entities of a cooperative process (e.g. documents or folders) in the electronic system. We have decided in favour of an object-oriented model, because the object-oriented paradigm has several advantages:
- a natural way of modelling real entities and processes,
- encapsulation of objects and their functionality,
- modularization and
- reusability.

We do not want to describe a specific CSCW platform, nor do we want to focus on the concrete selection of classes. This section proposes a concept for the design of CSCW systems.

With regard to the generic character of the system—modelling different forms of cooperation and transitions among them—it is important to realize the cooperation support functionality in a modular way. This allows the adaptation of the functionality to the users' needs in two ways: first, the form of cooperation can be specified by selection of basic functionality. Second, configuration of this functionality should be possible to allow fine-tuning. Our concept proposes the following solution:
- The platform offers a broad range of cooperation support functions, each encapsulated in single service objects.
- The interaction of the basic service objects can be modified during run-time.
- Since cooperation processes strongly depend on their context (as the organisation or the team), the model allows specification of the cooperation support functionality to be applied dependent on the context in which the objects are used.

The service objects are called *CSCW enablers*. Enablers encapsulate basic cooperation support functionality and provide this functionality to objects. The primary purpose of CSCW enablers is to make objects "cooperation-aware".

All enablers belonging to an object are administered by a *CSCW mediator*. The mediator encapsulates the interaction among the enablers. It takes on the responsibilities of a mediator as described in (Gamma et al., 1995, pp. 273-282).

Figure 1 shows how a method call on a target object is forwarded to its mediator. The mediator knows which enablers belong to the target object and invokes the cooperation support functions offered by the enablers in addition to the called method of the target. This concept is described in detail in the following sections.

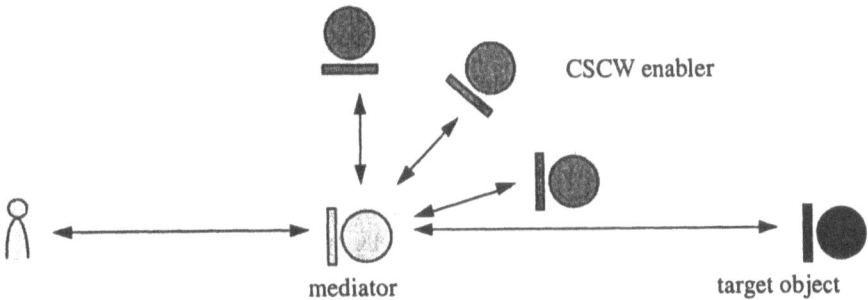

Figure 1: Dynamic enabling of a target object

CSCW Enablers

CSCW enablers encapsulate basic cooperation support functionality. They can modify the semantics of object methods on the target object as well as offer a different interface. The example of a container object that is enabled for use by several persons illustrates this. The methods of the container object can be enriched by an event mechanism which notifies changes to the users whenever a modifying method of the container object is called. In addition, the enriched object has to provide new methods, for example one to invite a person to take part in the sharing.

Ellis et al. (1991) distinguish three categories of cooperation support functionality: communication-enabling functionality, coordination-supporting functionality, and functions allowing the shared usage of common material. Based on this categorisation we want to identify basic functionality which can be encapsulated in CSCW enablers.

Communication

With regard to the required degree of synchronicity for communication, we can offer different communication enabling objects. Starting with an uncoupled communication between sender and receiver, functionality to exchange information on the basis of annotations or messages can be used. Enablers providing audio or video conferencing tools support a coupled form of cooperation.

The chosen form of communication is strongly dependent on two aspects. First, it requires that each cooperation partner has access to the technical equipment as well as the underlying infrastructure. The (technical) contactability has to be made visible in the system. Second, it depends on the social protocol, the style of cooperation that the group of cooperation partners has agreed upon. Just consider a team member that wants to contact another to clarify a question: is it convenient to interrupt by using a synchronous communication tool or is sending a message the "right" way?

Coordination

Different forms of coordination can be applied in a cooperative context. Here too the supporting functionality is dependent on the character of the cooperative process to be supported. With regard to a well-structured process, it may be suitable that the system offers explicit coordination support. Different strategies are possible: coordination can be realized by a human coordinator or—if a technical solution is more appropriate—by a token mechanism. The contrary approach is to neglect coordination support in the CSCW model and to leave it to the social protocol. Prerequisite here is that the cooperation partners have the chance to become aware of what is going on. This approach is suitable for processes that are less structured.

Sharing

The shared usage of common information requires several basic cooperation support services. Compared to multi-user access, shareability is defined in (Mariani and Prinz, 1993) as multi-user access which is supported by two additional services: first, information on who is locking the object is kept by the system and made available to others trying to access the object (identified locking). Second, the users are informed about past and ongoing activities (awareness).

Let us assume that two persons of a cooperating team want to edit a document. After the first person (A) has opened the document, the second (B) tries to do the same. Different design alternatives are possible, some should be mentioned here:

- The access is denied and information about the current user of the object supplied.
- The access is denied, user A is informed about B trying to access the object, user B is informed that A is the current user.
- Both persons get the chance to negotiate how to proceed.

Dourish (1995) presents a different approach which is based on "divergence and synchronisation between multiple, parallel streams" instead of considering single streams of activity.

Classes of Enablers

Based on the categorisation of cooperation support functionality introduced in the last sections, we can identify different classes of CSCW enablers (cf Figure 2).

They:
- provide synchronous and asynchronous communication facilities to users,
- support coordination among cooperation partners by allowing specification of sequences of activities,
- control access to information objects,
- lock an object and inform persons trying to access the object about the current user,
- generate events to provide awareness information,
- allow users to specify interest in events and collecting events on their behalf.

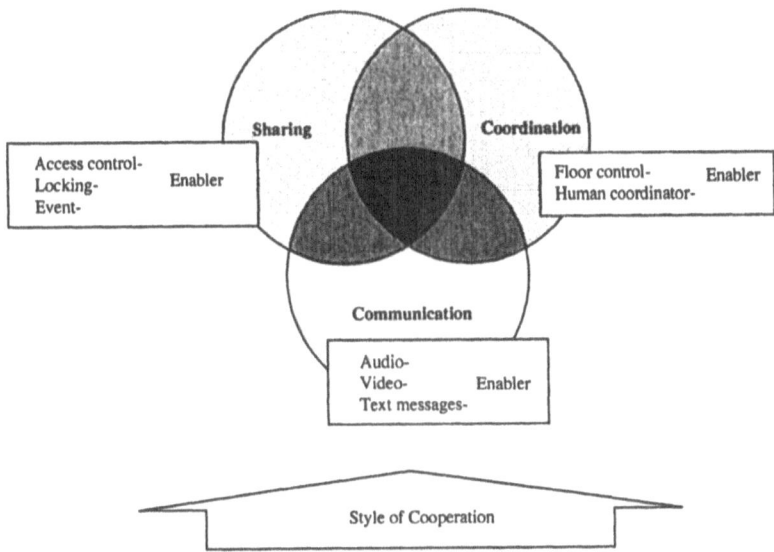

Figure 2: Different classes of enablers

Interface of a CSCW Enabler

In designing the interface of a CSCW enabler two aspects have to be taken into account: first, enablers are used to provide cooperation support to different kinds of objects. Second, the functionality provided by an enabler depends on which method is invoked on the target object.

For these reasons, all CSCW enablers offer a uniform interface (shown in Figure 3) that is independent from the interface of the enabled object. As will be shown in the next section, it is the task of the mediator to map object-specific methods onto methods provided by the enablers.

Each enabler method specifies how the corresponding method of the target object is extended. Additionally, the enabler interface provides the possibility to switch off this enabling functionality for single methods.

A closer look at the example of a shared workspace should illustrate this. Firstly, we have to clarify what we call a "shared workspace". A shared workspace offers its members a shared environment where they can store all documents they are working on. It is suitable to support less structured work processes, since it imposes no further processing rules on its members. Cooperation can be supported by providing awareness information to its members.

To realize this, an eventing enabler that informs the users about changes within the workspace is attached to the workspace object.

```
class eventingEnabler {
    delete (...);            //generates delete-event
    open (...);              //generates open-event
    openWithin (...);        //generates event indicating that an
                             //object within the workspace has
                             //been opened
    close (...);
    closeWithin (...);
    move (...);
    copy (...);
    share (...);
    add_object (...);
    remove_object (...);
    enable (method m);       //enabling the generation of
                             //specific events
    disable (method m);      //disabling the event generation
}
```

Figure 3: Interface of the eventing enabler

If a new object is added to the workspace, the mediator calls the corresponding method of the target object before invoking add_object() of the eventing enabler, which generates an event.

The users of the workspace may decide that they want to be informed when someone enters the workspace, but not when the person is leaving. In this case they disable the announcement of "leaving events" by using the method disable(close). Calling enable() reverses this again.

So far we have identified some basic cooperation support services that can be used to add cooperation awareness to an object model, transforming it into a suitable basis for a CSCW platform. In order to model complex cooperative processes we have to support a mechanism that allows the combination of these enabling objects.

CSCW Mediator

A mediator administers all CSCW enablers belonging to one target object and encapsulates their interaction. For this reason it keeps a handle to the target object and to all its enablers. The mediator provides an interface for the registration of new enablers and the removal of registered enablers. These methods allow to keep selection of enablers as dynamic as possible: CSCW enablers can be combined in an arbitrary way.

Initialisation

Whenever an object is created, a CSCW mediator for that object is instantiated and initialised according to a (default) configuration file. This allows specification of different policies by enumerating all CSCW enablers that are valid for the target object.

We differentiate between mandatory and optional CSCW enablers. Mandatory enablers are permanently assigned to an object, optional enablers can be removed from an object during run-time. This can be done under user control (cf Section "Configuration").

Figure 4 shows an example of a configuration file for an object that is enabled for the use as a shared workspace.

```
shared workspace :-   mandatory accessControl,
                      mandatory memberAdmin,
                      optional createShare,
                      optional communication,
                      optional eventing,
                      optional history.
```

Figure 4: Configuration file for a shared workspace

Invocation of a method

Whenever a method of an object is called, this call is first delegated to the mediator. The mediator calls the corresponding methods of the enablers that provide cooperation support functionality. Enablers invoked before the target object method is called provide pre-processing, whereas the remaining enablers allow post-processing.

Since the behaviour of an object is not only dependent on the object itself, but also on its context, the model provides a mechanism that takes this context into account. A method call to the target object first invokes the enablers attached to this target. If the target object is contained within an object, the mediator of this container object is called additionally and in turn invokes its enablers. This mechanism is applied recursively to further objects containing the container object.

Let us consider a simple example for illustration: if a document is deleted within a shared workspace, this has two effects: the document itself is deleted and it is removed from the workspace. According to this scenario, the invocation of the delete() method of the document should not only invoke the delete() method of all enablers attached to the document object, but furthermore invoke the remove_object() method of the enablers belonging to objects containing the document object. Seen the other way round, this mechanism allows specification of a method for handling access to a container's contents.

To summarise, a mediator

- first calls the corresponding methods of the CSCW enablers attached to the object and its containers providing pre-processing,
- then invokes the object specific method on the target object (in case that a pre-processing enabler has denied access to the object, no further methods are invoked) and
- finally calls the corresponding methods of the CSCW enablers (attached to the object and its containers) providing post-processing.

Example

Based on a concrete example, we show how a single-user container object can be used as a shared workspace and how it can be configured to the users' need with the help of enablers and mediators.

Our experiences with the usage of shared workspaces have shown that some users prefer to edit documents within their personal working environment and to put them back in the workspace afterwards (Prinz and Syri, 1996). As a consequence, the document is not visible to other members during this time. The example for solution proposed here automatically creates a 'share' (which is a new access point, a handle to the document object) to the document when someone tries to remove it from the workspace. Both, the editor as well as the other members of the workspace, have access to the document during this time.

Compared to an object representing a simple container, a shared workspace object has to provide access control and to administer a list of members. Furthermore it can be enriched by a notification and history service, communication facilities, and functions supporting shared usage. An example for the configuration file was given in Figure 4. In order to simplify the example, we now concentrate on the invocation of enablers directly attached to the workspace and ignore the calls to enablers belonging to its container objects.

Each time a method of the container is called, the call is sent to its mediator. The pre-configured mediator delegates this call to its enablers. A closer look at the example of the removal of an object from the shared workspace illustrates this (cf Figure 5; the numbers indicate how methods are enabled).

Technically, the call to the `remove_object()` method is first delivered to the mediator. The mediator calls the access control enabler of the workspace object, which checks that the user is allowed to remove the document object. If this right is granted, the object can be removed by calling the corresponding method (`remove_from_container()`) of the target workspace object. Before this method of the workspace object is called, the create-a-share enabler creates a 'share' to the document and stores it in the workspace. Finally the event enabler method `remove_object()` is called and generates a notification.

Calls to the other methods are handled in a similar way. The methods open(), close() and add_an_object() are complemented by functions that control access to the document and send notifications about ongoing changes.

Compared to a single-user container, the shared workspace offers additionally methods like invite_a_new_member(), exclude_a_member(), communicate() or get_history().

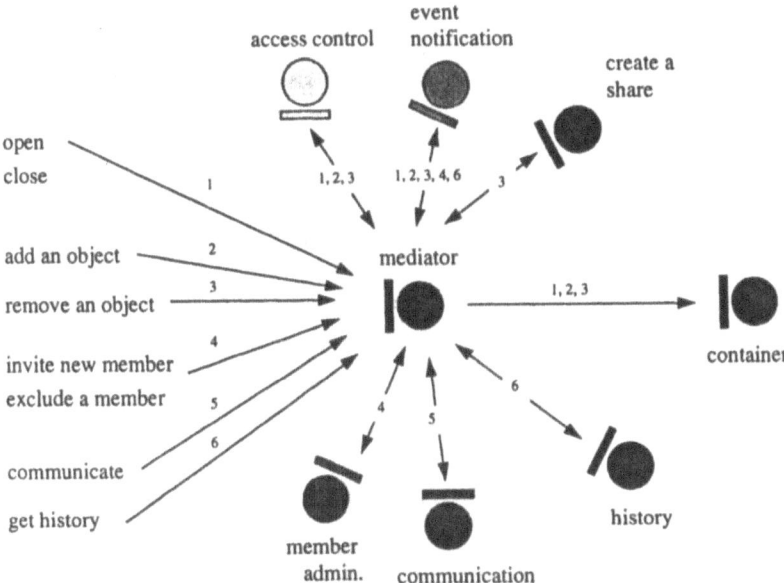

Figure 5: A container enabled for use as a shared workspace

This example shows how the combination of enablers allows the realization of a specific shared workspace behaviour. Having introduced the underlying concept, the next section shows how the basic cooperation support functionality can be adapted by configuration.

Configuration

Configuration of the cooperation support functionality is performed at different levels of abstraction: a default configuration can be specified in a configuration file, whereas a graphical user interface supports configuration during run-time.

The CSCW platform provides the underlying mediator pattern that supports the invocation of enablers. It is the responsibility of the designer of the platform to identify basic cooperation support functionality and to decompose this functionality into CSCW enablers.

The designer or system administrator can specify cooperation support functionality for an object or an object class through configuration files. In addition to this technical solution, we provide a graphical user interface that gives end-users the possibility to adapt the behaviour of an object to its concrete working context.

First, the user can assign a new behaviour to the object. Here pre-defined sets of enablers are illustrated with the help of metaphors: if the user wants to share a single-user container object with further persons, the user can give it a "shared workspace behaviour". If it should be used in a strictly sequential manner, a "circulation folder behaviour" is appropriate.

Second, after the instantiation of the object itself and its mediator and enablers, the user can add CSCW enablers to and remove enablers from the object. For this reason, the enablers are made visible at the user interface. Figure 6 illustrates this: The tree on the left contains the complete list of available enablers. The enablers that are valid for the object "Workspace" (identified locking and a keep-privacy-enabler) are shown on the right side. The functionality of the first enabler has already been described above. When a user decides to move a document out of the shared workspace to work on it privately before putting the document back into the workspace, the user may not want to have every single step of modification be recorded in the history of the object. The keep-privacy enabler allows to specify the level of detail of information describing activities in the private working environment.

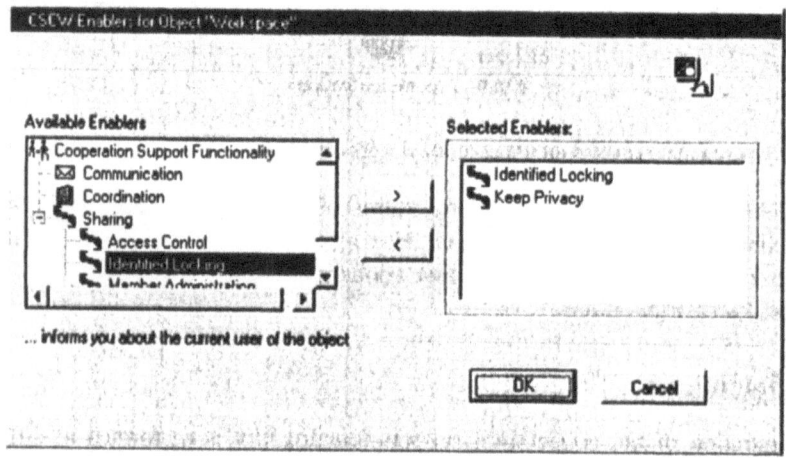

Figure 6: Specification of enablers for an object

To add more cooperative behaviour to the target object, the user moves the enablers from the left frame to the right. As a consequence, a corresponding enabler is initialised, attached to the object, and displayed within the right frame. To remove an optional CSCW enabler that is already assigned to the object, the user selects it on the right side and deletes it.

Third, the user can decide which activities are to be made cooperation-aware by enabling or disabling single methods of the CSCW enablers (the underlying methods were introduced in Figure 3). This is supported by context-sensitive menus attached to the enablers shown on the right.

Related Work

So far we have presented a concept for the design of a generic CSCW platform that allows the configuration of the cooperation support functionality. A lot of investigations have been undertaken with the aim to develop a CSCW platform, most of these developments concentrate on synchronous forms of cooperation. Representatives that can be mentioned here are RENDEZVOUS (Patterson et al., 1990), MMCONF (Crowley et. al, 1990), and GROUPKIT (Roseman and Greenberg, 1992). To portray these systems in simplified terms, the goal here is to provide the infrastructure for the distribution, initialisation and management of sessions.

Another group of CSCW-platforms is based on top of semi-structured messages or objects, as for example OVAL (Malone et al., 1992) or STRUDEL (Shepherd et al., 1990). The users interact by using semi-structured objects or messages; the structure of these entities is used to automatically invoke further functionality (such as the filtering of incoming messages or the modification of calendars). Configuration of the functionality is allowed by defining new message or object types, new structures and new rules. Nevertheless, a modular realization of cooperation support functionality is missing.

In (Navarro et al., 1993) the authors present a distributed environment, called MOCCA, for the design of open CSCW systems. This environment offers different services (e.g. a shared information space or an organisation information service) that can be used by CSCW applications realized on top of it. MOCCA differs from the approach presented here with regard to the level of abstraction: the first provides general services for CSCW applications, the latter allows tailorability of cooperation support functionality for single objects.

PROSPERO (Dourish, 1996) provides a framework for the development of CSCW systems. This development is supported by allowing the integration of application functionality into the framework itself. Whereas PROSPERO focuses on the development of CSCW systems, our concept concentrates on the configuration of the developed system during run-time.

COLA (Trevor et al., 1993) is an object-oriented platform supporting cooperative processes. It provides fundamental but basic mechanisms for the development of CSCW applications. The system uses a concept of object adapters (Trevor et al., 1994) to provide cooperation support for objects. Compared to COLA, the approach presented here focuses on a different level of abstraction, considering how the cooperative functionality should be provided, how it can be made visible to and tailorable by the users.

A different approach is presented by Bentley et al. (1992). The authors propose an architecture that allows the tailoring of multi-user displays by system designers in conjunction with users. Shared interaction objects, called user display agents, handle details about the interaction with and presentation of the shared information store. Thus the role of the user display agents can be compared to the role of mediators introduced in this work, but whereas the first deal with presentation issues, the latter focus on underlying cooperation support functionality.

Conclusion

In this paper we have presented an object-oriented concept for the design of a generic CSCW platform. This concept supports the modelling of cooperative processes by

- encapsulating cooperation support functionality into separate objects, called CSCW enablers,
- encapsulating the interaction of these enablers into a CSCW mediator.

Instead of hard-coding cooperation support into the object model, the concept allows to dynamically add or remove functionality by using enablers and mediators. This allows to flexibly combine basic enabler functionality in order to realize complex cooperation support functionality. Enabled single-user objects can show a new behaviour and be shared among users.

Configuration of this functionality can be done on several levels: first by selecting appropriate CSCW enablers, second by specifying their interaction and the policies employed. This configuration allows support of different forms of cooperation and the transition between different forms (by exchanging single enablers) as well as to represent context-specific norms (by adding further enablers).

There are still open questions that have to be examined concerning the configuration features provided by the concept. Different cooperation situations have to be looked at in order to identify typical configurations of enablers. The employment of metaphors that was briefly mentioned can provide support to make the configuration easier for the user.

Besides developing a CSCW platform from scratch, the concept allows to provide additional functionality to existing CSCW platforms as well. Prerequisite here is that the platform offers a programming interface. Two different approaches are possible: the modification of the underlying object model of the platform or—if this is not possible—the development of an external application which realizes enablers and mediators and makes use of the existing functionality of the platform via the programming interface.

This concept is implemented within the framework of the POLITeam project. However, we do not want our users to design their own cooperation environment, but to do the "fine-tuning". Having stressed the demand for the support of group conventions within a CSCW system, we expect that our users experiment with CSCW enablers representing conventions. The example of removing a document out of a shared workspace was mentioned before. How can this problem be solved? Should this removal be allowed or forbidden? If it is allowed, should the user be informed about the consequences of this action? Or should the decision be left to the user, but recorded? We are looking forward to how our users will use and evaluate this approach.

Acknowledgements

Thanks to Ludwin Fuchs, Wolfgang Prinz, and Markus Sohlenkamp for valuable discussions on many topics raised here. Thanks also to Richard Bentley and Gloria Mark for their constructive comments on earlier versions of this paper.

Bibliography

Bentley, R., T. Rodden, P. Sawyer, and I. Sommerville (1992): "An Architecture for Tailoring Cooperative Multi-User Displays", CSCW 92, Toronto, Canada, in: *Proceedings of the Conference on Computer-Supported Cooperative Work*, ACM Press, pp. 187-194.

Cole, P. and J. Nast-Cole (1992): "A Primer on Group Dynamics for Groupware Developers", in: *Groupware*, Marca, D. and G. Bock (eds.), Los Alamitos, California: IEEE Computer Society Press, pp. 44-57.

Crowley, T., P. Milazzo, E. Baker, H. Forsdick, and R. Tomlinson (1990): "MMConf: An Infrastructure for Building Shared Multimedia Applications", CSCW 90, Los Angeles, CA, in: *Proceedings of the Conference on Computer-Supported Cooperative Work*, ACM, pp. 329-342.

Dourish, P. (1995): "The Parting of the Ways: Divergence, Data Management and Collaborative Work", ECSCW 95, Stockholm, Sweden, in: *Proceedings of the Fourth European Conference on Computer-Supported Cooperative Work*, Kluwer Academic Publishers, Marmolin, H., Y. Sundblad, and K. Schmidt (eds.), pp. 215-230.

Dourish, P. (1996): "Consistency Guarantees: Exploiting Application Semantics for Consistency Management in a Collaboration Toolkit", CSCW 96, Boston, MA, in: *Proceedings of the Conference on Computer-Supported Cooperative Work*, ACM Press, Ackerman, M. S. (ed.), pp. 268-277.

Dourish, P. and V. Bellotti (1992): "Awareness and Coordination in Shared Workspaces", CSCW 92, Toronto, Canada, in: *Proceedings of the Conference on Computer-Supported Cooperative Work*, ACM Press, pp. 107-114.

Ellis, C., S. Gibbs, and G. Rein (1991): "Groupware: Some Issues and Experiences", *Communications of the ACM*, Vol. 34 (1991) 1, pp. 38-58.

Gamma, E., R. Helm, R. Johnson, and J. Vlissides (1995): *Design Patterns: Elements of Reusable Object-Oriented Software*, Addison-Wesley Professional Computing Series; Addison-Wesley Publishing Company.

Klöckner, K., P. Mambrey, M. Sohlenkamp, W. Prinz, L. Fuchs, S. Kolvenbach, U. Pankoke-Babatz, and A. Syri (1995): "POLITeam Bridging the Gap between Bonn and Berlin for and with the Users", ECSCW 95, Stockholm, Sweden, in: *Proceedings of the Fourth European Conference on Computer-Supported Cooperative Work*, Kluwer Academic Publishers, Marmolin, H., Y. Sundblad, and K. Schmidt (eds.), pp. 17-31.

Malone, T. W., K.-Y. Lai, and C. Fry (1992): "Experiments with Oval: A Radically Tailorable Tool for Cooperative Work", CSCW 92, Toronto, Canada, in: *Proceedings of the Conference on Computer-Supported Cooperative Work*, ACM Press, pp. 289-297.

Mambrey, P., G. Mark, and U. Pankoke-Babatz (1996): "Integrating User Advocacy into Participatory Design: The Designers' Perspective", PDC 96, Cambridge, MA, in: *Proceedings of the Participatory Design Conference*, Blomberg, J., F. Kensing, and E. Dykstra-Erickson (eds.), pp. 251-259.

Mariani, J. A. and W. Prinz (1993): "From Multi-User to Shared Object Systems: Awareness about Co-Workers in Cooperation Support Object Databases", in: *Informatik, Wirtschaft, Gesellschaft*, Reichel, H. (ed.), Berlin: Springer-Verlag, pp. 476-481.

Mark, G. and W. Prinz (1997): "What happened to our Document in the Shared Workspace? The Need for Groupware Conventions", INTERACT 97, Sydney, Australia, in: *Proceedings of the Sixth IFIP Conference on Human-Computer Interaction*, Chapman & Hall, to appear.

Navarro, L., W. Prinz, and T. Rodden (1993): "CSCW requires open systems", Computer Communications, Vol. 16, No. 5, pp. 288-297.

Patterson, J. F., R. D. Hill, S. L. Rohall, and W. S. Meeks (1990): "Rendezvous: An Architecture for Synchronous Multi-User Applications", CSCW 90, Los Angeles, CA, in: *Proceedings of the Conference on Computer-Supported Cooperative Work*, ACM, pp. 317-328.

Prinz, W. and A. Syri (1996): "Two Complementary Tools for the Cooperation in a Ministerial Environment", PAKM '96, Basel, Switzerland, in: *Proceedings of the First International Conference on Practical Aspects of Knowledge Management*, Workshop "Knowledge Media for Improving Organisational Expertise", Wolf, M. and U. Reimer (eds.).

Roseman, M. and S. Greenberg (1992): "GroupKit: A Groupware Toolkit for Building Real-Time Conferencing Applications", CSCW 92, Toronto, Canada, in: *Proceedings of the Conference on Computer-Supported Cooperative Work*, ACM Press, pp. 43-50.

Shepherd, A., N. Mayer, and A. Kuchinsky (1990): "Strudel - An Extensible Electronic Conversation Toolkit", CSCW 90, Los Angeles, CA, in: *Proceedings of the Conference on Computer-Supported Cooperative Work*, ACM, pp. 93-104.

Sohlenkamp, M., L. Fuchs, and A. Genau (1997): "Awareness and Cooperative Work - The POLITeam Approach", HICCS 97, Wailea, HI, in: *Proceedings of the Hawaii International Conference on System Sciences HICSS-30*, IEEE Computer Society Press, Nunamaker, J. F. and R. H. Sprague (eds.), vol. 2, pp. 549-558.

Trevor, J., T. Rodden, and G. Blair (1993): "COLA: a Lightweight Platform for CSCW", ECSCW 93, Milano, Italy, in: *Proceedings of the Third European Conference on Computer Supported Cooperative Work*, Kluwer Academic Publishers, Michelis, G. D., C. Simone, and K. Schmidt (eds.), pp. 15-30.

Trevor, J., T. Rodden, and J. Mariani (1994): "The Use of Adapters to Support Cooperative Sharing", CSCW 94, Chapel Hill, NC, USA, in: *Proceedings of the Conference on Computer Supported Cooperative Work*, ACM/SIGCHI, Furuta, R. and C. Neuwirth (eds.), pp. 219-230.

Doing Software Development: Occasions for Automation and Formalisation

Rebecca E. Grinter
Bell Labs, Lucent Technologies, United States of America
beki@research.bell-labs.com

Abstract: The use of workflow technology has created considerable discussion within the CSCW community. Although the debates have been grounded in theories of work, less has been written about specific organisational and social settings where workflow systems have been used. This paper presents findings from an empirical study where a workflow-like system was in routine use for some of the work. It draws conclusions about the circumstances that made this possible.

Introduction

The use of workflow systems to support work has generated much discussion within the CSCW community (CSCW, 1995). Workflow technologies aim to reduce the complexity of coordination in three steps. First, the work activities are categorised; in other words, they are reduced to their basic form. This categorisation usually removes details and specifics from the work and reduces the actions to objects like artefacts, procedures, and user roles. Second, these categorisations are formalised as a language that specifies permitted interactions and rules out non-permitted ones. The formalism makes it possible to embed the categorisation into a computer system. Finally, some parts of this formalism may be entirely automated by the system.

It is these three steps of categorisation, formalisation and automation that raise questions for some researchers. Many of the voices in the debate have asked questions about whom workflow systems serve, how well different formalisms support work, and how they affect the environment they are used in (CSCW,

J. Hughes et al. (eds.), Proceedings of the Fifth European Conference on Computer Supported Cooperative Work, 173-188.
© 1997 *Kluwer Academic Publishers.*

1995). Although the debate is highly grounded in theories of work, the discussions themselves have not focused so much on the empirical details about the companies and people using the technology and the kinds of uses these systems are being put to. Yet it is these details, as previous studies of groupware successes and failures remind us, that are so important to understanding the context in which the technology is embedded.

As the number of workflow systems grows and they are put into use inside companies a question arises as to what conditions support the successful adoption and on-going use of these kinds of systems. This paper examines three occasions when a workflow-like system helped reduce the complexity of work in a way that was helpful to those using the system. Specifically, it focuses on software development and the role of a workflow-like system — a configuration management tool — in supporting that work.

There is a growing body of literature that has examined the failings of groupware systems and as well as their successes. Within the CSCW community though empirical studies of workflow have tended to report the difficulties that people had working with them (Button and Harper, 1992). Even designers of workflow systems have also noted the difficulties of using these technologies (Abbott and Sarin, 1994).

However, despite these concerns workflow systems continue to be developed for a number of reasons. First, they continue to be a seductive technology to commercial corporations (Abbott and Sarin, 1994). Second, some popular management methodologies advocate the use of information technology to support work processes. Third, some successes have been achieved with workflow systems (Agostini, et al., 1994). Fourth, they present an interesting research challenge: to find ways to support the work of individuals in a useful and constructive manner (Medina-Mora, et al., 1992; Ellis and Wainer, 1994; Dourish, et al., 1996).

At the same time that workflow systems are continuing to be built, researchers are beginning to ask questions about the role of formalisms in collaborative work. For example, Bowers (1992) offers a number of counter-arguments against purely theoretical criticisms of formalisms. His counter-arguments also apply to workflow systems, and in this paper I shall provide some empirical support for two of them.

First, he argues that although some aspects of work maybe complex and uncertain other parts maybe routine and dull. The build process that I shall describe was a part of software development work that the developers in this study found less interesting than their development work and used the tool to automate the process.

Second, he observes that if there is such contingency in work then why can't formalisms be used in contingent ways? This paper describes two occasions when the formalisms generated by the system produced outputs that allowed the developers to develop an awareness of what their colleagues were doing and structure their activities in an uncertain environment. These examples highlight some uses of the system that support the contingent work of software development.

It is not my goal to say that workflow systems should always be used, or that they should never be used. Following the example of (Abbott and Sarin, 1994; Bowers, et al., 1995; Dourish, et al., 1996) I want to closely examine the potential of workflow systems for supporting work. Following the guidance set by Bowers (1996) at CSCW '96, it is time to "just go and see" whether there are occasions when workflow systems support work.

The paper begins with a description the domain of study, software development, the workflow tool used, a configuration management (CM) system, and the methods used to gather and analyse data. Next I describe the three cases when the tool supported and enhanced development work for the people using the system. Finally, some conclusions are drawn about why these occasions proved amenable to workflow systems.

Software Development and Configuration Management

In this section I describe the domain of study, commercial software development. I also describe one tool used to support software development work, a configuration management system. Configuration management systems have similar properties to workflow systems.

The Domain: The Development of Software Products

Modern software product development is a complex activity for four reasons. First, most commercially available software systems contain multiple components: pieces of software, libraries, documents, and utilities. These systems are built by a number of developers working on the same product simultaneously which creates coordination overhead (Brooks Jr., 1995). Moreover, software development is coordination-intensive as different parts of the system interact with each other, and so those responsible for these related pieces of code must continually align their efforts during development (Grinter, 1996).

Second, development usually consists of managing the development of multiple versions of the same product simultaneously. To appeal to enough customers most products need to work on a variety of different computer platforms and be compatible with different operating systems. While these differences do not require that the entire product be rewritten for each platform and operating system, part of the development process involves making multiple versions of components that interact with these substrate technologies. Each time the product is tested the correct version of the system needs to be assembled which requires coordinating what goes into the product as well as what stays out.

Third, software is an unusual product to develop because it is very malleable. Software can be changed by anyone, with the permission to do so, until the minute it is released. However, because of the dependencies between components of the system one change can potentially affect the functioning of other parts of the system. Developers working on other related parts of the software rely on a module of code behaving in the same way that it did before. Therefore developers need to coordinate their changes to ensure that they do not affect others' work.

Finally development times have dropped drastically in many sectors of the software industry. An increasing number of software development companies are under pressure to develop new releases of their products in much shorter times.[1] This compounds the previous problems by requiring that they all get resolved much more quickly. For all of these reasons software companies have looked for systems to help them organise their development environments. One class of tools that increasing numbers of development companies have turned to are configuration management (CM) systems.

The Tool: Configuration Management Systems

CM systems were designed to help companies who develop software organise their development environments by helping them to track the relationships among components, develop multiple versions simultaneously, and control changes made to software. The first generation of CM tools focused on controlling developers' abilities to make changes, by using a library metaphor of "checking out" software to revise it, and "checking in" software to indicate that the changes were complete.[2] When a developer had a piece of code checked out no-one else could make changes to it.

These systems had two disadvantages for commercial software development. First, they only worked for modules of code. Software systems contain more than just software, including libraries, test suites, and documents. Modern CM systems support these different types of components. Second, the check out state turned out to be very limiting because it prevented others from changing the same module at the same time. This slowed down developer's ability to get their work done because they had to wait to make their changes. Modern CM systems allow parallel development where two or more developers can check out the same piece of code make changes and then merge their versions back into a single integrated module.

Modern CM tools also address the problems of understanding the relationships among code and developing multiple versions by providing three other classes of functionality usually called *layers* (Caballero, 1994). The "configuration control"

---

[1] In my contacts with managers at various companies it was not uncommon for them to remark that systems development times had been cut in half during the last five years, while the number of variants necessary to be compatible with different hardware and software configurations has risen.

[2] Two early systems were Revision Control System (RCS) and Source Code Control System (SCCS) (Rochkind, 1975; Tichy, 1985).

layer maintains information about which components make a software product. Specifically it knows which version of each component goes into a certain release of the software system. It also maintains information about how those components relate to each other. The configuration control level allows developers to find out exactly which components belong to a specific hardware configuration.

The "process management" layer provides a "life cycle" for each type of component in the system. The life cycle consists of different states; for example, software can be checked-out, checked-in, unit tested, system tested, and released. When software is in these different states, certain people — who have corresponding roles — are permitted by the system to manipulate the software. For example, in the unit tested state only people assigned the testing role can access the component.

The "problem reporting" layer supports bug and enhancement tracking. All changes to the system components arise as a result of bugs being reported or enhancements being requested. These bugs and enhancements — collectively known as problems — follow a life cycle. The problem reporting layer also relates the problems with the software components that were changed.

CM systems are domain-specific workflow systems for the coding and testing parts of software development. They allow the formalisation of software development by categorising the artefacts and people involved in the work. Furthermore they support certain kinds of relationships among people and artefacts and only permit the artefacts to follow certain state transition models. Finally CM systems automate some elements of the work entirely.

Sites and Study Methods

The data reported in this study were gathered in 1994-1995 as part of a series of studies about configuration management. In this paper the data are drawn from two sites.

Tool Corp. is the vendor of a CM tool. They use their own CM tool to manage the development of the next versions of the tool itself. During the time I spent at Tool Corp. the development group varied in size from 14 to 18 people. The developers were all co-located working on one floor of one building. The product they built consisted of about 1 million lines of code.

Computer Corp. is the vendor of a computer operating system for specialised hardware. At the time of the study they employed 700 people to develop their software. Many of the software developers work at the company's headquarters in Silicon Valley, but they have developers located in other states, and other countries. The software consists of about 10 million lines of code. Computer Corp. had just started using Tool Corp.'s product in their software development work.

At both companies the development of the overall product was broken up into development teams that were organised by functional parts of the product. At

Computer Corp. there were many teams organised around the different operating system functions; for example, a kernel team, and an interface team. At Tool Corp. the software production effort was much smaller so the developers worked in two teams again related to a functional distinction between two parts of the product.

The data were gathered using a combination of interviewing and observation techniques. At Tool Corp. I had full access to the corporation and was given a cubicle among the developers which I used for three and a half months. I also had access to the tool and the software development environment provided through the system. I visited the headquarters of Computer Corp. and was taken to various parts of the corporation to meet different development groups. I also sat in on a class where developers were learning how to use the CM tool built by Tool Corp.

At both sites I was able to conduct interviews. At Tool Corp. I used unstructured and semi-structured interviewing techniques to gather information about the CM challenges that the developers faced (Bernard, 1988). I collected approximately 100 interviews of which 20 were taped and transcribed. At Computer Corp. 13 semi-structured interviews were conducted, and were taped and transcribed.

The data were analysed using grounded theory techniques (Glaser and Strauss, 1967; Strauss, 1987; Strauss and Corbin, 1990). Grounded theory consists of three stages. The first stage consists of analysing the raw data. The purpose of the analysis is to find as many conceptual groups — known as *categories* — that describe the events and phenomena in the data. The second stage focuses on filling in the categories; for example, characterising their properties, the events that caused them to happen, and any resulting consequences. Finally the third stage puts these substantive categories together to form the theory of action itself. Data analysis consisting of these three stages happens numerous times over the course of the study itself. Intitial gaps and questions surrounding the categories drive further periods of data collection.

In this study the initial cycles of gathering and analysis focused on the observational data gathered. As the theory started to form I used interviews to help inform and revise the categories developed. In the next three sections I describe the examples of the developers' tool usage. Discussion of these cases is deferred until the following section.

Case 1: Automating The Build

During the course of development, software components need to be gathered into the product to see whether they work together and function as intended. The process of putting the system together from the components is known as "the build." The time between successive builds decreases rapidly as development enters the final stages because the closer the product gets to release the more everyone wants to be absolutely certain that the software works.

The actual process of building the system consists of finding the latest changes of all the components and then compiling them. At both sites each development team had a developer known as a build manager who took responsibility for the job of ensuring that the build took place. However, there was a significant difference between the work that build managers did dependent on whether they used the tool or not.

The Build Managers

As Computer Corp. was still in the process of migrating all the teams to the CM tool, some groups still used manual build procedures. In these teams the build manager would take responsibility for the build as well as their development work. That person would visit every developer in the team, get their changes and compile them. Among these build managers there was a desire to have some kind of system organise this work for them. As one build manager put it,

It doesn't really track "am I getting the right version of this thing"... and unless you have, um, a system for doing that, which people have done in a manual way like writing down on bits of paper, talking to 18 different developers ... that are producers of their dependencies, there is no way.

and another described a similar manual procedure

I make them tell me stuff like what [files] to grab and what's the version number of them, what bug are you fixing and how am I supposed to know once I install it if that bug got fixed or not. What's the behavior I'm supposed to see and then, when it's necessary, I do the [recompile] and install and send out mail. ... I keep a track of it, and how I track is that every time I do an install I send everybody e-mail saying this is what I installed, this what is was supposed to fix and it's ready for you to use now or whatever... [3]

There is some benefit for doing this work. The build managers of the systems often end up knowing a lot more about the overall state of the system than the developers. Their continuous interactions with all the developers, to gather the latest changes of code, mean that the build managers have an up-to-date impression of what state the overall system is in.

Despite this advantage, the build managers do not enjoy the work of build management. Although they recognise the advantage of know what's going on, it does not compensate for the amount of time that it takes to do the work. This becomes especially true when the system enters the final weeks of development and builds may take place two or three times a day instead of once every two days or once a week. Build managers also dislike doing the job because they do not find it as challenging as their software development work.

Other teams at Computer Corp., and all the teams at Tool Corp. let the CM tool do the build. On command, the system would gather the latest code changes from everyone in the team and compile them. If the compilation was successful the tool

---

[3] Notes in square brackets represent references to artefacts and processes that might identify the company, so I have replaced them with more generic terms to maintain confidentiality.

would produce a new version of the product for testing and using in further development efforts. Otherwise the system would notify the build manager and provide them with information about where the problem occurred. The build manager would inform the developer responsible for the build failing.

The build managers who had worked in a manual mode and then switched to the CM tool all preferred the automated process. As one ex-build manager said,

> [The tool] makes it easy for the person in charge of the product to build the latest tested version of the product. It removes the manual process of the developer saying I've finished with this, you can use this now. That's a pretty big advantage, I was a build manager for a part of it, [team name], for a couple of months.

The tool reduced the amount of time it took to gather everything for the build. Also, it helped the build managers find the error that broke the build. Both of these activities are part of a manual build process but when automated improved the build managers' job.

The Developers

The developers also liked the automated procedure because of the guarantees it provided them. As one developer said,

> I come in in the morning and I [get a system update] I get the latest of everything and I generally don't even have to worry about it. I just know its going to be there and its going to work fine. Then I can just go about my business, having gotten everyone else's changes automatically.

Developers using the CM tool enjoyed the fact that the tool gathered their latest changes automatically, without them having to stop working. Furthermore it gave them everyone else's latest changes. The developers also described two weaknesses with the manual methods that affected their work. First, the time taken to manually gather the changes invariably meant that some developers had made revisions to their code since the build manager visited. This caused time delays in testing whether their new code worked, which were especially problematic during the final stages of development when teams wanted feedback very quickly. Second, changes often need to be tested in groups, as they represent a revision to the functionality of the sub-system. When only some of those changes get into the build, there's a high probability that the build will fail because the code depends on the other changes being there. The CM tool had a mechanism for ensuring that all the related changes got into the build or stayed out of it, which was the responsibility of the build manager in the manual groups. It was hard for the build managers in the manual groups to track the dependencies between changes, but failure to do so usually resulted in a failed build slowing down the testing process.

The build is one example of a case when automation benefits the build managers as well as the developers of the software. In this case the automated build generated positive reactions from the build managers because it reduced their workload and from developers because it supported their work. The trade-off between the formalisation of the build versus doing the build manually was acceptable to all using the tool.

Case 2: Awareness Created by the Formalism

In a paper about ways of creating awareness of others in CSCW systems Dourish and Bellotti (1992) describe an approach to collaboration they call *shared feedback*. Awareness of what others are doing is provided through feedback presented in a shared workspace. The CM tool provided this kind of awareness to the developers through the formalisms that the tool used to categorise the work of software development.

When the tool starts up the developers see the main view. To visualise the main view imagine a typical Mac folder with the files viewed by name. Each file in that folder has a name, size, type, and its date of creation. The main view of the CM tool has the same visual arrangement with the software component name, latest version number, the state of that component and current owner of the file (their e-mail handle).

Each team shares a collection of views, which correspond to folders of sub-system components. The main view that the developer sees when she launches the tool is the one corresponding to the folder — or as the developers call it the *directory* — of files she is currently working on, but it's very unlikely that she'll be working there alone. Other developers will be changing other files — or possibly the same file — in that directory, and that information is available to her.

The states that components move through were known to all the developers using the tool at both sites. This allowed the developers to read the information from the view and infer that their colleagues were working on certain components related to theirs, whether they were developing or testing them. Furthermore this view was not static. As developers changed components so their state changed in the life cycle and the version number was incremented by the system.

The CM tool allowed developers to update their main view at any time they wanted to, a process they called *reconfiguring* the view. I was alerted to the awareness created by the system when the developers talked about seeing things in the system. Two developers described their use of the shared feedback the system provided quite explicitly during interviews,

> In your own personal [sub-systems] you can see what the state of the parts of the project you are working on are because you get everyone's latest versions that others have checked in. When you reconfigure your [view of the sub-system] you see what versions you get, the dates on them, who owned them, who [changed] them, what changes they include.

> Sometimes I can tell from just reconfiguring my stuff and I can look and see what, who owns all the versions that I just got in. I can see that certain things have been changing.

The main view helped to make developers aware of the work going on around them. However, they also used the information to direct their own efforts. One thing that the developers did not enjoy doing was working on the same piece of code at the same time. Merging the two versions made back together turns out to be very difficult. However, the main view easily let developers see whether anyone else was working on the component that they wanted to change. As one developer put it,

> I'll look and see and if someone has it checked out, the module I want to modify and mine's not too difficult. I did this last night, I sent them mail and asked can you do this for me in your version...

The awareness provided by the main view comes from the tool's formalism. It would be impossible to display all the details of others work in a view like this, and for most of the developers it would not be useful. Often times they want a peripheral awareness of what others are working on, and when they need more they establish contact with their colleagues. The formalism provides them with a useful summary which often meets their needs and when it doesn't gives them a pointer as to who to contact.

Case 3: Tracking Problems

The CM tool that Tool Corp. and Computer Corp. used had an integrated problem reporting facility. Problems also had a life cycle starting from when they were entered into the system by managers or customer support. Every few days a team of people that consisted of the project manager, a tester and some senior developers, would meet and prioritise the problems in the system and assign them to developers. Once a developer has been assigned a problem the tool notifies the developer who has been assigned the problem.

Although the problem reporting facility sounds restrictive, the developers relied on it to tell them what they were supposed to be working on. The problem reporting facility thus became a scheduling system of sorts,

> It's nice, you come in in the morning and get a mail message, these are all the problems assigned to you, just look at all of them. No-one actually has to come to my office and say this is a bug, it has to be worked on, I just know because it's automatically generated and sent to me. So I look at that to figure out all the things I have to do.

At Tool Corp. the problem reporting facility was not free of some of the challenges of making workflow technologies work. Specifically the facility requires that all changes to the code must be associated — via hypertext links — to problems in the facility. This created a problem because the people who met to assign problems to developers could not meet frequently enough to prevent the developers from running out of problems and not being able to get any more work done until the next meeting.

The problem was solved when the managers decided to let the developers have the ability to create and assign themselves problems. In terms of the system this meant assigning the developers a supervisor role in the facility. This work around let the developers carry on using the system. Moreover, it had the unintended payoff of enhancing their use the problem reporting facility as a scheduling tool for organising their own work.

> I like to use the tool to organize my work. I use the [problem reporting] facility. I create tasks for just about everything I do.

With the ability to assign themselves problems, the developers could make notes to themselves about problems to be fixed in the future while working on other — possibly related — problems. Also the supervisor role now let the developers assign their own priorities to problems and make their own estimates about how long problems would take to complete.

> So it keeps track of all the problems which I have assigned to me and I can put priorities on them, so I know which ones I'm going to do first, also it has a field for estimated duration, so I can get an idea how long it will take me to do everything, and I can budget my time.

The problem reporting facility was used by developers routinely in their work. Its primary purpose was to give developers up-to-date information about the work assignments. This information was provided daily to them in the form of an e-mail message generated by the tool. However, at Tool Corp. the revised role assignment that developers took encouraged them into using the problem reporting facility as a place to put their notes about future work and a comprehensive scheduling system.

Discussion

These three cases are occasions when the workflow system — the configuration management tool — supported the everyday work of the developers. It is important to stress that this is not a recommendation that workflow technologies are universally applicable. Specifically, I have written about the limitations and failings of the same tool in other places (Grinter, 1995; Grinter, 1996). More generally, others have written about the failure of other tools to provide support for software development work (Button and Sharrock, 1994). However, in the three cases I describe the tool demonstrably supported the work of the developers and provided them with new opportunities to organise their actions in a changing environment. This section offers four reasons why the tool worked on those occasions: (1) understanding and accepting a model of work, (2) providing understandable and useful representations, (3) automating the "right" work, and (4) having a supporting company.

Understanding and Accepting the Model of Work

Like any workflow technology, the CM tool had a model of work embedded in the system. The developers had to understand and accept that model to really use the tool on these occasions. This became very explicit at Computer Corp. where developers were beginning to adopt the tool in their work.

At Computer Corp. I took part in a class where developers who were new to using the tool were learning about how the tool modelled the work of software development. During the adoption phase of the tool developers at Computer Corp. found that their old models of software development — usually based on other tools that they had used for configuration management and other professional sources — clashed with the new tool. Computer Corp. designed the class to help ease the adoption process by explaining the differences and similarities between the new tool and the old ways of work. It was an attempt to get the developers to understand and accept the model of work.

At both companies the developers who used the tool routinely both understood and accepted the model of their work. They understood the model well enough to know how the tool functioned and how it fit into their work. The developers also believed in the model enough to talk about their usage in positive ways as described in the three cases. For a workflow system to work, for any groupware system to work, both stages must occur.

Perhaps one reason why developers at both sites found the model acceptable enough to use the system stemmed from the fact that the developers had a good user model. The developers at Tool Corp. were both designers and users, perhaps the ultimate participatory design experience. The developers at Tool Corp. could use their own experiences of development to build a system that worked for them and their counterparts at Computer Corp.[4]

Understandable and Useful Representations

Developers used the main view and problem reporting facility in part because the tool provided an understandable and useful representation of the underlying model of work. By representation, I mean: the interface, the presentation of the content inside the windows, and way that the system updates that content. The main view relies on everyone understanding what they are seeing. As one developer put it,

> In [the tool] the system sets up everything in a standard way. It's easy to find out what is going on. There's rhyme and reason to it all.

This representation is maintained throughout the tool. Even when the developer changes their main view the new view they arrive at contains the same types of

---

[4] Although the developers at Tool Corp. contributed their own ideas about how development happens to the design of the system, other requirements still shape the development effort. The problem reporting facility; for example, contained a model of problem assignment that seems more appropriate for hierarchically organised software development. In my time at Tool Corp. I observed potential customers being attracted to this hierarchical model.

information and it still means the same thing.[5] To be used as a mechanism for peripheral awareness the developers had to trust the system to be telling them the same thing where ever they were in it.

However the main view was also useful because of its ability to provide peripheral awareness to the developers about the others' actions. The formalism provided that shared feedback because it reduced the details of peoples' work to a brief, consistent, and above all useful form. In the absence of the formalism it would have been very hard for the developers to find out what their colleagues were working on in such a concise way.

The use of the problem reporting facility also relied on it presenting information in an understandable and useful way. Beyond that the system was useful enough so that when they were given the opportunity to utilise more parts of it they did. When the developers had control over the scheduling functions of the problem reporting system they found it even more useful.

Automating The "Right" Work

The tool automated some aspects of the software development work almost completely. The build process was an example of this. It was also an example of picking the "right" work to automate because everyone supported the automation and some people benefited from it.

At both sites the build process was of concern to four distinct groups: developers, build managers, testers, and managers. The build managers supported the automation effort as a way of reducing the amount of time they spent doing that work. The testers and developers benefited from the automated build by being relieved of their part in the process. Moreover they enjoyed receiving up-to-date code from which to begin their own testing and development efforts with minimal effort on their part.

The managers at Tool Corp. and Computer Corp. were invested in getting new versions of the software released to the market as quickly as possible. They saw the automation of the build process as part of streamlining the development cycle and supported it.

A Supporting Company

At both Tool Corp. and Computer Corp. developers are viewed by managers as professional staff. This was visible in a number of ways. First, I did not see anyone keeping time records. At both companies it was assumed that the developers were putting in the required time unless they told someone otherwise.

---

[5] This is not an argument for making all interfaces consistent and arguments suggest that it can be problematic (Grudin, 1989). Instead the observation is similar to (Sommerville, et al., 1993) observation about how air traffic controllers look at the screens of their colleagues to understand what is about to happen in their own domain. In this case the screens are all shared inside the development environment.

Second, the developers were treated as professionals by their management. Finally, and most significantly, developers' opinions were taken seriously by their managers.

This kind of culture made it relatively easy for the developers at Tool Corp. to discuss their initial problems with the problem reporting facility and get permission from their management to simply change the role of developer into the role of supervisor. That change was simple to implement technologically, but in environments where users do not have that kind of control or ability to change their circumstances, the change is impossible to make.

Workflow system builders can not pick the companies that they sell their systems too. However, we can assume that companies who buy these kinds of systems would like them to function as intended, and potentially increase the efficiency of the work done. If the users can not use them or end up spending time working around the system to accomplish their work then these efficiencies will be much harder to attain.

Conclusions

Workflow technologies have generated an important series of discussions within the CSCW community. While these debates are grounded in theories of work, there have been few empirical studies of workflow systems in use. Those studies that exist often point to the difficulties of using these systems. This paper has reported on three occasions when the work of software development was supported by a workflow system.

In this paper I have outlined four reasons why this workflow system was used. They are: (1) understanding and accepting a model of work, (2) providing understandable and useful representations, (3) automating the "right" work, and (4) having a supporting company. These reasons highlight the *context-dependent* aspects of the use of workflow technologies in particular settings.

These empirical results provide a basis for grounding otherwise abstract and theoretical discussions about workflow technologies. In addition to talking about the theoretical hurdles to implementing workflow it is time to find out when the confluence of these positive forces creates opportunities to implement workflow rather than watching it happen badly without us.

Acknowledgements

I would like to thank the Engineering and Science Research Council for their financial support during the time I conducted these field studies. Many people have commented on this paper and I would like to thank Jim Whitehead, Jim Herbsleb, Neil Harrison, Jonathan Grudin, Paul Dourish, Peter Danielsen, Victoria Bellotti, Al Barshefsky and the anonymous reviewers for their suggestions. This work was inspired by Gunn, Megson, and Wark.

References

Abbott, K. and Sarin, S. (1994): "Experiences with Workflow Management: Issues for the Next Generation", in Furuta, R. and C. Neuwirth (eds.): *Proceedings of ACM Conference on Computer Supported Cooperative Work CSCW '94 , Chapel Hill, NC, October 22-26, 1994*, ACM Press, pp. 113-120.

Agostini, A., De Michelis, G., Grasso, M.A. and Patriarca, S. (1994): "Re-engineering a business process with an innovative workflow management system: a case study", *Collaborative Computing*, vol. 1, 1994, pp. 163-190.

Bernard, H.R. (1988): *Research Methods in Cultural Anthropology*, Sage, Newbury Park, California.

Bowers, J. (1992): "The Politics of Formalism", in Lea, M. (eds.): *Contexts of Computer-Mediated Communication*, Harvester Wheatsheaf, New York, 1992, pp. 232-261.

Bowers, J., Button, G. and Sharrock, W. (1995): "Workflow from Within and Without: Technology and Cooperative Work on the Print Industry Shopfloor", in Marmolin, H., Y. Sunblad and K. Schmidt (eds.): *Proceedings of European Conference on Computer-Supported Cooperative Work , Stockholm, Sweden, 10-14 September, 1995*, Kluwer Academic Publishers. Dordrecht, Netherlands, pp. 51-66.

Bowers, J. (1996): "PANEL: From Retrospective to Prospective: The Next Research Agenda for CSCW", in Ackerman, M. S. (eds.): *Proceedings of ACM Conference on Computer Supported Cooperative Work CSCW '96 , Cambridge, MA*, ACM Press, pp. 440.

Brooks Jr., F.P. (1995): *The Mythical Man-Month: Essays on Software Engineering*, Addison-Wesley Publishing Company Inc., Reading, Massachusetts.

Button, G. and Harper, R.H.R. (1992): "Taking Organisation Into Accounts", in Button, G. (ed.): *Technology in Working Order*, Routledge Press, United Kingdom, 1992, pp. 98-107.

Button, G. and Sharrock, W. (1994): "Occasioned Practices in the Work of Software Engineers", in Goguen, J. and M. Jirotka (eds.): *Requirements Engineering*, Academic Press Ltd., London, United Kingdom, 1994, pp. 217-240.

CSCW (1995): "Commentary on Suchman-Winograd Debate", *Computer Supported Cooperative Work: An International Journal*, vol. 3, no. 1, 1995, pp. 29-95.

Dourish, P. and Bellotti, V. (1992): "Awareness and Coordination in Shared Workspaces", in Turner, J. and R. Kraut (eds.): *Proceedings of ACM CSCW'92 Conference on Computer-Supported Cooperative Work , Toronto, Canada., October 31 - November 4, 1992.*, ACM Press, pp. 107-114.

Dourish, P., Holmes, J., MacLean, A., Marqvardsen, P. and Zbyslaw, A. (1996): "Freeflow: Mediating Between Representation and Action in Workflow Systems", in Ackerman, M. S. (eds.): *Proceedings of ACM Conference on Computer Supported Cooperative Work CSCW '96, Cambridge, MA, November 16-20, 1996*, New York, N.Y.: ACM Press, pp. 190-198.

Ellis, C.A. and Wainer, J. (1994): "Goal-based Models of Collaboration", *Collaborative Computing*, vol. 1, no. 1, 1994, pp. 61-86.

Glaser, B.G. and Strauss, A.L. (1967): *The Discovery of Grounded Theory: Strategies for Qualitative Research*, Aldine de Gruyter, Hawthorne, New York.

Grinter, R. (1995): "Using a Configuration Management Tool to Coordinate Software Development", in Comstock, N. and C. Ellis (eds.): *Proceedings of ACM Conference on Organizational Computing Systems , Milpitas, CA, August 13-16, 1995.*, ACM Press, pp. 168-177.

188

Grinter, R.E. (1996): "Supporting Articulation Work Using Configuration Management Systems", *Computer Supported Cooperative Work: The Journal of Collaborative Computing*, vol 5, no. 4, 1996, pp. 447-465.

Grudin, J. (1989): "The Case Against User Interface Consistency", *Communications of the ACM*, vol. 32, no. 10, 1989, pp. 1164-1173.

Medina-Mora, R., Winograd, T., Flores, R. and Flores, F. (1992): "The Action Workflow Approach to Workflow Management Technology", in Turner, J. and R. Kraut (eds.): *Proceedings of Conference on Computer-Supported Cooperative Work. CSCW '92*, *Toronto, Canada, October 31-November 4, 1992.*, ACM Press, pp. 281-288.

Rochkind, M.J. (1975): "The Source Code Control System", in (eds.): *Proceedings of 1st National Conference on Software Engineering*, *Washington, D.C., September 11-12, 1975*, IEEE Computer Society, pp. 37-43.

Sommerville, I., Rodden, T., Sawyer, P., Bentley, R. and Twidale, M. (1993): "Integrating Ethnography into the Requirements Engineering Process", in Finkelstein, A. and S. Fickas (eds.): *Proceedings of Requirements Engineering 1993*, *San Diego, California. 4-6 January*, pp. 165-173.

Strauss, A. (1987): *Qualitative Analysis for Social Scientists*, Cambridge University Press, New York, New York.

Strauss, A. and Corbin, J. (1990): *Basics of Qualitative Research: Grounded Theory Procedures and Techniques*, Sage Publications, Inc., Newbury Park, California.

Suchman, L. (1995): "Speech Acts and Voices: A Response to Winograd *et al.*", *Computer Supported Cooperative Work: An International Journal*, vol. 3, no. 1, 1995, pp. 85-95.

Tichy, W. (1985): "RCS: A system for Version Control", *Software Practice and Experience*, vol. 15, no. 7, 1985, pp. 637-654.

Introducing Third Party Objects into the Spatial Model of Interaction

Steve Benford and Chris Greenhalgh
Department of Computer Science, The University of Nottingham, UK

We introduce an extension to the spatial model of interaction for CVEs called third party objects that provides support for contextual factors in awareness calculations and that enhances scaleability. Third parties can have two effects on awareness: attenuation or amplification of existing awareness relationships; and the introduction of new aggregate awareness relationships. We propose a range of applications for third party objects including: world structuring regions, aggregate views, common foci, representational and group services, and dynamic load management. We present an implementation, the MASSIVE-2 system, focusing on its network architecture of a dynamic and self-configuring hierarchy of multicast groups.

1. Introduction and background

This paper extends the spatial model of interaction for Collaborative Virtual Environments (CVEs) as defined in (Benford, 1993) to include support for contextual factors in awareness manipulation and also greater scaleability. This is achieved through the introduction of third party objects, independent objects in a virtual world that can perform various awareness adaptations and aggregations. Third parties can be used to model a wide range of awareness manipulation mechanisms ranging from nested spatial structures such as rooms within buildings within regions, objects that act as common foci for interaction, through to mobile crowd aggregations. The paper also describes how this extended spatial model can be mapped onto an underlying network architecture based on a dynamic hierarchy of multicast groups. This mapping lies at the heart of the MASSIVE-2 system, a more scaleable and flexible successor to the MASSIVE system as described at EC-SCW'95 (Greenhalgh 1995). The paper describes the implementation of MAS-SIVE-2 and mentions several example applications including an arena where events can be staged in front of crowds of participants; a poetry performance and

189

J. Hughes et al. (eds.), Proceedings of the Fifth European Conference on Computer Supported Cooperative Work, 189-204.
© 1997 *Kluwer Academic Publishers.*

exhibition and a collaborative software visualisation tool.

However, before introducing the concept of third party objects, we first consider the background to this work in terms of the history of development of the spatial model, the current limitations of the model and also related work on spatially structured distributed virtual environments and multicast network architectures.

1.1. A history of the spatial model and its current limitations

The spatial model was first proposed as a way of managing awareness in CVEs through the mechanisms of aura, awareness, focus, nimbus and adapters (Benford, 1993) and was initially demonstrated in the DIVE system and then first fully implemented as the MASSIVE system (Greenhalgh 1995). MASSIVE has since been used to hold many virtual meetings and several papers have emerged from these experiences including studies of interaction within (Bowers, 1996a) and around (Bowers, 1996b) MASSIVE meetings and also mathematical analysis of system log data from an extended series of meetings (Greenhalgh, 1997). Recently, at CSCW'96, Tom Rodden proposed a generalisation of the spatial model to arbitrary "network" structured spaces that might map onto a range of CSCW applications (Rodden, 1996).

Having developed, implemented and extensively tested spatial model based CVEs, we have become aware of two major limitations:

Contextual factors in awareness - the original spatial model concepts of focus and nimbus (see section 2) were concerned with how an observer and observed could control the former's awareness of the latter. Beyond a limited notion of adapters (see below), there was no truly general consideration of how contextual (i.e. environmental) effects on awareness could be realised (e.g. the effects of boundaries in multiple nested spaces, crowds of participants or shared objects).

Scale - although the initial spatial model support scaleability in terms of awareness driven presentation of large volumes of information to an individual and the use of aura to limit connectivity, it still necessitated dealing with individual awareness relationships or aura collisions on a bilateral basis. This represented a major bottleneck to implementing CVEs that could support hundreds or thousands of simultaneous users. What was needed for some more fundamentally scaleable mechanism as a core part of the model.

The concept of third party objects, a much extended notion of the adapters in the original model, is intended to address both of these problems. Third party objects were first introduced in (Benford, 1997) which focused on their use for supporting dynamic crowds of participants in CVEs. This paper extends this work in two main ways. First, in section 3, it explores a broader range of possible applications of the third party concept. Second, in section 4, it describes how the extended spatial model has been implemented as the MASSIVE-2 CVE system with a particular focus on the mapping of the model onto an underlying multicast network architecture.

1.2. Related work on spatial partitioning for CVEs

The concept of third party objects also relates directly to other work in the field of distributed virtual environments. In particular, several researchers have been considering how to introduce some form of spatial partitioning into shared virtual worlds (typically involving notions of zones or regions) and then map this onto a underlying network architecture in an efficient way. For example, NPSNET (Macedonia, 1995) tiles the world with hexagonal cells, each with its own multicast group, so that observers need consider only near-by cells. The Spline system (Barrus, 1996) composes the world from arbitrarily shaped regions or "locales" that localise interaction and that may be "stitched" together by arbitrary 3D transformations. In a slightly different vein, RING (Funkhouser, 1996) scopes interaction and communication according to potential visibility in densely occluded environments (e.g. within buildings) while localising interactions at servers responsible for specific regions of the world. Other researchers have focused on alternative ways of exploiting multicast protocols, including the association of multicast hierarchies with the hierarchical composition of objects and collections of objects in a virtual world as implemented in recent versions of the DIVE system (Hagsand, 1996). The work described in this paper is intended to be sufficiently general so as to subsume previous spatial partitioning approaches. At the same time, it offers an interesting contrast to the strict "object hierarchy" approach. In the following section, we begin our discussion with a general introduction to the third party concept.

2. Third party objects and the spatial model

In order to understand third party objects, one must first be familiar with the original spatial model. The spatial model defines mechanisms for the spatial management of awareness and communication in shared virtual spaces such that the quality of one object's perception of another in a given medium is represented as the quantifiable concept of awareness. In turn, this awareness is enabled through collisions between auras and then negotiated through two further spatial fields, focus (observer's control) and nimbus (observed's control). Auras, foci and nimbi are defined as general spatial (and possibly non-spatial) fields that can have arbitrary shape and extent and can assume different values across their extent. They are also medium specific. The further concept of adapters involves the manipulation of awareness, focus, nimbus and aura as a result of interacting with other objects in the space and can be used to model simple spatial boundaries and communication aids such as podia and conference tables. However, the original adapters could only perform limited awareness manipulations (i.e. replacing focus, nimbus and aura) and there was no general definition of how they were activated and whether they might operate recursively (e.g. they could not be used to model nested boundaries within boundaries as one might expect to find in a large virtual building).

2.1. The concept of third party objects

We now introduce the concept of third party objects as an extension to the spatial model (Benford, 1997). A third party object is an independent object that affects the awareness between other objects (see figure 1 (a)). Two points should be noted about third party objects from the outset. First, as with focus and nimbus, all aspects of their operation as described below may be medium specific (e.g. they may operate differently in the audio medium than in the graphical, textual or video media). Second, as they are objects in their own right they might be embodied, have a configurable spatial extent, be mobile or fixed in the world, be dynamically or statically created and might apply their effects recursively to one another. This potential for recursive application is a key feature that enables the construction of complex nested virtual world structures and has profound implications for the network architecture of any implementation as we shall see later. Their ability to be mobile and resizeable is also important as this enables support for dynamic crowds in CVEs.

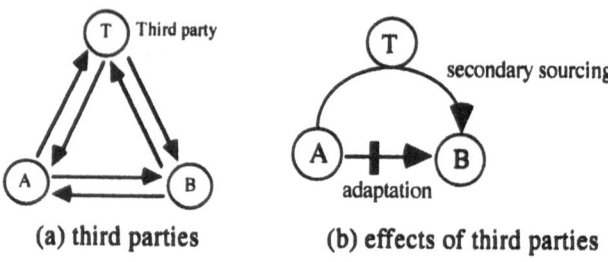

(a) third parties   (b) effects of third parties

Figure 1: Third Party Objects

There are two key aspects to the definition of third party objects: their effects (i.e. what they do to awareness relationships between other objects) and their activation (i.e. when and how these effects are brought into operation).

2.2. The effects of third party objects

Third party objects can have two general kinds of effect on awareness and these may be applied in different combinations (see figure 1 (b)).

Adaptation involves the manipulation of existing awareness relationships between objects. This includes attenuation (e.g. a third party acting as a barrier between objects) and amplification (e.g. increasing awareness between people who are accessing a common object).

Secondary sourcing involves the introduction of new indirect awareness relationships between objects in order to enable new transformed flows of information between them. Typically, secondary sourcing involves the consumption of information from an external object or group of objects, its transformation in some way and its subsequent re-transmission in order to provide an alternative view of the object or group (e.g. generating a single aggregate view of a crowd of people, a room or a region when seen from a distance). Various filters may also be applied at different stages of this process in order to reduce level of detail or to select key information. At the heart of secondary sourcing for groups lies the problem of creating a single aggregate view or stream of information from a number of sources. In general, there are three approaches to the aggregation problem: *selection* - switching between individual views or streams in some way (e.g. round robin, "loudest wins" etc.); *combination* - the direct composition of a new view from existing views (e.g. tiling multiple video windows); and *abstraction* - generating an entirely new representation based on statistical information describing the sources (e.g. mapping number of sources into size of representation, level of activity into colour etc.).

The combination of adaptation and secondary sourcing is the main reason why third party objects support scaleability in CVEs. Under appropriate circumstances, a third party can replace many individual awareness relationships with a single secondary source, thereby reducing the amount of information being transmitted across the network and processed by individual computers.

2.3. The activation of third party objects

Next we consider the circumstances under which different combinations of these effects are applied. The activation of a third party object is based on the awareness relationships between the third party and the other objects involved. Thus, referring to figure 1 (a), the activation of T depends on four possible awareness relationships: T's awareness of A and B respectively and their awarenesses of it. In figure 2 we identify three particularly interesting cases from among the various possible combinations of these awareness relationships.

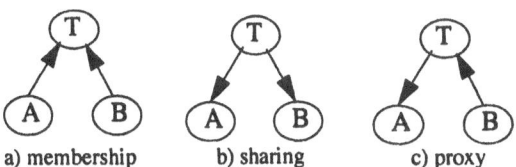

a) membership   b) sharing   c) proxy

Figure 2: Activating third party objects

Membership - cases where the third party is activated according to how aware it is of other objects.The third party's awareness of an object represents and expresses the degree of membership that object has of the third party. For example, one might become a member of a room or region by crossing its boundary, resulting in various changes in awareness (see section 3.1).

Sharing - cases where the third party is activated according to how aware other objects are of it. The third party is, in some sense, shared by the objects which, in turn, influences their mutual awareness. For example, two people focusing on a common data item in a 3-D information visualisation or working with the same 3-D design might experience an enhanced awareness of each other caused by the object of common interest (see section 3.3).

Proxy - cases where the effects of the third party depend on how much one object is aware of it and how much it is aware of another object. The third party consumes information from its members and makes it available to external observers as an aggregate view at a low level of awareness. At higher awareness levels, this view is unfolded, to be replaced by information from each of the individual member objects. This turns out to be a useful case for crowds as we shall see in the following section.

This concludes our introduction to the general mechanism of third party objects in the spatial model of interaction. The following section explores a wide range of possible applications of this concept.

3. Possible applications of third party objects

We propose that the third party objects can be put to a wide range of uses, including:

- **World structuring and regions** - including nested spatial structures such as virtual rooms, buildings and zones that introduce awareness manipulations and aggregations across their boundaries.
- **Aggregate views** - these include dynamic and mobile crowds of participants and data districts in three dimensional visualisations.
- **Common foci** - objects that, when shared by a number of people, affect the mutual awareness between them (e.g. working with shared 3-D designs or chance encounters in a 3-D information space).
- **Representational and group services** - embodying general services such as support for anonymity, non-local communication, subjective presentation, brokering and introduction, group navigation and floor control.
- **Load management** - the automatic creation and destruction of third party objects by the system to cope with computational and network load.

We now consider each of these in turn, with a particular focus on the first two.

3.1. World structuring through regions

One of the key uses of third party objects might be in partitioning shared virtual worlds into regions that apply different awareness effects across their boundaries. A typical region would be a membership activated third party as in Figure 2, case (a) above, where membership would be determined by the act of crossing its boundary. In terms of its effects, awareness relationships between members would remain as normal (i.e. subject to individual foci and nimbi). However, awareness relationships between members and non-members might be subject to a combination of adaptation (typically, attenuation) and secondary sourcing (typically, the region might offer an abstract view of its contents to those outside of it). A virtual world might then be divided into an arbitrary number of such regions of varying size and shape.

This basic structure might be extended in several ways. First, the effects of a region might be applied differently across different media, resulting in the kinds of boundaries proposed in earlier spatial model papers (e.g. "windows" that would be permeable to visual media and impermeable to audio, or "curtains" that would have the reverse effect). Second, regions might apply different combinations of effects for member to non-member awareness that for non-member to member awareness. In other words, the boundaries of regions could be defined to be directional (e.g. "one way mirrors"). Third, and perhaps most importantly, regions could be nested, allowing for the definition of arbitrarily complex virtual world structures such as virtual cities, divided into districts, divided into buildings, divided into floors, divided into rooms, all applying different awareness manipulations across their boundaries.

An example of regions is provided by the recent poetry performance that we staged using our MASSIVE-2 implementation of the spatial model; see section 4 for an overview of MASSIVE-2 and (Benford, Greenhalgh, Snowdon and Bullock, 1997) for a description of the event. The performance world was structured as a top level region that contained a stage area where poets performed to a virtual audience. This region contained four sub regions, each of which contained graphic designs and fragments of poetry that could be explored during breaks in the poetry. These regions incorporated one-way boundaries such that those inside could see and hear what was happening in the stage area, but those outside couldn't see or hear what was happening inside, thus providing semi-private zones for social interaction.

This application of third parties can also be related to other work in CVEs. Several existing CVEs support multiple disjoint virtual worlds linked by portals (e.g. DIVE and MASSIVE). These can be considered to be simple regions, although their only effect is to completely attenuate awareness across their boundaries. Other recent work has focused on spatial partitioning in virtual worlds. For example, the tiled cells of NPSNET correspond to simple regional third parties that have no adaptive effect, but that group their contents to give a unit of visibility or interest that can be mapped onto its own multicast group. Similarly, the localisation aspect of a locale in the Spline system also corresponds directly to a single region (although the spatial model does not attempt to address the issue of multiply-related coordinate systems as used in Spline). Scoping on potential visibility as in RING may be achieved by mapping rooms (or other basic open spaces) to regions, and either allowing each client to reason about what it might see according to a locally and hierarchically structured abstraction of the total environment, or by employing another third-party object (or objects) in a server-type role to determine inter-region visibility. Finally, regions need not be solely spatial in their determination, and regions with a non-spatial element (specifically "is-a-sub-object-of") can be used to realise object hierarchies, including the provision of different multicast groups for different sub-trees of the object hierarchy as prototyped in DIVE.

3.2. Aggregate views - crowds and data districts

Another application of regions is to define abstract views of dynamic collections of objects. The primary difference to regions is that these third parties might be mobile within a virtual world. We focus on two examples: crowds and data districts.

One of our first uses of third party objects has been to explicitly support crowds of participants in CVEs. This work is described in detail in (Benford, 1997). A crowd is a third party object that represents and manages a potentially large grouping of participants in a virtual world (e.g. audiences at virtual events or dynamic groupings of people in densely populated spaces). From the "outside" (e.g.when not a member or when perceived at low awareness) a crowd provides an aggregate image of its members across a range of relevant media. Typically, this aggregate would be generated dynamically and would provide information about the composition and current activity of the crowd. (Benford, 1997) proposes a range of crowd aggregation techniques for different media, including graphical visualisation of crowd statistics and the triggering of different media samples (e.g. audio and video fragments or texture mapped images). On the inside of the crowd, interaction with individual members becomes possible. Crowds are typically asymmetric; from the inside one can usually perceive the outside world in full detail (or even in amplified detail as in a crowd that amplifies awareness of a performer on a nearby virtual stage). Crowds may also be mobile (e.g. may follow or even pull their members around) or may be static (e.g. be attached to the virtual scenery in some way such as a bank of seating in a stadium).

We have implemented an application called the Arena to demonstrate crowds in the MASSIVE-2 system. The Arena provides a virtual world in which several participants may play a game of "Pong" (the classic computer tennis game) in front of a watching audience. Audience members are located in different crowd regions such that, those on the inside of a given crowd have normal awareness of one another, but those outside (e.g. the players or the members of other crowds) perceive an aggregate view. We have initially used two simple aggregation algorithms: a single graphical crowd body that grows in size according to the number of its members and the mixing together of audio streams coupled with the application of a low pass filter to produce a composite crowd rumble in the audio medium.

Outside of the Arena, we locate a number of mobile crowds. These are crowd objects (i.e. third parties) whose position in the world becomes the average position of their current members. People exiting the Arena typically fall into one of these crowds that then follows them and their neighbours around. These mobile crowds can be used to smooth the transitions of people around a world and to dampen down system load caused by many people moving at the same time. In order to test our application, we have also developed some simple "agents" that can be scripted to move through the world and that emit different utterances as they go.

Our second example of aggregate views is that of data districts. A data district corresponds to a dynamic grouping of information items in a three dimensional visualisation and the corresponding generation of an aggregate view that conveys the properties of the group as a whole. In addition, the aggregate might also convey summary information about the current users of the data items (e.g. might show how many other users are currently inside the data district). Our first example, implemented in MASSIVE-2, is a collaborative software visualisation. We have developed a three-dimensional hierarchical visualisation to show different relationships between the objects and classes in an object oriented software system (e.g. "inheritance", "using" and "aggregation" relationships). Collections of objects (e.g. class libraries or modules) can be defined as data districts whose detail is only expanded for those who are currently inside them or close to them. We are currently exploring other possibilities such as the use of "legibility techniques" applied to three-dimensional representations of the WWW (Ingram, 1996) to develop data districts of inter-linked WWW pages and the use of data-districts to provide aggregate views of relations (i.e. schema visualisations) in a relational database visualisation.

3.3. Common foci

Common foci are third party objects that affect the awareness between people who were using them. Unlike the above, they are activated according to how aware the participants are of the third party (case (b) from section 2.3). Thus, if two people both focus on the same object in the virtual world, then this object might have some effect upon their mutual awareness. Typically, this effect would involve amplification of their mutual awareness.

There are many possible examples of common foci. People working with a common 3-D design (or a common part of a large 3-D design), might experience heightened mutual awareness, perhaps resulting in the creation of an audio channel between them. People accessing the same data item in a visualisation might experience a similar effect. Thus, two people browsing the same page in a WWW visualisation might become aware of one another, or two software engineers who elect to modify the same component in our MASSIVE-2 software visualisation might automatically be put in contact with one another in order to resolve possible conflicts.

3.4. Representational and group services

Third parties might be used to embody and activate a range of other general services. Third party objects might provide transformed views of another object or objects to support, for example: anonymity - by concealing the identity of the indirectly viewed object; non-location communication - by generating the secondary source information at some distance from the object(s) being observer; or subjective views - via a personal third-party that provides a transformed view of the world. Third party objects might influence navigation, perhaps acting as group vehicles. On activating such a vehicle, one would be taken on a journey and would experience heightened awareness of the other passengers. As a final example, third parties might be used to implement more traditional floor control policies in group settings. In this case, one would loose direct awareness of others (adaptation) and this would be replaced by a secondary source channel where the aggregation algorithm implemented the floor control algorithm, switching between different participants (e.g. round robin, token passing or loudest wins).

3.5. Load management

Our final application of third parties operates at the system rather than at the application level. The scaleability offered by the replacement of individual awareness relationships with aggregate secondary sources might be exploited by the underlying system as a way of dynamically managing system load. Thus, when computational load or network traffic exceeds some threshold, the system might automatically introduce third party objects into the world, essentially re-grouping participants on the fly. The mobile crowds from the Arena application represent a pre-planned version of this. More generally, techniques have recently been proposed for pre-determining "social hot-spots" in virtual urban structures (Ingram, 1996). These might be used to automatically introduce third party objects at places in a virtual world where the population density might be expected to be high.

4. Implementation - MASSIVE-2

Having considered the definition and application of the third party objects, we now present one possible implementation of them in the form of the MASSIVE-2 system. MASSIVE-2 is, as its name implies, a successor to MASSIVE as described at ECSCW'95. Like MASSIVE, it provides a collaborative virtual environment within which a number of mobile and embodied participants can interact over a combination of graphical, audio and textual media, controlled by the spatial model. There are many important differences between MASSIVE-2 and MASSIVE, including MASSIVE-2's support for full interaction with the contents of the virtual world and provision of a general application development environment.

From the point of view of this paper, probably the most important difference between them is in their underlying network architectures. Whereas MASSIVE was based on a peer-to-peer unicast network architecture, MASSIVE-2 is based on a novel multicast network architecture. It is the mapping between the extended spatial model and the underlying multicast architecture that we explore in the remainder of this section. There are two main aspects to this mapping. First, enabling the transmission of information (e.g. state descriptions and state updates) between artefacts and observers in a virtual world. This is achieved through the introduction of a dynamic hierarchy of group objects, directly derived from the nested spatial structure of the world (as defined by third party objects), where each group provides one or more multicast addresses for distributing state and update messages for different media. Mechanisms are defined to enable transmitting artefacts to join and leave different groups as both move about the world, and for receiving observers to "page in" different groups as they move about the world. Second, the objects that are exchanging information in this way negotiate mutual awareness levels through additional protocol support for focus, nimbus and adaptation. Awareness is then used to tailor the presentation of the information received from the multicast groups (e.g. to control the volume of audio, quality of video or level of detail of graphics). We now examine each of these two aspects in more detail.

4.1. Spatially managed multicasting

As we saw above, the concept of third party objects allows us to define nested and evolving structures for virtual worlds through objects such as regions, bounded rooms and crowds, where these structures have direct effects on mutual awareness and information exchange. In MASSIVE-2, this spatial structure is mapped directly onto a hierarchy of multicast groups. The joining and leaving of these groups is automatically managed according to the movement of objects and structures in the virtual world. The aggregation effect of third party objects is supported by extending multicast groups to provide aggregate transmissions of their contents to their superiors in the hierarchy. There are four fundamental types of component involved in our architecture:

World - a single nominally infinite three-dimensional virtual space within which the other components can be situated. A world includes a configurable specification of media supported (e.g. text, audio, video, graphics) and also a mapping of these media onto multicast groups (e.g. all media sharing a single group, one group per medium or something in between).

Artefact - an object represented within the world that can be decomposed into medium-specific sets of attributes and streams of messages. An artefact is essentially a transmitter of information in the world.

Aura - is a device through which inhabitants perceive the world and takes the form of a scope or area of interest. Auras are defined by a world, location, spatial extent and set of relevant media. An aura is a receiver of information in the world. Thus, in order to participate in the world, a user will typically be represented by one or more artefacts and will observe the world through one or more auras.

Group - is a representation of a third party object from the spatial model. Groups are structuring tools for virtual space that introduce awareness adaptations and aggregations and that may contain one or multicast addresses so as to transmit information between artefacts and auras that are associated with the group. There are two separate classes of group membership: sending members (artefacts) and receiving members (auras). MASSIVE-2 groups are therefore a generalisation of multicast groups, in that they define their own membership mechanisms, support aggregation and may map onto several underlying multicast addresses.

We now discuss how these components work together, focusing on the mechanisms defined for managing artefact and aura membership of groups.

4.2. Groups and artefacts

Figure 3 shows how an example virtual world maps onto an underlying hierarchy of group objects. In our example, the virtual world is structured into an outer room that contains a further inner room. There are two dynamic crowds, one currently in the top-level world and one in the outer room. In this example, the rooms are fixed both in size and spatial location but the crowds may be mobile and resizeable. This structure maps onto to the hierarchy of group objects shown in figure 3(b). The eight participants in the world are represented by the artefacts a to h.

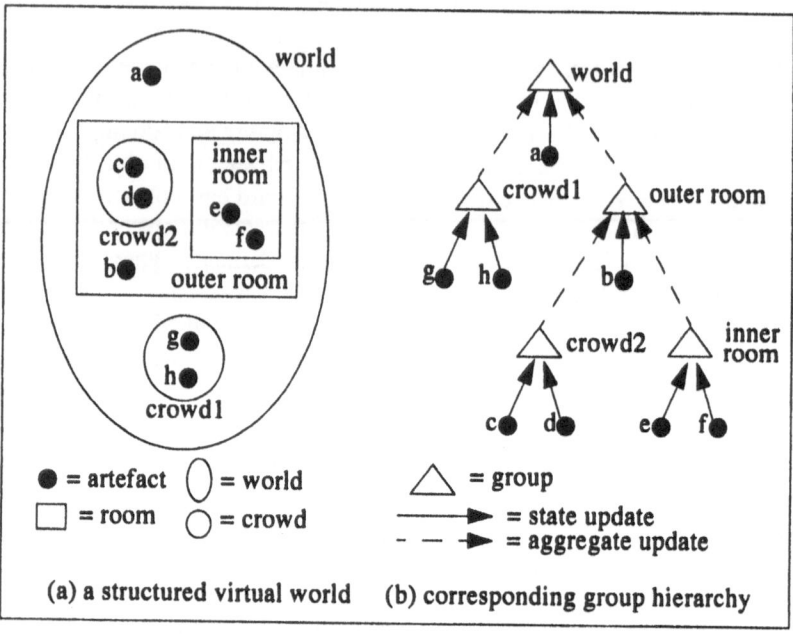

Figure 3: Spatial structure, group structure and sending updates

At any given moment in time each participant is deemed to be a sending member of its most local containing group. This means that the artefact associated with this participant sends its information (e.g. movement updates, audio packets etc.) to the multicast addresses associated with this particular group. As the participants move around the world, so they will pass through different spatial structures and, consequently, will be invited to join and leave different multicast groups as senders. Each group may also send an aggregated stream of information to its superior group in the hierarchy. Each artefact or group may only be a sending member of one other group at a time and membership as a sender is determined by strict spatial containment (i.e. an artefact or group has to be completely contained within a surrounding group in order to become one of its sending members).

As with participants, the movement of third party objects such as crowds around the world may cause the hierarchy of group membership to be automatically updated as spatial containment relationships change. Our architecture therefore results in there being an automatically self-configuring hierarchy of groups driven by movements in the virtual world.

4.3. Groups and auras

We now turn to the converse problem, that of dynamically managing the membership of auras within groups. In order to observe the world, a user (or other process) registers one or more auras in the world. An aura can have arbitrary (and changing) spatial extent and at any one time will overlap one or more third party structures. The effect of overlapping a group in this way is to join the aura as a receiving member of the group. Unlike artefacts, aura membership is based on spatial overlap not strict containment. Thus, an observer will receive information from potentially many groups depending upon the location and the extent of their auras. They may also dynamically resize their auras so as to increase or decrease the volume of this information. This is essentially a form of "spatial paging" of group objects - as one moves across the word, so different groups are paged in by one's aura and parts of the world are unfolded to different levels of detail. Thus, in figure 4, we see that two observers, X and Y, have each registered an aura in the world. X's aura currently overlaps the world, the outer room and crowd 2 and hence X receives updates from their associated group objects. Y's, on the other hand, overlaps the world and crowd 1, so they receive information from their associated groups.

As mentioned above, each MASSIVE-2 group object actually maps onto several underlying multicast groups. First, a world designer may choose to utilise different multicast groups for different media if they wish on a per-world basis. Second, different multicast groups are provided to handle different phases of joining and leaving a group as a receiving member. More specifically, the dynamic joining and leaving of groups raises an interesting problem. On joining a group, an aura will start to receive updates from a multicast group (e.g. movement notifications). However, without an initial snapshot of the whole state of the group these may not make much sense. In other words, a new aura joining a group has to first receive a (potentially large) state transfer before it can begin processing updates. This is handled by the introduction of a second multicast address that can be used to address the artefacts who are currently sending to the group (i.e. a back channel from auras to artefacts). This address is used by incoming auras to request a state snapshot from these artefacts. Thus, on joining a group, an aura first multicasts a state snapshot request to its artefacts. Once this has been received, these artefacts can then multicast updates to this state to the aura. As a further twist, the group may choose between unicasting and multicasting the state snapshot depending on how many requests are received within a given time (e.g. if many people enter a region of a world at one time, it may make sense to multicast the state update to them).

With reference to the underlying protocols, MASSIVE uses reliable multicasting for all communication except for "real-time" media (e.g. audio and video). The protocols are receiver reliable in that sequence numbers and heart-beats on messages allow receivers to detect errors and to request retransmission. Thus, MASSIVE-2 has been designed to be run over generally reliable networks.

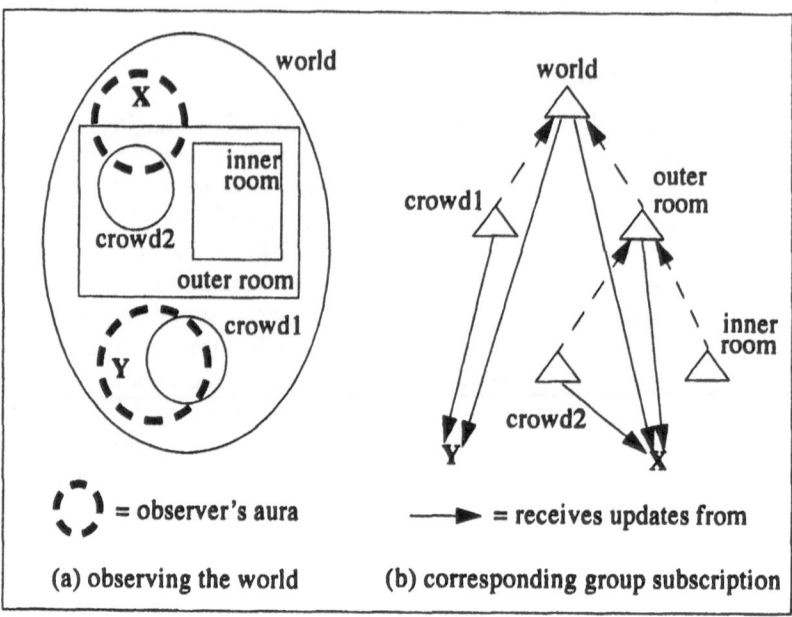

Figure 4: Aura and subscription to groups

4.4. Awareness negotiation

Having discussed in detail how groups, artefacts and auras combine to dynamically manage the multicasting of virtual world information, we now consider how objects negotiate detailed levels of awareness using focus and nimbus in order to manage the presentation of this information. This is achieved through specially defined awareness protocols.

Each artefact contains attributes that declare its specific focus and nimbus functions for different media. Default functions are provided based around a central region of maximum focus/nimbus that tails off according to a configurable distance and angle. However, other focus and nimbus functions can be added. Each artefact also contains attributes that list the groups of which it is currently a member, including a definition of the awareness adaptation effects of these groups. There are three such effects: a multiplier (that can amplify or attenuate awareness), a maximum awareness limit and a 'gate' threshold (an observer only becomes aware of the artefacts within a group once awareness of the group exceeds this threshold).

Each artefact provides methods that allow other artefacts to inspect its focus and nimbus functions, its current group memberships and also to sample its nimbus on another artefact. A further method is provided to interrogate an artefact about the value of its awareness of any other artefact. Evaluation of this method proceeds as follows. If we ask A about its awareness of B in some specific medium then:

- A samples the nimbus of B on A in that medium;
- A then asks B about its group memberships and compares them with its own, applying adaptation effects accordingly (again, taking the medium into account);
- Finally, A applies its local focus on B in that medium in order to calculate a final awareness level.

Awareness is then used to modify the presentation of the information that is delivered through the underlying multicast structure. For example, awareness may be used to control the local volume of an audio channel, the quality of service of video or the level of detail of graphics. This concludes of discussion of the MASSIVE-2 implementation of third party objects. As noted in section 3, MASSIVE-2 has already been used to develop a variety of CVE applications, including the public poetry performance described in (Benford, Greenhalgh, Snowdon and Bullock, 1997).

5. Summary

This paper has introduced an extension to the spatial model of interaction called third party objects, intended to support contextual factors in awareness and also greater scaleability of CVEs. Third parties are independent objects in a virtual world that can adapt existing awareness relationships between other objects and can also introduce new indirect awareness relationships corresponding to secondary sources of information. As objects in their own right, third parties can be mobile, resizeable, dynamically created and apply recursively to one another. These characteristics make them a powerful tool for defining CVEs. Our paper has explored a number of applications of third parties including: world structuring (e.g. defining nested rooms, buildings, regions and zones that apply different combinations of adaptation and secondary sourcing across their boundaries); providing aggregate views, especially of crowds and data districts; acting as common foci for shared interaction; embodying a range of more general representational and group services; and supporting dynamic load management.

We have discussed MASSIVE-2's implementation of this extended spatial model, focusing on how it maps the structure of a virtual world as defined by third party objects onto a underlying network architecture of multicast groups. Given the notion of secondary sourcing and also the fact that third parties may be mobile and resizeable, this multicast architecture has a number of highly novel features, namely, an automatically self-configuring hierarchy of multicast groups, with aggregated transmissions from children to parents in the hierarchy and with a "spatial paging" mechanism used to manage the joining and leaving of multicast groups.

As with the first version of MASSIVE, we intend the next few years to see a range of applications of this system, eventually leading to organised trials and evaluation of the system and underlying model. In terms of applications, we anticipate a strong focus on "citizen oriented" applications in areas such as entertainment, arts and performance. Indeed, a companion paper to this describes an early experiment with this kind of application (Benford, Greenhalgh, Snowdon and Bullock, 1997). In the longer term, we anticipate the development of CVEs that will be capable of supporting hundreds or thousands of simultaneous participants and believe that the mechanism of third party objects may provide one of the techniques required to achieve this.

References

Barrus, J. and Anderson, D. (1996): "Locales and Beacons." in *Proc. 1996 IEEE Virtual Reality Annual International Symposium (VRAIS'96)*, San Jose, 1996.

Benford, S. D. and Fahlén, L. E. (1993): "A Spatial Model of Interaction in Virtual Environments", *Proc. ECSCW'93*, Milano, Italy, September 1993.

Benford, S. D., Greenhalgh, C. M. and Lloyd, D (1997): "Crowded Collaborative Virtual Environments", *Proc. CHI'97*, Atlanta, Georgia, US, March 22-27, 1997 (in press).

Benford, S.D., Greenhalgh, C. M., Snowdon, D. N, and Bullock, A. N. (1997): "Staging a Poetry Performance in a Collaborative Virtual Environment", also submitted to ECSCW'97.

Bowers, J., Pycock, J. and O'Brien, J. (1996a): "Talk and Embodiment in Collaborative Virtual Environments", *Proc. CHI'96*, ACM Press, 1996.

Bowers, J., O'Brien, J. and Pycock, J. (1996b): "Practically Accomplishing Immersion: Cooperation in and For Virtual Environments", *Proc. CSCW'96*, pp 380-389, November 1996, Boston, ACM Press.

Funkhouser, Thomas A. (1996): "Network Topologies for Scalable Multi-User Virtual Environments", in *Proc. 1996 IEEE Virtual Reality Annual International Symposium (VRAIS'96)*, San Jose, CA, April, 1996.

Greenhalgh, C. M. and Benford, S. D. (1995): "Virtual Reality Tele-conferencing: Implementation and Experience", *Proc. ECSCW'95*, Stockholm, September, 1995, North-Holland

Greenhalgh, C, M. (1997): "Analysing movement and world transitions in virtual reality tele-conferencing, submitted to ECSCW'97.

Hagsand, O. (1996): "Interactive Multiuser VEs in the DIVE system", *IEEE Multimedia*, Spring 1996.

Ingram, R. J., Benford, S. D. and Bowers, J. M. (1996): "Building Virtual Cities: Applying Urban Planning principles to the Design of Virtual Environments", *Proc. VRST'96*, Hong Kong, July 1-4 1996, pp. 83-91, ACM Press.

Macedonia, Michael R., Zyda, Michael J., Pratt, David R., Brutzman, Donald P., and Barham, Paul T. (1995): "Exploiting Reality with Multicast Groups: A Network Architecture for Large-scale Virtual Environments", in *Proc. 1995 IEEE Virtual Reality Annual International Symposium (VRAIS'95)*, 11-15 March, 1995, RTP, North Carolina.

Rodden, T. R. (1996): "Populating the Application: A Model of Awareness for Cooperative Applications", *Proc. CSCW'96*, pp 67-76, November 1996, Boston, US, ACM Press.

Cooperative Work and Lived Cognition: A Taxonomy of Embodied Actions

Toni Robertson

School of Information Systems, University of New South Wales, Australia

Based on a field study of cooperative design in a distributed company, this paper identifies and defines the embodied actions of the designers that enabled a cooperative design process. These actions are considered as classes of cognitive practices that are simultaneously available to the actor and others in a shared physical workspace. The public availability of these actions to the perceptions of the participants in a cooperative process enables their communicative functions. A taxonomy of embodied actions is developed as a bridging structure between the field study of cooperative work and the design of technology that might support that work over distance.

> Boundaries are drawn by mapping practices; "objects" do not pre-exist as such. Objects are boundary projects. But boundaries shift from within; boundaries are very tricky. What boundaries provisionally contain remains generative, productive of meanings and bodies. Siting (sighting) boundaries is a risky practice.
>
> Donna Haraway, *Situated Knowledges*, 1991, p. 200.

Introduction

When people do not share a physical space, they are unable to see each other, hear each other speak, handle or look at the same thing, or perceive anything about the place where others are or what they are doing. This is a fact of human embodiment. Interaction just cannot happen when people are apart because there are no perceptual resources explicitly available and shared between them to form its basis. Unless, of course, they use some kind of technology to support, mediate, or even enable their interaction by providing some common basis for the creation

205

J. Hughes et al. (eds.), Proceedings of the Fifth European Conference on Computer Supported Cooperative Work, 205-220.

of shared meaning. Because CSCW technology can convey various kinds of information between arbitrary points, it can be used to support remote collaboration (Gaver, 1992). Exactly what information is needed, however, is by no means a foregone conclusion. This paper recognises the active and perceiving body as the essential basis of all human action and interaction. My starting premise is that the defining constraint in the design of technology to support interaction between people working in different places is the essential corporeality of human cognition. While many studies of the use of CSCW technology have recognised the implications of the corporeality of the users of technology, this paper focuses directly on the embodied actions of the participants in a cooperative process.

The empirical basis of this paper is a longitudinal field study of a small distributed company that designs computer based training and educational software products. This paper is not a descriptive account of the empirical research that inspired it (interested readers can find such accounts in Robertson, 1996a, 1996b). Instead, it attempts to structure the results of a field study of cooperative design in a way that might bridge the gap between the description of the work and the design of technology to support that work. A taxonomy is presented that identifies and defines the embodied actions of the designers that were observed in video tapes of cooperative design work within a shared physical space. The term "embodied action" is used here to name the publicly available, meaningful actions that people rely on to interact with others and their environment. Embodied actions are considered as classes of cognitive practices that are publicly and simultaneously available to the perception of the actor and others in a shared physical space. These include actions like talking, touching, drawing, looking and moving around in the environment, in order to accomplish whatever the person acting wants to do. It is the public availability of these actions that enables their communicative functions. It is these actions that need to be considered for technical support if the designers, in the field study, were to increase their options for robust and flexible communication while they are working apart.

Bodies, Spaces and Objects in the CSCW Literature

Interestingly, it is recent work on user embodiment in virtual spaces that has called for a greater understanding of the social and interactional role of actual bodies (Benford et al., 1995; Bowers et al., 1996a, 1996b). Benford et al. (1995) commented that in cooperative systems "embodiment often seems to be a neglected issue (It appears that many collaborative systems still view users as people on the outside looking in)" (p. 242). They identified some of the design issues involved in implementing virtual embodiment in two prototype systems, DIVE and MASSIVE. Bowers et al. (1996a) applied empirical techniques from interaction analysis and conversation analysis to the study of a meeting supported by the MASSIVE system. They found that the virtual embodiments seemed to have some social interactional role (p. 63). In a more recent paper, Bowers et al. (1996b) considered how action and interaction in the virtual and physical world inter-relate. Their analysis articulated the work that embodied subjects have to do within their local physical environment in order to manage their virtual body in its virtual environment.

Studies of the use of media spaces have revealed the interactional asymmetries between shared physical space and virtual space (Heath and Luff, 1991; Heath et al., 1995) as well as the effect on these interactions of the physical medium in which they occur (Gaver 1992; Gaver et al., 1995). Heath and Luff (1991) used ethnomethodology to analyse how technology transforms verbal and non-verbal conduct, particularly on the ways individuals used gestures and other forms of visual conduct to establish and preserve mutual involvement and to coordinate work tasks and activities. In a later paper, Heath et al. (1995) argued that the focus in media space research on supporting face-to-face communication does not allow participants the flexibility to align towards the focal area of their collaborative activity, for example a document, where coordination is achieved through peripheral monitoring of other people's involvement in the activity at hand. The taxonomy that is developed here encompass the whole range of actions observed within the shared physical workspace during cooperative work. Gaver's (1992) extension of Gibson's (1979) notion of affordances to media spaces highlighted the centrality of active perception to technology-mediated interaction. He argued that if social activities are situated in their environment (Suchman, 1987), then collaboration depends both on complex social relations as well as the physical medium in which these relations can work (Gaver, 1992, p. 17). More recent work investigated the constraints that media spaces placed on participants' ability to move through the environment (Gaver et al., 1995).

Studies of the use of physical objects in cooperative design have identified their role in design conversation (Harrison and Minneman, 1994, 1995). Harrison and Minneman (1994) found that interaction with 3-D objects in the design process objects "provides a rich source of information for the designer, is an integral part of the communications, alters the dynamics in multi-designer settings, and forms part of the pool of representations that are drawn on by designers" (p. 205). In a later paper reflecting on a range of studies of architects designing together in distributed workplaces, Harrison and Minneman (1995) argued that the use of representations and other objects involved in design work is dictated by and managed through the ongoing conversation of the designers.

Background to the Taxonomy

The field study that forms the empirical basis of this paper followed the design of a educational computer game from initial discussions through to the development of a prototype. The company studied is very small and the designers are professionals doing their normal work, within their usual work environment, over its actual time frame. The work environment included geographically separate workplaces, in fact the designers' homes, and a weekly gathering in a shared physical space. The designers used computer systems and communication technology, as well as highly developed communication skills and procedures, to enable them to work together despite being separated most of the time. My central conclusion from the field study was that the cooperative design of a software product was enabled and achieved by the work the designers did communicating with each other. Communication is used here in its widest and most active sense; where people interact to create, negotiate, maintain, share and review meaning, understanding and knowledge, to enable cooperation, to build and maintain relationships, and use whatever options for achieving this that they can. When the designers shared a physical space, the space itself enabled communication by supporting the mutual perception of their embodied actions, as they talked together and made and used various artefacts within the shared physical workplace. When they were apart, communication had to be supported by the interplay of specifically evolved work practices, with whatever communication technologies were available.

The taxonomy presented in this paper was developed as a possible bridging structure between the field study of cooperative work in practice and the design of technology that might support that work over distance. By definition, the design of any technology requires formalisation that, in turn, relies on categorisation and the setting of boundaries. Also by definition, formalisation distances the analysis from its basis in the lived corporeal world. This distancing is the source of the power of formalisation to structure that world. As Haraway (1991) observed "Siting (sighting) boundaries is a risky practice" (p. 200). For those seeking to design technology based on the lived experience of those who will use it, formalisation is always approached with caution. The taxonomy developed here is not concerned with any specific stage of the design process. Instead, in an attempt to tie it explicitly to the lived experience of the designers, the categories of embodied action are derived from the observation and analysis of the actions of the designers themselves. I should emphasise that this taxonomy defines categories that remain totally open and flexible in how and when people achieve and combine them in practice. This is an important point because it leaves open the possibility that people will evolve different ways to perform these actions; perhaps including ways to perform them in virtual spaces. The categories are definitely *not* suitable for implementation as explicit menu options. The following sections ground the taxonomy in the conditions of its development by accounting for its theoretical commitments and clearly stating its limits. In the remainder of the paper, categories of embodied action, for both individual actions and group activity are identified and defined.

Cognition as Embodied Action

Embodied actions are the actions of an active and perceiving embodied subject. The consideration of embodied actions as classes of cognitive practices recognises that human cognition depends on the "kinds of experiences that come from having a body with specific sensorimotor capacities" (Varela et al., 1991, pp. 172-173). These experiences are, in turn, always embedded within a specific social, historical and cultural context. Moreover, embodied sensory and motor processes, perception and action, are fundamentally inseparable in lived cognition and have evolved together over the lifetime of any particular individual (ibid). Perception and action are inseparable in this taxonomy because perception, as an active process, is achieved by motor actions at the same time that motor actions, as purposeful actions, are achieved by perception. The embodied actions identified and defined here are always, at the same time, both sensory and motor actions.

Perception as Lived Cognition

Merleau-Ponty (1962, 1968) provided an explanation of how our embodied actions enable us to create and maintain shared meaning between people. He recognised that our bodies are our sole means of communication with the world. Perception, as an active and interpretive, embodied process, immerses the human body in its lived world. For Merleau-Ponty perception is active, embodied and always generative of meaning. As such it belongs to neither body or mind but is constitutive of both. Over time, as it is lived by an embodied subject, the meanings generated during perception are continually shaped by what has been lived before. Central to Merleau-Ponty's (1962) account of perception is his insistence that bodies are both physical structures in the world at the same time as they are lived by the embodied subject. He called these two aspects of embodiment the phenomenological body and the objective body, "my body for me and my body for others" (p. 106). These two aspects of embodiment are continually interlinked by the fact that our objective body is perceivable by ourselves and, most importantly, by others. It is our phenomenological body, as a lived, experiential body that, through our awareness and control of our objective body, is able to act.

The Reversibility of Perception

Merleau-Ponty used the term "reversibility" to name the body's presence to itself as both perceiving and perceived (1968). Reversibility is the complex, reciprocal insertion and intertwining of the sensed and the sensing, that is the essential condition of our interaction with the world and with others. In a shared physical space a lived body can simultaneously see and be seen, touch and be touched, make sounds and be heard, move and reorient its perspective and cross over these sensory modes; that is, see *both* itself *and* others being touched or touching, moving, making sounds etc. The fact that we are able to perceive our own bodily surfaces at the same time as we live our acting bodies enables us to organise our actions (ibid). The public availability of these actions to the perceptions of others enables them to organise their own actions in relation to ours. In this way group activity is achieved that, in the field study, enabled a cooperative design process (Robertson, 1996a). Whatever the designers did was accomplished not just by internal cognitive processes, but by different combinations of their purposeful, embodied actions. Cooperation was achieved by the mutual perception, by the actor *and* others, of these actions as the basis for the ongoing creation of shared meaning.

The taxonomy of embodied action developed here assumes the reversibility of perception. It recognises that reversibility holds both reflexively to a single body (I can perceive at least some of my own body as the same time as I perceive with my body) and between bodies in a shared space (I can perceive others' embodied actions and they can perceive mine). This point is important when considering work that needs to be done in a shared space, whether physical or virtual, and work that does not. It also recognises that individual actions can be done when the actor is alone or when they are in shared space, where the availability of the action for others' perception may or may not contribute to the creation and maintenance of shared meaning. For this reason I have made a fundamental distinction between the embodied actions of an individual interacting primarily with physical objects, other bodies, or the workspace, and the activity of the group as a whole. The distinction recognises that the individual actions of group members enabled the activity of the group. But the activity of the group is something different from these actions and needs its own categories. This distinction becomes crucial in the design of CSCW technology to support work over distance. Individual participants in a cooperative process will always be acting in their local physical space. Some actions may be enabled by the technology, others will occur within their immediate physical environment. But all would need to be incorporated into the technologically-enabled, shared workspace if they were to be available to contribute to group activity.

Inclusion and Exclusion

I make no claim that the actions defined here are "natural", in the sense that they correspond to anything that is not culturally and socially produced. But any process of abstraction, by definition, excludes what is not explicitly included. My judgements about what is included and excluded by the categorisation, as well as how the taxonomy is structured, have been shaped by my perspective as a CSCW researcher concerned with designing systems that support remote collaboration. My aim is to identify those embodied actions, constitutive of shared meaning, that must be considered in any attempt to provide this support.

The categories emerged from an iterative process of viewing videotapes of group design work, identifying and then grouping the embodied actions of the participants. These were checked against further viewings and redefined. There were many iterations of this process until eventually the categories stabilised into those defined here. Some of these categories are already established in various disciplines that study different forms of interaction, including CSCW. I have identified other work I am familiar with, that is relevant to a category, or group of categories when I define the category.

These are not mutually exclusive categories in either the temporal or spatial dimensions. Individuals, or the group, were usually doing more than one of them at any one time. People talked at the same time as they looked at something or moved around the workspace. The actions are categorised separately because they are identifiably separate actions that would require different technological solutions if they were to be mutually perceivable over distance. The categories of group activity all require a range of individual actions occurring simultaneously. In this sense, they are another way of dividing the same analytic space as that of individual actions. While I would argue that the taxonomy accounts for the individual actions and activity of the group in this study, additional categories may be required in other contexts.

The Taxonomy of Embodied Actions

The major divisions in this taxonomy are
- individual embodied actions
  - in relation to physical objects
  - in relation to other bodies
  - in relation to the physical workspace
- group activities constituted by individual embodied actions

Individual Embodied Actions

These have been divided into individual actions performed in relation to objects, other bodies and the workspace. The "in relation to" recognises the indexicality of all embodied actions. Indexicality, in this context, is not used in a narrow linguistic sense, but in the ethnomethodological sense that all actions need to be interpreted within the context they occur (Garfinkel, 1967, pp. 4-7). This is the basis of ethnomethodology's focus on accounting for the "demonstrably rational properties of indexical expressions and indexical actions [that] is an ongoing achievement of the organised achievements of everyday life" (p. 34). I should also emphasise that actions defined in relation to objects and other bodies, have an implicit "in relation to" the physical space in which they occur.

Embodied Actions in Relation to Physical Objects

In their study of the role of 3-D objects in the design process, Harrison and Minneman (1994) argued that "a common thread that runs through all of the ways that objects were used is the relation of hand and eye" (p. 207). The actions in this section are defined from the "other side" of the relationship to the perspective of these studies. The focus here is the embodied actions of designers in relation to objects during that process.

1. Moving physical objects

Actions within this category make it possible for the designers to take advantage of the motility and immutability of physical objects (Seeley Brown and Duguid, 1994, pp. 21-22). Physical objects, including books, pieces of paper and computer disks are essential resources that the designers can move from place to place, as required by the specific unfolding of the design process.

- Moving a physical object into or out of the shared space
- Moving objects within individual workspace (within bodily reach)
- Making a physical object explicitly available, as a generator of meaning, during the current activity, e.g. passing it to someone else, holding it up or putting it somewhere so that it is available

2. Producing a private physical representation

These representations may or may not be available for the perception of others during production. Depending on how the work unfolds, they may or may not be made available during or after production via other actions.

- Drawing - usually on paper
- Writing - usually on paper

3. Highlighting some aspect of an object

Goodwin (1994) defined highlighting as those "methods used to divide a domain of scrutiny into a figure or ground, so that events relevant to the activity of the moment stand out" (pp. 609-610). In this way highlighting shapes "not only one's own perception but also that of others" (ibid). In highlighting, embodied actions are used to tailor the object, by framing, in some way, some part of it. In the study highlighting was done in relation to representations including those on the whiteboard, in books, on sheets of paper and on computer screens.

- Drawing a line around some part of an object with a pen, e.g. annotation, or by gesture alone
- Masking background of representation, or part of object, with one or more of: hand, arm, paper or other object

4. Personal use of a physical object

This action (like 2) may or may not lead into shared use of the object. It can also be a source of information that is then shared with the group

- Browsing through a book

- Working on a computer
- Reading
- Looking at a picture
- Holding object for some, not necessarily obvious, reason
- Touching (including when pointing) to some part of an object

Embodied Actions in Relation to Other Bodies

Kendon (1990) argued that "all aspects of behaviour in a situation must be seen at least, potentially, to have a role in the communication process" (p. 27). He observed that participants in interaction do not attend to all aspects of each others' behaviour in the same way, and do not place the same significance on every action. These distinctions make it possible for people to organise their actions in relation to others without having to explicitly do so. The mutual perception of these actions functions as a way of providing advance information that any one proposing to interact with another has to have (p. 262). Some of these actions are defined within other sections. But those defined here are central to the creation of shared meaning in that they enable the designers' conversation.

1. Emitting signs and monitoring signs
The embodied actions included within this category are those that enable individuals to monitor others' reactions to whatever is happening, as well as the actions that individuals make that indicate their own. These actions are continually performed by each individual. Their availability for mutual perception is an essential condition for the group activity of conversing.
- Visual indicators of individual involvement, attention and attitude including changes in body posture, changing facial expressions, changes in direction and intensity of gaze and other communicative movements like nodding, rolling eyes, gestures
- Oral/aural indicators of individual involvement, attention and attitude including speech and other sounds

2. Pretending to be another body
This category is defined to account for enactment that has been identified as a crucial activity in design (Tang, 1989; Robertson, 1996a). It is defined here as an action where an individual acts out the behaviour of someone else or animates the behaviour of an object. Enactment enables the individual to make and live within a temporal representation of some process or activity. A person, pretending to be another, makes various changes in their usual embodied actions. In a shared space, these changes shape the perceptions of others so that they are able to interpret the action as enactment and participate in it. As enactment is done through time, only a small part of the enacted process needs to be directly considered at any moment enabling the immersion of the participants in the process. This action was often done at the same time as actions in relation to objects.

- Pretending to be the user
- Pretending to be a character in the game
- Animating the behaviour of some inanimate object or process

Embodied Actions in Relation to the Workspace

The workspace includes not just the permanent physical features, such as doors and furniture, but the changing positions of other objects within it (including the bodies of others). These have been considered in previous categories. But the workspace also includes the physical medium through which actions can be performed and perceived - in this case air. The reversibility of perception (Merleau-Ponty, 1968) depends on air as the medium through which bodies intertwine perception and action. The communicative functions of all of the categories defined here depend on the physical properties of the space where the actions are done. Those in this section are defined specifically in relation to the properties of air that enable the embodied actions of moving through and looking through. Gaver (1992) analysed the differences between the affordances (Gibson, 1979) offered by media spaces for collaboration, with those of air. My concern here is the embodied actions of designers in relation to air, as a medium, during the design process.

1. Moving around

Gaver (1992) identified the ability of media spaces to support only static perception as a major interactional constraint. Our perception is seldom static. He argued "Successful systems must *afford* movement" (p. 21).

- To get a better view
- To change bodily alignment to something
- To get an object or put an object somewhere out of immediate reach

2. Pointing at something

The interpretation of what is being pointed at is dependent not just on the act of pointing but on other people being able to perceive what is being pointed at. Pointing is the classic example of an action used to maintain indexicality.

- At an object (including other bodies) somewhere in the workspace, e.g. "have a look in there"
- At something outside the workspace but perceivable from within it, e.g. "the green of that tree"
- As an indicator of direction, e.g. "they live over there"

3. Shifting direction of gaze

Gaver (1992) observed that air is isotropic with respect to light. Isotropism is a term from physics that refers to a material that has characteristics that are the same when measured along any axis (p. 22). Air is the medium through which we look, irrespective of the object or direction of the gaze. The gazer needs to be able to gaze at something and others have to be able to perceive what it is, or that the gazer is just gazing into space which is an indicator of action in itself.

- To look at the current speaker (in order to follow a conversation)
- To look at an object (including other bodies) for some reason
- To look at nothing in particular

4. Moving in or out of the shared space

Individuals would, for a range of reasons, temporarily leave the shared workspace. This category is defined separately to moving around within the workspace because absence from the workspace meant that the individual could not participate in the current group activity, whereas moving round within the workspace contributed to the current group activity. Temporary absences were perceivable, by others, as temporary and the individual's return was assumed.

- To prepare the group lunch
- To meet with a client in another room
- To attend to other responsibilities, including domestic responsibilities
- For no obvious reason

Group Activities Constituted by Individual Embodied Actions

These actions define shared activity in a shared physical space. All rely on the predictable availability of the individual actions of the designers for the perception of the other group members. They identify the different group activities that these individual actions made possible. Technology to support remote design collaboration needs to support these activities across the individual workspaces of the participants. In remote collaboration, the shared workspace is not a shared physical space, but one made possible by computer systems and communication technology. This space does not support the reversibility of perception, but mediates how the embodied actions of the participants are perceived by them.

1. Conversing

The literature devoted to the organisation of conversation is huge (e.g. Garfinkel, 1967; Goodwin, 1981; Suchman, 1987, pp. 68-97; Kendon, 1990). Conversational analysis, a branch of ethnomethodology, has examined the local organisation of human-human conversations in a variety of settings (Heritage, 1984). A number of principles governing the local sequencing of talk have been proposed including turn taking (Sacks et al., 1974) and repair (Schegloff, 1992). Interaction analysis (Jordan and Henderson, 1994) draws on these traditions among others. As would be expected, the organisation of conversation has been an important concern in CSCW research and product development (e.g. Heath and Luff, 1991; Heath et al. 1995; Bowers et al., 1996a). Harrison and Minneman (1995) argued that all the different elements of the design process are "held together by the conversation of the designers". Whatever work the designers did in meetings was accomplished by them talking together. Conversing is the major and essential category in this taxonomy of group activity.

- Maintaining a single conversation involving the whole group
- Maintaining more than one conversation involving different subsets of the group within the same space (individual involvement can vary over time)

2. *Looking at the same thing at the same time*

This activity made the design conversation more robust by enabling the inclusion in the conversation of some aspect of what was being looked at. Company members identified support for this activity, while working apart, as the most urgent requirement for CSCW support.

- Looking at a single shared representation, e.g. whiteboard, book, screen
- Looking at a series of shared representations one at a time
- Looking at a number of shared representations at the same time
- Looking at something in, or perceivable from, the shared workspace

3. *Organising shared communication resources*

These are actions that alter some physical aspect of the workspace in order to make communicative resources available to be the shared focus of group activity. This was done most frequently when the group needed to look at something on a computer and to organise the sequential viewing of files.

- Changing what the group is looking at
- Installing graphic files on the computer
- Installing software to enable group viewing

4. *Creating a shared representation*

Representations may be physical, or temporal/spatial representation. Bly (1988) suggested the importance of drawing activities are as important to collaborative design as the resulting artefacts (see also Tang, 1989). The creation of shared representations was used to express ideas, add meaning to the accompanying talk and to summarise work as it was done.

- Drawing - in the air, using the actor's body as the background, on paper or the whiteboard using a drawing tool
- Writing - using a writing tool, on paper or the whiteboard

5. *Shared physical use of an object*

This activity is distinguished from the others involving various kinds of sharing of objects because more than one individual is in physical contact with the same object in some way at the same time. The shared use of objects became more central to shared design work as the work progressed. This activity is severely compromised, if not impossible, in shared drawing systems that impose separate layers for each participant or those that impose locking systems to prevent or place conditions on shared use.

- Performing the same action, e.g. drawing

- Performing different actions, e.g. one person highlighting at the same time as another is drawing

6. *Focusing group attention*

This is usually initiated by one person's actions. But the group, as a group, perceives the action and reorients its attention. This category enables changes in group focus and is used as a way of structuring the conversation.

- Focusing on a shared object or representation
- Focusing on a speaker
- Focusing on a specific group activity

7. *Breaking into smaller groups and reforming*

When some aspect of the design work required it, people moved themselves and various objects in the workspace to form into smaller groups. The larger group would reform when this stage of the work was completed. People in different subgroups were peripherally aware of the activities of the other group/s and could participate in these at will. Interaction and movement between groups occurred with minimal overhead.

- To enable smaller groups to work on specific parts of the developing design, e.g. graphics, coding or planning
- To enable a smaller group to work on one project while monitoring the progress of another group

8. *Seizing the moment*

Group members took advantage of lulls in the group activity for the opportunistic use of time they were together to do something unplanned. The unplanned activity could include the whole group but was often done when one or more of the others was attending to an interruption, or to other work. At these times the main activity of the group was interrupted, providing opportunities for this activity.

- Asking a question about something else to do with work, e.g. technical information
- Used for explicit social interaction, e.g. to discuss movies, tell jokes

9. *Doing something else*

Individuals occasionally did something other than the group activity, while remaining in the same physical space. Those doing other work are aware of group activity, usually by listening, even if they are not actively participating. Should they wish to participate at any time, they can do so by changing their spatial position and orientation. Perceptual clues for this category include positioning the body to face away from the group and prolonged personal use of a physical object.

- Doing other work, e.g. meeting deadlines on other products
- Disinterest in current group activity
- Personal preference

Discussion

Mapping the actions defined in the taxonomy back onto the videotapes of cooperative design work revealed that irrespective of the stage in the development of the product, the same actions were used to achieve whatever specific work was being done. As would be expected, the spread, frequency and combination of the different actions varied, depending on what the specific work was. There were no occasions when the embodied actions of the designers were performed in any predetermined sequence. Nor were there any occasions when designers were performing individual actions in unison, even though they were participating in the same group activities. This is not to say that there were no patterns of interaction. Certain actions frequently occurred together, though not necessarily in any fixed sequence. For example, someone may leaf through a book to find a picture. When they find it they hold it up for the others to see, frequently highlighting some part of the picture. Other people move to get a better view and may point to the picture while discussing it. Highlighting connected physical objects with the design conversation, particularly when the group were looking at the same thing at the same time. These actions were performed purposefully and opportunistically by the designers as they worked to create and maintain shared meaning. Nevertheless they constituted the work of cooperative design at the same time as they enabled it to continue.

But the fact that these actions occurred throughout the cooperative design process, from early discussions through to the building of a prototype, demonstrates that people's embodied actions are not tied to specific functional stages of the design process, nor to any explicitly defined design procedure. This would suggest that technology, designed to support cooperative design over distance, might be more effectively directed to supporting the negotiation of shared meaning by the designers rather than attempting to structure the design process according to any functional categorisations of design work. The basic argument of this paper is that what needs to be supported, mediated and enabled by CSCW technology used to support design communication over distance is the mutual perception, for the actor and others, of the embodied actions of the participants in the process. All the categories of embodied action, defined in the taxonomy, function as communicative actions in shared physical space because physical space enables the reversibility of perception (Merleau-Ponty, 1968). Yet the reversibility of perception, a fact of human embodiment in physical space, is not a fact of virtual spaces.

In shared physical space we can predict how our actions are perceived by others because we can perceive them ourselves as we live them. In technology-mediated communication individual participants will always be acting in their local physical space at the same time as they act in virtual space. Self-perception, then, will require not just the assumed resources of the local physical space but the development of perceptual skills and the provision of perceptual resources to enable each individual to perceive their own actions as they appear to other participants. Put another way, a basic principle in the design of CSCW technology to support cooperative work over distance is that the perception by others of any individual's actions needs to be explicitly regarded as part of the same process, or act of perception, as that individual's perception of their own actions. I am perfectly aware of what a "big ask" this is. Developing technology to support the reversibility of perception of even one of these actions, with the finesse and flexibility of selection and combination available to embodied users in shared physical space, would be a major achievement in itself. But this does not mean that the provision of perceptual resources people need to organise their own actions in relation to others' actions ought not to be a central focus of technology design.

The taxonomy presented here is intended to structure the results of a field study of cooperative work in a way that might bridge the gap between the work itself and the design of technology to support that work if it were to be done over distance. Its immediate value may lie in enabling us, as researchers and designers of CSCW systems, to recognise the actions that our systems do not support and perhaps cannot support. On one level, this recognition may enable a clearer understanding of what our systems do, in fact, support in practice. On another it may lead to the development of perceptual resources in virtual space that are compensatory or even analogous to those provided by physical space.

Acknowledgements

My thanks, again, to the people whose work I have discussed in this paper. This research was partly financed by an Internal Research Grant from the University of Technology, Sydney and by the Telstra Fund for Social and Policy Research in Telecommunications.

References

Benford, S., Bowers J., Fahlen, L., Greenhalgh, C. and Snowdon, D. (1995): User Embodiment in Collaborative Virtual Environments. In *Mosaic of Creativity, Proceedings of CHI '95*, Denver, Colorado, USA, May 7-11, 1995. New York: ACM Press, pp. 242-249.

Bly, Sarah. (1988): A Use of Drawing Surfaces in Different Collaborative Settings. In *Proceedings of CSCW '88*. New York: ACM Press, pp. 250-256.

Bowers, J., Pycock, J. and O'Brien, J. (1996a): Practically Accomplishing Immersion: Cooperation in and for Virtual Environments. In *Cooperating Communities, Proceedings of CSCW '96*. Boston, Massachusetts, USA, November 16-20, 1996. New York: ACM Press, pp. 58-65.

Bowers, J., O'Brien, J. and Pycock, J. (1996b): Talk and Embodiment in Collaborative Virtual Environments. In *Common Ground, Proceedings of CHI '96*. Vancouver, British Columbia, Canada, April 13-18, 1996. New York: ACM Press, pp. 380-389.

Garfinkel, H. (1967): *Studies in Ethnomethodology*. Prentice-Hall, N. J.

220

Gaver, W. W., Smets, G. and Oberbeeke, K. (1995): A Virtual Window on Media Space. In *Mosaic of Creativity, Proceedings of CHI '95*, Denver, Colorado, USA, May 7-11, 1995. New York: ACM Press, pp. 257-264.

Gaver, W. W. (1992): The Affordances of Media Spaces for Collaboration. In *Sharing Perspectives, Proceedings of CSCW '92*, Toronto, Canada, October 31 to November 4, 1992. New York: ACM Press, pp. 17-24.

Gibson, J. J. (1979): *The Ecological Approach to Visual Perception.* Houghton Mifflin. London.

Goodwin, C. (1994): Professional Vision. *American Anthropologist*, 96, 3. American Anthropological Association. USA, pp. 606-633.

Haraway, D. J. (1991): Situated Knowledges. In *Simians, Cyborgs, and Women: The Reinvention of Nature.* Free Association Books. London, pp. 183-201.

Harrison, S. and Minneman S. (1994): A Bike In Hand: a study of 3-D objects in design. In *Analysing Design Activity - The Delft Protocols Workshop*, Delft University of Technology, pp. 205-218.

Harrison, S. and Minneman, S. (1995): Studying Collaborative Design to Build Design Tools. In *Proceedings of Computer-Aided Architectural Design Futures '95*, Singapore.

Heath, C., Luff, P. and Sellen, A. (1995): Reconsidering the Virtual Workplace: Flexible Support for Collaborative Activity. In *ECSCW '95 Proceedings of the Fourth European Conference on Computer-Supported Cooperative Work*, pp. 83-99.

Heath, C. and Luff P. (1991): Disembodied Conduct: Communication through video in a multimedia office environment. In *Proceedings of CHI '91*, New Orleans, Louisiana, April 28-May 2, 1991. New York: ACM Press, pp. 99-103.

Heritage, J. (1984): *Garfinkel and ethnomethodology.* Polity Press, Cambridge.

Jordan, B. and Henderson, A. (1994): Interaction Analysis: Foundations and Practice. The Journal of the Learning Sciences, 4: 1: 39-102.

Kendon, A. (1990): Conducting Interaction. Cambridge University Press. UK.

Merleau-Ponty, M. (1968): The Intertwining the Chiasm. In The Visible and the Invisible. Northwestern University Press, Illinios, USA. [France, 1964]. pp. 130-155.

Merleau-Ponty, M. (1962): Phenomenology of Perception. Routledge. UK. [France, 1945].

Robertson, T. (1996a): Embodied Actions in Time and Place: The Design of a Multimedia, Educational Computer Game. Computer Supported Cooperative Work: The Journal of Collaborative Computing, vol 5, no 4, pp. 1-27.

Robertson, T. (1996b): The Constraints and Resources of a Distributed Workplace. In Proceedings of Oz-CSCW 96. Brisbane, Queensland, August 30th, 1996. Brisbane: DSTC. pp. 57-65.

Sacks, H., Schegloff, E. and Jefferson, G. (1974): A simplest systematics for turn-taking in conversation. Language 50, pp. 696-735.

Seeley Brown, J. and Duguid, P. (1994): Borderline Issues: Social and Material Aspects of Design. In *Human-Computer Interaction* , Vol 9, pp. 3-36.

Schegloff, E. A. (1992): Repair after Next Turn: The Last Structurally Provided Defense of Intersubjectivity in Conversation. *American Journal of Sociology*, 97, 5, pp. 1295-1345.

Suchman, L. (1987): *Plans and Situated Actions.* Cambridge University Press, NY.

Tang, J. C. (1989): *Listing, Drawing, and Gesturing in Design: A Study of the Use of Shared Workspaces by Design Teams.* Xerox PARC Technical Report, SSL-89-3, Palo Alto, CA. (Doctoral Dissertation, Stanford University).

Varela, F. J., Thompson, E. and Rosch, E. (1991): *The Embodied Mind.* MIT Press. USA.

Aether: An Awareness Engine for CSCW

Ovidiu Sandor[1], Cristian Bogdan[1], and John Bowers[1,2]

[1] CID and IPLab, The Royal Institute of Technology, Stockholm, Sweden

[2] Department of Psychology, University of Manchester, Manchester, UK

ovidiu@nada.kth.se, cristi@nada.kth.se, bowers@hera.psy.man.ac.uk

Abstract: Extending and reinterpreting earlier work on the 'Spatial Model', this paper presents a generic model for supporting awareness in cooperative systems ('the AETHER model') and an implementation of a prototype awareness engine. The applicability of the approach is investigated by showing how some of the fundamental functionality in CSCW applications (e.g. versioning and access control) can be supported by the engine and by 'simulating' some other applications from the CSCW literature. The paper closes with a discussion of how the model facilitates the construction of flexible CSCW systems (e.g. workflow systems) supporting a variety of forms of awareness.

Introduction

The topic of awareness has received a great deal of attention in recent work in Computer Supported Cooperative Work (CSCW). Providing participants with mutual awareness of each other's activities is often seen as a important research and design goal (e.g. Dourish et al., 1992; Tollmar et al., 1996). The emphasis of much of this research is to provide an alternative way of supporting cooperative work to that found in, for example, workflow systems (e.g. Glance et al., 1996) where work activities are given a formal representation in terms of some workflow model which often stipulates how the contributions of different participants are to be coordinated. In contrast, in many awareness-oriented systems, the coordination between different activities is supported by giving participants an awareness of what each other are doing or have done so that participants can coordinate their work themselves. Many researchers would hope that, not only does this provide a 'truer' and more 'lightweight' sense for 'support', but would also make for more flexible applica-

221

J. Hughes et al. (eds.), Proceedings of the Fifth European Conference on Computer Supported Cooperative Work, 221-236.
© 1997 *Kluwer Academic Publishers.*

tions which are not liable to the usability criticisms (cf. Bowers et al., 1995) that can be made of more procedural-oriented approaches to CSCW.

Perhaps these arguments find their most detailed elaboration in work on Collaborative Virtual Environments (CVEs), where Virtual Reality (VR) technology is used to support cooperative applications such as virtual conferencing or collaborative information visualization and retrieval. Most notably, the COMIC project offered a 'Spatial Model' of interaction in shared virtual environments (Benford et al., 1994, 1995) which has provided the basis of a number of experimental applications as well as influencing the fundamental architecture of at least two VR systems: DIVE (Carlsson et al., 1992) and MASSIVE (Greenhalgh et al., 1996). The question arises, however, of how this research theme is to be further advanced as a major constituent of CSCW endeavour.

We would wish to argue that some of the most promising work currently on the theme of awareness in CSCW is concerned with one or both of two issues. First, there exist attempts to integrate support for awareness at fundamental levels of cooperative system architecture. We have already mentioned how the DIVE and MASSIVE VR systems implement awareness-oriented notions. Trevor et al. (1994) report on how a shared object service can be designed to facilitate user's awareness to the state of and changes in shared objects. Further attempts to 'build in' awareness as a foundational feature of cooperative systems are likely to be seen. Secondly, some of the concepts, models and notations elaborated in the development of awareness-oriented applications and systems will be found to have a broader utility. As an example of this, see Rodden's (1996) work showing how support for awareness can be added to workflow, shared databases and other cooperative systems.

In this paper, we attempt to address both these issues. First we show how concepts derived from the COMIC Spatial Model (cf. Benford et al., 1994, 1995) can be reinterpreted to have general utility beyond the domain of shared virtual environments which was their initial application. We present how we use the model and the new concepts we introduce. We describe the current implementation of an awareness engine, called AETHER, based on the suggested model. Our goal is to recognise awareness at a fundamental system level and to build other functions on top of it. In order to demonstrate the implementation, we present some small applications that we have developed as well as some ideas about how other systems can be implemented. The paper ends with plans for future development as well as drawing out the general implications of our work for CSCW research.

The Spatial Model

As the Spatial Model, largely developed in the European Communities' COMIC project (1992-1995), forms the basis for our work, we will spend a little time describing its essential elements. The Spatial Model supposes that objects (which might represent people, information or other computer artefacts) can be regarded as situated and manipulable in some space. The notion of space is very generally conceived only subject to the constraint that well-defined metrics for measuring position and orientation across a set of dimensions can be found. In principle, any application where objects can be regarded as distributed along dimensions such that their position and orientation can be measurably determined is amenable to analysis in terms of the Spatial Model.

The interaction between objects in space is mediated through the relationships obtaining between three subspaces: aura, focus and nimbus. It is assumed that an object will carry with it an aura which, when it sufficiently intersects with the aura of another object, will make it possible for interaction between the objects to take place. On this view, an aura intersection is the pre-condition of further interaction. For objects whose aurae intersect, further computations are carried out to determine the awareness levels the objects have of each other. The subspaces of focus and nimbus are intended as representing the spatial extent of an object's 'attention' and its 'presence'. Thus, "if you are an object in space, a simple formulation might be: the more an object is within your focus, the more aware you are of it; the more an object is within your nimbus, the more aware it is of you." and accordingly, "given that interaction has first been enabled through aura collision: The level of awareness that object A has of object B in medium M is some function of A's focus in M and B's nimbus in M." (Benford et al., 1994)

It is important to note that in the above definition, awareness-levels are defined per medium. Thus, the 'shape' and 'size' of each of the aura, focus and nimbus subspaces can be different, for example, in the visual (graphical) than in the audio-medium. In this way, I may be aware of the sounds made by another object but without being able to see it. Benford et al. (1994, 1996) go on to show how simple instantiations of this model can have a high degree of expressive power, for example enabling one to distinguish between different intuitively familiar 'modes of mutual awareness' on the basis of the possible relationships between A's awareness of B and B's awareness of A. However, perhaps the most important point emphasised in this work is the insistence that awareness is a joint-product of how I direct my attention to you (focus) and how you project your presence or activity to me (nimbus). Applications which recognise only one of these two components may well be experienced as too intrusive or too inflexible.

In recent work, various extensions of the Spatial Model have been reported. For example, Benford et. al. (1997) have introduced a concept of 'third party objects' which 'intervene' between objects and transform the nature and level of the awareness that the objects might otherwise have, and, importantly, Rodden (1996) has re-interpreted the Spatial Model in terms of spaces which can be represented as graphs of interconnected objects.

The AETHER Model

Our further development of the Spatial Model and the idea of an 'awareness engine' resulted from our previous studies like @WORK (Tollmar et al., 1996) and related projects such as CoDesk (Tollmar et al., 1995) where different awareness clues for supporting information sharing and casual interaction are provided. CoDesk was developed as an open environment where new applications could be added for specific tasks like editing or communication. Other systems have been taking similar approaches, e.g. GroupDesk (Fuchs et al., 1995) or TeamRooms (Roseman et al., 1996). We have been using CoDesk as a 'target system' for our awareness engine, so as an introduction to the Aether model we will present how the awareness engine would relate to the overall architecture of a system like CoDesk.

The Structure of the System

We place the awareness engine at a basic level of system architecture (Figure 1). The engine is intended to provide applications with the necessary information about what users are doing or have done.

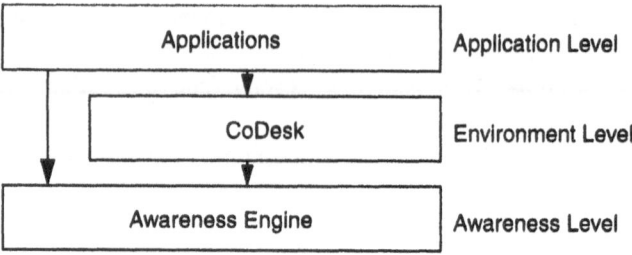

Figure 1. The Place of the Awareness Engine in the Structure of the CoDesk system.

The second level is that of the environment. This will include all the basic functionality: shared file access, access control, versioning, communication channels, etc. All these functions are to be built on top of the awareness engine.

The top level is the application level where specific awareness information is collated and presented to the user. Applications are written based on the functionality provided by the second level. They can interact with the awareness engine in two ways: by interacting with the environment or by directly accessing the engine.

The Semantic Network

Traditional CSCW systems usually keep a *structural network* of objects. For example, a classical shared file system can be represented as a tree structure by means of the 'containment' relation. Other kinds of relation can have their own representation. For example, ownership may be represented in terms of parameters associated with relevant files or folders. Inspired by systems like GroupDesk we also integrate representations of users and groups, as well as the result of their actions, into the structure obtaining a *semantic network* that forms a "representation of the working context" (Fuchs et al., 1995). This network made of *objects* interconnected by *directed relations* comprises the space in which awareness computations are done.

The *objects* in the network can be any entity (files, folders, applications, people, groups, sessions, whatever) defined by the environment and its applications. The awareness engine will treat all objects in the same way making no assumptions about the kinds of thing the objects represent. The *relations* that connect the different objects can also be of any type: structural relations (e.g. containment), user interaction relations (e.g. open file), property relations, and so forth. Once again it is up to the environment and its applications to define the specific type of relations. This semantic network creates a *space* in the sense similar to that suggested by Rodden (1996). This network will be the space in which aura, nimbus and focus are defined and in which the awareness levels between the different objects are computed.

Moving Away From Events

In many existing CSCW systems awareness information is obtained by means of *events*. User actions like file access, modifications, etc., are monitored, selected according to some criteria, and eventually recorded as event lists. For example, Fuchs et al.'s GROUPDESK keeps lists of events which are used to provide 'asynchronous awareness' even if some of the information in this event list duplicates information which could be derived from the semantic network. Events are discharged based on some distribution strategies defined in advance. As Fuchs et al. show, such event based systems seem to work satisfactorily for situations where workflow can be clearly defined in advance or if the application is known from the beginning.

However, as we remarked in the Introduction, much of the promise of awareness-oriented CSCW systems lies in their potential to offer a flexible alternative to strictly defined workflow approaches. So it would be somewhat ironic if an awareness mechanism only worked adequately in tandem with a system supporting somewhat rigid workflows. In contrast, systems like @WORK are intended to address groups of users with highly flexible working arrangements. This would make it hard to define appropriate selection criteria and distribution strategies in advance, an argument which is especially telling for systems (like CODESK) which provide an environment for new applications (and hence new user-actions and event-types) to be readily built. Thus, for the systems we are interested in, an event distribution approach for supporting awareness does not seem appropriate.

As an alternative we propose keeping all objects and relations in the net, even after their expiration, and using Spatial Model concepts to determine awareness levels for them. Instead of removing expired objects and relations we mark them as invalid. With this we have no need for event lists because the information that those contain is now in the objects and relations of the network. What we obtain is a semantic network containing both the actual state of the system as well as all history information. Of course, the disadvantage of this approach is the quick growth of the size of the net but later we discuss some ways for reducing this size.

Reformulating 'Time' and 'Medium' Spatially

By keeping the invalid relations in the network, we can compute meaningful aware-ness information not only about what happens right now but also about past events. In this way we can say that our space equally contains two aspects: the semantic and the temporal. Time now becomes one of the 'dimensions' of the space, the concepts of the Spatial Model equally applying to it as to any other dimension.

A cognate approach can be taken to the notion of a 'medium' of communication. In the original Spatial Model, medium was loosely defined based on an intuitive un-derstanding of this concept or, in Rodden's (1996) generalization, as a label on aura, nimbus and focus. In our case, as the space we have is not geometrical, we found it necessary to devote more attention to this concept. By medium we understand (a) a well defined type of information, (b) a subspace that has the capability to carry that specific information and (c) some objects that 'understand' that medium. Two ob-jects that understand the same medium can communicate though it. Information will be generated by one of the objects, will travel through the medium subspace and will be received by the second object. An analogy is radio, where an antenna trans-mits an electromagnetic wave that will propagate through all objects, even if these are not sensitive to it, while a radio, which can 'understand' the wave, will convert it to sound. For us, the medium's subspace is made of objects and relations, even if those do not understand that respective medium. Aura, nimbus and focus will be de-fined per medium subspace.

Medium also has a time component. For example, a medium can define a sub-space that contains only those objects and relations that have been valid during some time period. In this way we can obtain a time window. In this approach, a mo-ment can be defined by collapsing the time window. Thus, in a 'synchronous medi-um' the time moment of 'now' is achieved by filtering out everything that is in the past. The 'synchronous' becomes a subcase of the 'asynchronous'. We suggest that this will facilitate systems to provide smooth transitions between different forms of communication, a point we shall return to at the end of this paper.

Aura, Nimbus and Focus

Aura in our model is much the same as defined in the initial Spatial Model. It de-scribes the potential for collaboration between two objects. If there is sufficient aura intersection (e.g. collision) then there is potential interaction between them. Given our approach to the notion of a 'medium', aura is defined by the medium rather than objects themselves. Nimbus and focus in our system have much the same meaning as in the Spatial Model. Each object or relation can control its focus and nimbus to specify their 'willingness' to become aware of others or fall within their awareness. Given the temporal aspects of medium just argued for, it should be observed that aura, nimbus and focus also have a time component. Thus, a user can 'focus' on the present moment, on the past or even on the future. This is exploited in a prototype versioning system presented later on.

We considered that our engine would be most flexible if both objects and relations in our network could have aura, nimbus and focus. By allowing a relation to have nimbus we allow users to get notified about the presence of a relation. In this way the user is aware not only of objects but also of the activity of others to the extent that this is depicted in the relations and changes to them. As we shall shortly see, however, this necessitates a reconceptualization of how awareness can propagate through our space.

Presence

People and other agents can manifest a presence in the network space. Presence is defined as (a) the agent, (b) an application that the agent uses for manifesting its presence in one or more media and (c) the object where the presence is located in the net. For our purposes, an agent can be a person, a group of people, or a computer agent. We say that an application is present in a medium if it 'understands' that respective medium. The object defining the location is much like Rodden's (1996) definition of presence in non-geometrical spaces. Like him, we allow an agent to be present in more than one place in more than one medium at any given moment.

Medium Consumption

In the initial Spatial Model the level of awareness that an object A has of an object B in medium M is computed, if aura collision exists, as "some function of A's focus on B in M and B's nimbus on A in M" (Benford et al., 1994). That is, the awareness-level is obtained through a negotiation between A and B by means of controlling their respective foci and nimbi. We would like to add to this a new concept: space as an aura, nimbus and focus 'consumer'. Our point is twofold: first, that the level of awareness should not depend only on the two objects but also on the nature of the space between them, and secondly that space cannot be seen as an empty, passive 'container' for aura, nimbus and focus but rather become an actor in 'negotiation' of the awareness levels.

Fog provides a relevant analogy. Fog consumes part of the light and the sound passing through it, filtering out the fine details of objects perceived through a fog-filled subspace. Indeed, fog not only fills a subspace but also comprises a collectivity of very small objects, each one with a specific behaviour and a filtering effect. It is this conception of space as always 'filled' which motivates our choice of name: AETHER.

Accordingly, we redefine the level of awareness that object A has of object B in medium M, in case of aura collision, as being some function of A's focus in M *'filtered by'* the space between A and B and B's nimbus in M *'filtered by'* the space between B and A. This definition necessitates two remarks concerning our notion of spaces consuming focus and the rest. First, consumption is not necessarily symmetrical, that is, the consumption depends on the direction of the information flow. For example, the consumption of nimbus from A to B can be different to the one from

B to A. Second, consumption need not have only a diminishing effect as some elements in a space may also amplify aura, nimbus or focus.

The idea of consumption relates with other concepts of the Spatial Model used for manipulating aura, nimbus and focus. For example adapters (Benford et al., 1994) and third party objects (Benford et al., 1997) are mechanisms used for the same purpose. The main difference is that both concepts use objects for this manipulation. Our model is more general, space itself having this effect on aura, nimbus and focus, with space comprising not just objects but also their relations in a structured semantic network. Objects and relations in our system thus have a double role. First they are the ones manifesting their presence by generating aura, nimbus and focus. At the same time they form the space of the model so they will become consumers of aura, nimbus and focus. As such, any object or relation in our system can be seen, and used, as an adapter or third party object.

The consumption of aura, nimbus and focus also has a meaning in the time dimension. After all, time does have an effect on the importance of objects and relations. For example the importance of a certain user action might decrease in time; it might be important right now or five minutes later but it might have no importance at all in one month.

According to this new definition, the computation of the aura, nimbus and focus becomes a negotiation between the two objects or relations (A and B), the medium that both of them 'understand' (M) and the space between the two. The medium M defines the aurae of A and B while the aura consumption is defined by the objects and relations on the relevant path(s) between them. If the aurae intersect at some point at a high enough level, then focus and nimbus computations will take place. A will define its initial nimbus value, then the different objects and relations on the path(s) between A and B will consume it. B will define the initial value of its focus and again the objects and relations on the path(s) between the place B is focusing on and A will consume it.

The Percolation Mechanism

Before describing the implementation, let us explain how we see aura, nimbus and focus 'permeating the Aether'. Although there are a number of possibilities, we have explored a concept of percolation. Consider a case when the aura associated with an object A percolates from A (its 'source') through the objects and relations that belong to the relevant medium's subspace. The objects and relations which are neighbours of A will each consume the aura to some degree, as will, in turn, the neighbours of these neighbours. And so forth. The process of percolation stops wherever the aura level decreases to some threshold or below (zero in our case).

In Figure 2 we have an example of aura percolation. The numbers next to the different objects show the level of aura reaching it. We can see how the aura of the object labelled 12 is consumed from one object to another, except between objects labelled 9 and 15 where it is amplified. The relations or objects that do not belong to the medium M subspace are not taken into consideration in the percolation.

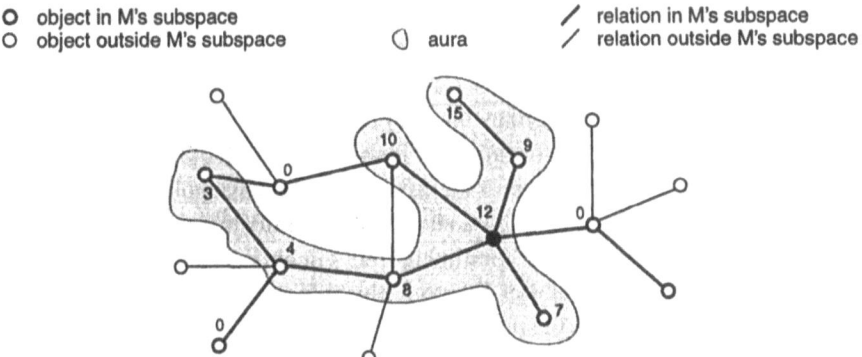

Figure 2. The Percolation of the Aura (or of the Nimbus).

We use the same percolation mechanism for nimbus but, for focus, we 'source' the focus not from the object whose focus it is but from the object(s) or relation(s) on whom focus is directed.

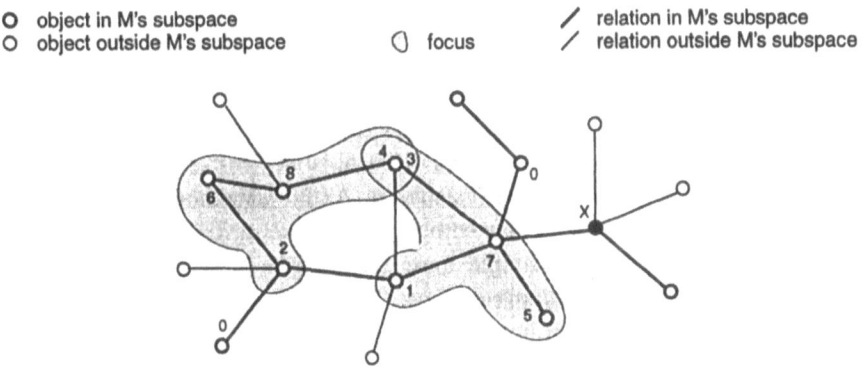

Figure 3. The Percolation of Focus.

In Figure 3 the focus of object X is made of two percolations, one centred in object 8 and one in object 7. The use of the percolation for focus is like saying "I am interested in these and what is around them."

Implementation

Currently a running implementation of the AETHER awareness engine is being experimented with. The engine maintains a network of objects and relations, though for reasons of parsimony and convenience, in our implementation the relations are defined as objects as well. Each relation points to two objects, a *from* and a *to* object to define the directionality of the relations. An object can point to none, one or more relations. In this way, what we have called 'objects' and 'relations' so far can be thought of as specializations of a *component* concept.

A component (object or relation) has a nimbus value and a nimbus 'strategy' attached. The nimbus strategy defines the way nimbus percolation will take place. Each component can also have one or more focus points, each of them with a focus value and a focus strategy. It is up to the environment or any application to set the focus point(s), the nimbus/focus values and to set or modify the nimbus/focus strategies. A percolation strategy, be it for nimbus, focus or aura, is defined as a function that answers the question "is object X part of object Y's nimbus/focus/aura?"

A medium in our implementation has to define (a) the medium's subspace and (b) the aura percolation strategy. The subspace is defined by means of a function that answers the question "is object X in medium M's subspace?". The presence of an agent is implemented by using a presence object. This object is connected to (a) a user, group or software agent by a 'represents' relation, (b) an application by a 'uses' relation and (c) a component in the net that defines the location by a 'visits' relation. Each component also contains the definition of the way in which aura, nimbus and focus are to be consumed. In the case of relations, consumption can vary according to the direction of percolation. Consumptions are defined as strategies that answer the question "how much of the aura/nimbus/focus value will remain?"

As we see, for each object the environment or the applications have to define a number of percolation and consumption strategies. In order to simplify things we have developed a number of basic strategies. These strategies can be logically combined in order to obtain more sophisticated ones. At the same time, any application can define new strategies rather than combine the pre-defined ones. In this way, it is hoped that the engine is both simple to use and flexible. An example of a pre-defined strategy is the 'now' medium subspace. The answer to "is object X in medium M's subspace?" will be "yes, if it is valid".

The Algorithm

Now we can define the awareness level computation algorithm. The computation is done for each medium separately. For a given object or relation (source), the engine starts from its neighbours as the first set of candidates, with a given initial strength. Each candidate is then checked as to whether it included in the medium's subspace, by asking the medium's subspace strategy. If it is, then the aura (defined in the medium), nimbus or focus (defined in the origin object) strategy is asked to confirm that candidate. If it gets accepted then the candidate's consumption strategy is asked to compute the new strength that reached it. If there is some strength left, the candidate becomes part of the computed subspace, having its membership characterized by this strength. Its neighbours will be considered as candidates in the next step. This process continues until no other candidates can be considered.

The awareness level between two objects A and B is defined as four strength values: A's focus on B, A's nimbus to B, B's focus on A, B's nimbus to A. If A's and B's aurae don't have common components (i.e. there is no adequate aura intersection), these values are null. After all the computations have been done, each presence object will get a vector of all components with whom it has aura collision and the respective awareness levels. As the intention is to provide as much generality as possible, the decision on how to interpret the four values is left to the application in question. One way would be to interpret them according to the 'modes of mutual awareness' as defined in Benford et al. (1994) and Bowers (1993).

The computation is repeated after any change in the network, that is after any user action that affects the state of the system. In order to reduce the data traffic between the engine and the applications, AETHER keeps track of the awareness level between every presence object and the other components. After each re-computation the new awareness levels are compared to the old ones and changes are reported to the applications.

We have defined an Application Programming Interface (API) for the AETHER engine to support communication between it and CODESK or the applications. The engine API is a very simple one, letting applications add, validate or invalidate relations and change strategies, and in the other direction, allowing the engine to announce awareness levels to the applications.

Computational Considerations

It is obvious that the AETHER model will raise issues concerning computing time and network size, especially if relations and objects continue to be stored after their invalidation time. We can address the computational complexity problem in several ways. The engine currently makes use of a number of techniques to reduce the number of computations, for example by performing multiple changes in the net before awareness level recomputation. Parallelization is another possible approach. As calculations in different media (and calculation of nimbus and focus in the same medium) can proceed independently of each other, CPUs can be allocated on a per medium (or per awareness-subspace) basis.

Computation time can also be facilitated by carefully managing the size of the network. In this regard, we suggest that from time to time certain objects and relations can be removed in a process much like garbage collection. The question is which objects and relations are important to maintain and which are of lesser significance and can be removed. Ultimately, 'importance' can only be properly defined at the application level, though we do provide a general technique at the awareness engine level which can be used quite flexibly in default of specific requirements made by the application.

In our model, the importance of a component is defined by its nimbus in time and our garbage collection algorithm periodically applies some consumption of this nimbus in terms of a function which reduces its value according to the distance in time since invalidation. The engine then removes the components whose nimbus falls below a given threshold. The system also removes relations connected to objects that have just been deleted and, if this now leaves objects without relations, then these are deleted too.

While this algorithm seems to work well for the applications we have experimented with, there is clearly scope for refining it. For example, we could relate the importance of an object to the number of times it has been 'visited' by users. An object visited often may be more important than one not visited at all. A visit could have the effect of incrementing the nimbus of the object, thus tending to increase its longevity.

Applying the AETHER Model

In order to demonstrate the feasibility of our approach we have developed a number of small applications. We have primarily concentrated on showing how services often thought to be fundamental to cooperative applications can be readily supported in the AETHER model, in particular, the management of versioning, history and access control. To demonstrate the generality of our model we have also simulated a version of Isaacs et al.'s (1996) PIAZZA prototype awareness system. We briefly discuss these applications in turn.

Versioning and History

Some kind of versioning is normally needed in CSCW applications. We will show one way of implementing it with the awareness engine. Each version of a document (say) is represented as an object in our net. A 'is-previous-version-of' relation binds the different versions into a version tree. A user can access the latest version or can focus on some previous time moment, by selecting the appropriate focus strategy, and access the versions that existed at that moment. Users could also have access to any other information about these documents, like for example who changed them and who's read them, by controlling nimbus and the focus.

In many cases, it is likely that after a while the number of versions would be too big and some would have to be removed. The point would be to remove the minor versions and to keep the important ones. For this, the versioning module would have to set the nimbus of the different versions in such a way that by applying the garbage collection algorithm the desired effect would be obtained. One way to do this would be to relate the level of nimbus in time with how much the new version differs from the previous one. In case of minor changes the nimbus would be small, while extensive changes would generate a high nimbus and would remain in the system for a long time.

History is a related problem but it refers to user actions over time instead of documents. Very many history events can be deduced from the time information of the different relations that represent user actions. By setting the focus strategy to some moment in time the user would be notified about the state of the system at that time around the point of focus. By displaying all the changes in the objects and relations (creation or invalidation) between two moments in time we could reconstruct a history of events. It may be that some components have been removed from the network but, as important events tend to be more long-lasting, this method of reconstructing history should be satisfactory for many purposes.

Access Control

Another important functionality needed in CSCW is access control. An interesting way to do this in the AETHER model is to have access control media. For example we could define a 'Top Secret' medium. The boundaries protecting an area that contains sensitive information could consume completely the aura, nimbus and focus of all other access media, except for the 'Top Secret' one. Only users that are allowed to use this medium would be able to notice the presence of those objects and access them. In this approach, boundaries can be realised by particular kinds of objects in the net which consume aura and the rest and can exert constraints on navigation through the net (cf. Bowers, 1993).

Another interesting approach would be to build on a suggestion in Benford et al. (1996). A 'Foyer' could be used for entering the system. One of the functions of the foyer is to "enhance security by providing a single point of entry... within which incoming and outgoing people are made publicly visible and hence accountable". The system could have such an entry point where all users would have to start and at which their capabilities (or 'strategies' in the sense used above) for manipulating and consuming aura, focus and nimbus would be defined. A guest, to give just one possible example, may have a more limited focus (so that they tend to access less) but a larger nimbus (so that other users are likely to be made aware of them and their activities) than a 'registered user'. As these capabilities can be defined on a per medium basis, a very flexible approach to access control is possible through the AETHER model. We refer to a given profile of awareness manipulation and consumption strategies as a 'character'. While taking on a specified character may be necessary to gain full access to a certain medium subspace, this is much more flexible than traditional approaches which typically give and withhold 'access rights' to 'roles'.

A Simulated PIAZZA

Our final test of the feasibility of the AETHER model and our awareness engine implementation is a 'simulation' of PIAZZA, an application prototyped by Isaacs et al. (1996), which provides users with information concerning "others who are doing similar tasks when they are using their computers, thereby enabling unintended interactions" (p. 315). PIAZZA comprises a number of sub-applications, two of which we have reimplemented using the concepts of the AETHER model: GALLERY which allows the user to get information about other group members, and ENCOUNTER, a component which can be added to any application and which makes users aware of others who may be "nearby" (see Isaacs et al., p. 319-321).

Our GALLERY is an application that sets its focus on the people selected by the user. The application uses a percolation strategy that will define the focus in terms of those relations around a person that show their current activities. When such activities exist, the application will present to the user what the others are doing and where in the network space they are. Our version of ENCOUNTER is a file browser that, in addition to traditional functionality, informs the user about the presence of others in the same subdirectory of the file system. The application sets the focus around the directory where the user is located and uses a strategy that monitors any other presence in that place. Our treatment of temporal relations as also being part of the network enables us to entertain extensions of Isaacs et al.'s work so that users can become selectively aware of others who have shared the same directory space at different past times. Accordingly, an ENCOUNTER application built upon our awareness engine may be able to support a richer set of "unintended interactions" and social encounters than Isaacs et al. currently discuss.

Discussion

We hope that we have demonstrated the feasibility of the AETHER model as a source of concepts for an awareness engine for CSCW. We believe that several forms of basic functionality for cooperative applications can be readily and flexibly implemented in an AETHER-style engine and have outlined our approach to versioning, history and access control. We have also shown how an existing prototype (Isaacs et al.'s PIAZZA) can be reimplemented (or 'simulated') in the AETHER awareness engine. As our approach can provide flexible solutions for basic CSCW functionality as well as have the capability of simulating other systems, we have a degree of confidence in both the relevance and generality of the AETHER model.

Future Work

In future work, we will investigate further applications of the model. For example, it is easy to see how the basic functionality we have discussed could be combined in, say, a flexible approach to workflow support. Rodden (1996) observes that most workflow systems depend at some level on a graph specifying transitions between states in the workflow. Such graphs can constitute a graph-space over which aura, focus and nimbus can be defined and manipulated. In this way, participants to a workflow can be made aware of activities 'upstream' which are about to become their responsibility as well of activities 'downstream' which follow on from what they have completed. In AETHER, we would add to the graph the documents in their various versions, representations of the users themselves, and any other object or relation of significance, and do so while the workflow is being enacted. In this way, the structure of a workflow can dynamically unfold and be enriched over time, with participants being present in and aware of various subgraphs as determined by the awareness computations. This approach has two attractive consequences. First, workflow graphs are no longer seen as stipulations of the states of the workflow. They become instead 'seeds' for a semantic net which will be added to as the workflow unfolds. Indeed, in some implementations, the pre-defined states might even get garbage collected if they are infrequently visited, that is, if they become irrelevant to the way the work has turned out. Secondly, as participants have points of presence within the graphs, which they themselves add to and manipulate their awareness within, the AETHER model could encourage workflow systems which support 'workflow from within', the self-organising and emergent structuring of work in response to contingencies, and not just mandate 'workflow from without', the execution of pre-defined procedures no matter what (cf. Bowers et al., 1995).

Other work on the AETHER model and our implementation of it will be devoted to optimising the performance of the engine by exploring different kinds of percolation and garbage collection algorithm. We will also need to develop methods for 'calibrating' these algorithms for different applications, so that, for example, the engine does indeed identify 'important' components and accord them longer life in a manner which matches user-requirements. Once this has been achieved and an appropriate application developed (perhaps a workflow application within the CoDESK environment), a program of user-evaluation will be necessary. We also intend to investigate parallel implementations of our algorithms. Experience with this would also inform further iterations of development with conventional machines (e.g. the appropriate use of background processing for awareness computations). Finally, we intend to explore ways in which the model can be mixed with geometrical models such as those associated with VR systems to obtain hybrids or in order to use geometrical (2D or 3D) interfaces to our model.

Awareness Beyond the Synchronous/Asynchronous Distinction

We want to finish by drawing out a general conclusion for CSCW research from the AETHER model. We remarked above that we treat time as another dimension in constructing the graph 'spaces' over which awareness computations are done, enabling various 'awareness windows' on past events to exist. Equally, by manipulating the form that focus takes, a user can broaden or restrict the extent of objects and relations of potential relevance to their work. This approach enables us to capture within a unified framework all of the forms of awareness in cooperative systems identified by Fuchs et al. (1995): coupled-synchronous (what is *currently* happening in the *actual scope of work*); uncoupled-synchronous (what happens *currently* anywhere else *of importance*); coupled-asynchronous (what happened in the *actual scope of work since the last access*); uncoupled-asynchronous (what happened anywhere else *of importance since the last access*).

'Actual scope' means, in our model, 'being in the focus of the user', 'of importance' means 'the user is in the nimbus of an object or a relation', 'currently' means 'the time focus is now', and 'since the last access' means 'in the time focus between the user's last access and now'. By manipulating the aura, focus and nimbus of the user and of the objects of the system, the awareness engine can generate awareness information for all these situations. But more than this. By translating the coupled-uncoupled and synchronous-asynchronous distinctions into concepts which admit of continuous variation, we can identify all the 'points in between'.

By offering a framework in which synchronous and asynchronous awareness can be supported equally, we 'deconstruct' this distinction in a unified approach. This is a powerful conclusion because the distinction between synchronous and asynchronous is used so very commonly - often as a way of distinguishing between different kinds of system. While the distinction may be clear at system levels where different communication protocols are discussed, perhaps we should not crudely transpose the distinction so that it classifies different types of awareness, still less different types of cooperative work. What matters to cooperative work *as it is experienced*, we suggest, is the *integration* of different streams of work which may be on many different time scales and show varying degrees of relevance to the matter at hand. Having a level of system architecture where different forms of awareness can all be supported together seems most appropriate to this image. The AETHER model and our experimental awareness engine comprise our attempt at this.

References

Benford, S., Bowers, J., Fahlén, L., Mariani, J. and Rodden, T. (1994): "Supporting Co-operative Work in Virtual Environments", *The Computer Journal*, 37, 8, pp653-668.

Benford, S., Brown, C., Reynard, G. and Greenhalgh, C. (1996): "Shared Spaces: Transportation, Artificiality, and Spatiality", in *Proc. of CSCW'96*, Boston, ACM Press, pp. 77-86.

Bneford, S., Bowers, J., Fahlén, L., Greenhalgh, C., Mariani, J. and Rodden, T. (1995): "Networked Virtual Reality and Cooperative Work", *Presence*, vol. 4, no. 4, pp. 364-386.

Bowers, J. (1993): "Modelling Awareness and Interaction in Virtual Spaces", in *Proc. of the 6th MultiG Workshop*, Stockholm.

Bowers, J., Button, G. and Sharrock, W. (1995): "Workflow From Within and Without: Technology and Cooperative Work on the Print Industry Shopfloor", in *Proc. of ECSCW'95*, Stockholm, Kluwer Academic Publishers, pp. 51-66.

Dourish, P. and Bellotti, V. (1992): "Awareness and Coordination in Shared Workspaces", in *Proc. of CSCW'92*, Toronto, ACM Press, pp. 107-114.

Fuchs, L., Pankoke-Babatz, U. and Prinz, W. (1995): "Supporting Cooperative Awareness with Local Event Mechanisms: The GroupDesk System", in *Proc. of ECSCW'95*, Stockholm, Kluwer Academic Publishers.

Glance, N., Pagani, D. and Pareschi, R. (1996): "Generalized Process Structure Grammars (GPSG) for Flexible Representations of Work", in *Proc. of CSCW'96*, Boston, ACM Press.

Greenhalgh, C. and Benford, S. (1996): "MASSIVE: A Virtual Reality System for Tele-conferencing", *ACM Transactions on Computer Human Interaction*, ACM Press.

Isaacs, E., Tang, J. and Morris, T. (1996): "Piazza: A Desktop Environment Supporting Impromptu and Planned Interactions", in *Proc. of CSCW'96*, Boston, ACM Press, pp. 315-324.

Rodden, T. (1996): "Populating the Application: A Model of Awareness for Cooperative Applications", in *Proc. of CSCW'96*, Boston, ACM Press, pp. 87-96.

Roseman, M. and Greenberg, S. (1996): "TeamRooms: Network Places for Collaboration", in *Proc. of CSCW'96*, Boston, ACM Press, pp. 325-333.

Tollmar, K. and Sundblad, Y. (1995): "The Design and Building of the Graphical User Interface for the Collaborative Desktop", *Computer and Graphics*, vol. 19, no. 2, 1995.

Tollmar, K., Sandor, O. and Shömer, A.(1996): "Supporting Social Awareness @Work - Design and Experience", in *Proc. of CSCW'96*, Boston, ACM Press, pp. 298-307.

Trevor, J., Rodden, T. and Mariani, J. (1994): "The Use of Adapters to Support Cooperative Sharing", in *Proc. of CSCW'94*, Chapel Hill, ACM Press, pp. 219-230.

Providing Flexible Services for Managing Shared State in Collaborative Systems

Hyong Sop Shim, Robert W. Hall, Atul Prakash, and Farnam Jahanian *
Department of Electrical Engineering and Computer Science,
University of Michigan, Ann Arbor, MI 48109-2122 USA
E-mail: {hyongsop,rhall,aprakash,farnam}@eecs.umich.edu

To effectively collaborate in Internet environments, it is critical to efficiently manage the shared state of collaboration. However, the management of shared state is highly situational; different collaboration semantics require different measures tailored to their specific needs. Hence, providing a general set of services that meet the management requirements of varying collaboration situations is challenging. In this paper, we discuss our approach to providing such services. The services are made flexible by allowing collaborators to choose appropriate services based on the needs of their collaboration tools and specific characteristics of their shared state. We present the shared state management services provided by our Corona server that embodies our approach and report experience with its use.

Introduction

Computer-supported collaboration often requires sharing of certain application context by geographically dispersed participants. The collaborators are able to *work together* over distance by making changes to a shared state and observing the changes made by others.

The semantics of shared state is *application-dependent*. For example, in a group-drawing tool, the shared state may be defined as the contents of the canvas. In a window-sharing environment, such as the one supported by DistView, the shared

---

*This work is supported in part by the National Science Foundation under cooperative agreement IRI-9216848.

J. Hughes et al. (eds.), Proceedings of the Fifth European Conference on Computer Supported Cooperative Work, 237-252.

state includes the attributes of a shared window, e.g., the size of the window, and the internal states of application-specific objects associated with the window (Prakash and Shim, 1994).

On the other hand, CSCW system developers need *application-independent* services for managing shared state and providing awareness information about its use. Critical issues concerning the management of shared state by application-independent services include:

- **Awareness:** In a computer-supported collaboration, a user may be unaware of the presence of other participants or their current status without explicit support from the underlying system. Collaboration awareness information such as when users join/leave a collaboration session, whether or not they are paying attention when connected (e.g. gone out of the office for coffee), or when they are disconnected from a session due to network or client failures plays an important role in managing shared state as it may dictate the interactions of collaborators. Such awareness information should be available for ready access.

- **Synchronization:** A shared state should be consistently synchronized for the entire duration of a collaboration. Furthermore, collaborators should be allowed to access and modify the shared state concurrently without disrupting each other's work.

- **Predictable Performance for Late-comers:** In synchronous collaboration, participants may join an ongoing collaboration activity. A late-comer should be able to receive a consistent state of collaboration in a "predictable" amount of time – independent of failures of or speed of other clients in the system. Our experience with CSCW systems indicates that users get impatient with a system if it takes them longer than "normal" to join a collaborative session, say, because of failures of other clients or slow bandwidth to a client that might have been selected by the system to transfer shared state. Users expect a "predictable" response time (i.e., limited largely by their bandwidth to the network and the size of the state) for state transfer when they join the system. Conversely, existing users do not want the joining of late-comers to be intrusive or disruptive to their on-going work.

- **Persistence:** A group activity may involve both synchronous and asynchronous collaboration. It is often the case that collaborators may not accomplish all their goals in a single session; they may have to adjourn a session and reconvene at a later time. In such cases, it may be necessary to save part or all of a shared state persistently to be retrieved for a later session. Persistence is beneficial to both synchronous and asynchronous collaboration.

- **Time-stamping:** Users may often want to know *when* an update to a shared state took place. In a chat application, for instance, users prefer that all messages be time-stamped by a reliable service. Time-stamping can also be useful if users want to know what has changed since the last time they participated in a long-term collaborative session. Hence, mechanisms should be provided to reliably time-stamp updates on the shared state.

- **Interactive Responsiveness:** Users expect collaborative applications to have similar response times as single-user applications. The ability to collaborate should not disrupt the fluidity of users' interactions with their applications.

- **Client-Based Semantics:** The interpretation of the semantics of a shared state should be the responsibility of collaborating application processes. This allows shared states to be scalable to a large number of collaborating processes, and processes of different applications may work over the same shared state (Patterson et al., 1996).

- **Robust Collaboration:** A collaboration session should be robust. It should tolerate various failures of collaborators' host machines and network connections and continue to support the work of non-faulty collaborators.

In addressing the above issues, different collaborative applications require different approaches to managing shared state based on their needs. For example, persistence may not be required in all collaborative applications. Also, different users in the same collaborative application may have different awareness needs. Nevertheless, it is highly desirable for the efficient development and widespread use of computer-supported collaboration technology to have a general set of shared state management services that adequately address all the aforementioned issues. Such services should be flexible in that the subscribers to the services are able to select only the services they need, with corresponding overheads.

In this paper, we present our approach to managing shared state. Our approach is realized in a set of shared state management services provided by our Corona server that we have implemented as part of the UARC project's Collaboratory Builder's Environment (Lee et al., 1996). The server supports both synchronous and asynchronous collaboration over the World Wide Web, where collaborating clients may be dynamically downloaded over the Internet. In an earlier paper, we discussed communication requirements supported by the Corona server and the scalability aspects of communication for different kinds of groups (Hall et al.,1996). In this paper, we focus on the management of shared state by the Corona server to address the above issues.

The remainder of the paper is organized as follows. We first discuss the motivation for our work. We then provide a detailed discussion of our approach. This discussion defines basic concepts fundamental to our shared state management services and describes each service in detail. We then report on the implementation status as well as some usage examples of Corona. We conclude the paper by comparing our work with existing systems and by outlining our future plans.

Motivation

Our work on the management of shared state in computer-supported collaboration has its origin in an NSF-sponsored project, called the Upper Atmospheric Research Collaboratory or UARC (Clauer et al., 1993). The UARC project focuses on the creation of an experimental testbed for wide-area scientific collaboratory work. This testbed is implemented as a large object-oriented distributed system on the Internet and provides a collaboratory environment in which a geographically dispersed community of space scientists perform real-time experiments at a remote facility in Greenland without having to leave their home institutions. This community of space

240

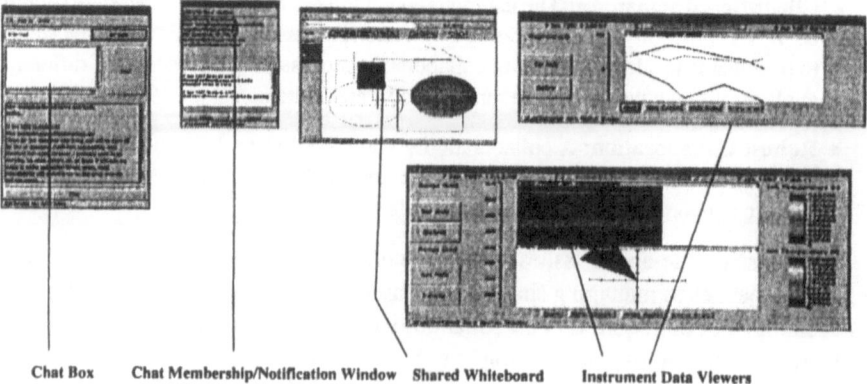

Chat Box   Chat Membership/Notification Window   Shared Whiteboard   Instrument Data Viewers

Figure 1. UARC Collaboration Tools

scientists has extensively used the UARC system over the last three years and has expressed a high degree of satisfaction with its mechanisms for remote collaboration. Figure 1 shows a snapshot of various UARC collaboration tools that enable space scientists to remotely conduct their science.

Consider two collaboration tools: the multi-party chat box for exchanging textual message and graphical images and a shared windows facility for viewing instrument data. These two collaboration tools have very different requirements for managing shared state. The chat box allows scientists to exchange textual messages and graphical images within the editing area of the chat box. All the messages are shown in the display area of the chat box. Made possible by our DistView toolkit, the shared viewer facility allows the selective sharing of the data display windows of instrument data viewers (Prakash and Shim, 1994). In order to share a window, a scientist first *exports* the window to a public repository. The exported window may subsequently be *imported* by any scientist who is interested in collaborating with the exporter of the window. Henceforth, the shared window provides the collaborating scientists with a synchronized view of the data being displayed and ensures that its physical appearance on the screen, e.g. its size, remains synchronized throughout collaboration.

The above two collaboration tools demand different strategies for managing shared state. The shared state of the chat box is defined to be the list of messages exchanged between participants. The shared state of a viewer includes the range of data being displayed in the shared window, the graphical display of the data itself, the settings of the display, and all of the graphical attributes associated with the window. In order to maintain the synchrony of its shared state, the chat box only needs to append each new message to its queue of exchanged messages; it does not have to re-send previously exchanged messages when updating its state with a new message.

In contrast, when a participant resizes a shared window, all instances of the window have to be resized. Likewise, when a scientist changes the display mode for the data being displayed in the window, the other replicas of the window have to reflect the setting change by overwriting their respective internal variables with the new value. Hence, keeping shared windows synchronized requires replacing part of its shared state with new values.

Another distinction concerns the degree of synchronization. The scientists are not very concerned about the total order of messages shown in the display area of the chat box, especially when the messages are timestamped. Instead, they want to interact with each other without delay by being able to exchange messages as freely as possible. When sharing a window, however, concurrent updates on the shared window should be serialized. Otherwise, the shared state of the window seen by different scientists may be inconsistent. For example, the shared window may be of different sizes, or the instrument data displayed in the window may be in different modes for collaborating scientists.

Over the years, the design of the UARC system has evolved through several generations. The current design is an applet-based architecture implemented in Java. It takes advantage of the widespread use of the World Wide Web and the platform-independence of Java applets. A key component of the UARC system is the Corona server. The server embodies our approach to shared state management; it is powerful and flexible enough to meet the varying shared state management needs of UARC applications as well as general collaboration environments.

Corona Shared State Model

Ellis, et al. (1991) define the shared state of applications in computer-supported collaboration as "...a set of objects where the objects and the actions performed on the objects are visible to a set of users". It follows that the management of a shared state may be defined as the management of actions, i.e. accesses and updates, on the objects that constitute the shared state.

We require each object in a shared state to have an identifier to distinguish the object from the others in the same shared state. The object should also be able to write its internal state to a stream as well as set its state upon receipt from a stream. The latter requirement is commonplace in object-oriented applications that utilize persistent objects. The identifiers for objects in a shared state may be automatically generated by a support system and may not incur extra programming efforts. For example, the object instances of the DistViewObject class in our DistView toolkit are automatically assigned such identifiers by the DistView runtime system (Prakash and Shim, 1994).

Corona Server Overview

In this section, we describe the basic approach of the Corona server to shared state management. We begin the discussion by defining the concept of *group*.

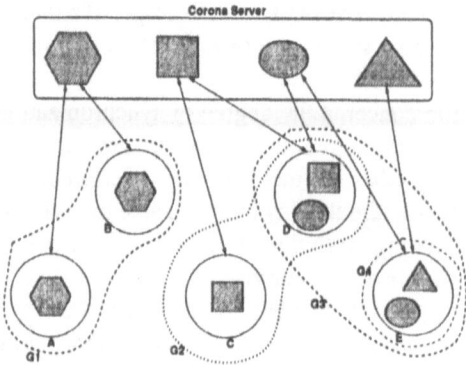

Figure 2. Overview of the Corona Server. Circles represent clients, dotted lines depict groups, and different shapes represent different shared states. Clients may belong to different groups; Client D belongs to both Group G3 and G4 etc. All the groups are stateful.

Group

The basic unit of collaboration in the Corona server is a group. A group is defined to be a set of application processes, termed *members*. A group may be characterized as *stateful* or *stateless*. A stateful group is associated with a shared state; the members of the group collaborate with each other by collectively accessing and modifying the shared state of the group. To participate, an application process has to join the group first. Once a member leaves the group, it no longer receives any update notifications on the shared state. A stateless group has no shared state and is used for group administrative tasks such as dissemination of group membership notifications. Figure 2 illustrates the group concept.

Groups may also be characterized as *persistent* and *temporal*. A persistent group exists even when it has no members; if it is stateful, the shared state of the group also persists. A temporal group ceases to exist when it has no members; if it is stateful, its shared state is also lost.

Note that our notion of group is distinct from the concept of a group of users who may be engaged in various collaboration activities. It may be viewed that our group represents a particular collaboration activity that a set of users is presently participating in.

Group State Management

The server manages a set of groups. A group is created by a qualified client sending a request to the server [1]. The client specifies the name of the new group and whether or not the group is stateful.

If a group is stateful, the client may also send the initial state of the group to the

---

[1] The server works in conjunction with our session manager, and the session manager determines who may have a privilege to create groups (Lee et al.,1996).

server. The server represents the shared state of a stateful group as a table indexed by object identifiers. Each table entry is a *byte stream* representation of the state of each object in the shared state. The server keeps the shared state table up-to-date as the group members update the shared state. When a new member joins the group, the server transfers the contents of the table to the new member. By default, a stateful group is persistent whereas a stateless group is temporal. The server allows groups to dynamically change their persistence status as needed.

Note that the shared state of a stateful group specifies *what* is shared but does not dictate *how* the shared state is actually used. Instead, the interpretation of the semantics of the shared state is left to collaborating processes. This is important because we want our shared state management services to be applicable to a wide range of collaboration situations. The lack of knowledge of the semantics of a particular shared state frees us from having to deal with its behaviors in a specific situation. Patterson, et al. (1996) describe this property as *client-based semantics*.

The Corona server takes a centralized approach to providing administrative services for maintaining shared state. A different approach would be to replicate management responsibilities among collaborating clients (Crowley et al.,1990, Knister and Prakash, 1990, Lauwers et al. 1990). In theory, such a replicated approach offers advantages over a centralized counterpart, especially in the issue of fault tolerance. However, in practice, a replicated approach would not be suitable in a wide-area, heterogeneous collaboration environment such as the World Wide Web. For example, maintaining the synchrony of replicated data among all the keepers of the data would be very expensive in such an unreliable environment. Further, clients may run on hosts of unpredictable processing resources and network connectivity. Hence, it would be unreasonable to expect clients to always perform shared state management tasks reliably.

A rationale for centralizing administrative services for managing shared state is that servers are designed to support multiple users and hence tend to be more reliable, allocated more resources, and run in a more controlled environment than clients (Patterson et al., 1996). Clients usually support the work of a single user and typically are not trusted to be reliable. Furthermore, a centralized service provider such as the Corona server can be made fault tolerant by having multiple replicas of the provider. There exist a number of well-known replication strategies, including a primary-backup approach (passive replication) and a state machine approach (active replication)(Budhiraja and Toueg, 1992, Birman and Joseph 1986).

Further advantages of a centralized approach are that it provides a single point of serialization and that it simplifies accommodation of latecomers (Crowley et al., 1990, Patterson et al.,1996). Further, the detection and handling of faulty clients is easier with a centralized approach than a replicated counterpart where all the clients would need to run a complex membership protocol to account for faulty clients.

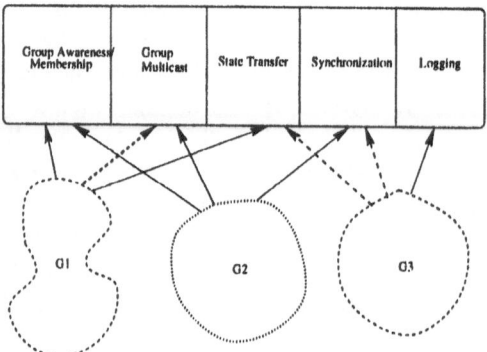

Group Awareness/ Membership	Group Multicast	State Transfer	Synchronization	Logging

Figure 3. Corona Services. The arrows represent subscriptions to services. Group G1 is subscribing to group awareness/membership, group multicast, and state transfer services. The dashed arrows show that Group G1 is using the group multicast service differently from Group G2 and that Group G2 is utilizing the synchronization service differently from Group G3.

Corona Services

The Corona server provides the following set of services for its groups: *group awareness*, *state transfer*, *group multicast*, *lock management*, and *logging*. Figure 3 graphically represents the Corona services.

Group Awareness Service

The group awareness service of the Corona server maintains information on the membership of groups. When a new client joins a group, the server sends a join notification to the other group members. Likewise, when a client leaves its group, the server notifies the other group members of the client's departure. The changes of member attributes are also notified; for example, when a member changes his or her username attribute, the change is broadcast to the other members. Furthermore, a member may indicate to the other members its participation status as *idle* or *active*. An idle member is unable or unavailable to participate in the group activities for some reason, e.g. has to answer a phone call, whereas an active member can fully participate. The server sends participation status notifications for the benefit of the group; the server does not distinguish idle members from active members. By default, a new member is active.

In some collaborative environments, it may be necessary to differentiate users based on the type of operations they can perform on the shared state. It may be desirable to grant only certain users the privilege to update the shared state while others are only allowed to view the changes on the shared state.

The Corona server supports the following member roles: *principal*, *observer*, and *membership-observer*. Principals have update privilege on the group's shared state. Observers and membership-observers are casual members who may only view the updates on the shared state or the changes on the group membership, respectively. Hence, principals need a higher level of awareness of each other's work and presence, and thus require a higher quality of service (QoS) from the server (Hall et al., 1996). For example, the server may have to ensure that a principal receives all of its notifications whereas it may notify observers without ensuring that all messages are reliably delivered.

By default, a client is a principal member. A client may also specify its role when it joins a group. Furthermore, the server allows group members to change their roles on the fly in response to collaboration needs or system events.

Group Multicast Service

Clients use the group multicast service of the Corona server to broadcast updates on a shared state; a client sends a message containing update information to the server, and the server broadcasts the message to the members of a group to which the sender belongs. Updates on a shared state may be characterized as either *memoryless* or *memoryful*. An update contains some value that represents a change of state of an object in the shared state. A memoryless update contains a value that *replaces* the old state of the object. In contrast, the value in a memoryful update is *added* to the existing state of the object. Hence, memoryful updates entail incremental changes to the state of the object whereas memoryless updates require overwriting the existing state of the object.

Memoryful updates are useful where the history of changes to the shared state is important to collaboration. In a group-drawing session, for instance, it is undesirable to remove existing shapes whenever a new shape is drawn on the canvas. On the other hand, memoryless updates are useful where the past history of changes is irrelevant to collaboration. For example, to know the current size of a shared window does not mandate knowing the past sizes of the window.

A group multicast message for an update specifies the group name, the object identifier to which the update applies, the byte stream encoding of the update value, and a flag specifying whether the update is memoryful or memoryless. Upon receipt of a memoryless update multicast, the server uses the object identifier to index into the group's state table and replaces the existing stream with the new update stream. Upon receipt of a memoryful update multicast, the server simply appends the update stream to the existing stream. The server then forwards the update message to group members.

The server provides two forms of group multicast: *sender-inclusive* or *sender-exclusive*. Sender-inclusive multicast is used when the server needs to perform additional operations on the message prior to delivering it to the clients, e.g. timestamping the messages of the chat box. With sender-exclusive multicast, the sender applies the update locally and then sends the update to the server which then forwards the update to the remaining group members. We use the phrase multicast instead of broadcast to highlight the fact that update messages may be sent to a subset of the total membership based on the roles of the individual group members.

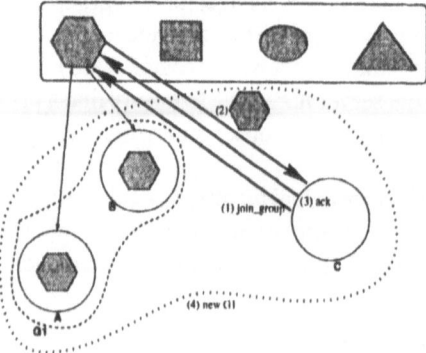

Figure 4. Fast State Transfer in Corona. A new client C is joining Group G1. The numbers represent the sequence of actions. C sends a join request to the server, the server transfers the current shared state of G1 to C, and C acknowledges the receipt of the state.

State Transfer Service

When a client joins a stateful group, the Corona server transfers the current shared state of the group to the new member. A decision has to be made as to what of the shared state should be transferred. Depending on the semantics of collaboration, the new member may be sent only part of the shared state. For example, the shared state of a shared window includes the states of all the user interface as well as application-specific objects associated with the window. Depending on particular collaboration needs, the importer of the window may be given the current states of both user interface and application-specific objects or of only the user interface objects. In the latter case, the importer would be allowed either to access the application-specific objects remotely or to only view others' updates on the window.

The decision also depends on the type of updates required. For the part of the shared state that requires memoryful updates, its current state as well as the accumulated effects of the past updates on it should be transferred to a newcomer. However, for the part that requires memoryless updates, only the current state needs to be transferred.

When a client joins a stateful group, the Corona server simply transfers the current shared state of the group to the new member without disrupting the work of the existing members. An authorized client such as a group creator may also specify to the server which objects in the shared state to be transferred based on the roles of new members. Figure 4 graphically illustrates the Corona state transfer protocol. The protocol is fast because a new member receives the current shared state of the group directly from the server.

State Synchronization Service

Ideally, the updates made by a user on the shared state should be instantaneously reflected on other collaborators. However, this may be impossible in practice due to constraints such as network latency. Hence, users will inevitably experience some inconsistencies in the shared state. Hence, the developers of synchronous collaboration systems often have to make design trade-offs between a desired degree of synchronization of the shared state and the fluidity of work on the shared state the end users are allowed to perform. The tighter synchronization implies that the users would be more constrained in their work (Greenberg and Marwood, 1994). At one extreme, the users are allowed to work as freely as they like as in a collaborative brainstorming session, and no synchronization processing is performed on the shared state. At the other extreme, only one user is allowed to make updates on the shared state while the others are forced to wait. The right balance depends on the requirements of a specific collaboration situation.

In order to provide a desired degree of synchronization and control concurrent updates on the shared state of a group, the Corona server allows locks to be associated with the objects in a shared state. By default, no lock is assigned to the shared state, allowing group members to work on the shared state concurrently. While this approach may lead to chaos in general, it has been found to be more efficient and useful in many practical collaborative scenarios (Greenberg and Marwood, 1994). For example, the design of the chat box in the UARC client allows the scientists to exchange messages freely without any concern for the total ordering on messages from distinct sources. Although messages were sometimes received out of order, the scientists did not find it confusing and often commented on the effectiveness of the chat box.

When concurrent access to shared state must be synchronized, the server allows a lock to be assigned to a set of objects in the shared state. The size of a *lock set* as well as its constituents are determined by group members based on collaboration needs. An object may not belong to different lock sets. Regarding the usage of locks, a client may acquire and hold onto a lock as long as the client actively updates the objects in the lock set associated with the lock. An advantage of this lock-set based scheme is that it allows a group to specify the degree of synchronization on the concurrent operations on the shared state. The flexibility stems from the fact that a lock set may be of any desired size and that a group may have several lock sets. Since a lock set is composed of object identifiers, not the objects themselves, the locks can be managed by the server regardless of whether the shared state is centralized or replicated.

This centralized approach not only simplifies the lock management but also frees the group members from the administrative burden of lock management. Patterson, et al. (1996) and Nichols, et al. (1995) also discuss the merits of such a centralized serialization point for their lock management and concurrency control strategies, respectively.

Logging Service

The logging facility of the Corona server consists of two complementary services: (1) a checkpointing service for taking a snapshot of the current shared state of a group periodically or on demand; (2) a record and replay service for logging group multicast messages containing update information on the shared state. Both facilities allow a group's shared state to be persistent and outlive the group itself. The first approach is particularly useful when the group members may have to adjourn their work to a later time. In the second approach, the server effectively records an incremental change to the shared state. This allows the server to replay the updates at a later time, detailing how the shared state has reached a particular state. The record and replay capability is especially useful for an end user who did not participate in a collaboration activity to find out not only the results of the activity but also how the results has been produced (Manohar and Prakash, 1995).

Implementation Status and Usage Examples

A prototype of the Corona server has been implemented as a multi-threaded Java application, supporting down-loadable Java applet clients. The server has been successfully tested and used in various UARC campaigns and project meetings, supporting numerous collaborative science and on-line group discussions. In two recent campaigns, approximately 40-50 participants (scientists and UARC developers) utilized our tools to conduct science on atmospheric phenomena over a three day period. The scientists were dispersed throughout North America and Europe, operating on a variety of platforms, including Windows 95, Solaris, and HP-UX with connectivity ranging from high-speed links to modems.

The initial development of the server has focused on its robustness and scalability; the server should accommodate dynamic client joins, leaves, and failures and tolerate varying network connectivity conditions. Hence, the prototype provides only the basic management services, including a group awareness service with limited role support and a state transfer service without the selective state transfer support.

Table I provides a partial overview of the client application programming interface to the Corona services. The Group Awareness/Membership interface allows clients to create, initialize, join, and leave groups. The interface also allows clients to pull awareness information such as group membership as needed. The group multicast interface allows clients to broadcast memoryful or memoryless updates on a group's shared state. The synchronization interface allows shared objects to be dynamically locked and unlocked.

The various collaborative tools discussed in Section are Java-based applets and access the Corona services through the interfaces of Table I. As of the present implementation, only the processes of the same tool form a group in the Corona server although the server itself does not impose such a restriction.

The different collaboration semantics that these tools are designed to support result in different usages of the Corona services. For example, A chat group uses the

Awareness/Membership Interface	
createGroup(gName)	creates a group named gName
initGroup(gName,gState)	initialize a group gName with its shared state gState
joinGroup(gName, aRole)	join group gName with role, aRole
joinAck(gName)	acknowledges the join completion of a member
leaveGroup(gName)	leaves group gName
deleteGroup(gName)	deletes group gName
changeRole(oldRole, newRole)	changes the role of a member to newRole
getGroupNames()	returns the names of available groups
getMembership(gName)	returns the membership of group gName
Multicast Interface	
mcastStateExcludeSender(gName,O_i stateMsg)	multicasts new memoryless state message for object O_i
mcastStateIncludeSender(gName,O_i stateMsg)	multicasts new memoryless state message for object O_i
mcastUpdateExcludeSender(gName,O_i, stateMsg)	multicasts an memoryful state update change to object O_i for group gName
mcastUpdateIncludeSender(gName,O_i, stateMsg)	multicasts an incremental change to object O_i for group gName
Synchronization Interface	
acquireLock(gName,L)	acquires a lock on an object whose id is in L
releaseLock(gName,L)	releases a lock on an object whose id is in L

Table I. Corona client application interface for group awareness and multicast services. $gState = \{(O_1, S_1), (O_2, S_2), ..., (O_n, S_n)\}$ is the set of shared state object identifiers O_i and their byte stream state representations S_i. $L = \{O_i, O_j, ...\}$ is a set of identifiers of objects for which a lock is to be acquired or released

mcastUpdateIncludeSender() to broadcast messages so that when a new chat joins the group, it is transfered all previously exchanged messages. Message are broadcast sender-inclusively so that messages are displayed with consistent timestamps. The chat group does not utilize the synchronization service so that users may freely exchange messages.

On the other hand, a shared windows group require a tighter synchronization of its shared state. Conflicting updates on the display mode of the shared window, for example, may result in confusion. Thus the shared windows group uses the synchronization service to acquire locks on one or more shared objects before performing updates. Further, it broadcasts updates through the *mcastStateExcludeSender()* interface.

Related Work

In its goals, Lotus' most closely resembles our Corona server. Both advocate centralized management of shared state and provide similar administrative services in its support (Patterson et al., 1996). The semantics of shared state is client-based in both systems so that their services are generalized to a wide range of applications. Further, the notion of Place in NSTP is synonymous with the group concept in Corona, and the Things in a Place correspond to the objects in a shared state of a stateful group in Corona.

However, NSTP and Corona differ in several aspects of their shared state management support. First, NSTP does not support the notion of incremental updates. Each update on a Thing always overwrites the old value of the Thing. This limitation would make the development of tools such as our chat box or draw applet difficult as the updates on the shared states of these tools are fully incremental. Instead, clients always access shared objects remotely. This may significantly degrade performance in user responsiveness in a highly interactive collaboration environment, especially over a wide area network. Finally, NSTP does not support any notion of persistence in its Things or Places. On the other hand, the Corona server does not support the Facade-like capabilities for viewing the shared states of groups before actually joining the groups.

Systems such as ISIS rely on clients for maintaining shared states (Birman and Joseph, 1987). As discussed earlier, a client-based approach may not be suitable for collaboration over a unreliable, long-haul collaboration environment such as the World Wide Web, where clients may not perform reliably. As a transport layer subsystem, ISIS supports the notion of process groups, notification of membership changes, and group multicast. It may be used to build our group awareness and group notification services. However, it lacks the notion of shared state and does not provide guarantees on delay when a client joins since the state transfer originates from another client.

Suite, Rendezvous, and Jupiter take a centralized approach to managing shared state (Dewan, 1991, Patterson et al.,1990, Nichols et al., 1995). In addition to managing shared states, the Suite, Rendezvous, and Jupiter servers run application code, potentially degrading user responsiveness. Corona is unique among systems that take a centralized approach in that it is application-independent and provides the state transfer service, allowing clients to interact with local copies of shared states. This facilitates user responsiveness, especially over a wide-area network.

Egret is structually similar to the Corona server in that it also supports an application-independent server that manages shared state that is replicated at clients (Johnson, 1996). While the Corona shared data model is generic, i.e. a set of objects, however, the Egret data model is schema-based and may not be easily applicable to applications that are not database-oriented.

The Corona server has provisions for both optimistic and pessimistic approaches to synchronizing shared state. By default, the server does not associate any locks to a group and allows the group members to freely interact with each other. This approach is synonymous in its intent with the optimistic synchronization approaches taken by Grove, Jupiter, and Coast (Ellis et al., 1988, Nichols et al., 1995, Schuckmann et al.,1996). The difference is that the server does not provide explicit conflict resolution mechanisms. For applications that wish to use locks, e.g. MMConf, DistEdit, and NSTP, the server provides support for acquiring and releasing locks

(Crowley et al., 1990, Knister and Prakash, 1990, Patterson et al., 1996).

Both IRC and Zephyr provide centralized messaging and notification services, which are similar to our group awareness and multicast services (Oikarinen and Reed, 1993, DellaFera and Eichin, 1988). However, neither of these systems has the concept of shared state or role distinction among members and is not intended to support general synchronous collaborative activities.

Conclusions and Future Work

This paper presented our approach to providing flexible services for managing shared state in computer-supported collaboration. We believe that both the efficient development of collaborative applications and the widespread use of computer-supported collaboration technology would be greatly benefited by such services. We have identified a set of general services fundamental to shared state management and discussed different design choices possible for providing these services. The services are provided by our Corona server whose flexibility allows clients to choose what services to receive and how the services are provided based on their particular shared state management needs. An initial prototype of the server has shown the applicability of our approach through the of development of several collaboration tools.

Our current research efforts are focusing on increasing the scalability and robustness of the server and examining the issues involved in a distributed implementation of the server.

References

Birman, K. P. and Joseph, T. A. (1987): "Exploiting Virtual Synchrony in Distributed Systems", *Proc. of 11th ACM Symp. on Operating Systems Principles*, Austin, TX, Nov. 1987, pp. 123–138.

Birman, K. P. and Joseph, T. A. (1988): "Low-Cost Management of Replicated Data in Fault-Tolerant Distributed Systems", *ACM Trans. on Computer Systems*, vol. 4, no. 1, Feb. 1986, pp. 54–70.

Clauer, C. R. et al. (1993): "A Prototype Upper Atmospheric Research Collaboratory (UARC)", *EOS, Trans. Amer. Geophys. Union*, vol. 74, 1993.

Crowley T., Milazzo P., Baker E., Forsdick H., and Tomlinson, R. (1990): "MMConf: An Infrastructure for Building Shared Multimedia Applications", *Proc. of ACM Conference on Computer Supported Cooperative Work*, October 1990, pp. 329–242.

DellaFera, C. A., and Eichin, M. W. (1988): "The Zephyr Notification Service", *Proc. of the USENIX Winter Conference*, Dallas, Texas, 1988.

Dewan, P. (1991): "Flexible User Interface Coupling in Collaborative Systems", *Proceedings of the ACM CHI'91 Conference on Human Factors in Computing Systems*, April 1991, pp.41–48.

Ellis, C.A., Gibbs, S.J., and Rein, G. L. (1988): "Design and Use of a Group Editor", *Engineering for Human-Computer Interaction*, North-Holland, Amsterdam, September 1988, pp 13-25.

Ellis, C.A., Gibbs, S.J., and Rein, G. L. (1991): "Groupware: Some Issues and Experiences", *Communications of the ACM*, January 1991, pp 38–51.

Greenberg, S. and Marwood, D. (1994): "Real-Time Groupware as a Distributed System: Concurrency Control and its Effect on the Interface". *Proc. of the Fifth Conf. on Computer-Supported Cooperative Work*, Chapel Hill, North Carolina, 1994.

Hall, R. W., Mathur, A., Jahanian F., Prakash, A., and Rasmussen, C. (1996): "Corona: A Communication Service for Scalable, Reliable Group Collaboration Systems", *Proc. of the Sixth ACM Conference on Computer-Supported Cooperative Work*, ACM Press, Nov. 1996, pp. 140–149.

Johnson, P. (1994): "Experiences with EGRET: An Exploratory Group Work Environment", *Collaborative Computing*, vol. 2 no. 1, Jan. 1994.

Knister, M. and Prakash, A. (1990): "DistEdit: A distributed toolkit for supporting multiple group editors", *Proceedings of the Third Conference on Computer-Supported Cooperative Work*, Los Angeles, California, October 1990, pp. 345–355.

Lauwers, J., Joseph, T., Lantz, K., and Romanow, A. (1990): "Replicated Architectures for Shared Window Systems: A Critique", *Proceedings of ACM Conference on Office Information Systems*, March 1990, pp. 249–260.

Lee, J.H., Prakash, A., Jaeger, T., and Wu, G. (1996): "Supporting Multi-user, Multi-applet Workspaces in CBE", *Proc. of the Sixth ACM Conference on Computer-Supported Cooperative Work*, ACM Press, Nov. 1996, pp. 344–353.

Manohar, N. R. and Prakash, A.(1995): "The Session Capture and Replay Paradigm for Asynchronous Collaboration". *Proc. of the Fourth European Conference on Computer-Supported Cooperative Work*, Kluwer Academic Publishers, Sep. 1995.

Nichols, D., Curtis, P., Dixon, M., and Lamping, J. (1995): "High-Latency, Low-Bandwidth Windowing in the Jupiter Collaboration System",*Proceedings of UIST '95*, Pittsburgh, PA, 1995.

Oikarinen, J. and Reed, D. (1993): *Internet Relay Chat Protocol (RFC 1459)*,1993. Available at ftp://ds.intenic.net/rfc/rfc/1459.txt.

Patterson, J. F., Hill, R. D., Rohall, S. L., and Meeks, W. S. (1990): " Rendezvous: An Architecture for Synchronous Multi-user Applications", *Proceedings of the Third Conference on Computer-Supported Cooperative Work*, Los Angeles, California, October 1990, pp. 317–328.

Patterson, J. F., Day, M., and Kucan, J. (1996): "Notification Servers for Synchronous Groupware", *Proc. of the Sixth ACM Conference on Computer-Supported Cooperative Work*, ACM Press, Nov. 1996, pp. 122–129.

Prakash A. and Shim H. (1994): DistView: Support for Building Efficient Collaborative Applications using Replicated Objects, *Proc. of the Fifth ACM Conf. on Computer Supported Cooperative Work*, Chapel-Hill, NC, Oct. 1994, pp. 153–164.

Schuckmann, C., Kirchner, L., Schummer, J., Haake, J. M. (1996): "Designing Object-Oriented Synchronous Groupware with COAST", Proc. of the Sixth ACM Conference on Computer-Supported Cooperative Work, ACM Press,Nov.1996, pp. 30–38.

Schneider, F. B., Budhiraja, N., Marzullo, K., and Toueg, S. (1992): "Optimal Primary-Backup Protocols", *Proceedings of the Sixth International Workshop on Distributed Algorithms*, 1992.

Supporting Groupware Conventions through Contextual Awareness

Gloria Mark, Ludwin Fuchs, Markus Sohlenkamp
GMD-FIT, German National Research Center for Information Technology
{gloria.mark, ludwin.fuchs, markus.sohlenkamp}@gmd.de

Abstract: Conventions are an important part of articulation work. They are a means to merge the various perspectives and workstyles that are involved in handling shared objects in CSCW. We report on convention use with a groupware system used in a government ministry. Our findings suggest that defining, establishing, and following conventions is aided by the visibility of other people's activities using the system. We describe a prototype that supports users in maintaining conventions by providing awareness facilities and an overview for shared objects.

Introduction

A groupware system, such as a shared workspace, is a social environment. People's actions do not occur in isolation; changes to shared documents and to file structures are not independent, and actions can, in fact, have adverse consequences for others. If someone removes a document from a shared workspace, renames a document, or rearranges files into new subdirectories, then others may have problems locating the documents.

Any cooperative activity involves reconciling individual work styles to achieve common procedures and representations (Gerson and Star, 1986; Schmidt and Bannon, 1992). Though shared workspace members may be spatially distributed, their actions do not occur in a vacuum, and even the simplest procedure often involves negotiations among group members. Conventions are a means to merge the various perspectives and workstyles that are involved in handling shared

253

J. Hughes et al. (eds.), Proceedings of the Fifth European Conference on Computer Supported Cooperative Work, 253-268.
© *1997 Kluwer Academic Publishers.*

objects. We consider conventions for a groupware system to be rules or arrangements established in the group, common and accessible to its members, that users need in order to cooperate effectively with the system. While conventions may include social protocols, i.e. common rules for behavioral interaction such as speaking turns, we concentrate on those that are based on explicit agreements on common procedures for using system functionality.

We examined the role of conventions with real users in the POLITeam project. POLITeam is a groupware system designed to supplement paper work processes with electronic work processes in a government ministry. The larger aim is to support telecooperation between Bonn and Berlin as the German government relocates. The main tools that POLITeam offers are a shared workspace and electronic circulation folders (Prinz and Kolvenbach, 1996). An already existing groupware system (LinkWorks[1]) was chosen and adapted to specific user and situation requirements. The system has been installed since January, 1995. For further information, see Klöckner et al., (1995), and Mambrey et al., (1996).

This study began as a result of a workshop discussion with the design team and users in June, 1996, during which the users reported that a major requirement for them was establishing conventions for the system use. Some examples of conventions that the users cited at the workshop as necessary were: *naming conventions for documents* (e.g. by creator vs. content and semantics); *storing old and current documents*; *shared task processes* (document changes, access rights, storage, editing, ownership, producing new documents, and document type); *and substitution rules* (when a workspace member is absent). Our users considered obligation to be a key word for conventions to make cooperation possible.

Conventions with Shared Objects

The standard approach taken in CSCW-systems is best characterized by the notion of a shared object[2]. A shared object gives a group of users access to common information together with facilities to manipulate the data. However, in an organizational work arrangement the same piece of data is subject to different specialized activities, opinions, perspectives and interests (see e. g. Star and Griesemer, 1989). According to Schmidt and Bannon (1992), cooperative work occurs when people are mutually dependent in their work; the role of systems support thus becomes far more complex than simply distributing the control or access points of the common data. Cooperative work involves setting procedures for coordinating a number of subtasks when using shared objects. This

---

[1] LinkWorks™ is a groupware product by Digital.

[2] We use the term "shared object" to distinguish it from the term "common artifact" (e.g. Robinson, 1993) to denote it as an object void of properties that are attributed to common artifacts, e.g. overview, peripheral awareness, etc.

articulation work forms the necessary overhead of coordination and cannot be prescribed formally in terms of task procedures; rather, a key characteristic of it is the continual flexibility in response to unanticipated changes and developments (Gerson and Star, 1986). One aspect of articulation work is establishing conventions so that the group can reach a shared understanding about the common usage of a shared object. The agreements must be consistent among users, yet robust and flexible enough to adapt and evolve, in response to local contingencies.

Individuals need to be aware of the activities of others in using a shared object to help them accommodate their own work styles to others in the group. Rogers (1993) reports on the use of conventions for managing files: group members checked out files by using a whiteboard in a common office as a mediating mechanism; each persons' activities were visible to the group. The convention enabled the group members to adjust their own work practices as they became aware of others' actions. Whereas Rogers' example illustrates explicit dissemination of awareness information, awareness may also result from implicit means, e.g. monitoring others' use of common objects (Heath and Luff, 1992; Hughes et al., 1992).

In addition to peripheral awareness, Robinson (1993) proposes other functional design considerations that address the multidimensional nature of shared object work: 1) the usage, function, and purpose of a shared object have to be clear and predictable, 2) a shared object must provide an overview; its presentation should convey its current state of use clearly, and 3) shared objects should include a dimension to account for both explicit and implicit communication.

Awareness information can complement and enhance these functional dimensions. First, it can enhance an object's predictability; it can help users to extrapolate an object's function in various circumstances by making its usage visible. This is sufficient according to Fischer (1991); a model of a system need not be technically accurate, but instead should be functional and fit for a purpose. Second, providing awareness information, e.g. the chronological usage of an object, can give an overview. With an overview, conventions can be formed around local contingencies: e.g. if a document is six months old, then file it in the archive. Third, awareness can complement the double level language facility of a shared object, by making salient "intuitive" access points for communication. For example, a system can provide facilities for clicking on a workspace member's icon to initiate a videoconference. If one sees that another is removing a document from a shared folder, then this can be a catalyst for informing the other of a broken convention. Thus, both awareness and multidimensionality in the design of shared objects can support conventions for an objects' use.

Awareness can be further qualified in terms of:

- *Reliability*: The dissemination of awareness information of the shared object needs to be clear and reliable. In Rogers' example, the convention functioned because the whiteboard made it clear to everybody in the group that all were aware of new files being checked out.

- *Cost and benefits:* Conventions for shared objects are like any aspect of cooperative system usage: subject to costs and benefits. Group calendars often fail if those putting in the extra effort are not those that benefit (Grudin, 1988). In Rogers' example, when peripheral awareness created an imbalance in costs and benefits, then the convention was broken. If the shared object actively collects and distributes awareness information, then following the conventions has a twofold advantage: sending information has no additional overhead and receiving it is not under the sender's control (Dourish and Bellotti, 1992).

- *Adaptation:* Providing awareness of others' work may potentially overload the user with information. In Roger's example, users were only peripherally aware of someone writing on the whiteboard, and were not disturbed in performing their task. Only by writing on the whiteboard did they became aware of exactly which files were checked out, an essential requirement for the convention to work, i.e. preventing file clashes. Thus, shared objects should smoothly adapt to changing work situations by providing differently focused awareness information. Since any notion of a work situation necessarily is subject to personal work practice, the system should allow users to individually tailor when, how, and where the awareness information is provided.

Research Setting and Methods

The focus of our study was done with users at the Federal Ministry of Family Affairs, Senior Citizens, Women, and Youth, located in Bonn, which currently has 12 primary POLITeam users: 1 unit leader, 6 ministry employees (responsible for specific content areas of the ministry), 3 typists in their own service unit, and additionally in Berlin, 2 users. The Bonn employees are distributed on two floors of the ministry and collaborate using the shared workspace and email. They perform services such as answering citizens' requests, doing tasks for the Minister, and collaborative speechwriting.

Our results are from a collection of material: workshops, site visits, design-team-user discussions, and user interviews. Initial semi-structured interviews were conducted before the system was introduced in order to learn about the potential users' work practice. Transcripts were also used from four workshops, in which the design team met with users: shortly after the first system version was finished, six months after the system introduction, in February of 1996 to present the new system version, and in June of 1996 to discuss specific new system features. A long list of user requirements for conventions emerged during this workshop.

This last workshop was followed after five months by a series of semi-structured interviews with the users, which lasted from 1 to 3 hours each. In these interviews, users were asked about: training and support, individual and collective work with the system, cooperation and use of information, the search facility, awareness of others, the shared workspace, and conventions: conventions the users had established and how, disturbing actions from others, conventions needed, violations, views on conventions, and their effect on work styles.

Information was also used from a log of reported problems and results from the user hotline and weekly site visits of design team members. Problems were categorized using content analysis (Holsti, 1969), into the categories of: computer hardware, POLITeam/related applications, individual work practices with the system, group practices with the system, and other. Coding was checked by a second coder with 93% agreement.

POLITeam provides shared folders and email to support communication and cooperation between two units in the ministry: the writing office and a ministry unit (referred to as Unit 57, not its real name). For document production and information exchange, the shared workspace has several purposes: First, it provides shared access to documents for the writing office and the Unit 57 members. The writing office either types a Unit 57 document from a dictation or written copy, or types in modifications. The workspace also provides access to a Unit 57 text for the production of a finished copy. Second, it enables Unit 57 members to exchange documents among themselves, such as when they coauthor documents. Third, it provides access for the unit leader to all documents that have been produced within the unit. Fourth, it provides access to common information sources about the ministry, which all users update.

Conventions in a Shared Workspace

Sharing a folder in POLITeam does not support articulation work. The shared folder gives only weak indications about it's accessibility in the group[3]. Communication and negotiation are complicated because each user has her own view on the documents in the folder. In this section we illustrate some difficulties that users had in using conventions with the POLITeam shared workspace.

Different perspectives and conventions

In the Ministry, we discovered that different groups using the shared workspace have different perspectives on how to organize the same information:
1) *The writing office view:* The writing office developed a solution to organize documents: first, according to the units and then, by members of a unit. Thus, each Unit 57 member has a workspace, shared with members of the writing

---

[3] Shared objects are labeled with different background colors. This, however, only indicates multiple access points, which could be from a single user (i.e. an alias) or from several users (i.e. a shared folder).

office. All these workspaces are contained in another folder, called the unit-folder, resulting in a two-level hierarchy. Whenever the writing office produces a document, it is placed in the appropriate unit/person workspace. This convention for how the shared workspaces are organized is logical for the work process of the writing office: their sorting and naming convention uses the name of the document owner and date of creation.

2) *The Unit members' view:* After some time of practical experience, the Unit 57 members found that it was easier for them to organize their documents according to their work processes. They collected documents produced by the writing office in task or process-specific folders, rather than according to Unit members. Their sorting criteria for documents in the workspace was based on the content of a document, e.g. a speech on an economic issue.

With the current configuration, only the writing office convention is supported. As a typist reports[4]:

> J has many subdirectories. Each have their own special names. When a document comes from J, it is very clear to us where the document should be placed back--she writes it on the paper document....However, we can't pay attention to and can't keep track of which subdirectories everyone has.

Thus, we discovered that the users structured their information using different methods, which correspond to their work roles, i.e. whether they type documents or write content. The problem for the group arises when the different users collaborate in a shared workspace which requires one common information structure for the groups' documents. Moreover, most users use a location-based finding strategy for documents (Wulf, 1997) and some Unit 57 members reported that they could not find documents among the vast array of information in the shared workspace because the system supported only the typists' view.

Multiple perspectives are intrinsic in many work situations and call for articulation. However, the process of reconciling different perspectives for the typists and Unit members is difficult since their individual perspectives are logical for their work roles and tasks. By having different file structures, the users lack a common overview. The problem here is that although a group reference would bring benefits, the cost of achieving it is that individuals would lose their individual overview.

Convention violations

Another difficulty with using conventions is that they are often violated. We describe three examples. First, in order to provide all users with access to the latest version of documents (the writing office especially needs to retain access to the latest electronic version of the document for further processing up the ministry hierarchy), a convention was set in the second workshop that a document must not

---

[4] All quotes are translated from German.

be removed from a shared folder. However, in practice, many Unit 57 members would drag the document out of the folder shared with the writing office into their task specific folder, violating the convention:

> It gets on my nerves, when people don't work on their things in the writing office shared folder. In the case of substituting, when you want to get these things, then it's really difficult.

Another violation occurs with file codes which serve as common references for electronic documents; the design team developed a system prompt for the users to enter the code. Yet, this convention is violated by all but one user:

> We [the writing office] give no file code. We type in 0000. Maybe they [the Unit members] give the correct file code afterwards.

> If I know the file code, I give it. Otherwise I use a fantasy number [rather than look it up].

> They don't type in the right file code. I must correct them. I must sort the documents into the right archive. And it must correspond with the file code. And that's annoying.

A third violation we observed is with the use of a shared address list. A convention was set which required that all members update the list. The users had methods for keeping addresses before POLITeam, such as storing lists in a drawer, and their personal lists provided most addresses for them, at least enough that they were unwilling to follow a group convention. As one user explains:

> It doesn't function yet, though, since we don't have conventions for it. Each one does something else. It functions only when all the users use this distribution tool. An address list functions only when all write it into a central place. It doesn't work when each one keeps a list in parallel.

Some users reported that the shared object did not exist before POLITeam, and they did not have previous conventions to carry over to it. According to one user:

> Not everything can be carried over into the computer work...Before, the address lists were organized so that you had it lying in the drawer in your desk. Now, it's being moved from the drawer in your desk into the public workspace as a share. Naturally, technology brings changes here. But it's a big advantage, that we can bring it from the private space into the public space.

Violations among agreements per se need not be detrimental to a task, such as in responding to changes in the environment (Beck and Bellotti, 1993) or if due to "productive laziness" (Rogers, 1993). In our cases, we feel that our users were simply unwilling to follow the conventions due to the overhead. And in these three examples of violations, breaking the conventions brings additional work and sometimes annoyance to others. Providing technical means to ease using the conventions, as with the file code prompt, was also not sufficient to get users to follow the convention. They still found a way around it. This demonstrates to us a gap between the designers' assumptions of user behavior and actual user behavior (e.g. Beck and Bellotti, 1993). And setting conventions via social means in the workshops, as was done with forbidding document removal and common address lists, also did not insure that the conventions would be followed.

Despite the fact that violations annoy some users, most users report that they do not want to be controlled to follow conventions. Nor does the Unit leader want to be an "enforcer". He argues for the users to inform each other of violations in "subtle and sensible ways". In the case of the file code, there is not a clear solution to this problem, but one possibility is to try providing software to make the file codes more available. In the case of using the shared address list, we believe it involves two factors: an imbalance in the overhead and benefits of using a shared object (Grudin, 1988), but it is also a problem concerning the lack of understanding of the properties of the shared object. One reason, as the above user mentioned, is that the address list is, by analogy to its use before POLITeam, thought of as a personal item, which indicates that the address list as a means to share is not clear for this user. However, in the case of removing the document from the shared folder, awareness information can inform group members of the consequences of their actions for the group, i.e. that removing a shared document from the workspace prevents others from having access to it.

Conventions carried over from nontechnological work

All the users have implicitly adopted a convention of distinguishing between public and private workspaces, and its use is quite similar across users. No one explicitly discussed borders of public and private workspaces. Private workspaces are respected; no one wants to search or look at anyone's private workspace, and conversely wants no one to search theirs. In the case of a person substituting, the substitute would not search private spaces. When questioned how this convention arose, many users pointed to their work practice experience before POLITeam:

> Private areas should be protected. It's good that I can't search L's desk. This corresponds to our earlier experience with our real desks.

> There are certainly private areas here. Such as my private workspace. If someone looks for a circulation folder here [pointing to the in- and out-box on her desk], they can search in the out-box, but not in the in-box. Similarly, what lays on my private desk, that is private.

> It [the distinction between public and private areas] was made very natural and implicit.

> It was obvious to us. The system is an exact technical reproduction of our work. You observed how work functions in the Ministry, and then you tried to reproduce it electronically. So it's no wonder that conventions used in our normal work are carried over.

This example of implicitly setting a convention shows that when the analogy is clear, conventions from nontechnological work before POLITeam can be easily carried over and applied to system use. Applying analogy from nontechnological work to technological work is a valuable learning tool, since people try to understand new processes in terms of a conceptual framework that they already know (Carroll and Thomas, 1982). In nontechnological face-to-face work, the public and visible nature of common artifacts make their uses clear (e.g. Hughes et al., 1992; Heath and Luff, 1992; Heath et al., 1993). Before POLITeam, the users had a clear distinction on their physical desks between public and private workspaces, e.g. private spaces being in-boxes or locked drawers. The visible nature of the distinction may have contributed to a formation of a common representation about public and private areas. The users apparently applied the same notion of public and private areas to their technological workspace; in fact, the metaphor itself of "shared workspace" could have facilitated this transfer. This example highlights for us that conventions formed in face-to-face nontechnological work which may be easy to form because of the visible usage of shared objects, can be carried over and applied as conventions in a CSCW system.

Emerging work processes

A shared folder opportunistically set up between ministry departments in Bonn and Berlin now enables documents to be accessed almost immediately, whereas before POLITeam, they were exchanged via regular mail. However, this emerging work process again points to the difficulty of knowing what conventions are needed, in particular, how the shared workspace between Bonn and Berlin should be organized. Since the easy and fast transaction of information between the two locations is a new experience, it is not clear yet what documents will be exchanged. As one Unit 57 member reported:

> When we use more information together with Berlin, then we must really think what [shared work areas] would be useful. E.g. should we have things where we pack five things inside, or something else? It also depends on what it is, what kind of information. I think that in certain folders, it must be this way. It is necessary. Otherwise we have chaos. Or someone has chaos for themselves.

The nature of this introduction of a shared folder illustrates how conventions cannot always be planned at the outset of a new work process. Orlikowski (1996) cites an example of how specialists, because of their experience, were able to recognize the need for some conventions to fit an emerging work process. However, with our inexperienced users, we see the need to provide awareness of others' activities to show who is using what public information; this could help users define the conventions for the organization of a shared folder.

It is not only with emerging work processes that conventions are difficult to define. Although the users recognize the need for conventions for many procedures, most users report that they do not have a clear idea of the activities of other users. The users themselves describe the lack of awareness of others' use of shared objects as one of the obstacles in defining conventions:

> We must think over, depending on the information that we have, which shared work areas would be sufficient. But I'm not in the situation where I can see that, i.e. where I get information other than that for my own workspace.

> For my own archive, what I set up myself, then I can look at my own example. But for a real archive [shared], that would be set up for others, then we must really think it over; what the system offers, and what is necessary. But I can't evaluate that at this point.

> There's always a certain openness of doing things and a certain stringency. These are the two poles....Each one arranges their desk in their own way, and that's their freedom....The problem is that we are in an evolutionary process here--we need conventions for our normal contact

262

with each other, our process. We need to find a balance between individual operations and conventions...There are things that must be reproducible. PoLiTeam's success depends on this.

The Development of Conventions

With new technology, coordination practices have been observed to develop over time in response to the changing nature of work (Orlikowski, 1996). We have also discovered through our user experience that developing an understanding of the use of a shared object takes time and also influences convention formation.

Stage	Time Span	Characteristics of stage: major problems/events
I. Learning basic functionality; mostly single-user idea of system	1st 6 months after system introduced	Problems with windows, hardware, basic computer skills: • struggling with text processing • transferring individual work practices to system • adapting group functionality to meet the group's needs
II. Discovering ways for structuring information	between 6 - 9 months	Developed own style for structuring information: • structuring information according to own work process • collecting information (finding semantic connections)
III. Developing awareness of group use of system	1 ½ years after system introduction	Developing awareness of cooperative work with system • discussed conventions for group use in workshop • discussed consequences of other members' actions
IV. Mature group working with system	?	We would expect the following: • new, unanticipated use of tools • conventions would be learned • implicit conventions would be developed

Table I. Proposed stages of user group development with PoLiTeam.

We have observed that since the introduction of the PoLiTeam system, our user work group has evolved in its use of the system. The data from site-visits, workshops, and interviews suggest that we can characterize the development of our user work group, with respect to its system use, in terms of rough stages. First, we see a trend in the problems reported at the site visits by members of the design team. The amount of problems concerning individual work practices declined sharply over time, as did hardware and software problems to a lesser extent. Early on, users requested help with their group work practices, and these mainly concerned adapting group functionality to fit their needs, e.g. setting up a shared folder or a common address list. However, in the last workshop, the users focused mainly on discussing group conventions, and it was at this time that they discussed the consequences of their actions as group members. Thus, initially, issues about group practices concerned setting up appropriate group functionality; 18 months later in the workshop, discussion about group practices concerned conventions about how to *coordinate* use of the functionality.

We have thus identified changes in attitudes toward the system over time, and even "milestones" in the system use. Through these, we distinguish stages. It is important to note that the time span of stages can only be roughly determined, since we interviewed users and held workshops at specific time points. We believe that although there was probably concurrence with some events, most likely the stages are sequential, i.e. users could not have discussed group conventions in the workshops without first learning system basics (Table I).

Thus, the users' requirement for convention support emerged after working with the system for roughly one and a half years (Stage III). This emphasizes to us that the recognition of many conventions is associated with the process of gaining an understanding of the function of shared objects in the context of work.

Design for Conventions

In this section we present the POLITeam awareness client, a prototype system, which emphasizes the mediating role of shared objects in order to support articulation work. Rather than attempting to formally capture the notion of conventions, the system includes technical means for providing overview and shared awareness in the usage of common objects to help define and maintain conventions. These facilities can help overcome some of the convention difficulties, by providing a group context of system use; it is thus a step towards the provision of common artifacts instead of shared objects (Robinson, 1993).

Awareness support has been one of the main goals of the POLITeam project from the very beginning (Sohlenkamp et al., 1997). A special client adding awareness features through a variety of mechanisms to the standard groupware functionality has been developed (Figure 1). The client is based on the standard desktop metaphor to build on existing skills of the users. Document hierarchy and the contents of opened containers are displayed in different windows. Users have the possibility to define different views on objects regarding sorting criteria and iconic or textual display, thus allowing for individual working styles. In the following we will concentrate on these facilities and give a perspective on their influence on the support of conventions in system use.

Peripheral awareness

The system supports a non-disruptive way of displaying others activities. Users do not have to focus on the information presentation explicitly, but rather they should be able to perceive it using peripheral vision; thus, conventions are reinforced via minor user interface cues. In POLITeam, cues include the representation of active users in a workspace, color changes, and the optical enlargement of objects that are the target of others' activities (Figure 1).

Synchronous actions of other users are indicated by annotating icons with actor-symbols. The colors used in icon overlays and for the actor-symbols correspond to the role based color assignment that is used in the ministry. Over time, these cues are gradually reduced, so the most current activities are more visible than older ones. These mechanisms provide overview at-a-glance of the shared usage of objects: users can easily spot activities, while still allowing them to work normally with their documents because the hierarchy and the relative positions of objects remain unchanged.

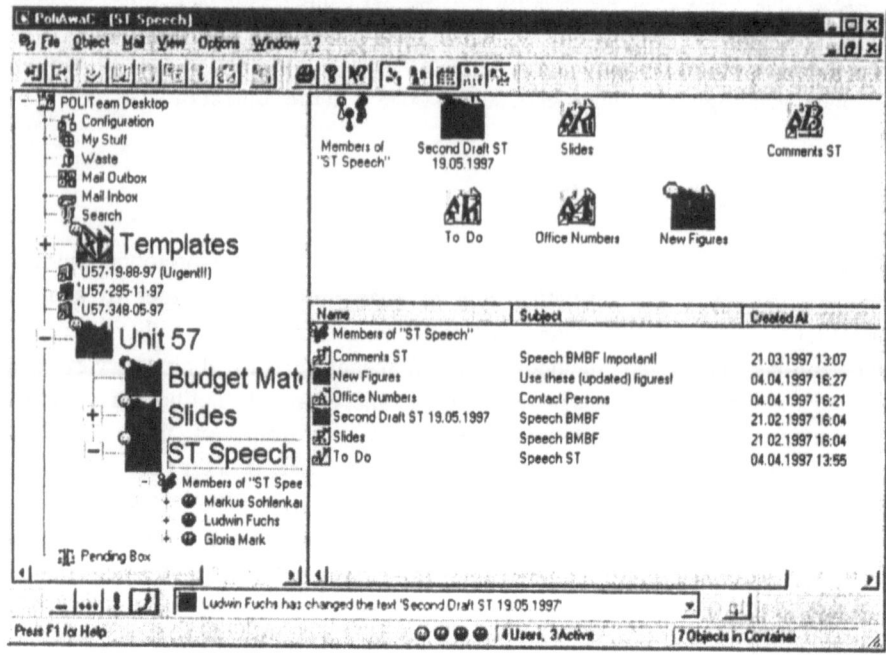

Figure 1. The POLITeam awareness client

Chronological overview is facilitated by an *event bar*, a drop-down text box, that can be opened to display the list (latest first) of all events for an object. The event bar is also used as a textual presentation medium, that always shows the latest event that is of interest to a user, displayed in the color associated with the user that generated the event. The event bar can be attached to the client main window (Figure 1), or as a stand-alone window (Figure 2). In stand-alone mode, it can be used to monitor cooperative activities, even if the working focus is on other applications.

Additionally, users can enter text in the text box, which will be distributed as a message associated with the currently selected object to all other users. This allows users to provide awareness information that cannot be collected automatically by the system (e.g., the rationale behind a convention violation). Informal communication facilities, e. g. launching a video conference, are attached to the actor symbols in the display of awareness information. In this way the system implements an intuitive integration of double level language communication.

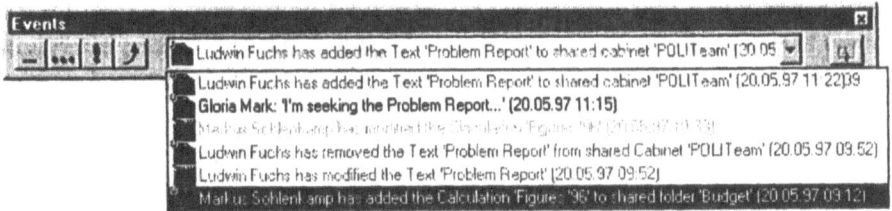

Figure 2. Expanded history list

Figure 2 shows an example how the event bar can be used to support conventions. The drop-down list has been expanded to show the complete set of current events. It can easily be determined who performed which actions on which documents. In this example, a user violated a convention by removing a document from a shared workspace. Some time later, another user reacts to this by asking for the document. This, in turn, results in the document being reintroduced into the workspace by the first user, allowing others to access it again.

Contextual awareness: supporting individual working styles

In POLITeam, the filtering of awareness information can be applied on the basis of individual work practice or on a common work practice of the group. To accomplish this, the system uses the metaphor of a situation to allow users to specify awareness profiles.

Work situation	System provides awareness information
"Working on the document"	when the user opens the document
"Accessing the parent container"	when the user opens the folder, that contains the document
"Accessing any parent container"	when the user opens any higher-level folder containing the document
"Immediately"	immediately, regardless of the user's current activity
"Working on the same process"	when the user accesses another document that shares the same file code

Table II. Work situations in which users may receive document-related awareness information.

An object, such as a document, defines a number of activities as well as a variety of work situations in which it may be involved, both of which can be selected by the user to tailor her personal awareness preferences to her individual work practice. Work situations are highly dynamic and need not be restricted on actions performed on the target object itself but include actions on objects that share certain relationships or similarities in terms of the application domain. Table II lists the work situations for documents in which users may receive document-related awareness information.

These details of awareness preferences can be defined using awareness profiles, which can be attached to single objects, collections of objects, or whole classes of objects. The system gives notifications about events only in situations that conform to a user's subscribed set of profiles. In this way it is possible for users to set up their interest in awareness information in a natural way, in terms of domain specific work patterns, e. g.: "whenever I open any document I want to see what happens to other documents, that belong to the same process".

Enforcing group awareness

Awareness profiles are shared objects. Users can create new awareness profiles and jointly subscribe to existing ones. Thus, awareness profiles not only enable individual diversification of system feedback, but also provide means for reliable awareness information, by enforcing joint subscription of profiles in a group.

For example, one of the conventions concerning the shared unit folder is not to remove any object from the shared folder. To support this convention, users can use a common awareness profile for the unit folder. This profile issues a notification if a user removes a document from the shared folder. The notification situation of the profile is "Working on the unit-folder", which applies as long as a user has opened the folder. Thus, awareness about the violation of this convention is only supported among users performing similar tasks, which increases the chances to create a shared awareness about conventions. As the visibility of activities on those objects is enhanced, the group may be more likely to apply social protocols to govern their actions.

The awareness profiles allow group members to keep a balance between tailoring the information needs according to their individual sense of work practice and receiving feedback about activities of other users.

Conclusion

Conventions for using a shared workspace like PoLiTeam are *vast*; they encompass all aspects of operations with the system, ranging from managing shared activities to document storage. Whereas we cannot generalize beyond our users, conventions appear to be unique within a work group, and in fact, may even be unique across work groups using the same system.

The current model of organizational life is that of flexibility and learning, reflected in much research focusing on the role of the situated nature of work. Applying such a model makes sense for referring to groupware conventions: conventions are dynamic and can be unpredictable. Changes in organizational structure, work practices, and group membership all call for conventions to adapt to fit the environment. With our users, new information exchange patterns were emerging, as new shared workspaces were set up for different groups of people. Along with the opportunity to exchange information easily and fast, however, is uncertainty as to what conventions are needed in order to manage the shared workspace. With time, users can realize what information is beneficial to exchange; the conventions will also take time to develop. Even after nearly two years of system use, the users are still discovering work operations for which conventions are needed. Conventions needed for shared archives did not become clear until a large quantity of electronic documents built up over time.

In our experience we found that some conventions failed. One reason is due to an imbalance in costs and benefits. Yet even when a technical solution was implemented to make it easier for users to follow conventions, users still found a way around them, which points to the gap between the designers' assumptions and users' behavior. The method by which some conventions were formed, via social means in workshops, could also have contributed to their failure. Workshops bring people out of their everyday work context, which has advantages, e.g. for focused training and discussion. But discussion alone does not suffice; as Gerson and Star (1986) illustrate with coordination. Grounding discussion in the work context is necessary, and in our case, it supplies the essential information for forming conventions.

Although the need for conventions may be recognized, it is not always clear to the users how conventions should be defined. When a shared object lacks the properties of clear usage, overview, and awareness of others' activities, then it is difficult for users to mesh procedures. The users themselves reported a need to understand better the work practices of the other group members in order to define the conventions. These experiences suggested to us the requirement of enhancing a shared object with additional information to make people's activities with the object visible and reproducible.

Our approach was to support conventions implicitly through non-directive technical means, by supplying users with awareness information about ongoing activities in the system, through feedback and event information. Future empirical research is called for, to track with long-term observation the effect of awareness information on convention use, as well as other social implications of convention use, such as violations, and their development in the face of emerging change.

Acknowledgements

We thank Uta Pankoke-Babatz and Konrad Klöckner for their help in our research. We also thank Wolfgang Prinz, Mike Robinson, Volker Wulf, and our reviewers for their valuable comments.

References

Beck, E. E., and Bellotti, V. (1993). "Informed opportunism as strategy: supporting coordination in distributed collaborative writing", *Proceedings of ECSCW '93*, September 13-17, 1993, Milan, Kluwer Academic Publishers, Dordrecht, pp. 233-248.

268

Carroll, J.M. and Thomas, J.C. (1982): "Metaphors and the Cognitive Representation of Computing Systems", *IEEE Trans. On Systems, Man, And Cybernetics*, vol. SMC-12, no. 2.

Dourish and Bellotti, V. (1992): "Awareness and coordination in shared workspaces", *Proceedings of CSCW '92*, October 31- November 4, 1992, Toronto, ACM press, pp. 107-114.

Fischer, G. (1991): "The importance of models in making complex systems comprehensible", in M. J. Tauber and D. Ackermann (eds.): *Mental Models and Human-Computer Interaction 2*, North-Holland, Amsterdam, pp. 3-36.

Gerson, E. M. and Star, S. L. (1986): "Analyzing due process in the workplace", *ACM Transactions on Office Information Systems*, vol. 4, no. 3, July 1986, pp. 257-270.

Grudin, J. (1988) "Why CSCW applications fail: Problems in the design and evaluation of organizational interfaces", *Proceedings CSCW '88*, September 26-29, 1988, Portland, pp. 85-93.

Heath, C., Jirotka, M., Luff, P., and Hindmarsh, J. (1993): "Unpacking collaboration: the interactional organisation of trading in a city dealing room", *Proceedings of ECSCW '93*, September 13-17, 1993, Milan, Kluwer Academic Publishers, Dordrecht, pp. 155-170.

Heath, C. and Luff, P. (1992): "Collaboration and Control: Crisis management and multimedia technology in London Underground Line Control Rooms", *Computer Supported Cooperative Work (CSCW), An International Journal*, vol.1, pp. 69-94.

Holsti, Ole R. (1969): *Content Analysis for the Social Sciences and Humanities*. Addison-Wesley, Reading.

Hughes, J. A., Randall, D., and Shapiro, D. (1992): "Faltering from ethnography to design", *Proceedings of CSCW '92*, October 31-November 4, 1992, Toronto, ACM press, pp. 115-122.

Klöckner, K., Mambrey, P., Sohlenkamp, M., Prinz, M., Fuchs, L., Kolvenbach, S., Pankoke-Babatz, U., and Syri, A., (1995): "POLITeam - Bridging the Gap between Bonn and Berlin for and with the Users", *Proceedings of ECSCW '95*, Stockholm, September 10-14 1995, Kluwer Academic Publishers, Dordrecht, pp. 17-31.

Mambrey, P. Mark, G. and Pankoke-Babatz, U. (1996): "Integrating User Advocacy into Participatory Design: the Designers' Perspective", *Proceedings of the Participatory Design Conference '96*, Boston, November 13-15, pp. 251-259.

Orlikowski, W. J. (1996): "Improvising Organizational transformation over time: a situated change perspective", *Information Systems Research*, vol. 7, no.1, March 1996, pp. 63-92.

Prinz, W. and Kolvenbach, S., (1996). "Support for workflows in a ministerial environment", *Proceedings of CSCW'96*, November 16-20, 1996, Boston, ACM press, pp.199-208.

Robinson, M. (1993). "Design for unanticipated use.... " *Proceedings of ECSCW '93*, September 13-17, 1993, Milan, Kluwer Academic Publishers, Dordrecht, pp.187-202.

Rogers, Yvonne (1993). "Coordinating Computer-Mediated Work", *Computer Supported Cooperative Work (CSCW), An International Journal*, vol. 1, pp. 295-315.

Schmidt, K. and Bannon, L. (1992). "Taking CSCW Seriously: Supporting Articulation Work", *Computer Supported Cooperative Work (CSCW), An International Journal*, vol. 1, no. 1-2, pp. 7-40.

Sohlenkamp, M., Fuchs, L., Genau, A. (1997). "Awareness and Cooperative Work: The POLITeam Approach", *Proceedings of HICSS 30*, Jan. 9-11, Wailea, Hawaii, IEEE Computer Society Press, pp. 549-558.

Star, S. L. and Griesemer, J. R. (1989): "Institutional Ecology, 'Translations' and Boundary Objects: Amateurs and Professionals in Berkeley's Museum of Vertebrate Zoology", 1907-39. *Social Studies of Science*, vol. 19, pp. 387-420.

Wulf, V. (1997). "Storing and retrieving documents in a shared workspace: experiences from the political administration". To appear in *Human Computer Interaction: INTERACT 97*, Chapman & Hall, UK.

Supporting the Flow of Information Through Constellations of Interaction

Tony Salvador
Intel Corporation, USA
tony_salvador@ccm.jf.intel.com

Sara Bly
Sara Bly Consulting, USA
sara_bly@acm.org

Abstract: In field studies designed to uncover opportunities for computationally-intensive business applications, we observed an interaction pattern we term "constellations" in which people depend on a variety of people and information sources to perform the duties of their employ. Constellations are significant for several reasons: constellations extensively cross organizational and corporate boundaries, the value of a constellation depends on the individual being appropriately *in sync* at any one time with the elements of the constellation, constellations are uniquely defined in terms of the individual who draws maximum benefit from that particular collection of people and information, and the value from a constellation derives from all of the elements existing in a particular work context to support the individual who is the hub of the constellation. From a design perspective, the implications are for CSCW technologies that do not assume well-defined organizational and corporate boundaries, but rather that support individual access to and management of personal connections and interactions.

Introduction

In the past few years, much has been said about the value of studying actual practice in context to inform the design of computer technologies (Blomberg et al, 1993; Holtzblatt et al, 1993; Hughes et al, 1994; Plowman et al, 1995; Shapiro, 1994). Such methods in the high tech industry provide a closer look at actual user activity and the ways in which novel technologies might support those activities (Lewis et al, 1996). However, unlike traditional ethnographic studies, the intent

269

J. Hughes et al. (eds.), Proceedings of the Fifth European Conference on Computer Supported Cooperative Work, 269-280.
© *1997 Kluwer Academic Publishers.*

here is not so much to seek general principles about society but rather to identify data that is applicable for design. Such studies are one way of identifying opportunities for new technologies. For a business that knows its general area of interest but has flexibility in its product range, studies of real world work practice can be an excellent method for eliciting opportunities for designing new products.

In the work reported here, our goal was to identify opportunities for business applications that take advantage of today's computing power. We set out two phases of field work: first to explore a range of domains and work activity that already use intensive computational power and second to observe current business practices that might utilize more computing power, particularly as drawn from experiences in the first exploration. Our goal was to translate the work activity into design ideas.

Our basic finding suggested that not only did people rely on their computing power for their jobs, but more significantly, they relied on interactions with other people and information sources to at least as great an extent. Specifically, we identified a persistent pattern of such interactions that we call *constellations* as sets of people and information sources connected to a specific individual, which cross organizational and corporate boundaries and which exist in a particular work context. That is, constellations differ from personal "networks" in that the people and information sources provide value in an immediate and specific context, and constellations differ from teams in that the constellation members may not know each other and only contingently share common goals.

The purpose of this work was to identify new opportunities for computing power. However, examining our data through our "designerly eyes" (Henderson, 1993), we see constellation interactions not only as a major aspect of accomplishing work but also as an opportunity, and indeed a need, for CSCW technologies to recognize these interactions. These interactions demonstrate a need not to support teams (viz. groupware) or personal networks (viz. personal information managers—applications and processes that view the individual either in isolation or as merely a part of a formal organization—but rather to support constellations. Specifically, low-level system architectures too often assume a fixed, a priori arrangement of access to people and information, focusing largely within organizational boundaries and limiting the ability of an individual to access, manage, organize and view ever-changing information in a unique constellation from an individual work context.

In the following paper, we describe the field work, give examples of the interview data, and suggest the relevance of our study for design of CSCW technologies.

Study Plan

Our primary goal in the study was to gain an understanding of the ways in which intensive computing power supports an individual's work. Thus, we wanted to get broad exposure to a variety of work environments and tasks in the first exploratory phase of our study. We interviewed 25 participants in five organizations using open-ended questions about their work, their tools, and their interactions.

Participants

We chose organizations and participants within those organizations based on work that would utilize computing power. We brainstormed a list of tasks that would need intensive computing such as multimedia applications, image processing, and simulations. From our list, we choose areas of rapid information summarization, large data sets, and complex calculations as those most relevant to the business environments and computing intensive application focus we needed. Our domains for study were a government scientific laboratory, a bank equity trading department, a division of a government intelligence community, a high-tech product business, and a service that provides research findings to elected officials. The duties of our participants included stock traders on a trading floor, portfolio managers, scientific researchers, market researchers, a branch manager, expert consultants, information analysts, and people whose job it is to collect information from far-ranging sources.

Method

We scheduled 1 to 1 1/2 hour unstructured, observational interviews with each of our participants in their work environments. With the exception of the three buyers on the stock market trading floor, we interviewed participants individually. Two interviewers were present. Our data consists of audio tapes and transcripts, notes, and occasional still photographs.

Our questions were initially open-ended to the extent that we asked two primary questions: 1) What are your responsibilities? 2) Describe in detail a recent project on which you've worked. From each of these, we used artifacts in the work environment and further questioning about tools and sources of information to determine who, what, why, how, where and when work was accomplished to the extent that interview time permitted. Questioning was guided by our ultimate purpose: to understand their environment sufficiently to develop useful computing concepts.

Data Interpretation

With our data, we were looking for emergent patterns that cut across all or most of the interviewees in the sample. In fact, we were specifically trying to build a model for our data that we could then use to derive useful product concepts. That is, as practitioners, we were not intent on representing our subjects' experiences in their own terms, but rather we focused on identifying an appropriate transformation of the data that retained the context and veracity of the subjects' experience but which is useful for designing computing products. An example of this approach is represented in Mateas, Salvador, Scholtz and Sorensen (1996).

In this particular case, we were looking pointedly for new uses of computing power among information and knowledge workers. Thus, we were looking for a common model to describe the data as well as one that would make sense to designers and engineers. The constellation interactions was an emergent pattern among all the interviews. And, in fact, all of the subjects' individual environments can be viewed through constellation lenses. However, from the perspective of each user, the constellation model might not best explain any one subject's environment. It is important to note that the constellations emerged as an opportunity for design rather than as a careful description of the work environments.

Specific examples of our data illustrate our observations and the emergence of constellations.

Dwight the Physicist

Dwight's job is to perform complex numerical calculations to help define the flexibility and limits of a multi-national agreement for monitoring underwater nuclear tests. Dwight describes his work as very computer-centric:

> D: "...Most of my time is spent sitting in this chair...I've shifted gradually into doing computer simulations of physical phenomena...another way of describing my work is that it focuses on shock waves and hydrodynamics. Most of the time in my career I've been using the Crays because that was the place for a long time, the only place where you could get lots of good CPU time and the Crays are still faster by an order of magnitude than anything we do on our regular computers...."

However, we quickly start to hear ways in which Dwight also depends on others

> D: "...And we have what's called a boundary condition in an attempt to try to understand that surface. If - imagine hypothetically, though, I could shift from a condition which I ignored the waves to another one in which I simulated the waves. One of the results might change a little bit or maybe even quite a lot.
>
> One of the things that I'm supposed to be doing that's a major part of the requirements of my job is to know when I'm going to get into a situation where things are going to change drastically.
>
> T: "So you're looking for one of the prime effects on the wave? Well, what conditions you have to pay attention to -

D: "Yeah, that's right. And some combination of knowledge and experience *and talking to other experts to know what's critical and what's unimportant.* This plot here, which you can have a copy of if it matters, is an example of what I'm calculating. Energy total means the energy in the wave. This is time and you see there are several different lines here. They all come down - this is a log scale here so they drop a lot. This is from original energy represents perhaps 10 tons of explosion. It's dropping in order of magnitude about here, but interestingly, these calculations represent finer and finer zoning *and as John pointed out, it's getting so that this last one is almost level and in fact the calculation represented here may form, should form another line that's out about here, closer to level.* So the point is that I do repeated calculations of something. I can't take the first calculation and assume that's the answer, I have to do repeated calculations...."

Dwight works in a small group of other scientists, particularly with John, as their work often has similar goals which enables them to look at, understand, and comment on each other's results. That is, Dwight and, in this case, John, are not simply colleagues, but colleagues who at this time are sharing the ongoing context of the work they are doing. Further, Dwight is specifically working with John in this example, and John is in the same organization as Dwight. In this regard, Dwight also mentions regularly interacting with his boss and his assistant post-doc. All of this seems rather straightforward.

However, we also learn that Dwight is responsible not only for his own work, but for certain input to the multi-national task force. That is, Dwight needs to understand where his research intersects with the test ban treaty negotiations especially when it comes to offering technical details for the decision making. Dwight has contact with certain individuals who are responsible for bringing Dwight's work into their discussions and on whom Dwight relies for knowing the requirements and context for his work.

D: "...but my stuff feeds into a study to try to understand if the explosion occurs here, how does it propagate and what do these things, which might represent barriers, like for instance right here is a very significant barrier ...."

In addition to the content of his work, Dwight depends on understanding the software he uses to calculate the simulations of physical phenomena. In this case, the primary wave code he was using for this work at this time was written not by him, but by someone else at a different organization. Dwight knows the author, and they have interacted frequently and, again, in the context of the actual work. Dwight refers to him casually, as if he were an obvious member of the "team".

D: "Yeah, well because of the fact that Andy's at NRL he gave us a version of [the code] and we've been making mostly quite minor changes to it."

Other pieces of code were written by people in other divisions in the government laboratory where Dwight works.

D: "Well, in solar luminescence the guys in [another division] we're dependent on. But one of the nice things for me personally is [the wave simulation code] is almost entirely self-contained and if Andy fell under a truck why we could manage pretty well. Now that's not true of the typical code effort around here where usually one organization or one group is developing a code and other people are using it. And there's all sorts of psychological *questions about whether or not you're close to the developers either psychologically or physically. For instance, it's a real hassle if you can't discuss anything about the code over the telephone...If I want to just ask something pretty simple about how do I get this plot, I can call somebody. But still they're over on the other side of the lab. Annoying. And it tends to be that they tend to do things when they make an update or an improvement they tell the 2 dozen other people in their hallway and we never hear about it.*

In fact, Dwight continually works to understand the code and to maintain his "in sync'ness" with that element of his constellation. Notice also that Dwight wanted to discuss not the code per se, but the result of the code in the form of his particular plot. This implies that Dwight is not necessarily interested in code the same way in which the developers would be interested. In fact, Dwight's issues with the code reflect the value *he* gets from the code, i.e., his perspective, rather than the perspective of the developers. Thus, his particular issues may well force the developers to evaluate their work in Dwight's context.

In this particular example, we also see a case of non-reciprocity. While Dwight holds these people in his constellation, the others clearly do not consider Dwight to be a part of theirs—at least not to the extent that they would provide him updates, etc. The value relationship is one way; Dwight is primarily interested in the code because of the plots that he can produce, i.e., his perspective. Furthermore, the value Dwight is drawing from the developers is mostly unilateral.

Dwight routinely depends on a variety of people and information sources on a regular basis: John and others in his group provide feedback on results, his manager provides direction and priorities, simulation code experts (from two different organizations) provide specifications and constraints of the software, expert colleagues (both collocated and physically separate) provide knowledge about boundary conditions on the simulation, and the US negotiating team members provide insight into the committee perspective and needs. Note further that Dwight needs to stay in sync with all of these people only to the extent that his current project continues, i.e., so long as he remains in the current context. These people are not on the same "team" as Dwight, nor are they simply a part of his personal network. Rather these people are bound to Dwight such that they provide significant and specific value to Dwight, albeit to greater and lesser extents. Dwight relies on these other people and information sources to accomplish his job — and for all this we see limited technological support.

Chuck the Congressional Analyst

In contrast to Dwight, Chuck is a biologist responsible for public and environmental health issues at a research service that exclusively serves the Congress of the United States. Chuck's main responsibility is to be a non-partisan expert on a number of public health issues, including the nation's blood supply and tobacco. In this case, non-partisan refers not only to a lack of political bias, but also to a lack of personal bias, that is, Chuck does not perform any of his own research, but continuously amasses information from a variety of sources and summarizes that information as objectively as possible. As expected he uses a number of sources and, not surprisingly, relies on personal contacts:

> C: "...I'm just handling more information because I'm learning more and I know more, but also because the actual sources, of that information are growing. See, when I started, you know, we relied mostly on paper and the telephone. But to that we have added in the last year e-mail and Internet so now in addition to paper, which is - which are the journals that cross my desk, the newsletters that cross my desk, the clippings that we get, the mail that comes, and in addition to the telephone messages, I now have the e-mail messages which is - and the Internet. So two more sources of information and the day hasn't grown - the number of hours in the week has not grown any more so I spend more time interfacing with these various sources of information and I spend less time reading books and lengthy documents. *I still think the telephone is the most - single most important source of information by far."*

> T: "Why? Other than because you like to talk?"

> C: "Because it is specific...Because the telephone is the only way you can access exactly what it is that you want."

> S: "Can you say some more about that?"

> C: "Well, the - when I want to find - and I should point out that I was both as a graduate student and then as I university teacher, which I was for a couple of years before I came here - George Mason - and I continued to teach...on the side to help earn money I was a freelance science journalist and I wrote magazine articles...did some television...and when I wanted to know something I picked up the telephone and that's the way I still operate primarily. *When I want to know something and confirm something, I still use the telephone.*

When Chuck wants to know something specific, that means he is working on a specific problem, in a specific context. He does not just pick up the phone and call anyone. In fact, if he is concerned with a specific element of the nation's blood supply, e.g., the prevalence of some disease, he calls the person whom he knows personally and whom he knows understands the issue. The point is that Chuck has members of his constellation around the blood supply who are most knowledgeable given the particular context of a specific blood supply issue.

However, Chuck does not limit himself to the phone as evidenced by a quick look about his office. Nevertheless, his point about the growth of information sources and the relative stability of the number of hours in a day is well taken if a bit ironic. The finding and understanding of specific issues is increasingly difficult, which again pushes him to specific people and sources he knows.

> C: "E-mail is getting more helpful. The problem with the Internet is that it is 99% garbage. Now given that I probably have access on here to - I don't know - 10, between 10 and 50 million pages or maybe 100 million now it might be potentially - somewhere out there - 99% of it as far as I'm concerned is probably complete crap. *The other problem with the Internet is that - the Internet is that it is unedited.* The Internet is great and we use it daily. The Internet is great *if you know who - if you're familiar with the source of the information.* So the Internet is terrific for going into the home page of the Centers for Disease Control [CDC], the government public health agency, and it's a place that we use a

lot. Because we know about CDC, we know who they are, we know the caliber of the work they do and we know that we can rely on the information they put in their home page and so it is with a lot of other places. *So if you already know something about the people - them at the other end - then that can be very useful.*

Chuck holds not only the information at the CDC Home Page as a part of his constellation, but also certain people at the CDC as related to a specific topic. Moreover, Chuck does not simply rely on information he sees, he needs to be aware of its source and the quality of the information.

Finally, and not surprisingly, much of the swapping and sharing of information comes from relationships of trust, giving as well as getting, although perhaps over an extended period of time:

> C: "I have had 4 or 5 phone calls in the last 3 days for information from a woman who is a staff member on a house subcommittee. She has written an oversight report ... And word is out that she is doing this, but there's plenty of people out there who would like to know what she has said and she will call me up - ... - she called up, she wanted - it's an article from Science Magazine and she wanted some clarification... So I just did some calculations saying where I get them from, where the numbers come from... Now the - that little interaction between us is a) confidential. Well, that's the most important thing about it. And b) in this case was done over a Xerox machine. But it's - but it illustrates the nature of the relationship we have with the staffers that they can call us - you know, the very fact that she wants to talk about [a topic] would be of interest to other people because she - that by extension she's interested in how effective these antibody tests are and whether a...test would be better and blah, blah, blah. But she knows when she calls me up that I'm not going to, you know, divulge. This in itself is just a small piece but if you string together all the 2 dozen or so interactions Susan and I have had over the past 10 weeks, then you can begin to see what the hell she's up to - you know, as her -...not foes, but the [scientific] community is kind of anxious to know what the hell she's going to say in this damn report. And obviously I have a fairly good idea...."

This example shows a nice situation of reciprocity. Chuck's contacts with her offer him a chance to "begin to see what the hell she's up to". More directly, Chuck is reflecting on his role as a member of *her* constellation. That is, his expertise in the blood supply (an expertise he maintains through reliance on his "blood supply constellation") and his specific role relative to congress render him particularly useful to this subcommittee staffer who's writing a report. Over time, then, the staffer and Chuck develop a relationship around this particular context -- the staffer comes to trust not only Chuck's technical knowledge, but also his discretion in these matters. It is likely that once the staffer is finished with the report, Chuck will no longer be included in the staffer's active constellations. In fact, Chuck will be relegated to "network" status. Similarly, Chuck's constellations evolve as he finds better and more efficient sources of information related to his evolving sets of issues.

Like Dwight, Chuck routinely depends on a variety of people and information sources on a regular basis. He has established a number of written sources for which he knows the authors, their accuracy, and their biases. More importantly, he feels comfortable calling sources whether or not he knows them personally, but often based only on reputation and Chuck's own particular needs at that time. But finally, he has developed a set of relationships which he both feeds and which feed him in a regular and ongoing way.

Design Implications

Although our focus was on individual workers and on the ways in which they utilized computing power, we found that the most noticeable aspect of the work was not the information processing itself but the ways in which people accessed information. This is not surprising, and much can be found in sociology and descriptions of work that describe the value of interactions and trust relationships (e.g., Schrage, 1995). The significance of constellations as such, i.e. the need to be in sync, the cross-organizational relationships, and the individual-centric sets of contacts, is a set of design opportunities. For example, only Dwight can define this constellation of people and information sources; no organizational boundaries exist that include all the pieces. Equally importantly, any other person in Dwight's constellation has his or her own constellation of people and information sources that may overlap but is not defined by Dwight's constellation.

While constellations are actively maintained by each of our interviewees, the tools for doing so are person-to-person technologies like the telephone and email. Underlying databases of support are oriented toward individual networks of relationships with little or no support for flexibly recognizing daily interactions and connections. Email distribution lists recognize groups but most often from the perspective of an organizational entity, not from an individual use.

The constellation relationships and the need to be in sync require the regular awareness and informal interactions currently being discussed in CSCW technologies. But more importantly, the individual-centric aspect of a constellation offers opportunities for further CSCW development. Currently many CSCW systems such as media spaces (Bly et al, 1993) assume that the day-to-day interactions are shared primarily by a well-defined group of colleagues. Yet for any individual in a media space, the environment only supports a segment of the daily interactions. Problems in expanding systems like media spaces can, in part, be explained by constellations. For a given group of people, it is highly unlikely that their constellations will be completely overlapping. Yet efforts to expand media spaces have typically assumed a large and public collection of people. Security and privacy, however, are meaningful at the constellation level. There is at best little support for small overlapping but non-merging collections of people.

On the other hand, the cross-organizational aspect of constellations is often constrained by current technologies. Firewalls and intranets, while important for protecting a company's concerns, also contradict the reality of the work accomplished through constellations. Technologies like the World Wide Web offer a breakdown of such constraints but, as yet, without good filters and management tools. It will be important to merge the necessities of both the Intranet and the Internet to move toward support of constellations as they already exist in working life.

Summary

In his book, *At Home in the Universe*, Stuart Kauffman discusses his ideas about self-organizing properties of biological systems. We see constellations defined from the perspective of an individual and arising, in a nearly self-organizing fashion, from an individual's particular work context. Adopting a biological metaphor, one may think of a constellation as akin to a self-organizing system of ideas. It is defined by and centered around an individual who derives the maximum value from the total set of interactions and from the total collection of ideas focused on that individual's context. The interactions arise initially, almost serendipitously, from among people who comprise teams and networks and relationships as yet undetermined. That is, constellations form around an individual with an expressed need, drawing support from other people and information sources as they are found to be valuable for so long as they continue to be valuable. Should the need diminish or the individual depart, so too would the constellation.

While the individual or hub of the constellation draws value from the assorted constellation elements, many of the people that comprise a particular constellation may not necessarily know other members of that constellation and may not even know of their own existence as a member of a constellation. In fact, the individual hub probably does not even recognize that there is such a thing as a constellation, only that there are people and resources on which he/she relies. Some elements of a constellation are more valuable than others, acquiring, organizing and eliminating information more efficiently. And more often than not, constellation elements with maximum value were external to the corporate entity to which the individual hub is a member. These characteristics are quite different from a team, where sources are shared and where members know each other and each other's value.

Given the contextual nature of the constellation, its real value is apparent only when the individual around whom the constellation revolves is in sync with the constellation elements. To be in sync means that an individual has a continuing basis for communication, ease of access, and an ongoing awareness of the status, availability, and information content from the various elements of the constellation. However, constellations are variably persistent in time, coming and going, expanding and declining as information needs present and remove opportunities to provide value.

Constellations offer an opportunity to rethink assumptions about CSCW technologies. Constellations reflect a change of perspective to consider systems based on individual-centric, cross-organizational collections of people strongly interlinked and frequently changing. Constellations suggest personal information and interaction management as indispensable to open, shared environments and appropriate incoming and outgoing pathways as essential to corporate boundary management.

Acknowledgements

We always appreciate the willingness of individuals to share with us descriptions of their work activity and environments. We thank Bill Gaver, Bob Anderson, and Bob Hughes for their discussions about our work and the conference reviewers for their thoughtful and useful comments on our paper.

References

Bly, S., Harrison, S., and Irwin, S. (1993): Media Spaces: Bringing people together in a video, audio and computing environment. *Communications of the ACM*, 36(1).

Blomberg, J., Giacomi, J., Mosher, A. and Swenton-Wall, P. (1993): "Ethnographic Field Methods and Their Relation to Design". In *Participatory Design: Principles and Practices*, D. Schuler and A. Namioka (Eds.). Hillsdale, NJ: Lawrence Erlbaum Associates, pp. 123-154.

Henderson, A. (1993): "Views of Work, the Foundations of Architecture", In *Proceedings of Software-Ergonomie '93*, Stuttgart, Germany: B.G. Teubner, pp. 31-50.

Holtzblatt, K. and Beyer, H. (1993): "Representing Work for the Purpose of Design". In Representations of Work, L. Suchman (Ed.). HICSS Monograph (Hawaii International Conference on System Sciences).

Hughes, J., King, V., Rodden, T. and Andersen, H. (1994): "Moving Out from the Control Room: Ethnography in System Design". In *Proceedings of the Conference on Computer Supported Cooperative Work*, R. Furuta and C. Neuwirth (Eds.). Chapel Hill, NC: ACM Press, pp. 429-439.

Kauffman, S. (1996) *At Home in the Universe*. Oxford University Press. New York, New York, USA.

Lewis, S., Mateas, M., Palmiter, S. and Lynch, G. (1996): "Ethnographic Data for Product Development: A Collaborative Process". Interactions, 3(6), p. 52-69.

Mateas, M., Salvador, T., Scholtz, T., and Sorensen, D. (1996): "Engineering Ethnography in the Home". In *Proceedings of the Conference on Computer Human Interaction 1996: Companion*. p. 283-284.

Plowman, L., Rogers, Y., and Ramage, M. (1995): "What are Workplace Studies For?". In *Proceedings of ECSCW'95*.

280

Schmidt, K. (1994): "The Organization of Cooperative Work: Beyond the "Leviathan" Conception of the Organization of Cooperative Work". In *Proceedings of the Conference on Computer Supported Cooperative Work*, R. Furuta and C. Neuwirth (Eds.). Chapel Hill, NC: ACM Press, pp. 417-428.

Schrage, M. (1995) *No More Teams*. Doubleday, NY, NY, USA.

Shapiro, D. (1994): "The Limits of Ethnography: Combining Social Sciences for CSCW". In *Proceedings of the Conference on Computer Supported Cooperative Work*, R. Furuta and C. Neuwirth (Eds.). Chapel Hill, NC: ACM Press, pp. 417-428.

Supporting Cooperative Working Using Shared Notebooks

Phil Turner

The MARI Group Ltd, UK

pat@mari.co.uk

Susan Turner

Department of Computing, University of Northumbria at Newcastle, UK

susan.turner@unn.ac.uk

This paper discusses the use of a shared cooperative notebook by a group of software engineers and support staff distributed over two sites. The design of the notebook is described and results of the pilot trial reported. It was found that the system was an effective means of sharing information for the non-technical staff but required much greater integration with other information systems and the actual rather than perceived working practices of users. Issues which appeared to influence the results were the distinction between formal and informal information and the parallel rather than genuinely cooperative work patterns of the technical staff.

Introduction

This paper discusses some of the work of the DUCK project in supporting co-working between members of a distributed group. DUCK aimed to provide, in the first instance, a cooperative toolset for the practice and management of engineering design. The development of the toolset was driven by detailed requirements engineering and by longitudinal pilots situated in the actual working environments of the users.

J. Hughes et al. (eds.), Proceedings of the Fifth European Conference on Computer Supported Cooperative Work, 281-295.
© 1997 *Kluwer Academic Publishers.*

The DUCK project's user company was a large supplier of engineering and software services and consultancy with many sites distributed across the length and breadth of the United Kingdom, and a significant number of cross-site teams. In the second phase of the project the particular focus was the creation and evaluation of tools to support distributed, cooperative software design, build and testing. This work forms the subject of this paper[1].

Resources for mutual awareness

From early requirements elicitation work with the teams involved in software development, it emerged that a potential function for technological support would be to keep team members aware of what their colleagues were doing, particularly those located at a different site. The technology should support such mutual awareness as appropriate. Where members of workgroups share a physical workplace, they are continually aware of what their colleagues are doing through the everyday processes and cues of co-presence. It is easy to pass on information in an *ad hoc* way when the situation demands it, and to glean information useful to oneself. For example, a designer passing a colleague's desk may recognise part of a prototype, recall that problems had been found with a similar module in an earlier project, and suggest an alternative. A further piece of information afforded by the encounter is that work on this part of the project is far from finished, and therefore the first designer's task on an interfacing module can be postponed for a while. In a more active exploitation of co-presence, a code fragment which 'just doesn't look right' can be passed across the desk for someone else to check. The key points about these types of interaction is that they are unscheduled, informal and demand very little extra effort beyond that required for the main task in hand.

Similar low key exploitations of co-presence have been described by researchers working with, for example, air traffic controllers (Bentley *et al*, 1992) and London Underground staff (Heath and Luff, 1991). Such cooperation usually relies on the affordances of common artefacts such as screen displays (Underground control rooms), flight strips (air traffic control rooms) and whiteboards (engineering design office - Rogers, 1993). We were interested to know if a shared technical notebook could provide similar affordances for software teams.

Uses of technical notebooks

One of the main loci for the work of designers, managers and others in technical domains is the notebook, daybook, logbook, journal or laboratory book. In its prototypical form, this is of A4 size with hard covers. The notebook is used for a wide range of activities - for engineering designers, for example, these include

---

[1] For more details of DUCK see Turner and Turner 1994; and Turner, Turner, Green and Mayne, 1997.

recording and exploring ideas in words and sketches, notes of discussions, calculations, records of trials, keeping lists of tasks and so on. Notebook contents comprise not just the book's original pages, but frequently other items are attached or simply interleaved. Our own anecdotal knowledge of notebook use is supported by two surveys conducted as part of the early requirements work in the DUCK project. These consisted of (i) a questionnaire survey of 200 engineers, managers and support staff at the DUCK user company and (ii) a smaller scale analysis of the use of notebooks at a software house. Of the 200 people surveyed 103 responded and of these 90 were engineers or (technical) managers. It was found that the major uses to which the notebooks were put were for notes of discussions (34%), 'to do lists' (28%), and calculations (22%). Of the software house survey 25 software engineers, designers, and software project managers were interviewed and it was found that the notebooks were used for 'technical purposes' (52%), 'to do lists' (30%), and as a diary (11%). The major findings were that although the profiles of usage from the two studies do vary, there remain a number of key commonalities. Notebooks are not used exclusively for technical matters; and they are used for both formal and informal information. Notebooks thus provide the repository for much of the stream of work which is the subject of informal interactions of the sort discussed above. Consideration of the notebook as a resource for work-in-progress suggested that sharable on-line notebooks could support cooperation where opportunities for mutual awareness and the casual exchange of information are restricted.

The Collaborative Notebook System

The collaborative notebook system (CNS) is the software implementation of a shared notebook. The CNS is built on a LOTUS NOTES™ platform thus giving it all the necessary facilities to support both group and distributed working. The CNS presents the user with pairs of pages separated by a 'binder'.

The right-hand page

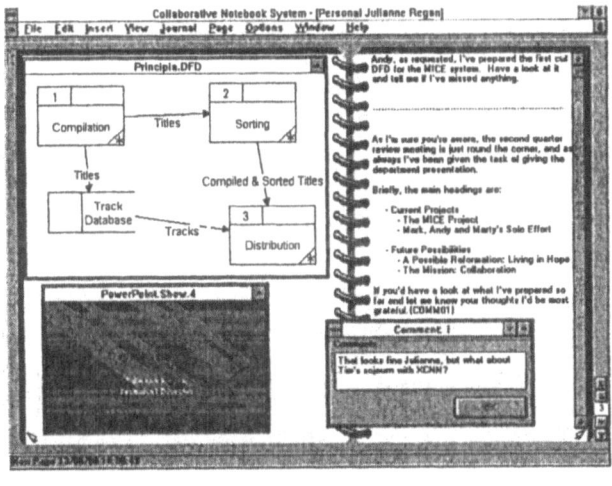

Figure 1 - A pair of notebook pages

284

supports simple note taking, and the ability to add comments, identified by a marker and between and within notebook 'hyper-links'. The left-hand page is a OLE-enabled page into which any OLE capable document can be embedded. Figure 1 is a screenshot of a typical pair of notebook pages.

New (empty) notebooks or ready populated notebooks created from user-specified keywords are easily created. For example, a user could ask for a new notebook to be created from all notebook pages to which he or she has access containing the words 'bug report' or 'management meeting' and so forth. The on-line notebook also supports full text searching (using the LOTUS NOTES search engine), printing, a contents page and page *publication*. Publication is the mechanism whereby a page from one notebook is made available to a second notebook. Figure 2 illustrates the mechanism of publication as implemented in the CNS. As can be seen from this figure, notebook A consists of five pages while notebook B consists of four pages. There is one common page (the shaded figure) which can be thought of as being published from notebook A to notebook B.

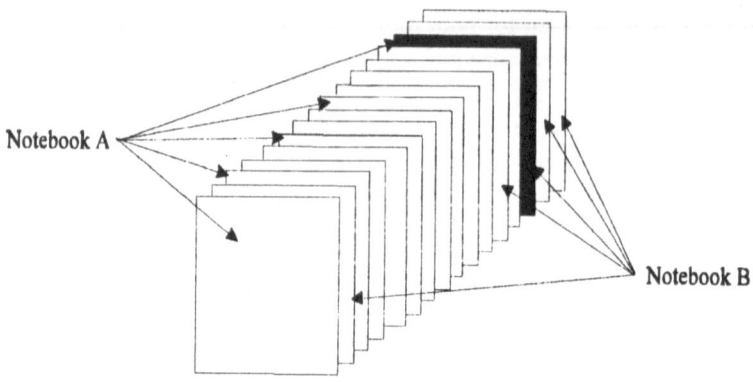

Figure 2 - The mechanism of publication

The dialogue whereby a page may be published from a notebook to one or more other notebooks is illustrated in figure 3 (overleaf). Published pages are then rendered read-only but comments may be added. Access control also allow users to specify who has access to their notebooks and the nature of the access, e.g. reader or writer. The recipient of a published page is notified by an automatically generated email message.

The final CNS as described above was developed in close conjunction with the potential users prior to its first release, and then in response to change requests and the evaluation exercises described below. Comments made in response to pre-pilot demonstrations resulted in the original, fairly crude approximation of notebook appearance being replaced by something that looked much more like the real-world object. Hyperlinks were also introduced at this stage. After the one-month evaluation the original functionality embodied in the left hand page, a simple sketching tool, was replaced by the OLE-enabled page described above and the final phase of enhancements, after the three-month evaluation, provided integrated email and publication notification (described above).

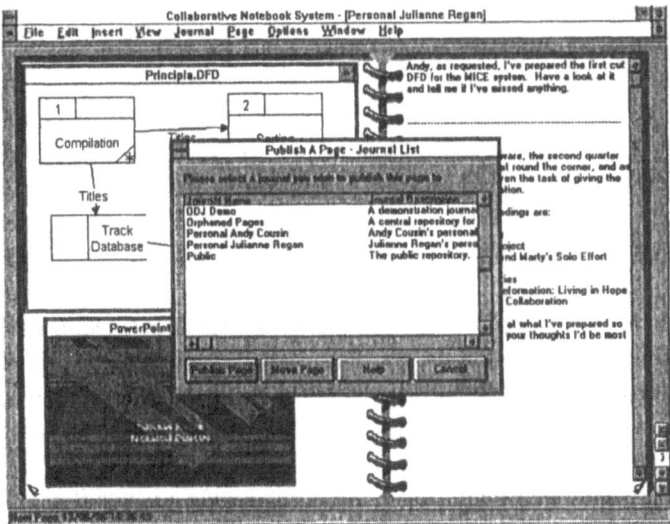

Figure 3 - Page publication in action

The pilot trial of the CNS

The context

To validate the CNS an extended pilot was set up across a pair of test sites selected from the DUCK project's user company's offices. These test sites were geographically remote being located in London and Glasgow (some 400 miles apart) but shared responsibility for the user company's software product range. The design of the pilot followed the recommendations of Opper and Fersko-Weiss (1992) who have argued that the pilot introduction of CSCW technology should be divided into two phases - an experimental and then an expanded pilot. In the former, which is the case under report, the group itself is heavily involved in the evaluation of the system and actively observe changes in their own behaviour and working practices. It should be noted that this was not intended to be a formal experimental trial of the software: indeed the pilot was run to address a real-world business problem.

The users at both sites were groups of software designers, developers, support staff, sales staff, and a management team, all of whom were very IT literate. In all there were eight users in London and three in Glasgow. Most took part in the initial pre-release demonstration and discussions and were supported by hands-on training in the CNS. Once the software was installed on individual machines, they were asked to experiment with the system and to use it in any way they found useful in support of their normal activities,

As a group they were initially very enthusiastic about the CNS and its potential to resolve a number of information sharing issues that existed between the two sites. Overall, these groups were responsible for the continued software development of their product range of CASE tools. The development drive came from a number of sources but most immediately from customer feedback. This feedback took a variety of forms but centred around change requests and bug reports.

However the information sharing issues faced by these groups were much broader than that, as in addition to change requests and bug reports, requests for support, sale enquiries, training enquiries and so forth for the full product range frequently arrived at either site. This happened despite the fact that the support of these products is explicitly demarcated between sites. It was therefore envisaged that the CNS would play an informal role in supporting a range of such activities.

Evaluation objectives, methods and schedule

In parallel with the pilot was an evaluation activity, the purpose of which was to produce a measure of the usefulness of the CNS. To this end the three key dimensions along which the CNS was evaluated were identified. These were (in brief):

1. Is the CNS a better technological solution to information storage and management than a paper notebook?
2. Does using the CNS make the individual user more productive / effective in their day-to-day work?
3. Does using the CNS make the group using it more productive / effective in their day-to-day work?

Each dimension was then further divided into sub-issues and questions generated. The users of the CNS were interviewed at four points: immediately before the start of the pilot as to their expectations of the CNS; after one month and after three months, using semi-structured interviews and administered questionnaires; and finally after six months using semi-structured group discussion.

Results

This section first reports quantitative data obtained from users' ratings of the software then amplifies this material with the less structured material obtained from user interviews.

Ratings of the CNS

What follows are the core results from the rating scales which formed part of the administered questionnaires.

Technological effectiveness

Eight of the original 11 users[2] were interviewed after the pilot had been running for one 1 month. The items to be scored (on a scale of -3 to +3) were:

1. How reliable did you find the CNS?
2. How responsive did you find the CNS?
3. How well integrated with other applications did you find the CNS?
4. How effective is the analogy between the CNS and an A4 notebook?
5. Would pen-based technology make the CNS easier to use?
6. How useful did you find publication?
7. How secure did you find your (i) pages, (ii) your journals.

The first three items were repeated at the three months stage; it was considered that data on the remaining four items would be less meaningful at this point. Figure 4 (overleaf) illustrates the mean scores for the technology component of the evaluation of the CNS.

As figure 4 shows, after one month (i) the technology was performing quite well in terms of its reliability and responsiveness, although (ii) the CNS did not particularly look, feel and behave like an A4 notebook. The main reasons for this were two-fold: firstly portability - as the CNS was only installed on desktop PCs it was not portable. Secondly, a number of users pointed out that a real notebook may be opened in the middle, towards the end and so forth. The CNS always opened at the first page, although comprehensive page navigation facilities were available thereafter. Next, (iii) pen computing was not perceived as a useful addition to the CNS largely on the grounds that it was another operating system to learn; (iv) publication, that is, the primary means by which information is shared using the CNS, was seen to be useful but not overwhelmingly so. This may be due to the relatively short period of time the CNS had been in use. Finally, (v)

---

[2] The other users continued to participate in the pilot, but were unavoidably not available for interview,

288

integration. The CNS did not offer integration with other Windows™ application except at the most simple level (i.e. cut and paste using the clipboard). It will be recalled that the requirement for integration was realised in the final version of the CNS.

Mean scores for the technology component

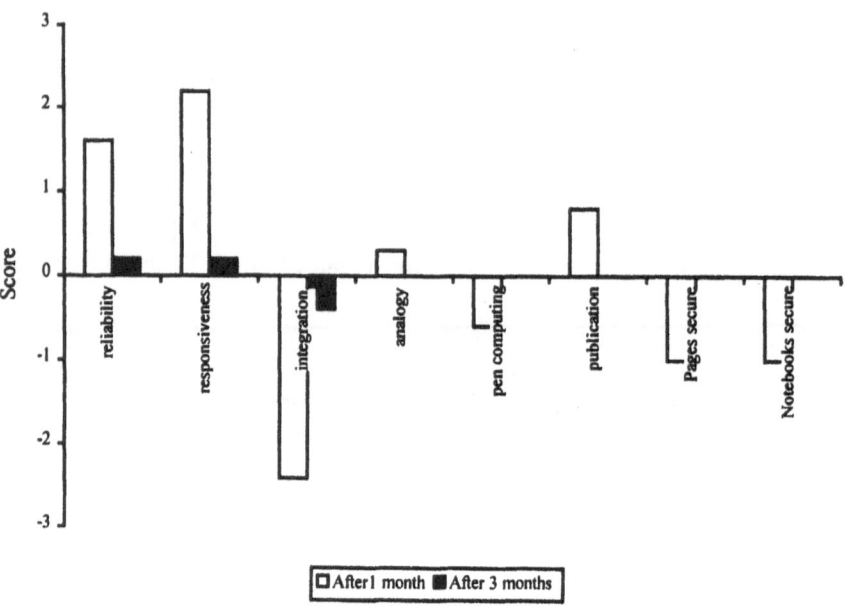

Figure 4 - mean scores for the technology component of the CNS at one and three months.

After three months, while integration problems had been ameliorated, there had been a corresponding drop in perceived responsiveness and reliability. Responsiveness and reliability were however no longer identified as problems in the group discussion session at six months.

Individual and group working using the CNS

Users were similarly asked to score the CNS (on a scale of -3 to +3) along dimensions designed to elicit perceptions of overall usefulness for individual and group working. (The underlining corresponds to labels on the graph overleaf.)

1. How would you score the usefulness of the CNS for individual work?
2. Has using the CNS improved your productivity when working alone?
3. Has using the CNS made your job easier?

4. In the context of group working, how would you score the usefulness of the CNS for keeping <u>in touch</u> with other people's work in the office?
5. In the context of group working, how would you score the usefulness of the CNS for <u>sharing information</u>?
6. In the context of group working, is the <u>flow of information</u> better or worse?
7. In the context of group working, does the CNS provide the features which allow you to <u>work with others</u>?
8. Has using the CNS improved your productivity as a <u>member of a group</u>?
9. Has using the CNS improved the productivity of <u>the group as a whole</u>?

From figure 5 (below), it is clear that after one month using the CNS had made individual work a little more productive. Turning to the groupworking measures, there was a more positive assessment of the CNS as a means of supporting collaborative working. For both conditions there was a small negative response to 'Has using the CNS made your <u>job easier</u>?', but this may be an effect of the overhead of learning to use the system. The major change from the one month evaluation point to three months point is the perception that the CNS had improved the <u>productivity</u> of the group and the individual while the support for individual and groupworking *per se* remained approximately constant.

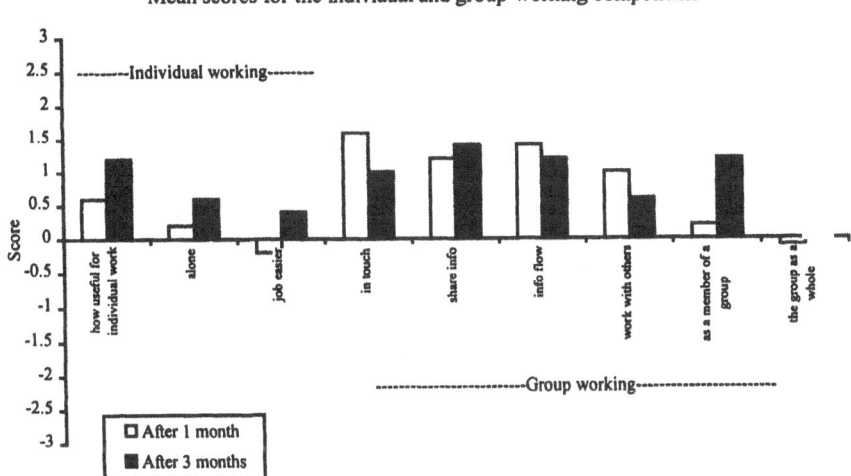

Figure 5 - Mean scores for the individual and group-working components

Supplementary material from semi-structured interviews

Pre-pilot findings

Each of the sub-groups within the pilot sites (i.e. technical staff, salespersons, managers and support staff) foresaw a clear role for the CNS in their range of day-to-day duties. For the technical staff this was product support activities; and for the sales staff, marketing activities and so forth. For the managers it would be used for all of these.

After 1 month of use

The software engineers uniformly failed to use the CNS. In contrast, other staff at the test sites used the CNS extensively, particularly those individuals supporting their software products. Further analysis of the evaluation data revealed that there appeared to be an antagonism between the clarity and ease of information sharing that the CNS offers - no more *Chinese whispers*, as one individual put it, with the apparent transformation of informal to formal information when committed to an electronic medium. Informal information exists without a written record or time and date stamped, while information within the CNS is necessarily written and time and date stamped. Yet, users did find the CNS useful for jotting down ideas and for managing unstructured information. In all the software engineers appeared to resist using a means of communication perceived as formal for information which they considered informal. In contrast the managers and sales staff were using the CNS as they had indicated at the pre-pilot stage.

After 3 months of use

Four major issues emerged after this extended period of use, (i) all groups of users reported greatly improved information sharing between the two sites, but (ii) the transition from their current working practices to CNS was proving to be very slow, which was being hampered by (iii) software reliability problems. The users finally noted (iv) that there was a clear need to integrate the CNS with other information sharing tools such as MSMAIL and MICROSOFT SCHEDULE+.

After 6 months of use

The users after six months believed that they had fully explored the CNS's potential and uniformly found it useful if not 'too powerful' for their immediate needs. The CNS was variously described as 'only' an information sharing tool; as a tool for supporting cooperative working; and as a medium for sharing formal information while 'feeling' like an informal system (this dichotomy was attributed to the *situated* nature of the PCs on which the CNS ran which were perceived as group resource located at the users' place of work whereas notebooks are personal and owned by an individual). Use of the CNS was seen to have greatly improved cross-site communication where email (and fax, and telephone) had proved to be insufficient. Finally, a small number of users said that they would not return to their paper notebooks after the pilot.

Overall many of features of the CNS were not used, which is not in itself surprising except to note that this includes the publication mechanism. Users shared information by creating public notebooks to which all had access. In the main private notebooks were created, experimented with and then discarded in favour of the public notebooks. On being asked why this was so, users, excepting the overall manager, described themselves as having a peer relationship with respect to technical information.

Discussion and conclusions

Technology push

That the transition from current working practice to the CNS was very slow is understandable and is a well-known problem faced by many if not all CSCW projects - the reports by Orlikowski (1992) and Bowers (1994) are two of numerous examples. In our case existing working practice at the pilot sites was proven, well understood and familiar and the need to migrate to a new system in this instance was due to technology push rather than an identified set of problems. Moreover, take-up may have been adversely affected by performance problems during the middle phase of the trial.

Our experience may be compared to the major example of a 'shared notebook' used in real-world contexts, the VIRTUAL NOTEBOOK SYSTEM (VNS), (Brunet *et al*, 1991; Fowler *et al*, 1994). The VNS is a much heavier-weight instantiation of the notebook concept, supporting large repositories of information in several media. The system has been found to be most valuable where its introduction is hand-in-glove with process re-engineering, thus facilitating adoption of information sharing resources. This supports our observation that the adoption of the CNS may have been limited by the attempt to infiltrate the notebooks into existing work patterns.

Technical and non-technical staff

Prior to the pilot users were asked to estimate how much of their work normally fell into each of the following categories: independent[3], sequential[4], reciprocal[5] and team working[6] (Categories drawn from Van de Ven and Delbecq, 1976). The mean percentages of work allocated to the four categories were:

	independent	sequential	reciprocal	team
Technical	70%	0%	13%	17%
Managers/sales/support	37%	15%	28%	20%

If these data are graphed (summing sequential, reciprocal and team percentages to arrive at an overall percentage for cooperative work):

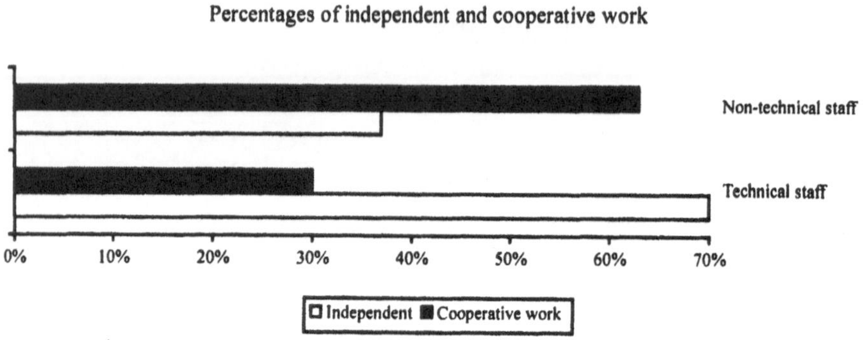

Percentages of independent and cooperative work

Figure 6 - Percentages of independent and cooperative work

From the above data and very clearly from figure 6, it can be seen that the relative proportions of independent and cooperative work are virtually mirror images of each other. The style of work between technical and non-technical staff may be assumed to differ. Moreover, as Reder and Schwab (1990) note:

"...we observe that some occupational groups, such as artists, architects and mechanical engineers (designers of physical objects whose development is shared in posted drawings or sketches) tend to prefer open workspaces through which colleagues are encouraged to browse. Other occupational groups (e.g. software engineers, academics, writers) tend to prefer more enclosed and private workspaces which offer fewer intrusions and interruptions."

---

[3] Independent working: work is performed by you independently and does not involve anyone else in the team.

[4] Sequential working: work flows between you and one or more other members of the team, but only in one direction.

[5] Reciprocal working: work flows between you and one or more other members of the team in a reciprocal 'back and forth' manner.

[6] Team working: you and one or more other members of the team problem solve and collaborate as a group at the same time to deal with the work.

While Reder and Schwab refer to the physical workplace, this observation appears very pertinent to our findings. Technical work of the type under discussion may simply offer less of an opportunity for collaboration technologies than managerial or support activities.

Premature information sharing

The pilots teams' preference for the use of group journals rather than the publication mechanism may be partly explained by the relative ease of doing this, but more interesting factors may be at work here. As we have observed elsewhere (Turner and Turner, 1995) technical staff are frequently reluctant to commit partially formulated information (i.e. informal information) to publicly available media in case it is used prematurely and attributed to its originator. A similar observation has been made by Citera *et al.* (1995), in their study of creating databases to record design rationale. One might speculate that that information contributed to a *group* notebook is perceived to have a weaker link to its originator than information on a page published from an *individual* notebook. The moral here is perhaps that considerations of privacy, responsibility and ownership remain very important in implementations of this type even when information sharing is discretionary. Indeed the whole issue of responsibility for the integrity of information once electronically available is one that warrants further study.

Not another box on my desk

A key observation to be made lies with the dichotomy between personal and shared (or business) information systems. The identified need to integrate the CNS with other tools was not unexpected. This is consistent with our experience elsewhere, in the context of real-time, multi-media information sharing (Turner and Turner, 1992) that users prefer integration with existing tools to standalone innovations, a point of view put succinctly by one potential user as 'not another box on my desk'. The existing personal information system we sought to replace here was the A4 notebook which may be characterised as being (i) easy to use; (ii) portable; and (iii) secure or easily secured. In contrast the corresponding characteristics on a shared and / or business information system are: (i) integration with (other) information systems; (ii) integration with messaging systems / calendaring / scheduling (iii) integration with business applications; and (iv) that it is secure. The CNS attempted to bridge this dichotomy but only partially succeeded as it matched some of the former characteristics but few of the latter. The evidence therefore suggests that CSCW applications must bridge the gap between personal and shared (or business) information systems.

Were the users actually cooperating?

We suspect that there may be a difference between the users' perceptions of their patterns of work compared with the actual patterns. Our informal observation of the technical users suggests parallel but linked working. While it will be recalled that the technical staff reported that they spent around 30% of their time in team work, this may be an over-estimate of the true situation and/or much of this work may actually consist of co-ordinated, but relatively independent activities. The team members are working towards a common goal, but this is at a higher level of organisational activity: for example, to get the next release of the software out on schedule. Individual goals may not be shared, and the object of apparently 'cooperative' work may be so subdivided as to be no longer a common artefact in any meaningful sense. Comments elicited from individuals at the six-month evaluation illustrate this: *"We work individually."* and *"We work as individuals not as a team."*. In such circumstances the information sharing supported by the CNS may be to some extent an irrelevance at this level, and the lesson for designers of similar technologies may be that information only needs to be shared at the boundaries of individual tasks.

Postscript

This note is based on a series of informal observations made of the use of the CNS outside the DUCK project. At the first author's place of work a software development project was being conducted at two of the company's sites which were separated by a distance of 10 miles or so, two developers at one site and a developer and a manager at the other. Until the CNS became available to the team, co-ordination was achieved by means of frequent meetings (twice weekly as a minimum) as email (and phone and fax) had proved to be insufficient.

The team decided to adopt the CNS as a means of bridging this gap. What emerged over a period of six to eight weeks was strikingly familiar: the publication mechanism was not used. Instead public notebooks were used to shared information which largely consisted on site reports, meeting minutes and 'to do lists'. The CNS was described as being useful for 'braindumps' and for storing information which did not neatly fit elsewhere.

Acknowledgements

The DUCK project (Designers as Users of Cooperative Knowledge) was supported by funding from the United Kingdom Department of Trade and Industry and the Engineering and Physical Sciences Research Council. The consortium comprised MARI Computer Systems, BAeSEMA Ltd and the University of Paisley. DUCK was a three year project ending in December 1996. Thanks are due to Adrian Gordon of the University of Northumbria for his helpful comments on an earlier version of this paper, and to the anonymous ECSCW reviewers.

References

Bentley, R., Hughes, J. A., Randall, D., Rodden, T., Sawyer P., Sommerville, I. and Shapiro, D. (1992): "Ethnographically-informed systems design for air traffic control", in J. Turner and R. Kraut R. (Eds.): *CSCW'92 Conference Proceedings*, ACM Press, New York, pp 123-9.

Bowers, J. (1994): "The Work to Make a Network Work: Studying CSCW in Action", in R Furuta and C Neuwirth (Eds.): *CSCW'94 Conference Proceedings*, ACM Press, New York. pp. 287-298.

Brunet, L. W., Morrissey, C. T. and Gorry, G. A. (1991): "Oral History and Information Technology: Human Voices of Assessment", *Journal of Organizational Computing*, vol. 1, pp. 251-274.

Citera, M., McNeese, M.D., Brown, C.E., Selvaraj, J.A., Zaff, B.S., and Whitaker, R.D. (1995): "Fitting Information Systems to Collaborating Design Teams", *Journal of the American Society for Information Science*, vol. 46, no. 7, pp. 551-559.

Fowler, J., Baker, D.G., Kouramajian, V., Gilson, H., Dargahi, R., Long, K.B., Petermann, C., and Gorry, G.A. (1994): "Experiences with the virtual notebook system: Abstraction in hypertext", in R Furuta and C Neuwirth (Eds.): *CSCW'94 Conference Proceedings*, ACM Press, New York, pp. 133-143.

Heath, C. and Luff, P. (1991): "Collaborative activity and technological design: Task coordination in London Underground control rooms", in L. Bannon L *et al* (Eds.): *Proceedings of the Second European Conference on Computer-Supported Cooperative Work EC-CSCW '91*, Kluwer, Dordrecht, pp. 65-80.

Opper, S. and Fersko-Weiss, H. (1992) *Technology for Teams - Enhancing Productivity in Networked Organisations*, Van Nostrand Reinhold, New York.

Orlikowski, W. J. (1992): "Learning from Notes: Organizational issues in groupware implementation", in J. Turner and R. Kraut R. (Eds.): *CSCW'92 Conference Proceedings*, ACM Press, New York, pp 362-369.

Reder, S. and Schwab, R. G. (1990): "The Temporal Structure of Co-operative Activity", in *CSCW'90 Conference Proceedings*, ACM Press, New York, pp 303-16.

Rogers Y. (1993): "Coordinating Computer-mediated Work", *CSCW*, vol 1, 295-315.

Turner, P. and Turner, S.E. (1992): *"Report on the non-functional requirements capture exercise for the BMST"*, (UNOM project deliverable ref UMAR520010PPGI02)

Turner, P., Turner, S.E., Green, S. and Mayne, P.J. (In press) "Collaborative Notebooks for the Virtual Workplace", to appear in M. Igbaria and M. Tan (Eds.): *Technology for the Virtual Workplace*, Idea Press.

Turner, S.E. and Turner, P. (1994): "Expectations and experiences of CSCW in an Engineering Environment", *Collaborative Computing*, vol. 1, no. 4, pp. 237-254

Turner, S.E. and Turner, P. (1995), *"Best Practice in the Management of Technical Information"*, MARI Computer Systems, internal report.

Van de Ven, A. H. and Delbecq, A. L. (1976): "Determinants of Coordination Modes within Organizations", *American Sociological Review*, vol 41, pp.322-338.

Does "roomware" matter ?
Investigating the role of personal and public information devices and their combination in meeting room collaboration

Norbert A. Streitz, Petra Rexroth, Torsten Holmer
IPSI - Integrated Publication and Information Systems Institute
GMD - German National Research Center for Information Technology
Dolivostr. 15, D - 64293 Darmstadt, Germany
{streitz, rexroth, holmer} @darmstadt.gmd.de

Abstract: We report about an empirical study that investigates the role of different "roomware" configurations on the products and processes of meeting room collaboration. The configurations were realized by different combinations of providing computers and a large interactive electronic whiteboard. In this study, 48 subjects working in teams of four were assigned to three experimental conditions: four workstations networked and mounted in the table (WS), a LiveBoard (LB), and a networked combination of computers and LiveBoard (WS+LB). The results show that the teams in the WS+LB condition produced better quality work, in particular, generating more ideas than in the other two conditions. They also employed a more effective distribution of different cooperation modes.

1   Introduction

Research and development in the area of CSCW aims at the support of cooperation, communication and coordination of groups, but a large number of studies and development efforts in this field result in design decisions for software running on a computer on the desktop of an individual. The design focuses on what

J. Hughes et al. (eds.), Proceedings of the Fifth European Conference on Computer Supported Cooperative Work, 297-312.
© *1997 Kluwer Academic Publishers.*

happens on the screen of this computer and how to interact with the software. Of course, the software supports multiple users and the interface has special cooperative features, but the desktop computer in an individual office is more or less the default situation. This trend is even increasing in the age of networked computer systems and Internet-based applications, where people do not have to be in one physical location in order to work together but can be distributed over multiple locations, in a multitude of individual offices. This way, people can share information and interact with one another although being apart. There are, of course and without any doubt, a number of serious advantages of software support for these settings bridging physical distances. We have worked and are still working ourselves in this area, e.g., on support for so called "virtual organizations" (Streitz, 1996; Johannsen et al., 1996).

The case of distributed cooperation settings covers only part of the full range of group work situations. We have argued before (Streitz, 1994) that comprehensive real world group activities involve all four combinations of the well-known same/different matrix of time and place and that system design should also address the transitions between different cooperation situations. For example, real face-to-face meetings (same time, same place) still play an important role, especially in the initial and later on often in critical phases of group work. Face-to-face meetings require a certain physical setting, usually a room which can accommodate all group members participating in the meeting. Beyond a certain size a traditional meeting room requires some furniture (tables, chairs, etc.) and some standard equipment (e.g., flipcharts, whiteboards, overhead projectors, etc.) providing the functionality needed to conduct meetings. It is known that the ergonomics of the physical design of these rooms including size and shape of the table, issues of lighting and acoustics, etc. are important for the quality of meetings.

Introducing computer-based technology into such a setting results in what has been called "electronic meeting rooms" (e.g., Nunamaker et al., 1991). It requires that the physical design of meeting rooms and the arrangement of equipment in the rooms have to be viewed from a new perspective. While the traditional ergonomic aspects are still important, one has to make new decisions on: which kind of computer equipment, how much of it, and where it should be positioned? Since computers are not the only type of equipment to be considered, we speak in general of "information devices", i.e. devices allowing information to be created, edited, and displayed. In order to have a term for the combination of information devices, furniture, walls, etc., we call the sum of these physical objects and their relationships constituting these settings "roomware".

We emphasize the general point that it is not sufficient to design only software when designing computer-based support for group work settings but that one has to pay equal attention to the roomware. We cannot discuss the role of all items making up the roomware in general in this paper. Instead, we will focus on those aspects relevant for the experiment reported in this paper.

In a face-to-face meeting situation, one can, in principle, distinguish between two kinds of "information devices" available to meeting participants:

- *personal devices*: these are usually available and visible only to one person. Examples are paper and pencil; paper documents brought along by a specific person; personal computers, notebooks, PDAs with documents in electronic form.
- *general/public devices*: these are used for displaying information so that it is visible to all people present in the room. Examples are whiteboards, the projection of transparencies via an overhead projector/slide projector, TV monitors showing video tapes or large screens for showing movies. Since some time, projection units are used for displaying the content of computer screens. Usually, they allow only to passively display information to the audience/participants. More recently, there are also devices which allow to interact with the displayed information using the hand or a cordless pen, modifying or creating new information. Examples are the Xerox Liveboard (Elrod et al., 1992) and the SMART Board (SMART Technology).

Different scenarios for electronic meeting rooms have employed different roomware configurations. For our purposes, we distinguish between three major configurations: networked computers only, large passive or interactive public displays, and the combination of these two sets of information devices. There are situations in which only or primarily networked personal computers are provided to the participants (e.g., Olson et al., 1993; Nunamaker et al., 1991), in most cases one computer for each participant. In other configurations, an additional large passive display is provided showing the content of one participant's window or a general public window. Examples are the CoLab (Stefik et al., 1987) and the CaptureLab (Mantei 1988). In some cases, the public display is operated by a moderator/facilitator (Nunamaker et al., 1995). Other scenarios provide an active large electronic whiteboard/blackboard. An early version is the electronic blackboard in the NICK experiment (Rein & Ellis, 1989). While the NICK experiment included also a condition which provided only workstations for the participants, there was no condition with a combination of all devices. Most scenarios involving interactive electronic whiteboards concentrate on providing and using only one large display (Pedersen et al., 1993) operated with a pen, sometimes additionally operated by a scribe using a notebook on the table (Moran et al., 1996). There is also the obvious but seldomly realized configuration of providing a large interactive display *and* personal computers to all participants and networking all devices with each other. This is the standard setup in our OCEAN-Lab at GMD-IPSI (see figure 1 in the description of the experiment). The functionality of the software used in the different scenarios differs also widely. It differs in the degree of and mechanisms for sharing information between different screens, the range of information types available (ascii text, scribbles, hypertext/media nodes and links, multimedia, etc.), and the types of interaction possible (keyboard/mouse-based, pen-based, etc.). Since this experiment does not investigate and compare software features of meeting support systems, we do not elaborate this aspect.

People keep asking what really is necessary for setting up a computer-augmented meeting room - not only when they visit us and see the OCEAN-Lab configuration. There is no easy answer. Although there has been a lot of discussion for and against different roomware configurations, it is difficult to compare existing configurations because of many differences in other variables. There is - at least to our knowledge - no comparative study of defined roomware configurations with respect to information devices under controlled conditions, i.e. keeping the software, the task, the furniture, and the room constant. Therefore, we decided to design and run such an experiment comparing three different configurations. We will specify them in more detail when we describe the experimental conditions.

2 The Experiment

Based on the considerations in the introduction, we set out to investigate different roomware configurations. Our specific interest in this experiment was to focus on combinations of different *computer-based* information devices and keep other variables as constant as possible. Furthermore, in this experiment we do not compare computer-based information devices with non-computer-based devices such as traditional whiteboards/blackboards, overhead projectors or paper-and-pencil only.

2.1 Experimental questions and hypotheses

We had a number of hypotheses we wanted to investigate. One hypothesis was that the availability of personal devices for each group member would enable and increase the potential for individual and parallel work in subgroups. This should increase the number of ideas generated and have a positive impact on the quality of the final result. Another hypothesis was that the provision of a public device in the form of a large interactive whiteboard would provide a focus of attention for the group facilitating coordination and updating knowledge about information changes. A "public device only" condition should result in a more collective work style involving the whole group and less individual or parallel work phases. Finally, we expected that the combination of both personal and public devices would provide the group with the respective functionality to the benefit of the group. Thus, we had the hypothesis that the overall quality of the final result would be better than in the other two conditions. Of course, this would require that the group would be able to develop a work style which could make appropriate use of both types of devices in a complementary manner. This was an open question we could not answer beforehand and was therefore also a subject of the investigation.

In order to test our hypotheses, we needed a task and software with the potential that the group could actually develop different types of cooperation behavior.

Thus, the choice of the task was determined by the following requirements: It should be a realistic task and a situation which was easy for the subjects to identify with, at least in a role playing mode. It should have a clear objective but still be an open problem in the sense that there is not one definite answer or a predefined outcome. It should also be complex enough so that working on its solution could take advantage of the capabilities of the DOLPHIN software (Streitz et al., 1994) - we intended to use - which supports these different work styles.

2.2   Method

2.2.1   Setting

Since the experiment's goal was to investigate the effects of different configurations of personal and public devices, the setting was different in the experimental conditions. The experiment took place in our computer-augmented meeting room, the OCEAN-Lab. Figure 1 shows a picture of the OCEAN-Lab as it was used in the experiment. It shows the setting in the full WS+LB condition (see below). The papers used by the subjects in this picture are the task instructions and the software manual.

Figure 1. View of the OCEAN-Lab with the full WS+LB Condition

People were seated around a rectangular table (1,20 m x 2,80 m) and had different devices available, depending on which condition they were assigned to. The following information devices were available:

public device:
- a large interactive, electronic whiteboard was realized by a Xerox Live-Board (LB) with a 67 inch color screen (back projection) and a cordless pen for directly interacting with the content on the screen while standing in front of it. A keyboard and a mouse was also available which could be placed on the table.

personal devices:
- four compact SUN Voyager workstations with flat 12 inch color LCD screens were integrated into the meeting room table and provided with keyboard and mouse. They were networked with each other and in the WS+LB condition (see below) also with the LiveBoard.
- paper and pencil

2.2.2 Experimental Design

In order to investigate the effects of different roomware configurations, a between-subjects design was used. Subjects worked in groups of four, with four groups in each of the three conditions resulting in a total of 48 subjects. Groups were assigned to the following three conditions as shown in Figure 2.

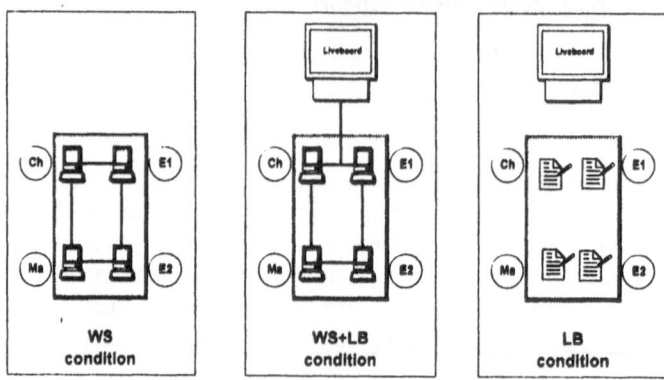

Figure 2. Schematic view of the three experimental roomware configurations

   WS condition: Each member of the group was provided with an individual but networked compact workstation (WS) mounted in the table. The LiveBoard was not available. No paper and pencil was provided.

   WS+LB condition: Here, the LiveBoard (LB) was added to and networked with the workstation configuration available in the WS condition. Subjects could work at their workstation but were also free to use the LiveBoard. The LiveBoard was available for everybody. No specific assignment of a person to the LiveBoard was made. No paper and pencil was provided.

   LB condition: In this condition, the group had only the LiveBoard available. No specific assignment of a person to the LiveBoard was made. It was available for everybody. In addition, each member of the group was provided with a pencil and sheets of paper. (The workstations were not visible. They were hidden below the table. The holes were covered by fitting wood segments resulting in a table with a standard flat surface.)

Due to the table construction and the arrangement of the flat LCD screens of the mounted workstations, the group members had unobstructed views of each other also in the WS and WS+LB conditions. Thus, they were well able to see and talk to each other with no problems while using the computers. There were no relevant differences with respect to the visual and acoustic communication situation between the three conditions.

2.2.3 Task

The subjects were instructed to form a team which had the task of developing concepts and a proposal for the program of a new TV channel. The prospective new channel should specialize in families as its target group. The instructions for the team required two sets of activities. There was a global part which addressed the team as a whole and there were specific parts which specified the assignments of roles for each member of this team of four people. There were three different roles with the following responsibilities: One chairperson (Ch) supervising and coordinating the team, one marketing person (Ma) responsible for advertisement, PR activities, design of a logo, etc., and two editors (E1, E2) creating the content and the structure for the new program. The instructions recommended to organize the task as a project with the phases of brainstorming, assessment of ideas, elaboration and integration of ideas into a common proposal, and its final presentation based on the electronic document created during the project. The subjects were instructed to work through all phases but were free to decide the organizational and temporal arrangement on their own.

2.2.4 Software

We used the DOLPHIN cooperative hypermedia system (Streitz et al., 1994, Bapat et al., 1996) in the following ways: as a pen-based system on an interactive, electronic whiteboard and as a multi-user application shared between the networked computers and the LiveBoard.

DOLPHIN provides operations for creating, editing, selecting, moving, copying, pasting and deleting scribbles, text, geometrical objects (circles, lines, rectangles), hypermedia nodes and links. We explain the functionality of DOLPHIN available at the time of this experiment by describing different windows and elements of an example document with content from the experiment as shown in figure 3.

DOLHIN documents begin with a top node. Nodes consist of a title and a content which is called a page and displayed in a DOLPHIN window. The upper left window (labeled "Top Page") shows the group browser where all group members are currently working together. At the top of this window, the group members are represented by icons showing their face and name thus providing awareness information on who is currently sharing this content. Pages are composites that contain text elements, rectangles, nodes and links. Nodes are represented by gray boxes with a text label, e.g. "Image" or "Logo". Links connect different nodes. The content of the node "Logo" is displayed in a separate DOLPHIN window (the upper right window in figure 3). This window (labeled "Logo") contains some ideas and a sketch for the design of the signet for the Family TV channel. Users can create scribbles, text, nodes and links to other nodes. A scribble is a freehand writing or drawing such as the logo "F-TV".

DOLPHIN offers the possibility for users to work in parallel, either privately in an individual space or sharing a space with a subgroup. These spaces are separate nodes which can be viewed and edited in parallel to the public window (in

304

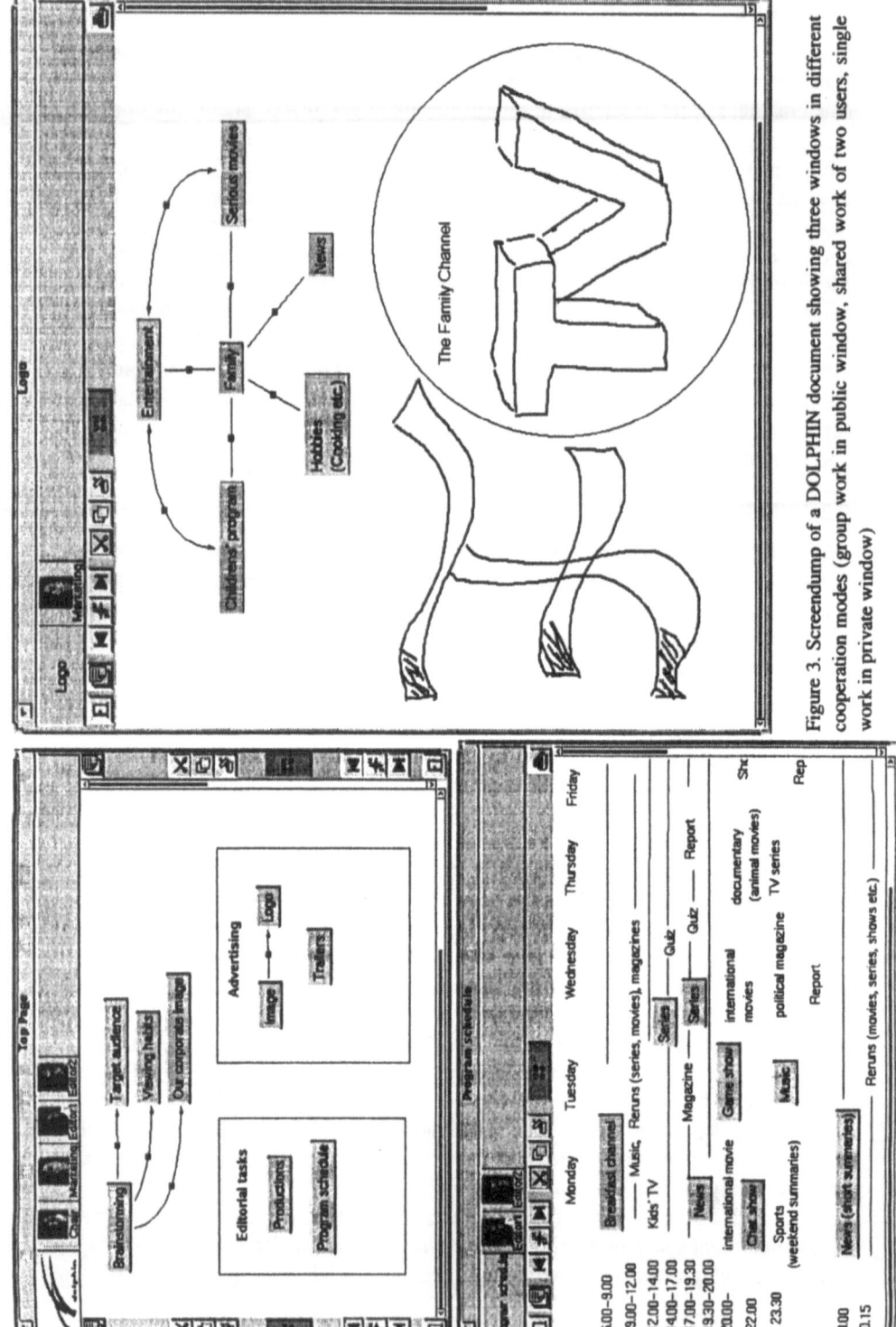

Figure 3. Screendump of a DOLPHIN document showing three windows in different cooperation modes (group work in public window, shared work of two users, single work in private window)

this example the Top Page). The bottom left window (labeled "Program schedule") shows an example for a shared session of the two editors working together. If a user wants to work privately, there is the alternative to open a node with a single session. The upper right window in which the marketing person is working on the page of the "Logo" node is an example of this. Within a shared workspace, DOLPHIN supports concurrent operations performed by different users. Shared access and active update/synchronization of concurrent DOLPHIN windows displaying the same node's content are provided by a cooperative hypermedia server. All changes to the DOLPHIN hypermedia document are reflected in the hypermedia server and made persistent.

Using the above types of objects and operations, users may create different structures, ranging from hierarchically nested structures, i.e. each node at a higher level of the hierarchy contains the nodes of the next lower level (thus forming tree-like structures) to nonlinear structures where nodes are included in the content of several other nodes (thus constituting nonlinear graph structures). The pen-based user interface of DOLPHIN provides gestures for creating, deleting, moving, and selecting objects as well as for opening a node's content. Further technical information on DOLPHIN can be found in (Streitz et al., 1994).

2.2.5 Subjects

The experiment took place between December 1995 and April 1996. A total of 48 subjects were recruited from students of the Technical University of Darmstadt. Their age varied between 19 and 24. There was the explicit requirement to have basic computer skills in order to participate in the experiment. These skills were primarily in the area of text processing, drawing programs, spreadsheets, and e-mail. No subject had prior experience with the DOLPHIN software or the task.

2.2.6 Procedure

All subjects received a 45-minute training session on the functionality of the DOLPHIN system. Subjects were shown examples of information structures on the LiveBoard and how to create and edit them using DOLPHIN. The training included a 15 minute period in which the subjects could practice on their own. After the training, the group started its work on the experimental task. The time of working on the experimental task was 4 hours, organized in two phases of 2 hours each separated by a lunch break of one hour.

2.2.7 The data collection infrastructure

Speaking time and cooperation time: The total view of the meeting room was videotaped. In order to differentiate how much time each subject spent speaking and how long he/she was engaged in different cooperation modes, we developed a new coding tool called COPROT. It was used for obtaining these times by viewing the video tapes. Figure 4 shows what its interface looks like. There are four categories for recording the speaking time by clicking on the buttons for the Chairman (Ch), the Marketing person (Ma), and the two Editors 1 (E1 and E2) when this team member was speaking. In addition, there are 15 categories for different cooperation modes coded by selecting the icons at the bottom of the interface. For the different categories see section 2.2.8 on measures.

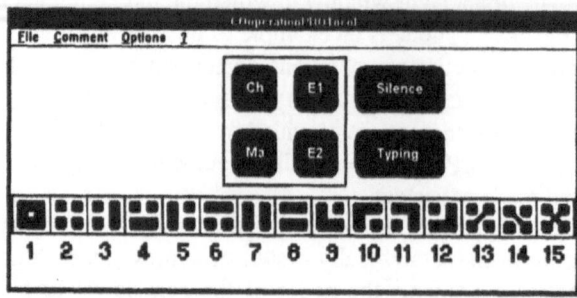

Figure 4: The interface of the COPROT-Tool with buttons for recording speaking time of team members (Ch, Ma, E1, E2) and recording different cooperation modes (1 to 15).

Logging of system interactions: All system interactions of the subjects with the DOLPHIN system at all four workstations and the LiveBoard were recorded in logfiles. This was possible by using a special version of the DOLPHIN software with a built-in logfile functionality. It allows recording each interaction and storing it in a data file, categorised and marked with a time stamp and information about the actor, time, location and if other users are in the same node at this time. The categories of the interactions are content production (typing, drawing), content structuring (moving, resizing, color change), navigation (opening nodes and windows) and hypertext operations (creating nodes/links).

Capturing of ideas on paper: In the LB condition, each subject was also provided with paper and pencil. In order to also obtain in this condition information on how ideas and concepts were generated and developed over time, we used stacks of paper sheets with carbon copy sheets in between. Subjects would always write on the top and keep this top sheet. Every thirty minutes, we removed sheets from below showing copies of the current state of the top sheet created by the carbon copy. Thus, we obtained 8 "snapshots" for each subject.

2.2.8 Measures and Coding

The choice of our measures was guided by the hypotheses and the design.

Qualitative measures: Two experts judged the overall quality of the final electronic documents created by each team. This was done separately. In a few cases, they resolved some differences afterwards in a common discussion. Criteria were the originality of ideas, quality of the information structure and quantitative aspects as, e.g., number of ideas. All documents were rank ordered by this quality measure.

Quantitative measures: Quantitative measures for assessing the production process of each team were obtained by using the data in the logfiles of the system interaction. This included interactions for navigation, for creation of hypermedia nodes and links, text editing, and scribble creation. Furthermore, two experts counted how many ideas were generated. For the LB groups, the experts also counted the number of ideas created on paper.

Speaking times for each member of the team based on the COPROT data.

Time spent in different cooperation modes. This measure was obtained from the data recorded with the COPROT tool. Depending on the group size, there are many combinations of possible cooperation and communication patterns between the group members. In this experiment with four members, we distinguished between 15 different cooperation modes. The different combinations in which the members can communicate and cooperate are illustrated by the different icons (1 to 15) in figure 4.

A typical situation is cooperation mode 1. The group works together and all members have the same focus. In contrast to this is mode 2 which shows no cooperation. Nobody is speaking to anybody else. Everybody is working on a separate task. Cooperation modes 3 to 15 represent the different subgroup modes where one or more group members are working on their own separated from the rest of the group or two subgroups are working independently from another. For the particular evaluation reported in this paper, we clustered the 15 modes into the following three categories: "group mode" (= mode 1), "single mode" (= mode 2), and "subgroup mode" (= modes 3 to 15). There are more detailed analyses possible and interesting to look at but not within the limits of this paper.

Duration of individual work: In the cooperation modes "single" and "subgroup" some members are not communicating with the rest of the group. These subjects are engaged in individual work. We examined how much time is spent in a group in individual work vs. in collective work. This measure was derived from the coding of the time spent in different cooperation modes.

3   Results

The statistical procedures used in analyzing the data of this experiment were analysis of variance and t-test using a significance level of 1% or 5%.

The *overall quality of the teams' product* is measured by the quality of the proposal in terms of the final electronic document created by each team. As figure 5 shows, it differed significantly between the three conditions [$F(2,11)=7.52$, $p<0.05$]. The mean rank of the document quality was 7.63 in condition WS, 9.13 in condition WS+LB, and 2.75 in condition LB. The configurations WS+LB and WS are clearly superior to the LB only condition [$t(WS,LB) = 2.59$, $p<0.05$, $t(WS+LB,LB) = 5.01$, $p<0.01$].

Quantitative measures. While the overall quality of group work is a combined measure, the *number of ideas in the electronic documents* is a measure which can also be compared to other studies in the field. Figure 6 shows that it differed significantly between the three conditions [$F(2,11) = 5.52$, $p<0.05$]. The mean number of ideas created per group was: 251 in condition WS, 403 in condition

308

WS+LB, and 134.5 in condition LB. The WS+LB condition created the most and had the largest difference to the LB condition [t(WS+LB,LB) = 2.92, p<0.05].

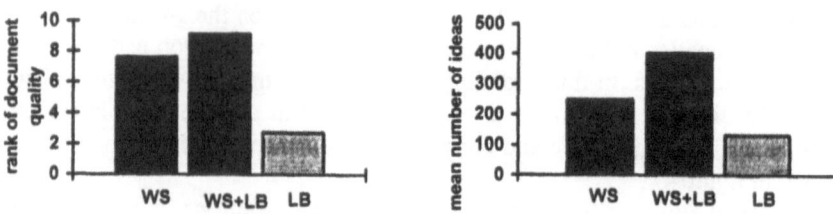

Figure 5. Mean ranks of document quality in the three experimental conditions

Figure 6: Mean number of ideas per group in the three conditions.

The groups in the LB condition had the possibility to generate ideas on paper before using them as part of the electronic document on the LiveBoard. Figure 7 shows the result of comparing the number of ideas on paper (mean = 350) with the number of ideas created per group as part of the electronic documents (mean = 134.5). One can see that the electronic documents contain only about one third of the number of ideas created on paper. These numbers do not refer to exclusive ideas, i.e., some ideas created on paper are also found in the electronic documents and vice versa. There were also ideas in the electronic documents which were combinations and/or modifications of ideas previously created on paper.

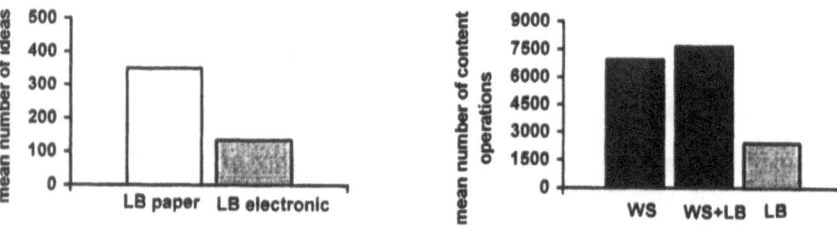

Figure 7: Number of ideas created on paper vs. in the electronic document for the LB condition

Figure 8: Mean number of content operations per group in the three conditions.

While the previous results are indicators for the final product, we now report some results on *variables reflecting the process*. One variable is the number of content operations which were detected by the logfile tool. The mean *number of content operations* per group was: 6953 in the WS condition, 7665.25 in the WS+LB condition, and 2435.5 in the LB condition. As one can see from figure 8, it differed significantly between the three conditions [F(2,11) = 7.73, p<0.05]. t(WS,LB) = 2.78, p<0.05. Again, the largest difference was between the WS+LB and the LB conditions [t(WS+LB,LB) = 5.43, p<0.01].

Since we expected differences in the modes of cooperation, we now report the *proportion of the time the group as a whole spent in one of the three cooperation modes* (defined in section 2.2.8). Figure 9 shows that the teams in the LB condition spent more time in "group mode" (69.4%) than the teams in the other conditions (57.8% and 64.3%) . This is mainly due to the differences in the time spent in the "single mode" (2.9% for LB vs. 9.5% and 17.9% respectively) while the proportion of activities in the "subgroup mode" is very similar.

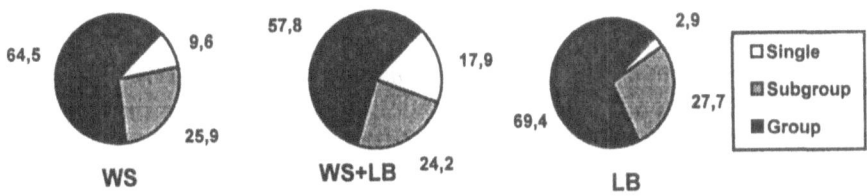

Figure 9: Relative proportion (%) of different cooperation modes: single, subgroup and group.

With our analysis tool, the different cooperation modes can be traced down to the behavior of the individual team member. Of special interest are differences between team members with different roles in the team. Figure 10 shows therefore the *duration of individual work for particular roles,* i.e. averaged over those members who had the same role and were in the same experimental condition.

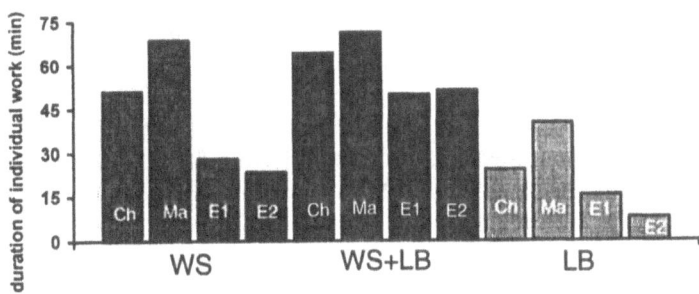

Figure 10: Duration of individual work for the roles: chairperson, marketing, editor1 and editor2.

Although there are significant differences between the conditions [$F(3,47) = 3.58$, $p<0.05$] with respect to the absolute time, there is a common pattern for the different roles irrespective of the conditions. Individual work is done especially by the marketing person (Ma) and also by the chairperson (Ch), while the two editors (E1, E2) work significantly less in this mode [t (Ma, E1) = 2.84 $p<0.01$; t(Ma, E2) = 2.85 $p<0.01$].

In figure 11, we now show the proportion of individual work with respect to the total time by distinguishing only between *individual work vs. collective work.*

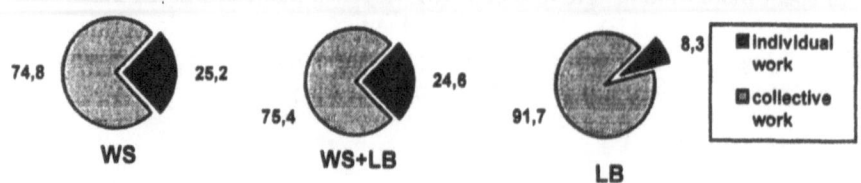

Figure 11: Proportion of time working alone vs. working together with other group members.

There are significant differences between the conditions [F(2,11)= 3.94, p<0.01]. The members of the LB teams spent less time in individual work situations than the WS and the WS+LB teams [t(WS+LB,LB) = 3.32, p<0.05]. In order to illustrate this result, we convert it in minutes. The members of the LB condition worked only less than 20 minutes alone while the WS teams and the WS+LB teams spent more than one hour working alone. For comparison: the total time of work in the experiment was 4 hours.

4   Discussion of results

The results of this experiment show that most of our hypotheses were confirmed or were pointing in the right direction. Those groups which were provided with a combination of both personal and public information devices, as realized in the WS+LB condition, produced higher quality products than the groups which had only one type of information device available. In particular, these groups produced significantly more ideas than the groups in the other conditions. With respect to the work process, the teams in the WS and WS+LB conditions had a similar high level of activity creating/editing content and were significantly more active than the teams in the LB condition. But in terms of number of ideas, the WS+LB teams did better than the WS teams. The availability of the LiveBoard provided a means for improving the elaboration and integration phase. It served the purpose of providing a focus for the discussion and coordination activities of the whole group. For example, it was used for the presentation of intermediary results.

With respect to the cooperation modes, the results show that the provision of both types of information devices was used by the WS+LB teams in an effective combination. On an average, they spent about half of their total time in the full group cooperation mode, and the other half in subgroups and in individual, single work. The other groups, especially the LB teams, spent more time in the full group cooperation mode so that not much time was left for individual work. Comparing the results on the proportion of cooperation modes (figure 9) with the results on the overall quality measure (figure 5) one can see that these results are running parallel. The more single work - but still maintaining enough subgroup and full group activities - the better is the quality of the final product. This can be explained by the following interpretation. Individual work is primarily used for generation of ideas and the number of ideas provides a major contribution to the overall quality measure. This is reflected in the correlation $r = 0.73$ ($p < 0.01$) we found between the cooperation mode single and the number of ideas generated computed over all groups and conditions.

The opportunity for individual activities (single mode), parallel activities (subgroup mode), and public activities (group mode) are mainly provided by the potential of the DOLPHIN software to work in these different modes. The hypermedia functionality provides nodes for private and public work spaces and the cooperative functionality means for sharing information. This is in line with previous results from an earlier experiment in which we investigated how hypermedia structures enabled parallel work and the division of labor (Mark et al., 1995; 1996).

One interesting way to look at the results is the following. One takes the full WS+LB condition as the starting point (these results are always in the middle of the figures 5 to 11). Looking to the left side (-> WS condition) one can see the effect of removing the LiveBoard from this roomware configuration. Looking to the right side (-> LB condition) one can see the effect of removing the networked workstations from this roomware configuration.

5 Conclusions and future work

There has been a large amount of work in CSCW that investigates the role of organizations, the social composition of work groups, the impact of situational factors on how to design multi-user information systems and appropriate interfaces supporting group work. We think that it is now time to look (again) at the physical settings and roomware variables of group work and its impact on products and processes of cooperation and communication. The reported experiment regarding different roomware configurations is one contribution to this direction.

In the future, we will extend this line of research in different directions. One direction is to design, build and investigate computer-augmented cooperation activity rooms populated by a variety of information devices ranging from very small to very large and being attentive, active, and adaptive (A^3-Rooms). This requires also new interaction paradigms and new visualization metaphors. Another direction is to provide the cooperation activities within the room with additional information sources: in terms of corporate memory knowledge, external world-wide available information or other people. The latter is a continuation of our work on distributed meeting rooms and ubiquitous meeting environments (Johannsen et al., 1996; Streitz, 1996). Here, we are coupling two or more meeting rooms via ATM networks and complementing the shared work spaces by conference control and high quality audio and video communication.

6 Acknowledgements

The authors thank the following people for their invaluable help and support: A. Bapat, J. Geissler, J. Haake, C. Schuckmann, and D. Tietze, esp. for commenting on an earlier version of the paper.

7 References

Bapat, A., Geißler, J., Hicks, D., Streitz, N., and Tietze, D. (1996). From Electronic Whiteboards to Distributed Meetings: Extending the Scope of DOLPHIN. *Video Proceedings of the ACM CSCW'96 Conference,* Boston, MA., November 16-20, 1996.

Elrod, S. et al. (1992). Liveboard: a large interactive display supporting group meetings, presentations and remote collaboration. *Proc. of CHI'92 Conference, Monterey,* pp. 599-607.

Johannsen, A., Haake, J., Streitz, N. (1996). *Telecollaboration in Virtual Organisations - The Role of Ubiquitous Meeting Systems,* GMD Arbeitsberichte No. 974.

Mantei, M. (1988). Capturing the Capture Lab Concepts: A case study in the design of computer-supported meeting rooms. *Proceedings of the CSCW '88 Conference, Portland,* pp. 257-268.

Mark, G., Haake, J., Streitz, N. (1995). The use of hypermedia in group problem solving: An evaluation of the DOLPHIN electronic meeting room environment. *Proceedings of the E-CSCW'95 Conference,* Stockholm, Sept. 10-15, 1995, Kluwer Publishers, pp. 197-213.

Mark, G., Haake, J.M., and Streitz, N.A. (1996). Hypermedia Structures and the Division of Labor in Meeting Room Collaboration. *Proceedings of the ACM CSCW'96 Conference,* Boston, MA., November 16-20, 1996, pp. 170-179.

Moran, T.P., Chiu, P., Harrison, S., Kurtenbach, G., Minneman, S. & van Melle, W. (1996). Evolutionary Engagement in an Ongoing Collaborative Work Process: A Case Study. *Proceedings of the ACM CSCW'96 Conference,* Boston, MA., Nov. 16-20, 1996, pp. 150-159.

Nunamaker, J.F. Briggs, R.O. & Mittleman, D.D. (1995). Electronic Meeting Systems: Ten Years of Lessons Learned. In: David Coleman & Raman Khanna (Eds.), *GROUPWARE: Technology and Applications.* Prentice-Hall Inc., pp. 149-193.

Nunamaker, J.F., Dennis, A.R., Valacich, J., Vogel, D. & George, J. (1991). Electronic meeting systems to support group work. *Communications of the ACM,* vol. *34, no. 7,* pp. 40-61.

Olson, J., Olson, G., Storrosten, M., Carter, M. (1993). Groupwork close up: A comparison of the group design process with and without a simple group editor. *ACM Transactions on Information Systems, special issue.* T. Malone & N. Streitz (Eds.), vol. 11, no. 4, pp. 321-348.

Pedersen, E., McCall, K., Moran, T., Halasz, F. (1993). Tivoli: An electronic whiteboard for informal workgroup meetings, *Proc. of the InterCHI'93 Conference, Amsterdam,* pp. 391-398.

Rein, G. L., Ellis, C. A. (1989). The Nick experiment reinterpreted: Implications for developers and evaluators of groupware. *Office: Technology and People,* vol. 5, no. 1, pp. 47-75.

SMART Technology. http://www.smarttech.com

Stefik, M., Foster, G., Bobrow, D.G., Khan, K., Lanning, S. & Suchman, L. (1987). Beyond the chalkboard: Computer support for collaboration and problem solving in meetings. *Communications of the ACM,* vol. 30, no. 1, pp. 32-47.

Streitz, N. (1994). Putting objects to work: Hypermedia as the subject matter and the medium for computer-supported cooperative work. In: M. Tokoro & R. Pareschi (Eds.), *Object-Oriented Programming.* Proc. of the 8. European Conf. on OO-Programming (ECOOP'94), Bologna, Italy, July 4-8, 1994. Lecture Notes in Computer Science 821. Berlin: Springer, pp. 183-193.

Streitz, N. (1996). From individual work and desktop-based collaboration to ubiquitous meeting environments. In: Brusilovsky, P. Kommers, P., Streitz, N. (Eds.), *Multimedia, Hypermedia, and Virtual Reality: Models, Systems, and Applications.* Lecture Notes in Computer Science 1077. Heidelberg: Springer, 1996, pp. 149-163.

Streitz, N., Geißler, J. Haake, J., Hol, J. (1994). DOLPHIN: Integrated meeting support cross Liveboards, local and remote desktop environments. *Proceedings of the ACM CSCW'94 Conference,* Chapel Hill, N.C., pp. 345 - 358.

Analysing movement and world transitions in virtual reality tele-conferencing

Chris Greenhalgh
Department of Computer Science, University of Nottingham, U.K.
c.greenhalgh@cs.nott.ac.uk

In this paper we make use of automatically generated logs of user activity from 6 meetings held using the MASSIVE-1 virtual reality tele-conferencing system to determine a number of characteristics of user movement and world transition. These results are applied to a consideration of four issues for CVE system design and resource requirements: the amount of network bandwidth and computation required to handle movement within worlds; the degree of look-ahead required when moving; whether world transitions by groups of participants could benefit from special handling (e.g. some form of multicast state-transfer); and whether caching of world state would be useful in these contexts. In each case the implications are quantified for the meetings analysed.

1. Introduction

Within the BT/JISC-funded Inhabiting The Web (ITW) project 17 meetings have been held using the MASSIVE-1 virtual reality tele-conferencing system. MASSIVE-1, which was presented at ECSCW'95 (Greenhalgh and Benford, 1995a), supports real-time 3D graphical, audio and text interaction between geographically isolated users at graphical workstations and is based on the spatial model of interaction, which was presented at ECSCW'93 (Benford and Fahlen, 1993). In MASSIVE-1, each participant is (graphically) embodied and can move freely and independently within a connected universe of virtual worlds, talking to other participants that they meet.

MASSIVE-1 has been the subject of at least three previous analyses: our own reflection on the use of the system (at ECSCW'95); and two studies by Bowers, O'Brien and Pycock (1996a and 1996b) which employ social scientific methods (employing talk and virtual body movement transcription) and ethnographics ob-

313

J. Hughes et al. (eds.), Proceedings of the Fifth European Conference on Computer Supported Cooperative Work, 313-328.
© *1997 Kluwer Academic Publishers.*

servation to investigate social interaction in CVEs, and the concurrent interactions which occur in the real and virtual worlds. All of these analyses have been qualitative, and have focused on particular (characteristic) incidents or experiences.

In contrast, in this paper we make use of automatically generated logs of user activity in the virtual worlds, which are analysed mathematically to explore the full range and occurrence of movement and world-transition behaviours over a relatively long period of time (6 meetings). This analysis of overall characteristics has direct application to system design and network requirements for CVEs in general. In this paper we show how this information can help to determine:

- the amount of network bandwidth and computation required to handle movement within worlds;
- the degree of look-ahead required when moving;
- whether world transitions by groups of participants could benefit from special handling (multicast state-transfer), and what delay this would introduce; and
- whether caching of world state would be useful in these contexts and on what time-scale.

In the next section we give some further information about the meetings which occurred, and which the subsequent analysis is based on. Section 3 describes the nature and handling of the data. Section 4 presents the direct results of the data analysis, while section 5 goes on to consider the four questions above. Finally, section 6 presents the overall conclusions and acknowledgements.

2. The meetings

This section gives some details of the nature and form of the meetings which occurred over the course of the ITW project using the MASSIVE-1 CVE.

Over the course of the project 17 official virtual meetings were held using MASSIVE-1 over SuperJANET, the UK's high-speed academic network. The meetings involved between 5 and 9 simultaneous participants based at BT and at (some or all of) the five participating UK Universities: Nottingham, Lancaster, Manchester, Leeds and UCL.

Each trial lasted approximately one hour. The first 11 were concerned primarily with familiarising the participants with the technology and with ensuring consistent and acceptable performance of the system. The remaining 6 meetings combined project management activity (for the ITW project itself), informal social interaction and organised games and activities. The data in this paper is based on these last 6 meetings. For the 6 meetings in question, in addition to project management, the organised activities and meeting attendance were:

- team word games (14th August 1996, 8 participants, 6 sites);
- team anagrams and other word games followed by hide and seek in the maze (21st August 1996, 9 participants, 6 sites);
- multi-world exploration and problem solving in teams followed by a maze

race (4th September 1996, 5 participants, 4 sites);
- team exploration of a noisy environment requiring control of focus (18th September 1996, 6 participants, 4 sites);
- two individual games (balloon debate and discussion) (25th September 1996, 8 participants, 5 sites); and
- an end-of-trials party with a dance contest, obstacle race and discussion (2nd October 1996, 8 participants, 6 sites).

In the next section we consider in more detail the actual information captured during meetings and way in which it has been analysed.

3. The data

Having described something of the nature of the meetings that were held, we now describe the information that has been captured and the way in which it has been used in this paper. There are five main sources of data about the meetings:
- log files generated by the MASSIVE-1 user client programs;
- network logs for audio data captured using the UNIX utility "tcpdump";
- videos of the meetings from the perspective of one or more participants;
- questionnaires completed after the meetings; and
- personal reflections on the meetings from those involved.

This paper is based primarily on the first of these only, since they are amenable to automated analysis and include all of the information required for this analysis of the movement and world transition. Specifically, these log files from the MASSIVE clients include information about: position and orientation within worlds; and transitions between worlds.

Log files are available for approximately 70% of participants at the 6 meetings in question. For the 6 meetings there are a total of 35.9 hours of log files (from individual participants) covering approximately 8 hours of meetings.

3.1. Example meeting: 25th September 1996

Figure 1 illustrates the available log data for the meeting held on 25th September 1996. Time runs from left to right with time of day values recorded at the bottom of the graph. At the left is a column of labels which identify virtual worlds ("presentation-world", "balloon", etc.), and within each virtual world identify participants (by the IP number of the machine which they were using, e.g. "128.16.8.225", "128.243.22.16"). Thus the horizontal area at the top of graph between the first pair of horizontal lines represents activity in the "presentation-world"; in this case the participant using machine "130.88.13.171" enters that world at about 15:10 from "meeting-world" and returns almost immediately. The second horizontal area represents activity in the world "balloon", and so on. The activity of each participant is recorded by a horizontal trace which evolves with time from left to right. When

316

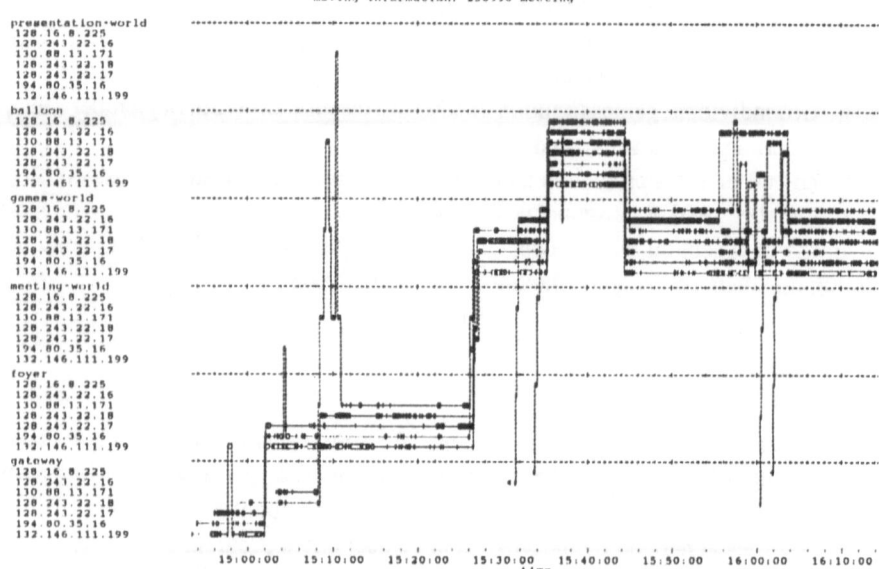

Figure 1. Visualisation of data from 25/9/96 meeting.

the person is stationary the trace is a thin line; when the person is moving the trace
becomes a thick line or a box; when the person moves directly to another world (via
a portal) this is indicated by a dashed vertical line.

Key events which may be seen from the graph include: participants arrive in
"gateway" from 14:53 to about 15:02, when most of them move into the "foyer"
world; the project management phase of meeting runs from then to about 15:26,
when everyone moves on to the "games-world"; the balloon debate runs from about
15:35 until 15:44 in the "balloon" world and is followed by a discussion and the introduction of next task which runs from about 15:55 to about 16:04; the meeting
ends at about 16:14 when everyone finally leaves the world (and the system).

3.2. Data handling

All data processing and analysis was done using in-house tools developed for the
purpose. The key events used in the analysis are: participants entering and leaving
the system; participants moving between worlds; and participants starting and stop-
ping moving. All of the results are presented as distributions of measures extracted
from the data, such as time spent moving, time spent in a world, etc.

The next section presents the actual measures derived from the data, i.e. the basic
results, while section 5 goes on explore the implications of these results.

4. Results

In this section we present the basic results of this paper, based on the analysis of logged data from 6 meetings. The specific issues addressed by the analysed data are:

- How much of the time do participants spend moving?
- Do people all move simultaneously or do they move independently?
- How quickly do participants move about within the virtual worlds?
- Do participants move to new worlds in groups or individually?
- If moving between worlds in groups, how spread out are those groups?
- Do participants revisit worlds, and if so with what time lapse?

In the section 5 we go on to consider the implications of these results for CVE system design and resource requirements. While these results form the foundation for the implications it is possible to read skip directly to section 5 and refer back to individual results as they are considered in that section. In this section we take each of the above issues in turn.

4.1. How much of the time do participants spend moving?

The first results concern the fraction of the time which individual participants spend moving while in the virtual world. I.e. how long do people spend moving and how long are they stationary? MASSIVE-1 uses a mouse-based navigational interface in which participants click on different parts of the graphical window to move in different directions.

For all participants and all six later meetings (subject to available log files) the average percentage of time spent moving was 19.6%. Figure 2 shows the distribution of percentage of time spent moving for a single participant during a single visit to a single world. I.e. each visit of a participant to a world has been considered independently, and a percentage value calculated for the fraction of time which they spent moving while in that world on that occasion. The upper curve is the cumulative distribution while the lower jagged line is the point distribution with a bucket size of 1%.

Analysing the same data by participant over all six meetings (all worlds visited) reveals that average movement rates for individual participants vary from 7.2% to 28%. Similarly, average movement rates for particular worlds (all participants) vary from 7.5% to 54.6%. Both of these extremes occurred in the final meeting which included the end-of-project virtual party; the lowest movement rate occurred in the classical music world while the highest movement rate occurred in the disco world (home of the disco-dancing competition). The average movement rate in the formal meeting world was 16.7%.

This result, like the others, is simply presented in this section: reflection is reserved until section 5.

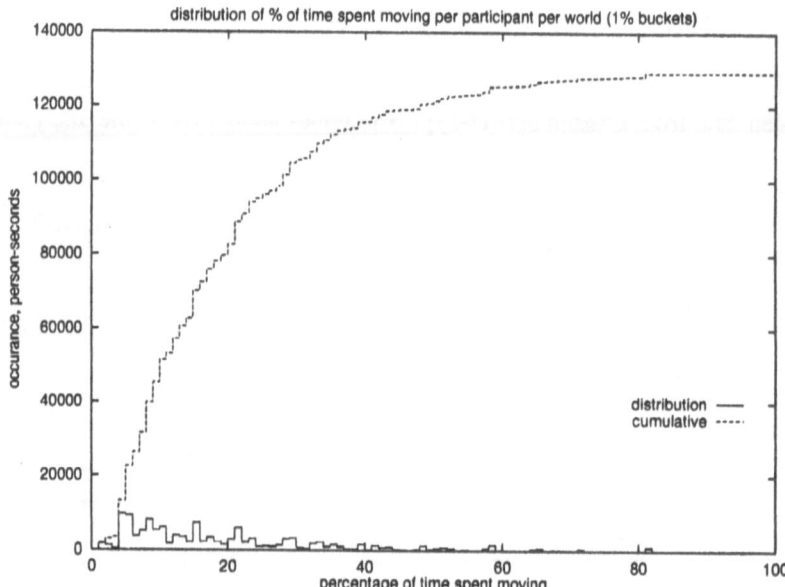

Figure 2. Distribution of percentage of time spent moving, all log files.

4.2. Do people all move simultaneously or do they move independently?

The second result considers whether people in a single world tend to move simultaneously or not. I.e. if one person is moving is everyone likely to be moving? (following?)? Or are people more likely to be stationary instead? (watching?) Or is there no connection?

For all six meetings and all participants the groups or participants simultaneously present in a world has been considered to establish the distribution of numbers of participants moving concurrently. Figure 3 shows this distribution (the solid line). There were over 9000 seconds of logged activity in which exactly one person was moving in a world. The incidence of larger numbers of participants moving simultaneously falls off smoothly. For comparison, the dashed line shows the distribution that would be expected if movement were completely independent, e.g. random.

It is apparent that the incidence of larger numbers of people moving concurrently is rather higher than chance, indicating that (at least some of the time) people coordinated their movement activities. This would clearly be the case when, for example, the meeting moves together from one world (and activity) to another.

4.3. How quickly do participants move about within the virtual worlds?

The third result concerns the speed with which participants move about in the virtual environment. Movement in MASSIVE-1 is not constrained by any particular

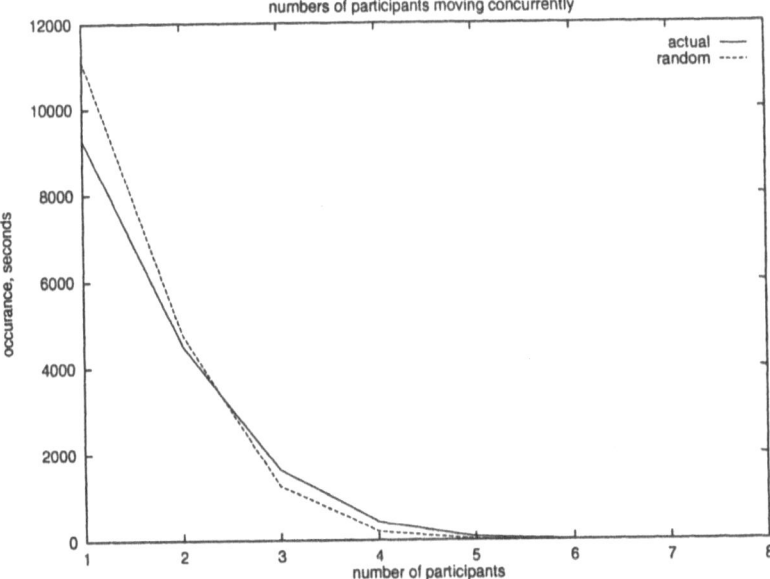

Figure 3. Distribution of numbers of people moving concurrently.

physical model or real-world analogy. According to where on the screen users click the mouse buttons they move at different speeds. The nominal maximum speed is 8 units per second, though higher speeds may occur as a result of uneven frame rates (i.e. where drawing subsequent graphical images takes significantly different lengths of time). A unit is approximately equivalent to a metre (based on scale size of embodiments and world geometries).

Figure 4 shows the cumulative distribution of speeds of movement for all participants in all (6) meetings. The average speed overall (including periods when stationary) is 0.18 units per second. The average speed when moving is 1.04 units per second. The distribution is a smooth curve with higher speeds decreasing in likelihood. Note that the vertical axis of the graph does not start at zero: the high incidence of being stationary (80.4% of the time - see section 4.1) is not displayed.

4.4. Do participants move to new worlds in groups or individually?

The fourth measure concerns the question of whether participants tend to move between worlds in groups or as isolated individuals. From the nature of the meetings we expect that group transitions will occur, as when the meeting moves from the "games-world" to "balloon" world in the example meeting (section 3.1). Here we will quantify this effect to help us establish its general significance (the next result will address the spread of group transitions).

For this measurement we have identified the occurrences of two or more participants moving from one world to another so that at some point in time all are in one world and at a later point in time all have moved directly to the other world and are

320

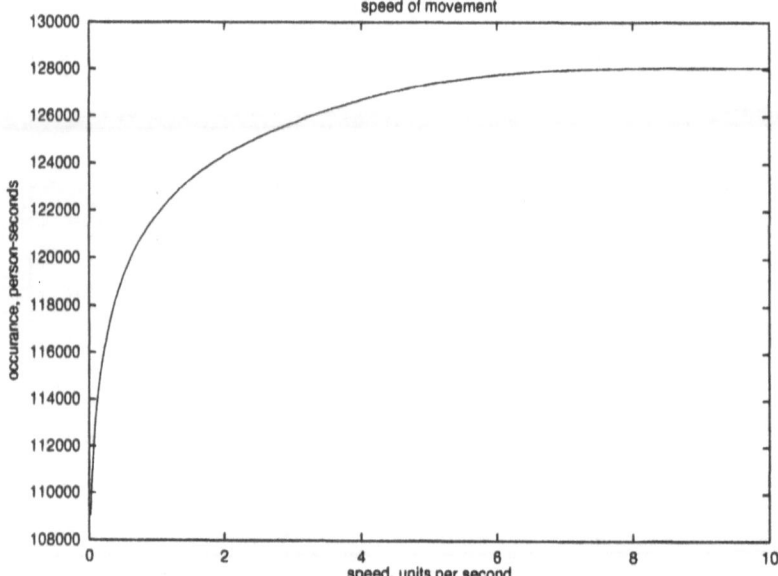

Figure 4. Distribution of speed of movement.

still there. This reflects a group moving together to another world. Figure 5 shows the incidence of group world transitions for different group sizes. The upper

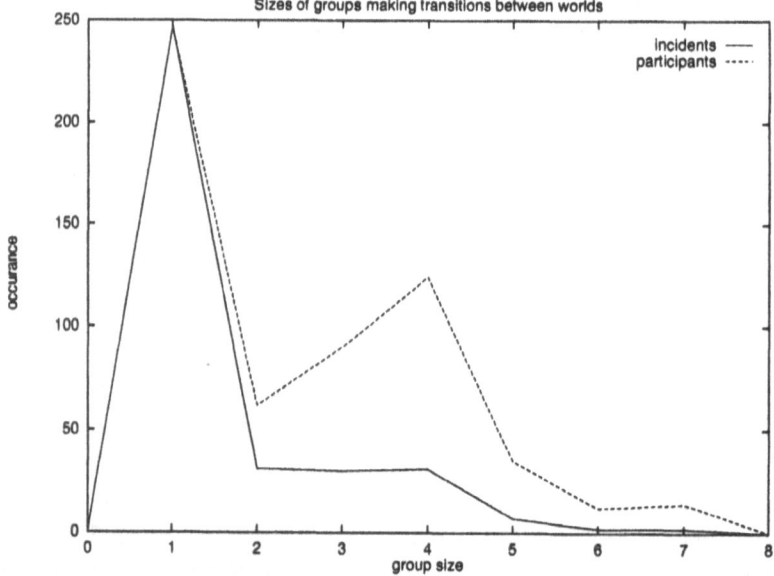

Figure 5. Distribution of sizes of group moving between worlds.

(dashed) line is weighted by the number of participants in the group, while the lower line shows just the number of incidents. The upper curve is representative of the importance of this effect as it the number of participants involved A participant entered a new world 584 times in the available data. 337 (58%) of these person-transitions were in groups of 2 or more participants. In total there were 350 incidents: 247 (71%) solitary transitions and 103 (29%) group transitions occurred. The average group size for group transitions was 3.27; for all transitions (including solitary transitions) the average group size was 1.67. The largest group making a transition had 7 members (constrained by available log files).

4.5. If moving between worlds in groups, how spread out are those groups?

Having established above that indentifiable groups move between worlds, we now consider how spread out in time those groups are. I.e. from start to finish, how long does it take a group to make a world-transition through a single portal. There is no collision detection in MASSIVE-1, so that participants could in principle all move through the portal simultaneously.

Figure 6 shows the distribution of world entry delays for group members lagging behind the first group member to make the transition. I.e. the time on the graph is

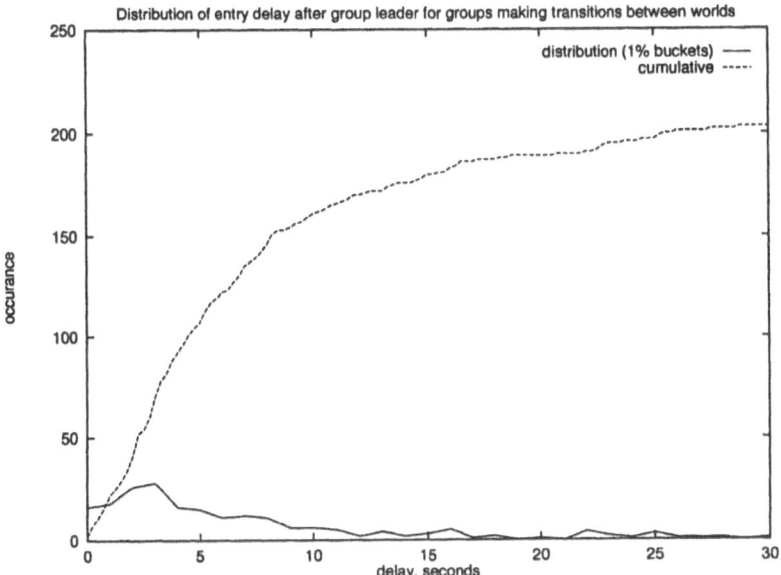

Figure 6. Distribution of world entry delay for group members.

the time which has elapsed since the first member of the group entered the new world. The graph shows delays of up to 30 seconds which account for 203 (87%) of the 234 participants who follow another participant into a world. 104 (44%) of these occur within 5 seconds while 159 (67%) occur within 10 seconds of the first group member making the transition.

4.6. Do participants revisit worlds, and if so with what time lapse?

The last result concerns participants who visit a world more than once during a single meeting. In particular, when a participant does visit a single world twice in a meeting, how much time elapses between those visits?

Figure 7 shows the cumulative distribution of times between repeat visits to a world for all participants in all meetings. Return visits occurring after more than 24

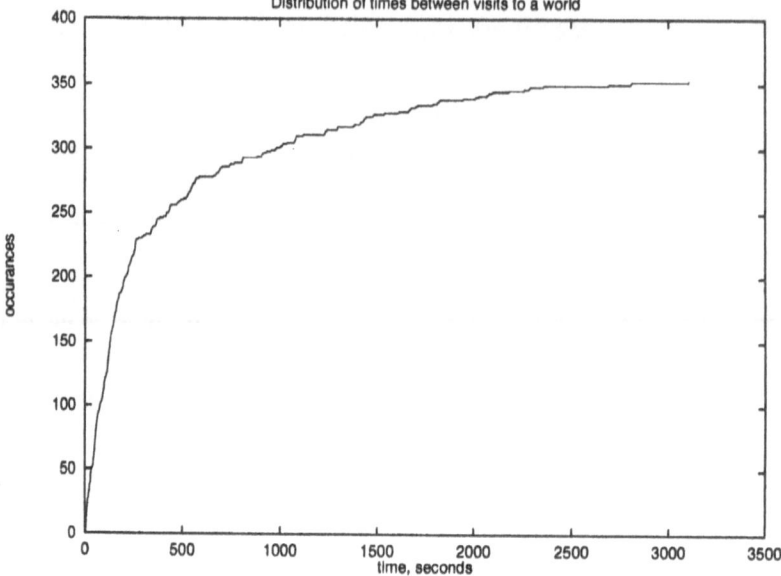

Figure 7. Distribution of times between return visits to a world.

hours are not shown (i.e. only return visits occurring in the course of a single meeting are shown). There are 353 occurrences in total, with an average delay of 427 seconds (just over 7 minutes) between visits. Half of these return visits occur within 162 seconds (less than 3 minutes). 231 visits to worlds do not feature in this distribution because they were the first visit to a world during that meeting, i.e. 60% of world transitions were return visits within a single meeting.

We have now seen all of the basic results obtained from analysing the logged statistics from 6 of the ITW meetings. We now move on to consider the implications and applications of these results.

5. Implications

In this section we use the results from the previous section's analysis of the meeting data to reflect on four implementation issues for CVEs: the amount of network bandwidth and computation required to handle movement within worlds; the degree of look-ahead required when moving; whether world transitions by groups of participants could benefit from special handling; and whether caching of world state would be useful in these contexts. We consider these issues in turn, and refer to individual results from section 4 as appropriate.

5.1. Handling movement within worlds

The first issue which we consider is that of handling movement with virtual worlds: handling movement in virtual worlds consumes network and computational resources since user movements are non-deterministic and so must generate network traffic to inform other participants, and this traffic and consequent world cache updates require computation resources from recipients. Consequently, when assessing the number of participants which a system may support or the resources required to support different numbers of participants it is important to know how much participants move and whether the system should be expected to cope with all participants moving simultaneously.

From section 4.1 we observe that in the meetings considered participants move on average 19.6% of the time, and we might use this figure in calculating expected average bandwidths produced by a large number of participants. (The model of network traffic for MASSIVE-1 described by Greenhalgh and Benford (1995b) used a value of 25% based on earlier in-lab use MASSIVE-1 for lab meetings.) This aspect of movement traffic behaviour is normally ignored when modelling resource requirements of CVEs, and a single long-term average traffic rate used, (e.g. Macedonia, Zyda, Pratt, Barham, and Zeswitz,1994).

From section 4.2 we observe that participants do move together more often than chance within common-purpose groups. For example, 6 participants moving simultaneously was observed for 11.3 seconds in the test data compared with an expected value of 1.1 seconds for independent movement. So the system should be able to cope with simultaneous movement of members of coherent groups being more common that might be expected for completely independent (and isolated?) participants.

The above values will be affected by techniques such as update rate limiting and dead reckoning which reduce the (worst case) amount of traffic needed to communicate movement information. For example, if positional updates are sent no more than once per second then the effective time spent moving is increased to 33.4% (from 19.6%). This is because short periods without movement are effectively swallowed up by the surrounding periods of movement.

5.2. Spatial look-ahead

The second issue with design implications is spatial look-ahead in virtual worlds: to enhance the scalability of large virtual worlds some form of spatial coherence can used (e.g. NPSNET (Macedonia, Zyda, Pratt, Brutzman and Barham, 1995), MASSIVE-2 (Benford, Greenhalgh and Lloyd, 1997), PARADISE (Singhal and

Cheriton, 1996)). Depending on the organisation of the system more distant participants and parts of the environment may need to be acquired (e.g. paged into memory) as a participant moves about. This paging may take a significant period of time
(e.g. several seconds) especially when it must be acquired across the network or it
contains a very large amount of information. Therefore to avoid or reduce abrupt
discontinuities in the participants view of the environment it may be necessary to
anticipate their future requirements and to begin paging in regions before they are
needed. The degree of anticipation required will depend (amongst other factors) on
the speed with the participant is expected to move.

In the meeting considered here, which involved relatively small virtual spaces
comparable in size to large rooms or small halls, the average rate of movement was
1 virtual metre per second (section 4.3) - a slow walking pace. Participants had interfaces which allowed them much greater speeds (at the expense of accuracy), and
speeds of 6-8 (the nominal maximum) virtual metres per second are uncommon
(occurring only 0.25% of the time). We may suggest from this that in normally
scaled room structures people adopt a normal speed of movement - approximately
walking pace, and look-ahead may be tailored accordingly.

However it is unlikely that this result will generalise to large or exterior spaces.
After all, the average speed of movement on a road is more like 25 metres per second (and this often feels frustratingly slow).

5.3. Group world transitions

The third issue we consider concerns group world transitions and the potential utility of multicast state transfers.

Virtual reality systems often exploit a metaphor of multiple disjoint virtual
worlds connected by gateways or portals (e.g. DIVE (Carlsson and Hagsand, 1993),
MASSIVE-1 and VRML worlds). On moving to a new world a process (e.g. a participants interface) must acquire initial information about that new world. This may
be by means of a unicast state transfer from a peer process (as in DIVE) or processes
(as in MASSIVE-1); it may be by means of a unicast state transfer from a server (as
in VRML); it may emerge over time from watching activity in the new world (as in
DIS 2.x with periodic entity state transmissions). If groups of participants tend to
move to other worlds together than there is a clear opportunity to make use of multicasting where a specific state transfer phase is present. This is especially true if
those groups can be identified in advance, for example within another virtual world
heading towards a portal.

In the six meetings under consideration there were 584 occurrences of a participant entering a new world, and of these 337 (57%) involved travelling in a group of
2 or more (section 4.4). It can be argued that the fact that group transitions occur is
just a reflection of the application and the way in which the meetings were organised - a different application of CVEs might not involve (coordinated) world transitions at all. On the other hand, it can be argued that structuring the meeting into

distinct phases involving different virtual worlds was found to be useful and effective and so is likely to be used in a broad range of applications. Also, group transitions may be observed within structured worlds as well as between worlds (e.g. entering a room or building, leaving a concert - see (Benford, Greenhalgh and Lloyd, 1997)) and the same techniques will be relevant.

Given that group transitions occur (in whatever context) it is also important to understand how well defined they are and how long they take. For example, if a multicast state transfer were employed then all group members would effectively reach the new world (or region) at the same time, although they may have set off at different times. This will necessarily delay the earlier members and/or require speculative state transfers to those participants who are *expected* to follow. Referring to section 4.5, if every group transition used multicast state transfer then 337 unicast state transfers would be replaced by 103 multicast state transfers (eliminated 69% of unicast state transfers), however the longest resulting delay would be 13 minutes! More realistically, we might constrain the maximum delay (i.e. the period over which group members may arrive and still use the same multicast state transfer). For delays up to 5 seconds 104 unicast state transfers would be eliminated (30.8%); for delays up to 10 seconds this rises to 159 (47%); for delays up to 30 seconds it rises to 203 (60%). No longer delay is likely to be acceptable except in very specific applications.

On the negative side, the management overhead for the multicast state transfer may well include a component for every recipient; so multicast state transfers will be increasingly attractive where larger quantities of state have to be transferred. MASSIVE-2 uses multicast state transfers when participants arrive in quick succession, and unicast transfers otherwise. However performance data is not yet available to assess the effectiveness of this implementation.

5.4. World state caching

The final issue which we reflect on concerns the possibility of caching world state between visits. CVE systems which use state transfer on world (or region) may repeat this transfer each time a participant returns to the same world (or region) (e.g. MASSIVE and DIVE both do this). Clearly, the participant could (resources permitting) retain a local cache of some or all of this state information between visits, alleviating or eliminating the requirement for a new state transfer. In order for this to be effective some or all of the state information from the previous visit must still be valid. I.e. the world cannot have changed; or if it has changed then it must have changed only in limited and well-defined ways which can be updated independently. Shortage of resources (for caching) and the potential volatility of world information may dictate that caching be limited in extent and duration. Information from the ITW meetings is relevant to this second limitation of duration. Ideally, we would like to keep information only for those worlds which will be returned to. One heuristic by which we can attempt to consider the likelihood of returning to a world is the time since it was last visited (this will also impact the likely usefulness of the cached data).

In the meeting data under consideration there were 353 occurrences of participants returning to a previously visited world within the course of a meeting (section 4.6). The average delay was just over 7 minutes, but half of the incidents occurred within 3 minutes of leaving the world. This discrepancy between mean and median indicates that returning to a world within a few minutes is relatively common, but that above about 6 minutes (67% of occurrences) the return times spread out much more. I.e. we can make a rough division between return visits which happen within a few minutes and which account for the majority of incidents, and the remainder which happen over much longer periods. In the appropriate circumstances this could be an appropriate cut-off point for short-term caching of worlds visited.

Again, it can be argued that we are just seeing the effects of the particular choice of meeting agenda and universe structure. Certainly, more data would be needed to generalise these results to a broader range of scenarios. On the other hand at least some of the return visits reflect the choice to structure the meeting worlds as common hub or access worlds with multiple activity worlds "hanging" off them. This is a general structuring technique (c.f. hierarchical file stores) which might be expected to recur in many systems and applications, and to encourage (or require) repeated return to the hub world(s), making this effect wide-spread.

This completes our reflection on the implications of the participant movement and world-transition data obtained from the later ITW virtual meetings. The final sections presents our conclusions in a more succinct form and outlines future work.

6. Conclusions and future work

In this paper we have analysed data captured automatically during the BT/JISC-funded Inhabiting The Web (ITW) trials of the MASSIVE-1 virtual reality tele-conferencing system. These concern structured meetings with 5-9 participants in a combination of group management, unconstrained social interaction and organised games and activities. Using this data we have produced answers to the questions:

- How much of the time do participants spend moving?
  About 20%, though there is considerable variation between individuals (7% to 28%) and between worlds (7% to 55%). This value is also sensitive to bandwidth reduction techniques like rate-limiting and dead-reckoning.
- Do people all move simultaneously or do they move independently?
  People move simultaneously more than we would expect from independent movement, though the drop off in incidence of simultaneous movement with numbers is still very marked.
- How quickly do participants move about within the virtual worlds?
  About walking pace (1 virtual metre per second on average) within the room-scaled environments used in the ITW project.

- Do participants move to new worlds in groups or individually?
  They move in groups on average 58% of the time, the average group size being 1.67 (or excluding solitary transitions, 3.27). The largest size group observed making a world transition was 7 participants.
- If moving between worlds in groups, how spread out are those groups?
  Transition times of up to 5 seconds account for 44% of the participants who follow another participant into a world; times up to 10 seconds account for 67%; and time up to 30 seconds account for 87%.
- Do participants revisit worlds, and if so with what time lapse?
  60% of participant visits to worlds were return visits during the course of single meeting. The average return time was just over 7 minutes, though 50% of return visits occurred within 3 minutes and 67% of return visits occurred within 6 minutes.

The four design and resource issues which we have considered are:

- Network bandwidth and computational requirements to handle movement within worlds -
  must account for movement at least 20% of the time (depending on the use of other bandwidth-limiting techniques and the individual character of the world), with an independent movement model being unsuitable for coherent groups of individuals.
- The degree of look-ahead required when moving -
  may use normal "real-world" movement speeds as a heuristic expectation in small interior virtual worlds.
- The scope for using multicast to handle transitions by groups of participants -
  there is significant scope for using multicast state-transfers to handle group world transitions which accounted for 58% of world transitions; delays in the range 5-30 seconds may be chosen, trading off delay and effectiveness of multicasting (44%-87%).
- Whether caching of world state would be useful in these contexts and on what time-scale -
  caching of world state would have accounted for 60% of world transitions in these meetings, and a relatively short cache expiry time of 6 minutes would have accounted for the majority of these (67%); this is clearly potentially beneficial.

The scope of these answers will be limited by the specific range of activities occurring in the meetings under consideration. Future work is needed to extend these results and reflection to include:

- larger numbers of simultaneous participants;
- other uses or applications, e.g. spontaneous meetings and unstructured (or self-directed) use; and
- other virtual geographies and topologies such as large exterior spaces.

Other issues which remain to be addressed from this same data set may include:

- characteristics and requirements of audio interaction;

- suitability of dead-reckoning and other movement bandwidth limiting techniques for user movement without simulated "real-world" constraints; and
- characterisation of network traffic and behaviour for further modelling, including consideration of burstiness and systematic variations (e.g. with task).

Acknowledgements

We would like to gratefully acknowledge the support of British Telecommunications plc. in funding and participating in this research, which has been carried out within the BT/JISC funded Inhabiting The Web (ITW) project. With thanks to all those who participated in the meetings: Jolanda Tromp, Gail Reynard, Steve Benford, Rob Ingram, David Lloyd and Lucy Smallwood at the University of Nottingham; Dave Small at the University of Leeds; John Cook and Adrian West at the University of Manchester; Angeline Lim at UCL; Jason Morphett, Paul Shumake, Charanjit Sidhu and Natasha Upal at BT; and especially Adrian Bullock at Nottingham for making sure that the meetings happened and for collecting the data.

References

Benford, S. and Fahlen, L. (1993): "A Spatial Model of Interaction in Virtual Environments", in *Proc. Third European Conference on Computer Supported Cooperative Work* (ECSCW'93), Milano, Italy, September 1993.

Benford, S., Greenhalgh, C., and Lloyd, D. (1997): "Crowded Collaborative Virtual Environments", in *Proc. 1997 ACM Conference on Human Factors in Computer Systems* (CHI'97), Atlanta, Georgia, March 22-27 1997, ACM Press.

Bowers, J., Pycock, J. and O'Brien, J. (1996a): "Talk and Embodiment in Collaborative Virtual Environments", in Proc. CHI'96, New York: ACM Press, 1996.

Bowers, J., O'Brien, J. and Pycock, J. (1996b): "Practically Accomplishing Immersion: Cooperation in and for Virtual Environments", in *Proc. CSCW'96*, New York: ACM Press.

Carlsson, C. and Hagsand, O. (1993): "DIVE - A Multi-User Virtual Reality System", in *Proc. VRAIS'93, IEEE Virtual Reality Annual International Symposium*, pp. 394-400.

Greenhalgh, C., and Benford, S. (1995a): "Virtual Reality Tele-conferencing: Implementation and Experience", *Proc. Fourth European Conference on Computer Supported Cooperative Work* (ECSCW'95), Stockholm, September, 10-14 September, 1995, Kluwer Academic Publishers, Dordrecht, pp. 165-180.

Greenhalgh, C. and Benford, S. (1995b): "MASSIVE: A Virtual Reality System for Tele-conferencing", *ACM Transactions on Computer Human Interfaces* (TOCHI), Volume 2, Number 3, pp. 239-261, ISSN 1073-0516, ACM Press, September 1995.

Macedonia, Michael R., Zyda, Michael J., Pratt, Donald P., Barham, Paul T., and Zeswitz, Steven (1994): "NPSNET: A Network Software Architecture for Large-Scale Virtual Environments", in *Presence*, Vol. 3, No. 4, Fall 1994, pp. 265-287, MIT Press.

Macedonia, Michael R., Zyda, Michael J., Pratt, David R., Brutzman, Donald P., and Barham, Paul T. (1995): "Exploiting Reality with Multicast Groups: A Network Architecture for Large-scale Virtual Environments", in *Proc. 1995 IEEE VRAIS'95*, 11-15 March, 1995, RTP, North Carolina.

Singhal, Sandeep K., and Cheriton, David R. (1996): "Using projection aggregations to support scalability in distributed simulation", in *Proc. of the 1996 International Conference on Distributed Computing Systems*, IEEE.

Designing for Cooperation at a Radio Station

Finn Kensing, Jesper Simonsen, and Keld Bødker
Dept. of Computer Science, Roskilde University, Denmark
{kensing, simonsen, keldb}@ruc.dk

Abstract: We address computer support for work and its coordination in one of the radio channels of the Danish Broadcasting Corporation. Based upon ethnographically inspired analysis and participatory design techniques, we propose design solutions now implemented or under implementation. We focus on cooperative aspects within and among the radio channel's editorial units, and between editorial units and the editorial board. Finally, we discuss technical and organisational aspects of the design, seen in light of recent CSCW concepts.

Introduction

Design of CSCW-systems can be related to at least two different design contexts. When a software company develops a CSCW product for a large market, "product development" (Grudin, 1991), the product will be used in and among various user-groups within an organisation, and/or between different organisations. When we design within an organisation, "in-house development" or "contract development" (Grudin, 1991), we benefit from thinking about the design and the use of the system in terms of *specific* cooperating ensembles of users (Schmidt and Bannon, 1992). This is what we aim for in this paper.

We use the term "design" in the same way as architects do - focusing on the analysis of needs and opportunities, and the preliminary design of functionality and form. Therefore we see results of a design project to include a conceptual design in terms of a written document, sketches, mock ups and/or prototypes. Also we consider an evaluation of consequences of implementing the design, as well as a plan for the implementation, to be parts of the result. Based upon a design proposal, it should be possible for the organisation to proceed in purchasing and/or developing the proposed design.

J. Hughes et al. (eds.), Proceedings of the Fifth European Conference on Computer Supported Cooperative Work, 329-344.
© *1997 Kluwer Academic Publishers.*

We describe a design project from one of the radio channels in the Danish Broadcasting Corporation, DBC. The project took place in 1995, and the objective was to design a coherent vision of computer support for the planning, production, broadcasting, and administrative follow up of radio programs. A majority of the proposed design is now implemented. For some design proposals however, a final decision was not reached, but was left until during and/or after experiments and negotiations were made during implementation. We used the MUST method, which we have developed over the last six years (Kensing et al., 1996). The method is inspired by ethnographic approaches (see e.g. Hughes et al., 1992; Blomberg et al.,1993) and by participatory design approaches (see e.g. Greenbaum and Kyng, 1991; Muller and Kuhn, 1993) and it aims at combining these approaches (like e.g. Kensing and Winograd, 1991; Hughes et al., 1993; Blomberg et al., 1996; Mogensen and Shapiro, 1996).

Previous studies of CSCW-systems in use have dealt with organisational issues (see e.g. Bullen & Bennett 1990; Orlikowski, 1992; Okamura et al., 1994; Ackerman, 1994; Rogers, 1994). In most cases the product development oriented CSCW contributions have not taken organisational issues into account. Our design project demonstrates how technical and organisational issues can be dealt with by combining ethnographically inspired analysis and participatory design. Thus it adds to the, according to Plowman et al. (1995), small body of papers describing workplace studies and specific design guidelines. The project's design report addresses technical and organisational issues, and it evaluates the consequences for the various cooperating ensembles of users. This was discussed as part of the channel's evaluation of the report.

When we strive to understand the problems and needs for computer support and elicit requirements in an organisation, we become engaged in a complex situation where various cooperative ensembles of users may or may not share like problems and potential solutions. In this paper we consider two types of such cooperative ensembles within the Danish Broadcasting Corporation's Channel 3. Editorial units are comprised of journalists, technicians, and administrative staff responsible for a daily or weekly program. The editorial board comprises managers at different levels, with different backgrounds, who have a formal meeting once a week to do overall planning. The editorial units and the editorial board represent multiple, different, and reconfigurable groups, which have conflicting interests (in some cases) and which also have to work together in an remarkably dynamic way to produce 24 hours of constant radio programming. How the editorial units and the editorial board are maintained, and how management exerts its ideas for contents in the various programs are both interesting questions to consider. In such a context, artefacts take on a crucial role in facilitating the cooperation. In the paper we focus explicitly on coordination mechanisms within and among editorial units and between editorial units and the editorial board. We relate our experiences to recent concepts developed in the CSCW-community, regarding coordination and computational coordination mechanisms.

We present our analysis of work practices at the channel, which is followed by a presentation of the proposed design. The paper is concluded by a discussion of technical as well as organisational aspects of the suggested computational coordination mechanisms in the light of the entire design.

Analysis of Needs for Computer Support

The structure of DBC is briefly described first, including some recent management initiatives. Then one of the radio channels, Channel 3, is described. Finally we focus, in greater detail, on one of this channel's editorial units, Station X, responsible for a daily radio program.

A design team was comprised of the authors, two internal IT-consultants, and three user representatives. A steering committee was comprised of the chairman of the editorial board, two staff members, and the IT manager. The design team was responsible for the investigation of IT-support for Channel 3.

The analysis below of the organisation and its needs for computer support are a result of applying tools and techniques suggested by the MUST method. For a more detailed analysis see (Kensing et al., forthcoming). The analytic activities were comprised of *observation* of the planning, production, broadcasting and administrative follow up of radio programs, as well as of management meetings and of the work of several employees on staff; *interviews* which were recorded, partly transcribed and corrected by the interviewed persons; *document analysis* of the corporation's strategic reports, and of material used for research, production, broadcasting, and administrative purposes; *thinking aloud experiments* where employees were asked to describe what they were doing while working; *drawing rich pictures* of current work practices; *analysis of existing software*; and *information modelling* for the purpose of prototyping and time/cost estimates.

These analytic activities were conducted by the design team and approximately one third of the total 140 employees from Channel 3 were involved. They allowed the design team to develop a common understanding of current work practices and to locate potential areas for computer support and/or organisational changes, and to relate these to management strategies. E.g. a lot of rewriting of information took place in various media, the distribution of information among the channel's employees was cumbersome, and the coordination within and among editorial units often failed or was considered confusing and full of disturbances. Concrete design ideas also started to emerge during the above listed activities with users and during the design teams subsequent analyses of the material, e.g. ideas for computer support for the producers' planning of programs, for journalists' research purposes, and for automatic reports for the editorial board as well as for each of the editorial units.

The Danish Broadcasting Corporation

DBC is a public, national station founded in the twenties. Since the eighties it has been running as a limited company for which, by law, every radio and TV-set owner has to pay a license fee. DBC produces and broadcasts TV and radio. The radio station consists of three national radio channels, one news group, and nine regional channels.

The following management initiatives had recently taken place or were under implementation when we started. Our design had to take these initiatives into account.
- Layoffs, expanding the hours of broadcasting, computerised selection of music titles and computerised broadcasting from midnight to 6 A.M.
- The editorial board of Channel 3 wants to shift from "after broadcasting monitoring" to a "forward planning process."
- Self steering groups and integration/loosening up professional demarcations.
- A channel should be perceived as a whole by the listeners, rather than as a collection of individual programs.
- Workgroup computing, and as little in-house development as possible.
- From analogue to digital technology for production and broadcasting.

Before the design project started, the unions had already been forced - by layoffs and by management hiring younger, less specialised employees - to accept these initiatives. It was clear that the project should be seen as part of implementing the initiatives, and the employees accepted these premises of the project.

Channel 3 - A Radio Channel

At Channel 3, 140 journalists, technicians, administrative staff and managers are involved in the production, broadcasting, and administration of 24 hours of radio programming each day all year. The profile of the channel, which broadcasts nation wide, is a mix of music and features for a young or young-minded audience. The channel cooperates with the station's news group that also serves other channels. Channel 3 is organised around some 25 editorial units (1 to 15 people), an editorial board, a couple of staff units and an administrative staff, all under the management of a chief editor. An editorial unit - comprised of journalists (some of which are freelancers), technicians and administrative staff - is responsible for a radio program that is broadcasted on a daily or weekly basis. Each unit had only very little computer support: a few PC's and terminals to access a wide range of mainframe systems and news agencies.

Each radio program has its own concept, but when e.g. a new CD is released, or during larger political, sport, and musical events, competition may take place between editorial units, though the editorial board tries to coordinate it. Cooperation in terms of discussions of various angles on stories, including advertisements and referring to each others programs is encouraged by management and happens on a regular basis.

Our design project focused on activities related to the production, broadcasting and administration of radio programs, rather than on managerial and general administrative work. This is why the work of one of the editorial units will be described in greater detail below. Of course we noticed many differences between editorial units, some of which relate to their needs for IT-support. This will be touched upon in the conclusion, and not dealt with in the description below.

Station X - A Radio Program

Station X is a program than runs Monday through Thursday from 4 P.M. to 6.30 P.M. It is staffed by two producers, two hosts, and four reporters. As a consequence of the integration policy, two technicians and two assistants are part of the editorial unit too. The content of the program is a mix of popular music and features (reportage, interviews, telegrams, gimmicks, etc.).

A typical weekly schedule starts on Fridays when the producer of the coming week and a reporter meet to establish an overview of next week's four programs. They spend 2-3 hours reading newspapers and magazines. They run through the suspension files into which everybody in the editorial unit puts ideas for a specific date. They read a list of upcoming events relevant for the channel. The list is produced and photocopied for all editorial units by a staff member. The list also reflects events and ideas promoted at the last editorial board meeting. They receive a list of news of general interest from external news agencies. Sometimes they order books from the library and tapes from an archive of earlier broadcasted material. They are informed by this week's producer of arrangements that are set up for the coming week. They finish by sketching potential features for the coming week.

At 8 o'clock, Monday through Thursday, a reporter starts running through the newspapers of the day and writes a list of headlines for the producer. He shows up at nine, turns on a computer with access to a news agency, NEWSSTAR. Since he finds the editor in NEWSSTAR as insufficient, the producer starts WORDPERFECT on another computer to make up the list of potential stories for the day. He looks into a paper file to see who is going to work on the day's program. Reflecting the concept of the radio program, he runs through the reporter's list, looking for stories that are adequate for montage, for the mobile recording unit, for mixing sound or music, and for inviting guests for telephone interviews. He prints out a list of about 20 potential stories for the day, makes photocopies and gathers the unit for a meeting to discuss which six or seven stories that the reporters will pursue. At 10 o'clock, back at the desk, the producer sorts out the list and takes print-outs for himself and the host, who is briefed when he shows up. During the day they both annotate the print-outs for individual purposes. He creates a new document rewriting the stories in the order he prefers. He takes into account which programs will be broadcasted before and after his program, and at what time guests can give interviews. The technicians show up to learn the schedule. The person operating the mobile recording unit calls to find out if, when, and where he is needed. The producer coordinates current status with the reporters to know if and how the stories will materialise or if new ones have to be researched. He checks with the editor responsible for daytime programs during the week to find out what other editorial units are working on. He keeps the schedule for the two studios. He, the assistant, and the host find the music for the program, taking the stories into account.

The reporters work on their stories. During the day reporters constantly check stories and angles with the producer and with each other, and they discuss the length of their feature to make them fit into the schedule of the program. For pre-recorded broadcasting reporters use a tape recorder for interviews and for recordings of their own talk. They go to the studio where the material is edited for broadcasting assisted by a technician. They brief the host and deliver a tape to the producer, who makes a final check.

At 2 o'clock the producer, the host and the assistant (the group that works as a team during broadcasting) make up the final plan of the program including all features and music to be played. The assistant rewrites the plan on his computer adding minutes and seconds for each story and additional data for each music title, for the purpose of e.g. statistics and paying royalties. These processes finish close to deadline, and they are further stressed by reporters (coming and leaving) who have to check with the producer and to brief the host. The producer checks all pre-recorded stories and sometimes he has to make cut-downs in order to make them fit the time schedule. The news group calls to coordinate, since every full hour the program is interrupted by the news. If the producer has a story that the news group has overlooked - or he wants them to overlook - he does not mention it, or he moves the story to before the news break. He makes a final check on NEWSSTAR for any big news before he leaves for the studio. During the entire process of producing the program the producer plays the role of a "center of coordination" (Suchman, in press). This gives the producer valuable information, while he considers some of the interactions as disturbances.

During the day the assistant is responsible for reporting on the day before's program. This involves collecting data from the reporters - data they were supposed to have delivered the day before. Furthermore he fills out forms for paying reporters' travels, artists whose music has been played, and experts who have given an opinion during the program.

During broadcasting the host is in a studio, while the producer, the technician, and the assistant are in an adjacent room. They can communicate by gestures through a big window, by microphones and loud speakers (the host has an ear piece), and they may meet, but only when the host is not on the air. They each have a paper copy of the final plan of the program, which they all individually annotate for personal use. The assistant notes the precise actual time and length of the broadcasted features and music titles (information needed for paying royalties). They each continuously update their copy of the plan when changes are made due to e.g. a prolonged live interview.

The description above of the previous work practices at Station X illustrates parts of our analysis at Channel 3. To sum up, we found the following areas as candidates for computer support for the entire channel:

- Coordination within and among editorial units. This type of coordination is a central part of the daily work mediated through meetings, phone calls and paper. Most employees interviewed found large parts of this coordination cumbersome. Also, management wanted enhanced coordination among all editorial units for the channel's profile to be perceived as more distinct, to avoid individual "kingdoms" of programs.
- Coordination between editorial units and the editorial board. This type of coordination was mediated mainly through the editorial board's weekly meetings, the editors responsible for a group of programs, and by the weekly paper list of upcoming events. Our analysis clarified that this type of coordination did not support management's request for a "forward planning process".
- The process of planning, production, broadcasting, and administrative follow up of the various elements that make up a radio program. Very early on during our observations we were led to believe that if the program elements, each consisting of one piece of music or one feature, were represented electronically, all data needed only be typed in and recorded once and could then easily be rearranged by the producer and accessed by several employees.
- Electronic access to material for research purposes. Observations and interviews highlighted a need for faster access to audio and written material.
- Digital recording, editing, and broadcasting. The planned shift from analogue to digital production and broadcasting would allow journalists to work on program elements in the same digital media from early planning until final broadcasting.

In the following, we focus especially on the first three candidates for computer support, addressing coordination within and among editorial units and between editorial units and the editorial board.

Design for IT-use in Channel 3

The results of the analysis in terms of problems, needs, and candidates for computer support were described and proposed in a report. It was presented to all employees at a hearing and to the steering committee and management of the channel. The purpose was to check the degree to which we had understood their work and to point out potential areas for IT-support. The users gave valuable feedback, which helped the steering committee to prioritise. After some minor changes we went further on to design, which comprised the following activities: *Two visits abroad to radio stations* using state of the art technology. This provided the design team with a shared reference for discussing and developing design ideas. *Design workshops,* where the design team collectively sketched future work practices on large sheets of paper. *Sorting out design ideas*, writing them down on stacks of post-it's and grouping them on a wall to provide an overview and to account for design ideas. And finally *data modelling* as a basis for the subsequent development of *demonstration prototypes* of all key design ideas.

These design activities caused the design team to revisit the result of the analysis to check or account for the design ideas. Also a couple of additional interviews had to be conducted to cover discovered holes in our understanding.

The design was presented to all employees at a hearing and to the steering committee and management of the channel. We demonstrated the prototypes and presented a report consisting of the analysis, a vision of the proposed suite of systems and their relations to the envisioned new work practices. The report also included a functional description of each system, a scenario of their future use, an evaluation of consequences for management and the employees, an implementation plan including organisational development and a required training program, and finally an economical estimate.

The overall design criteria has been to facilitate new types of coordination and to allow for qualitative improvements of work processes and of programs by providing easier access to existing and new research material and to reduce the time spent on routine tasks. In addition the design reflects major parts of the management's initiatives mentioned above. The design was proposed to be realised for the entire channel within 2 years. The employees were satisfied with the design, and management decided to purchase, develop, and implement the design.

In the presentation below we restrict ourselves to give only a very brief description of the proposed suite of systems, describing in some detail only two of the systems for the purpose of highlighting new ways of cooperation.

The Overall Design

In line with the business- and IT-strategy, we suggested a client/server solution with multimedia workstations connected to a LAN with access to the Internet. MICROSOFT OFFICE was proposed since this was part of the corporation's IT-strategy too. The overall design consisted of fifteen systems. Two of these focused especially on coordination within and among editorial units and between these and the editorial board. They are in the following referred to as the *Event Calendar* and the *Program Manager*, and are described in further detail in the following.

The Event Calendar

The Event Calendar satisfies a need for electronic access to research material and for coordination voiced during the analysis. It is maintained by a staff member, who creates and updates an electronic version accessible to everybody at the channel. It contains information that is mailed to him about concerts and CD releases, and e.g.

political or musical events he finds in magazines and newspapers. It also reflects events and ideas promoted at the last editorial board meeting. He might indicate for which radio programs a certain event is relevant, and leave it to them to book events and indicate an angle on how they plan to cover the event. He may also indicate if he wants to be notified when an event is booked.

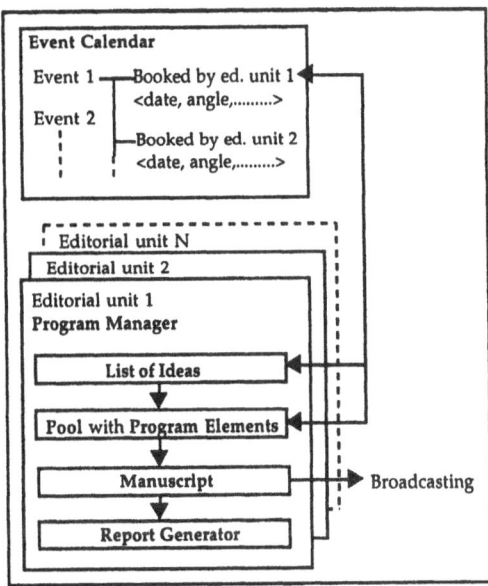

Figure 1. Illustration of the Event Calendar, the Program Manager, and the linking between them. Editorial units book events and indicate an angle. Data from the Event Calendar can be dragged to the List of Ideas in the Program Manager. Ideas evolve into Program Elements and are linked to the Manuscript, broadcasted and finally used by the Report Generator.

The Event Calendar also allows for the requested coordination among editorial units. Several editorial units might book the same event, but then they have to negotiate angles, thus preventing adjacent programs to bring the same stories. Data of an event (contact persons, date and time, type and genre, etc.) can be 'dragged and dropped' to the List of Ideas or a Program Element (see figure 1). By allowing for this type of coordination, the Event Calendar also works against the tendency voiced during the analysis, that each editorial unit thinks of its radio program being *the* channel instead of seeking to cooperate across programs.

Finally the Event Calendar supports the editorial board in maintaining an overview for editorial purposes as it had requested. They might also decide that they want an event covered by a certain editorial unit. The system allows them to electronically notify the unit by putting an event into its List of Ideas - one way to obtain "visible management" as some employees had asked for.

In addition, since the events are linked to the List of Ideas and Program Elements (see figure 1) the editorial board may, if access is allowed, monitor the current status of features at all times until broadcasting (and even listen to pre-recordings). This provides the technical means for supporting the "forward planning process."

The Program Manager

The Program Manager, which is linked to the Event Calendar, supports individual work as well as coordination between producer, host, reporters, technicians, and administrative staff in the editorial units. Seen from the perspective of an editorial unit such as Station X, this is the central part of the design. The Program Manager is comprised of five elements:

- A *List of Ideas*. Each editorial unit has its own list where members of the editorial unit write general ideas and ideas for specific dates. Editorial units may suggest ideas to each others' lists of ideas also, and the editorial board may mark an idea as "mandatory".
- A *Pool*. This is the work space where journalists work on features for the day's program from "idea" to "ready for broadcasting". Ideas are dragged to the Pool where they are embodied in Program Elements (see below). All data about an idea is automatically inserted into specified fields in the Program Element. The Pool contains all Program Elements to be produced for the actual program.
- A *Program Element* gradually contains all data and sound for an element to be produced and broadcasted. A Program Element can be one of different types like feature, music (one title), jingle, spot, trailer, etc. Program elements are used to register both administrative, technical, and personal data (e.g. the script for the host). It holds a link to the sound file to be broadcasted if the Program Element is pre-recorded. The status of Program Elements may be inspected by the editorial board.
- The *Manuscript* is a template for the program where mandatory elements (e.g. the news every full hour, jingles, and spots advertising other programs) are present when initiated. Program elements from the Pool are linked to the Manuscript in the order decided by the producer. When the Program Element is linked to the Manuscript, the start/end times according to its current location in the Manuscript, and the (estimated or fixed) time for broadcasting the Program Element, are automatically calculated. The Manuscript gradually evolves from a plan for the program into the final version of Program Elements ready to broadcast. When the program starts the Manuscript is used directly from the studio for semiautomatic broadcasting.
- A *Report Generator*. Since all data, including a digital copy of the broadcasted program, are stored in the Manuscript, reports can be generated automatically.

The system allows an editorial unit to keep for themselves the content of a program until they choose to make it public (by using a "make public"-button), after which the editorial board and everybody else working at the channel may orient themselves into the plans of that editorial unit for the purpose of coordination.

The Program Manager saves the journalists a lot of multiple rewriting of information. It provides an editorial unit with a common overview of a program in progress. And it supports journalists in collecting - in one media - all the information relevant for themselves, the producer, the host, and the assistant. It saves the assistant a lot of time in gathering the various information needed for producing reports and for paying royalties. These are all requirements that stem from the analysis. In addition to such functional descriptions of the suggested systems, the design report holds a scenario of their use, data models, and an estimate of resources needed to develop and implement the design (see Kensing et al., forthcoming).

Discussion

We now turn to a discussion of the design, focusing on elements for supporting individual work, cooperative aspects, and the relation between technical features and organisational considerations. For this purpose, it is important to remember that the project was not about designing a single artefact, rather the design was a combination of organisational development and development of a suite of systems - some of which were purchased as standard systems while others were developed as customised systems. In the discussion we relate findings from the project to recent CSCW concepts: Computational coordination mechanisms as developed by Carstensen (1996), Schmidt and Bannon (1992), and Gerson and Star (1986); technologies of accountability as suggested by Suchman (1994); and Workflow from within and without as proposed by Bowers et al. (1995).

In an organisation such as Channel 3, constituted by a large number of cooperating ensembles of users, coordination is very complex. We have shown how it was based on various physical artefacts - and on human agents' social and professional skills. We suggested a distinction between coordination among editorial units, between editorial units and the editorial board, and within an editorial unit.

Coordination Mechanisms

The Event Calendar and the Program Manager incorporate computational coordination mechanisms. They enable a dynamic program planning process - in two dimensions, vertical and horizontal.

- Among Editorial Units

Horizontal coordination among the editorial units was raised as a concern by journalists and management during the analysis. Therefore the Event Calendar was designed as a computational coordination mechanism which provides an overview of events and bookings. An editorial unit which tries to book an event is notified by the system if that event is already booked. Either it has to give up the event or it must negotiate angles with the one that booked first. The Event Calendar is also seen by management as a way of reducing "the small kingdoms" by promoting co-operation between the editorial units.

- Between Editorial Units and the Editorial Board

Vertical coordination addresses the relation between the editorial board and editorial units. Some journalists had asked for more "visible management" and the editorial board wanted to exercise "forward planning" instead of the previous "after broad-casting monitoring". Therefore the Event Calendar was designed as a computational coordination mechanism that enables the editorial board to promote or enforce ideas by changing dynamically the contents of the Event Calendar, instead of just updat-ing the paper based version at the weekly meeting. On the other hand the Event Calendar and the Program Manager are tools by which the editorial units are able to dynamically inform the editorial board of the content of programs in progress - or the systems are "technologies of accountability" to use a term coined by Suchman (1994). However, during the analysis the design team became aware of a tension between on the one hand editorial units who want to work independently ("self steering groups" was also a management policy), while on the other hand they do acknowledge the editorial board's right to intervene. The questions were when and how editorial units need to account for their actions, and when and how it shall be possible for the editorial board to give orders/feedback on e.g. events covered, or whether or not the channel's music policy was followed. The design team raised this issue by implementing "make public-buttons" in the prototypes and by describ-ing their use in the scenario of future use of the envisioned design. The degree to which the editorial board should be allowed access to plans was still discussed when we finished our design and thus left to the experiments during implementation and use. This reflects an understanding of design similar to Suchman's (in press): ".... professional design needs to be understood not as an end point but as a start-ing place, or a platform, for the ongoing processes of "lay" design or design-in-use that are both inevitable and necessary for an effective working environment."

- Within Editorial Units

The Program Manager incorporates computational coordination mechanisms to be used within an editorial unit. It facilitates coordination in relation to planning and production of the program between the producer and the reporters, and among the reporters. And it eases the handing over of information from the journalists to the assistant as well as his production of reports. These features aim at the other sense of accountability - the ethnomethodological sense - that Suchman (1994) attributes to technologies. The reporters use the List of Ideas to store ideas for any member of the editorial unit as well as for other units to take up. The reporters store their ready made features in the Pool for the producer to link to his Manuscript. During broad-casting, the Manuscript facilitates coordination between the producer, the host, the assistant, and the technician. The coordination takes place partly via the Manuscript, partly via other coordination mechanisms (electronic communication, gestures, etc.). Thus this system addresses the predominant request for computer supported coordination raised by all editorial units during the analysis.

Coordination Mechanisms in an Organisational Perspective

- Workflow from Within and Without

Bowers et al. (1995) introduce an important distinction between workflow systems which reflect methods that are internal to the work (workflow from within) and systems which seek to order the work according to e.g. a general communication theory or a process model (workflow from without). Taking previous critiques of workflow systems (Orlikowski, 1992; Suchman, 1994; Bowers, 1995) into account, the Program Manager's workflow aspects were designed to mirror or reflect methods that the analysis showed were internal to the work. In addition we added new ways to access information for research purposes and new ways of coordination which the analysis showed were needed, but which the indigenous work practices did not support.

- Linking of Mechanisms

Gerson and Star (1986) denote coordination mechanisms as 'local and temporary closures'. Empirical studies by Carstensen (1996) suggest that coordination mechanisms might also have a more global character, functioning as a kind of workflow system that has evolved over time in a bottom up manner, that has grown out of practice, and he suggests that coordination mechanisms may also be linked - they may inter-operate. Our analysis of the work practice at Channel 3 clearly supports this. The producer's list of ideas that through many rewrites gradually evolved into a manuscript used by the team during broadcasting and by the assistant afterwards for the production of reports and for paying royalties was cumbersome and it often lead to breakdowns. Therefore the systems were designed to allow for coordination that goes beyond the previous paper based artefacts' ability to support coordination. The Event Calendar and the Program Manager each work as computational coordination mechanisms and they are linked (see figure 1). Since they are, or may be made, accessible to people outside the editorial unit, they enable new ways of coordination which the paper based coordination mechanisms did not allow for. It follows from the description above that the mechanisms are more than local and temporary closures in as much as they allow for more enduring and more extended kinds of closure, that reach beyond an editorial board, which the analysis of the previous work practice called for.

- Dealing with conflicts

The design of computational coordination mechanisms in an organisational context may entail conflicts. The editorial board wants to promote and enforce a "forward planning process" instead of "after broadcasting monitoring." On the other hand, the editorial units want to retain their autonomy - though they do acknowledge the editorial board's right to give suggestions and intervene, they still want to decide for themselves which events to cover and how.

To design computational coordination mechanisms and the linking of them are not just a matter of taking a set of technical criteria into consideration. It is also a question that resides in the realm of political discussions characterised by power, norms, and traditions for how such issues are dealt with in the organisation. What kind of computer support do we want - systems for control or for support, and support for whom? And who is the "we" who decides?

These issues have been dealt with in previous studies of CSCW-systems in use (see e.g. Bullen & Bennett, 1990; Orlikowski, 1992; Okamura et al., 1994; Ackerman, 1994; Rogers, 1994). In most cases the product development oriented CSCW contributions have not taken organisational and political issues into account. However, design in a specific organisational context of coherent systems has to be organisationally feasible. This is why organisational issues have to be an integrated part of the design and implementation. We have demonstrated how technical and organisational issues can be dealt with during a project in an organisational context. The role of a design team is neither to cover up nor to solve political conflicts. Rather it should unveil such conflicts and help the parties to formulate technical and/or organisational ways of dealing with them, and leave it to them to solve the conflicts in the proper fora. During the project, organisational aspects were an integral part of our interactions with the management and employees of Channel 3. The project team's final report addressed such issues and evaluated the consequences for the various parties. Some controversies were solved as part of the evaluation of the report at the hearing and at the final steering committee meeting. Some were left to experiments and negotiations during the implementation.

Channel 3 Conceived as Cooperating Ensembles

Finally, what do we get from conceiving a complex organisation as cooperating ensembles of users when we design computer support for an organisation? The conception of Channel 3 as cooperating ensembles of users leads us to acknowledge the differences among the 25 editorial units and between these and the management. Some units are quite small and may eventually just comprise one person. Such persons are often "lonely riders" who don't fit into a group. They are allowed to work alone producing a weekly or biweekly program. Some units have very particular domains of interest, others are more general programs.

From this follows that there are differences in terms of work domain and workplace culture, and thus also differences in the perceived need for computer support, both in general and in terms of coordination in particular. Above we have focused on Station X, one of the larger editorial units. We expect the future use of computer support for individual work to be more or less identical among the editorial units.

However, we expect the future work practice in relation to the coordination aspects of the systems to be quite diverse. This does not present a problem in relation to the design - as long as it is conceived of as consisting of a suite of systems. Individual users can choose which parts of the systems they want to use as long as a minimal set of reporting procedures, supported by the design, is followed.

The design facilitates improved managerial control of the content of programs. Though some conflicts were postponed to experiments and negotiations during development and implementation, the employees generally accepted the design because it also offered support for their individual and cooperative work.

To summarise, we have presented findings from a design project in an organisational context which involved detailed work practice studies of cooperating ensembles of users, and the participatory design of computer support for collaboration and individual work. Finally, these findings were discussed in terms of computational coordination mechanisms and related to politics at the organisational level.

Acknowledgements

We are very grateful for valuable comments by the anonymous reviewers and by Jeanette Blomberg, Susan Newman, Lucy Suchman, and Randy Trigg to a prior draft of the paper. Also we want to thank all the employees at Channel 3, the two designers, and their manager for a most valuable collaboration.

References

Ackerman, M. S. (1994): "Augmenting the Organizational Memory: A Field Study Of Answer Garden", *Proceedings of the Conference on Computer-Supported Cooperative Work,*, ACM, New York, 1994, pp. 243-252.

Blomberg, J., J. Giacomi, A. Mosher, and P. Swendon-Wall (1993): "Ethnographic field methods and their relations to design", in Schuler, D. and A. Namioka (Eds.). *Participatory Design: Perspectives on System Design*, Lawrence Erlbaum, Hillsdale, NJ, 1993, pp. 123-154.

Blomberg, J., L. Suchman, and R. Trigg (1996): "Reflections on a Work-Oriented Design Project", in *Human-Computer Interaction*, Vol. 11, 1996, pp. 237-265.

Bowers, J., G. Button, and W. Sharrock (1995): "Workflow from Within and Without", in H. Marmolin, Y. Sundblad, and K. Schmidt (Eds.), *Proceedings of the Fourth European Conference on Computer Supported Cooperative Work*, Kluwer, Dordrecht, 1995, pp. 51-66.

Bullen, C. V. and J. L. Bennett (1990): "Learning from User Experience with Groupware", *Proceedings of the Conference on Computer-Supported Cooperative Work*, ACM, New York, 1990, pp. 291-302.

Carstensen, P. (1996): *Computer Supported Coordination*, Ph.D. Thesis, Department of Computer Science, Roskilde University.

Gerson, E. M., and S. L. Star (1986): "Analyzing Due Process in the Workplace", *Transactions on Information Systems*, Vol. 4, No. 3 July 1986, pp. 257-270.

Greenbaum, J. and M. Kyng (Eds) (1991): *Design at Work: Cooperative Design of Computer Systems.* Lawrence Erlbaum Associates, Chichester, UK.

344

Grudin, J. (1991): "Interactive Systems Bridging the Gaps between Developers and Users", *IEEE Computer*, April, 1991, pp. 59-69.

Hughes, J. A., D. Randall, and D. Shapiro (1992): "Faltering from Ethnography to Design", *Proceedings of the Conference on Computer Supported Cooperative Work*, ACM, New York, 1992, pp. 115-122

Hughes, J. A., D. Randall, and D. Shapiro (1993): "From Ethnographic record to System Design: Some Experiences From the Field", in *Computer Supported Cooperative Work (CSCW): An International Journal*, Vol. 1, No. 3, Kluwer, Dordrecht, 1993, pp. 123-141

Kensing, F. and T. Winograd (1991): "Operationalizing the Language/Action Approach to Design of Computer-Support for Cooperative Work". In R. K. Stamper et al. (Eds.) *Collaborative Work, Social Communications and Information Systems*, North-Holland, 1991, pp. 311-331.

Kensing, F, J. Simonsen, and K. Bødker (1996): "MUST - A Method for Participatory Design", in Blomberg et al. (Eds.), *PDC'96: Proceedings of the Participatory Design Conference*, CPSR, Palo Alto, 1996, pp. 129-140.

Kensing, F, J. Simonsen, and K. Bødker (forthcoming): "Participatory Design at a Radio Station", submitted to *Computer Supported Cooperative Work (CSCW): An International Journal*, Kluwer, Dordrecht.

Mogensen, P and D. Shapiro: "When Survival is an Issue: PD in support of landscape architecture", in Blomberg et al. (Eds.), *PDC'96: Proceedings of the Participatory Design Conference*, CPSR, Palo Alto, 1996, pp. 55-62.

Muller, M. J., and S. Kuhn (1993) : "Participatory Design. Introduction", in *Communications of the ACM*, June 1993, Vol. 36, No. 4, pp. 24-28

Okamura, K., M. Fujimoto, W. J. Orlikowski, and J. Yates (1994): "Helping CSCW Applications Succeed: The Role of Mediators in the Context of Use", *Proceedings of the Conference on Computer-Supported Cooperative Work,*, ACM, New York, 1994, pp. 55-65.

Orlikowski, W. J. (1992): "Learning from Notes: Organizational Issues in Groupware Implementation", *Proceedings of the Conference on Computer-Supported Cooperative Work,*, ACM, New York, 1992, pp. 362-369.

Plowman, L., Y. Rogers, and M. Ramage (1995): "What Are Workplace Studies For?", in H. Marmolin, Y. Sundblad, and K. Schmidt (Eds.), *Proceedings of the Fourth European Conference on Computer Supported Cooperative Work*, Kluwer, Dordrecht, 1995, pp.309-324.

Rogers, Y. (1994): "Exploring Obstacles: Integrating CSCW in Evolving Organisations", *Proceedings of the Conference on Computer-Supported Cooperative Work,*, ACM, New York, 1994, pp. 67-77

Schmidt, K. and L. Bannon (1992): "Taking CSCW Seriously: Supporting Articulation Work", *Computer Supported Cooperative Work (CSCW): An International Journal*, Vol. 1, Nos. 1-2, Kluwer, Dordrecht, The Netherlands, 1994, pp. 7-40.

Suchman, L. (1994): "Do Categories Have Politics? The language/action perspective reconsidered", *Computer Supported Cooperative Work CSCW): An International Journal*, Vol. 2, No. 3, Kluwer, Dordrecht, The Netherlands, 1992, pp. 177-190.

Suchman L. (in press): "Centers of Coordination: A case and some themes". To appear in L. Resnick, R. Saljo, and C. Pontecorvo (eds.) *Discourse, Tools, and Reasoning*. Springer-Verlag, in press.

A Group-based Authorization Model for Cooperative Systems

Klaas Sikkel
GMD-FIT, German National Research Center for Information Technology
klaas.sikkel@gmd.de

Requirements for access control in CSCW systems have often been stated, but groupware in use today does not meet most of these requirements. There are practical reasons for this, but one of the problems is the inherent complexity of sophisticated access control models. We propose a general authorization model that emphasizes conceptual simplicity and show that several issues—in particular negative access rights and delegation of rights—can be solved elegantly in this model.

1 Introduction

Traditional access control models from the operating systems and database world do not meet the needs of groupware systems. This was stated by Greif and Sarin (1986) more than a decade ago. Since then, some work on access control has been done in the CSCW community, but limited progress has been made. A handful of access control models specifically designed for collaborative environments has been published. Some have gained acceptance at least as a theoretical contribution to the field, notably the model of Shen and Dewan (1992); none enjoy large scale usage as part of a widely used CSCW system.

The requirements for access control are known, but these seem to have had little impact in the construction of actual systems. What are the obstacles that prevent system designers from supplying groupware with adequate access control?

Firstly, as has been observed by several authors (Ellis et al., 1991; Shen and Dewan, 1992), access control models for groupware tend to be rather complex. It

345

J. Hughes et al. (eds.), Proceedings of the Fifth European Conference on Computer Supported Cooperative Work, 345-360.
© 1997 *Kluwer Academic Publishers.*

is far from trivial to design a user interface that offers the user an adequate set of access control operations and is easy to understand.

A second cause is of a more mundane nature. In prototype systems—and the large majority of systems discussed in technical CSCW literature are prototypes—access control is a feature that can always be added "later." A prototype without proper access control can be employed in first tests, whereas access control without a running prototype doesn't show very well... Hence the natural tendency *not* to make access rights a priority.

A telling example is the development of our own system, "Basic Support for Cooperative Work" (*BSCW*), offering shared workspaces on the World Wide Web (Bentley et al., 1995; Bentley et al., 1997). Thousands of users accept its shortcomings because it provides some essential features not found in other systems: simple cross-platform data sharing in distributed groups, within one's regular working environment. User feedback showed a need for more powerful and easy to use access control, yet it took more than a year after the system's public release before we started designing the access control model that is currently being implemented.

Although our work has been motivated by the immediate needs of the BSCW system, the access control model presented in this paper is of a general nature. We address several issues in groupware authorization—in particular negative rights and delegation—at a fundamental level and propose general, simple solutions.

After reviewing some important issues in Section 2 we present the authorization model in Sections 3 and 4; Section 5 briefly discusses access control in BSCW. Conclusions follow in Section 6. A more formal and more elaborate presentation of the model can be found in a technical report (Sikkel, 1997).

2   Issues in authorization and groupware

A distinction is made between *authentication* (verifying that you are who you pretend to be) and *authorization* (what it is that you are allowed to do). There is also a distinction between *access rights* (here used as a synonym of authorization) and *access control*: ensuring that the rights are not violated. We focus on authorization.

The following issues are commonly mentioned in relation with access rights for CSCW systems:

- *Application-oriented access rights.* Traditional authorization models originate from the operating systems and database worlds. The emphasis is on protection of data against unauthorized access, cf. (Salzer, 1974). An operating system defines access rights on the level of OS operations, but access rights should relate to the operations available to the user (Greif and Sarin, 1986). Synchronous groupware, in addition, may offer various levels of object sharing (Patterson at al., 1990).

- *Flexibility and ease of use.* Access rights in groupware may depend on who is doing what and therefore are highly dynamic (Trevor et al., 1994). Edwards

(1996) states that access rights should dynamically adapt to changes in the real world. Access rights modifications to be explicitly performed by the user should be easy to carry out and easy to understand.

- *Roles.* Authorization should be given to roles (e.g. teacher, assistant, student; designer, programmer, project leader; superuser), rather than to individual users. Users should be able to take multiple roles and change roles dynamically. On the other hand, users should not have to change roles explicitly when the system can infer their roles. Shen and Dewan (1992), Dewan et al. (1994), and Kanawati and Riveill (1995) argue that a user's permission should be the sum of the permissions of his roles. In a more security-oriented approach, cf. (Lampson et al., 1992; Coulouris and Dollimore, 1994b), the level of trust should be based on the intersection, not the union of the authorizations of a person's actual roles.

- *Delegation.* The system should allow delegation of rights from one person to another (who, depending on the type of delegation, may or may not further delegate it), with the possiblity to revoke delegated rights (Coulouris and Dollimore, 1994ab; Kanawati and Riveill, 1995).

- *Negative rights* are often stated as a requirement and present in several systems and models (Saltzer, 1974; Satyanarayanan, 1989; Shen and Dewan, 1992; Härtig et al., 1993). When a system allows complex hierarchical group structures, negative rights are required in situations where it is essential that some users (groups) are excluded from some rights.

And, of course, access control should be implemented efficiently, i.e., without noticeable loss of performance for frequently used operations.

Shen and Dewan (1992) state that authorization models satisfying these requirements are necessarily rather complex, but in Section 4.1 we will argue that their model is more complicated than needed. One of the issues we wanted to investigate is how complex an authorization model really needs to be. Hence Occam's Razor[1] has been used as a main design principle.

In Section 3 we present the basic model. It extends the canonical authorization model with a *single* concept: hierarchical group structures. in Section 4, we add several orthogonal extensions. These can be included in particular implementations, or—when an application does not need one of these extensions—left out, so as to reduce the complexity of the underlying model.

3   A simple authorization model

Authorization commonly involves three parameters: a *subject* (also called principal) has a *right* to perform an operation on an *object*. A classical way to organize this is

---

[1]*"Entia non sunt multiplicanda praeter necessitatem."* (Entities ought not to be multiplied except out of necessity.) – William of Ockham (1285-1349)

the *Lampson matrix* (Lampson, 1974), enumerating subjects in one dimension and objects in the other. Each cell contains all the rights given to the particular subject on the particular object. The Lampson matrix can be split into rows (columns) along either dimension, yielding *capabilities* (all rights on all objects for a given subject) or *access control lists* (*ACLs*) (all rights for all subjects on a given object). Sophisticated authorization models can be designed by adding structure to the dimensions of the authorization space.

Our model is ACL-based. For every object there is a structure describing which subjects have which rights. We use set theory for building these structures but talk about *groups*, rather than sets.

Leaving out all semantics, a group is a set, an unordered collection of entities, comprised in a single structure so that you can refer to it with a single name. Groups are used for different purposes.

Firstly, users may be organized in some group structure according to their position in an organizational hierarchy A project is composed of teams, a team of subteams, etc. In the literature groups are often called *roles*. In Section 4.3 we will differentiate between roles and groups, for the moment we consider them equivalent: for each role there is a group of persons that may act in this role, or reversed, for each group there is some role that all members of the group may act in.

A second type of group could be called *access group*. Suppose you are collaboratively working on a paper. You may distinguish between "writers", "annotators" (proof-readers giving comments) and "readers" of this paper. Each of these groups may perform an appropriate set of operations on the paper. The allowed operations as well as the composition of the groups may change over time.

3.1 User groups

In order to define user groups, we assume the existence of a domain of **users**, e.g., *tom, dick, harry*, etc., or more abstractly, $u, v, \ldots$. **User groups** are recursively defined as follows:

- A (single) user is a user group.
- A set of user groups is a user group.

Empty user groups are allowed in principle. A user group may not, directly, or indirectly, be contained in itself.

For convenience we have defined single users to be user groups as well. In the remainder of the paper we can refer to "a user group" meaning "an individual user or a group of users." In the rare cases where we need to refer to a composite group, not an individual user, we call this a **proper user group**.

User groups form hierarchical structures. If user group g is contained in user group h (i.e. $g \in h$), h is called a *subgroup* of g (and g a *supergroup* of h). The subgroup relation defines a directed acyclic graph with users as leaves and proper user groups as non-leaf vertices. An example is shown in Figure 1. Subgraphs can be shared: a user group can be a subgroup of different supergroups.

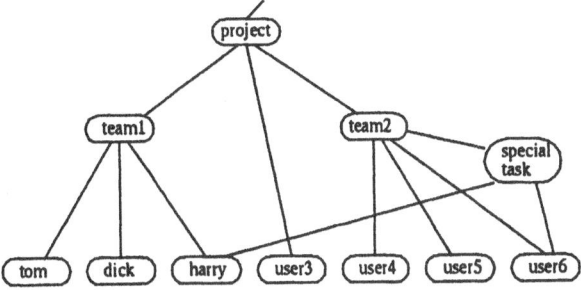

Figure 1: A hierarchical group structure

Members of a user group are those users who are, directly or indirectly, contained in the group (i.e., descendant leaves in the graph). Note the difference between subgroups and members. For example, in Figure 1, we have

team2.subgroups = {*user4, user5, user6, special_task*},
team2.members = {*user4, user5, user6, harry*}.

It is possible to perform operation on groups. We describe only those operations that change the state of the system (as opposed to functions, like, e.g., *members*, that merely retrieve values). [*In brackets the operations are defined in terms of graph operations.*]

- **NewGroup** creates a new (empty) user group [*creates a new node*].
- **AddSubgroups** adds a set of user groups as subgroups to a given group [*adds edges*]. AddSubgroups fails if a group would (indirectly) be included in itself [*a cycle would be created*].
- **DeleteSubgroups** deletes subgroups from a user group [*removes edges*].
- **RemoveGroup** removes a user group from the system [*removes a node with its incident edges*]. This may cause its supergroups to lose some members.
- **DissolveGroup** removes a user group from the system without affecting the membership of other groups: subgroups of the dissolved group are added as subgroups to its supergroups [*removes a node; incident edges are replaced, linking each predecessor directly to each successor*]. This is illustrated in Figure 2; (a) shows part of a group structure; user group *g* has been removed in (b) and dissolved in (c).
- **RenameGroup** changes the name of a user group [*changes the label of a node*].

Additional composite operations, like splitting, merging, or inserting (the reverse of dissolving) user groups can be added as required. Note that RemoveGroup is not a primitive operation. It can be composed from DeleteSubgroups and DissolveGroup,

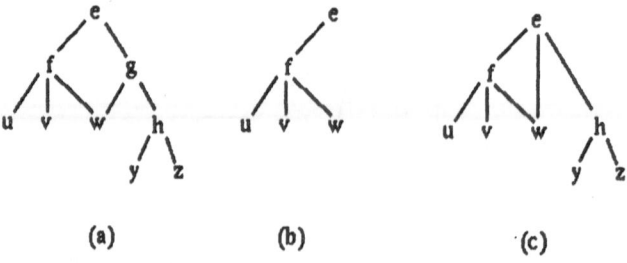

Figure 2: RemoveGroup (b) vs. DissolveGroup (c)

hence it could be discarded. It has been included, however, in order to point out the difference between removing and dissolving.

3.2 Objects and user groups

Access rights are to be defined for (classes of) objects, typically stored in a database of some kind. In general, such a database may hold different kinds of information. Disregarding *metadata*, used for the system's organization and not accessible to the user, we distinguish two categories of objects:

- Ordinary objects: documents, containers, programs, etc. Here we call them *regular objects*. These are the objects for which access rights have to be defined.

- In addition, the system may contain objects that cannot be accessed independently and appear to be attributes of other objects. We call these *attributed objects*.

  An example of an attributed object in the BSCW system is the "description" that an object (say, a document) may have: typically a line of text describing its nature, contents, or purpose. The description is regarded as an attribute of the document. Access to the description (see it, edit it) is governed by access rights defined *for the document*. Also, its existence depends on the existence of the document: if the document is deleted from the system, the description ceases to exist.

To which of both categories do user groups belong?

In the database world it is common to separate regular data and access rights, so that accessing data and changing access rights are regulated by different administrative procedures (Sandhu et al., 1996). In an object-oriented approach it seems rather more natural to see user groups as regular objects. There is an argument of elegance and simplicity: Groups themselves have to be accessed and manipulated, hence there is no reason why rights on user groups should be organized differently from rights on other objects.

We will use groups of either category. The issue of independent existence applies to groups in the same way it applies to other objects.

- A regular user group (*Rgroup*), is a regular object.
  Examples of Rgroups (cf. Figure 1) are *project* = {*team1*, *team2*} and *tom*.

- An attributed user group (*Agroup*) is an attribute of a regular object.
  As a consequence, accessing the Agroup is only possible through (and controlled by) the object to which it is attributed. Moreover, when that object is removed from the system, the Agroup ceases to exist.
  An example of the use of Agroups are the "writers," "annotators," and "readers" groups for a particular document.
  As a practical notation, we write, e.g., *obj.writers*, *obj.readers* for Agroups of an object *obj*.

Individual users are Rgroups, proper user groups can be of either type. Rgroups can be subgroups of Agroups and vice versa. For example in *obj1.readers* = {*obj2.writers*, *team1*} an Agroup is composed of an Agroup and an Rgroup. The group properties defined in Section 3.1 (having members, subgroups, etc.) are not related to the distinction between Rgroups and Agroups.

3.3 Rights

For each regular object we assume a set of rights $r_1 \ldots r_k$ where the number of rights k depends on the (class of the) object (k need not be fixed; it is conceivable that new rights for new operation are added to an object during its lifetime). The semantics of these rights, i.e., which operations they allow, are of no concern here.

For each right, an Agroup is defined. We write $obj.r_i$ to denote the Agroup that has right r_i on object *obj*. The individual users that have these rights are given by $obj.r_i.members$ as defined in Section 3.1.

Agroups have no access rights for themselves. Accessing an Agroup amounts to accessing an attribute of some object, which is controlled by one of the rights on that object. This avoids a recursion of rights on rights, rights on rights on rights, etc. *Modification* of access rights is discussed in Section 3.5.

In Figure 3(a), part of the ACL of some imaginary object is displayed. It is a directed acyclic graph with the rights to the object (the graph's sources) at the top and the users (the graph's sinks) displayed left. Auxiliary nodes a, b, and c have been introduced to improve the structure of the graph. The Agroups corresponding to rights $r_1, \ldots, r_4$ have a common subgroup a which has a single subgroup *special task*. The same distribution of rights to users could have been obtained by adding *special task* directly as a subgroup to each of these four rights.

Figure 3(b) shows a conventional matrix-shaped ACL with a rights distribution that has the same effect. The essence of our model is that we have replaced this matrix by a graph.

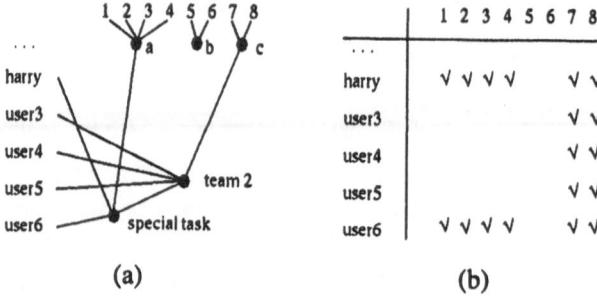

Figure 3: ACL in our model (a) and as a matrix (b)

3.4   Views

The groups *a*, *b*, and *c* in Figure 3 exemplify the notion of a *view* on an object: a subset of the rights defined for that object. Views can be used to organize large sets of access rights into managable proportions. An example: In the BSCW system, an object of type *folder* has 12 different rights: $5\times$ *add* (for different types of objects), *delete* (from the folder), *cut* (i.e. relocate) the folder, *edit description*, *edit banner*, *get* (folder contents), get *info* about the folder, and *rename*. In order to simplify things in the user interface, we could partition these rights into 4 views:

- *read* (get, info),
- *add* (add any kind of object),
- *edit* (edit description, edit banner, rename), and
- *dispose* (delete, cut).

Views may overlap. We could, for example, add a view *annotate* (get, info, and *add article*, i.e., create a note to which others can reply).

The possibility to organize rights into views is a *consequence* of the model, not part of its definition. In the structure of Figure 3 we have simply created an Agroup *obj.a* and defined $obj.r_i = \{obj.a\}$ for $i = 1, 2, 3, 4$.

In a practical system we can employ views and their subgroups to show (and have the user interact with) access rights. Listing these against each other, we obtain a conventional —but much smaller—access rights matrix, see Figure 4. Of course the user should have additional means of finding out who are the members (subgroups) of a group and which are the rights gathered in a single view.

	a	*b*	*c*
team 2	√		√
special task			√

Figure 4: Simplified presentation of the access rights in Figure 3

3.5   Control

For purposes of system maintainance there must be some notion of *responsibility* for objects. E.g. if obsolete objects have to be deleted to free disk space, somebody should be told to do so. Also, it should not be possible that a user creates a "zombie" object that does not allow further access to any user, including its creator.

These problems have be dealt with by introducing some conventions into the model. There are various ways of doing this; the following is simple and general.

- *Responsible.* Every object *obj* is associated with a particular user who is responsible for it. We write *obj.responsible* to denote this user.

- *Control right.* Every object *obj* has an access right r_c, that allows any access on any of the access right groups $obj.r_1, \ldots, obj.r_k, obj.r_c$.

- *Control group.* The control right of an object *obj* is granted to members of the control group $obj.r_c$. In addition, the control right is also granted to *obj.responsible*, irrespective of his membership of $obj.r_c$.

If a group were to be responsible, the question remains which group member is accountable when something is wrong. To avoid that, we have laid responsibility with an individual. Some policy has to be laid down to transfer responsibility for objects when users are removed from the system.

4   Extensions to the basic model

We define negative rights (4.1), conditional authorization (4.2), and explicit role switching (4.3) as extensions to the basic model. Delegation (4.4) is supported by the model without further extensions.

4.1   Negative rights

A straightforward model of negative rights is used in the Andrew system (Satyanarayanan, 1989). Rights exist both in positive and negative form. When both apply, the negative right overrides the positive right. In this way, negative rights can be used to immediately revoke a permission in a distributed system where propagation of changes may take a while.

Shen and Dewan (1992) do not have an a priori bias for negative rights, but let other factors decide which, in case of conflict, is the more important. In principle this is a good idea, but it has dramatic consequences for the complexity of their model: several conflict resolution rules have to be introduced *solely* to solve ambiguities caused by positive and negative rights applying simultaneously.

We can keep the flexibility of Shen and Dewan's model but avoid its complexity, by introducing negation at another level. Rather than negative rights, we introduce negative group membership. *Excluding* somebody from a user group, as opposed to deleting him as a member, has a different modality, stating that "this person cannot be member of the group." If another person tries to make him a member (e.g. by adding him to a subgroup), this is overruled by the exclusion.

As an example, consider again the group structure in Figure 1. Tom and Dick are organizing a surprise party for Harry. Team 2 will be involved at some stage, and perhaps some other people, but it is essential that Harry is not a member of the group of persons who know about the party. In Figure 5 a new user group has been created from which Harry is excluded (dotted line marked "X"). Whether Tom and Dick have realized that Harry is indirectly a member of team 2 is not relevant—even if he were not, currently, somebody could add him to (a subgroup of) team 2 any time. Hence specific exclusion, rather than non-inclusion, is needed.

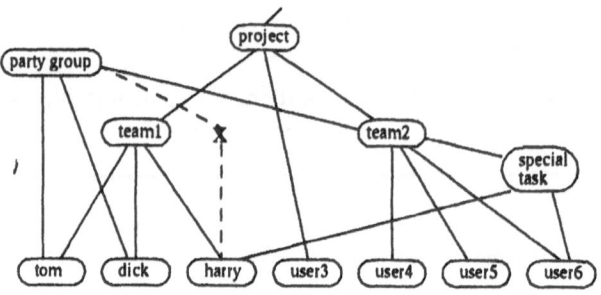

Figure 5: Exclusion from group membership

The model is therefore extended as follows. Each proper user group g has attributes $g.subgroups$ and $g.excluded$; both are (possibly empty) sets of user groups. Members of a group are defined as the members of its subgroups, with the exception of those users that are also members of an excluded user group. In order to be precise, we define the following function *members* on user groups (for compatibility with the rest of the paper we do not use the conventional functional notation $members(g)$ but the object-oriented notation $g.members$):

$$u.members \stackrel{\text{def}}{=} u \quad \text{for users } u, \text{ and}$$

$$g.members \stackrel{\text{def}}{=} \bigcup_{h \in g.subgroups} h.members \setminus \bigcup_{h \in g.excluded} h.members$$

for proper user groups g.

Exclusions can be nested, an example will be given in Section 4.4.3.

As in Section 3 it is required that the group graph is acyclic. We have a labelled graph now, each edge carries a label "subgroup" or "excluded". The type of label is not relevant for the acyclicity constraint. Acyclicity of the graph guarantees that the recursion in the definition of *members* is finite.

We need two more operations to change the state of the system (in addition to those of 3.1): **AddExcluded** and **DeleteExcluded**, with the obvious semantics.

4.2   Conditions

So far we have assumed that the rights to access an object are stored with the object and do not depend in any way on the state of the system—or the state of the real world outside the system. "Context" can be handled by introducing *conditional access rights*.

Again we will adopt a more general solution and attach conditions to groups, rather than access rights. Every user group (Rgroup or Agroup) can be supplied with an attribute *condition*, a boolean function to be evaluated at the moment of access. If the condition evaluates to *false* the system behaves as if the group does not exist.

Some examples of conditions:

- *Only from a workstation within the building*, not over a telephone line or remote login.

- *Only in case of emergency*. E.g.: protected patient data in a hospital can be retrieved by any staff if there is an emergency. (Note that some protocol is required to decide what is an emergency. For example, the user may *declare* an emergency by answering the question "Is this an emergency?" with "yes"; emergency accesses are logged and the user is held accountable for such accesses.)

- *Only until March 31st* (for a temporary user group).

- *"Dynamic roles"*: Edwards (1996) proposes a similar scheme to dynamically include persons in a group by run-time evaluation of a function. In our model, one could grant access to "everybody" and then use a condition to prevent everybody from getting in all the time.

A design choice in our model, motivated by security considerations, is that conditions can only be used to *deny* access that, in different circumstances, would have been granted. The evaluation of a condition might call arbitrary code outside the realm of access control (as in Edwards' model). In order not to open the system to abitrary access, conditions should only allow access within clear limits defined in the access control component.

Indirect membership via a chain of subgroups may lead to a conjunction of conditions; membership via multiple chains of subgroups to a disjunction of conjunctions. When conditions have no side effects this is unproblematic. But if, for example, evaluation of a condition may require interaction with the user, a policy has to be specified that defines the order of evaluation.

4.3   Roles

Roles are modelled as user groups. A user can act in a number of different roles. Most of these are trivial (e.g., *harry* may act as a member of *team1* and as a member of *team2*) and the system should keep track of this. This is what we have modelled in Section 3. There are, however, less trivial roles that should require a conscious act on behalf of the user in order to take on that role. A typical example is the role of system administrator. The person administering the system has, in principle, superuser capabilities. But in his regular work these should not be effective, so as to prevent accidents by unintended use. If the user wants to take on such a role, some action on behalf of the user is required.

In our model, a role is a user group that requires additional authentication. This could be anything from checking a box "I want to have role R" to authenticating yourself with a personal chip card. The important thing is that a role does not become effective without the user knowing that he is taking on the role. Roles (as any other groups) can be subject to conditions. For example, in order to take on the role *superuser*, it might be required that the user is working from (and not remotely logged in on) a workstation within the building.

Which roles should be tracked automatically and which roles should require explicit adoption of a role? An indication is the awareness information that one would like the system to generate for other users. If, for example *tom* has edited a document that belongs to the user group *project*, at some place you want to see a line

```
<doc> modified by tom
```

and you don't want to be bothered with the trivial information that *tom* is a member of *project* via *team1*. If, on the other hand, an obsolete object is removed by the system administrator, it is more appropriate to get a line such as

```
<obj> removed by tom as sysadm
```

stating which role licenced the operation (and who was acting in that role).

4.4   Delegation

Several delegation models have been proposed in the literature. We show how these are supported by the authorization model presented above.

The user should not have to perform the complicated group operations "manually," and it is obvious that additional delegation functionality in the user interface is required when delegation of rights is to be included in an application. The purpose of this section, however, is to make clear that the authorization model needs no further extensions to support delegation.

For the sake of simplicity we assume that the responsible is the only person with control right and call him, more conventionally, the *owner*. (Joint ownership does not affect any of the following.) As a convenient shorthand we write g_u to express that user u is the owner of a user group g.

4.4.1   Single-step delegation

A user u has been told to do something with an object. To that end, the owner of *obj* has constructed a view

$$obj.view = \{\{u\}_u, \ldots\}.$$

The view has a subgroup that contains u and is owned by u. However, u wants to delegate the job to v.

In the simplest case, the delegate can perform the task, but may not further delegate it to somebody else. To this end u extends $\{u\}_u$ to $\{u, v\}_u$, yielding

$$obj.view = \{\{u, v\}_u, \ldots\}.$$

This gives user v access to the view, but he cannot change the user group to which the view is granted. Moreover, u can revoke the delegation by deleting v again.

4.4.2 Recursive delegation

In other scenarios a delegate may further delegate a right. For example in the work flow in a German ministry (Mambrey and Robinson, 1995): an object moves down several layers of hierarchy, is processed by somebody, and then moves up the hierarchy in reverse direction. Starting from the same situation as above, user u now adds a user group that contains v and is owned by v:

$$obj.view = \{\{u, \{v\}_v\}_u, \ldots\}.$$

Hence v can delegate the view to w in similar fashion. Any person in such a chain of delegations may revoke the delegations he made, including further delegations made by his delegates.

4.4.3 Delegation within a trusted group

Coulouris and Dollimore (1994a) present a case study of examination preparation at a university college. A task (viz., typing of the exams) can only be delegated within a predefined group of trusted persons. In order to model this, we assume negative rights (see 4.1). We write

$$g = \{\ldots, \neg x\}$$

to denote that x is excluded from user group g. Further, we denote "everybody in the system" by a special constant E.

Let t be the group of trusted persons. Then we define "nontrusted persons" as "everybody in E who is not in t", denoted

$$n = \{E, \neg t\}.$$

Having an expression for nontrusted persons, we can now define groups from which *"nontrusted persons are excluded."* Thus the owner of object obj creates a view

$$obj.view = \{\{u\}_u, \neg n\} = \{\{u\}_u, \neg\{E, \neg t\}\}$$

(assuming u is member of t). User u may delegate his right in one of the ways explained above. Delegation (whether single-step or recursive) to a person who is not a member of t is overruled by the exclusion of nontrusted persons; see (Sikkel, 1997) for a more detailed treatment.

5 Realization in BSCW

An implementation of the presented authorization model in the BSCW system ("Basic Support for Cooperative Work") is currently under development. A public release of a BSCW version offering full access control is due Autumn 1997. BSCW (Bentley et al, 1995; Bentley et al, 1997) is based on the notion of a "shared workspace." A workspace is a repository for shared information, accessible (only) to group members. Workspaces may contain different types of objects (documents, folders, threaded discussions, etc.). It offers some awareness facilities: one can see what other members in the workspace have been doing; soft locking can be used to prevent simultaneous editing by different users. Support for synchronous cooperation is being integrated (Trevor and Koch, 1997).

The BSCW server is realized as an auxiliary component to a WWW server. All interaction takes place via the Common Gateway Interface (CGI) hence the BSCW server is not dependent on any particular WWW server. BSCW runs on must UNIX variants and on Windows NT. A public server is available free of charge at GMD.[2] The user interacts with a shared workspace using an ordinary WWW Browser. One of the advantages of the system—and probably one of the reasons for its success—is that a BSCW user can join a working group without any prior installation of software.

Authentication in BSCW employs the Web's "basic authentication" scheme, the only Web-wide standard. Users authenticate with user name and password.

A prime consideration in the implementation of access control is efficiency. In the context of BSCW, the following queries to the access control component have to be efficient:

(1) Has user u right r_i on object obj?

(2) Which rights does user u have on object obj?

(3) Which users have right r_i on object obj?

In order to address all of these, the computation of $obj.r_i.members$ has to take minimal effort. To that end, a list of group members is stored with the user group. It probably suffices to maintain membership lists for Rgroups, because that is where most of the nesting is to be expected. When the composition of a user group is changed, the membership lists of its supergroups are to be adapted accordingly.

Our main concern for the near future is in designing and testing a user interface that our users find easy to work with.

6 Discussion and conclusions

In this paper we have investigated the foundations of access control in groupware. We have drawn up an authorization model that addresses many of the issues in

---

[2]http://bscw.gmd.de

access control.

The treatment of negative rights is as general as in (Shen and Dewan, 1992). It is simpler, however, because no conflict resolution rules are needed. Further, we have shown how various models of delegation, drawn from case studies in cooperative work, are supported by the general authorization model.

Not addressed in this paper is the variety of different rights needed in the context of groupware systems (see (Dewan et al., 1994) for an elaboration in the context of joint editing) and, more prominently, a user interface that supports the appropriate functionality and conveys a suitable mental model. An implementation of access control in the BSCW system based on this authorization model is, at the time of writing, still under construction.

Given the inherent complexity of the matter, we have stated simplicity as an important goal. The presented model is *minimal*: each concept that has been introduced is evidently needed to satisfy legitimate practical requirements. In addition, the model is *modular*: extensions not needed in a particular application can be discarded, yielding a simpler model.

Acknowledgements

I am grateful to Uwe Busbach, Wolfgang Appelt, Jonathan Trevor, David Kerr, Gerd Woetzel, Richard Bentley and two anonymous referees for discussions and feedback on previous drafts.
This work was partially supported by the Ministry of Science and Research of North Rhine-Westphalia.

References

Bentley, R., Appelt W., Busbach U., Hinrichts E., Kerr, D., Sikkel, K., Trevor, J. and Woetzel, G. (1997): "Basic Support for Cooperative Work on the World Wide Web." *International Journal of Human-Computer Interaction*, special issue on novel applications of the World Wide Web, 1997 (in press).

Bentley, R., Horstmann, T., Sikkel, K., and Trevor, J. (1995): "Supporting collaborative information sharing with the World Wide Web: The BSCW Shared Workspace system." *4th International WWW Conference*, Boston, December 1995, pp. 63–74.

Coulouris, G. and Dollimore, J. (1994a): "Requirements for security in cooperative work: two case studies." Technical Report 671, Dept. of Computer Science, Queen Mary and Westfield College, University of London.

Coulouris, G. and Dollimore, J. (1994b): "A security model for cooperative work." Technical Report 674, Dept. of Computer Science, Queen Mary and Westfield College, University of London.

Dewan, P., Choudhary, R. and Shen, H. (1994): "An Editing-Based Characterization of the Design Space of Collaborative Applications." *Journal of Organizational Computing*,

Vol. 4, pp. 219–239.

Edwards, W.K. (1996): "Policies and Roles in Collaborative Applications." *ACM Conference on Computer-Supported Cooperative Work (CSCW'96)*, Cambridge, Mass., pp. 11–20.

Ellis, C.A., Gibbs, S.J. and Rein, G.L. (1991): Groupware: Some Issues and Experiences. *Communications of the ACM*, Vol. 34, No. 1, January 1991, pp. 38–58.

Greif, I. and Sarin, S. (1986): Data Sharing in Group Work. *ACM Conference on Computer-Supported Cooperative Work*, Austin, Texas, 1986.
An extended version appeared in *ACM Transactions on Office Information Systems*, Vol. 5 (1987), pp. 187–211.

Härtig, H., Kowalski, O., Kühnhauser, W. (1993): "The BirliX Security Architecture." *Journal of Computer Security*, Vol. 2, pp. 5–21.

Kanawati, R. and Riveill M. (1995): "Access Control Model for Groupware Applications." In Allen, G., Wilkinson, J., and Wright, P. (Eds), HCI'95: People and Computers. School of Computing and Mathematics, University of Huddersfield, UK, pp. 66–71.

Lampson, B.W. (1974): Protection. *ACM Operating Systems Review*, Vol. 8, pp. 18–24.

Lampson, B., Abadi, M., Burrows, M. and Wobber E. (1992): "Authentication in Distributed Systems: Theory and Practice." *ACM Transactions on Computer Systems*, Vol. 10, No. 4.

Mambrey, P. and Robinson, M (1995): "Preparing a speech for the minister: Notes towards understanding the role of artefacts in a flow of work." Unpublished manuscript, GMD-FIT, Sankt Augustin, Germany.

Paterson, J.F., Hill, R.D., Rohall, S.L. and Meeks, W.S. (1990): "Rendezvous: An Architecture for Synchronous Multi-User Applications." *ACM Conference on Computer-Supported Cooperative Work (CSCW'90)*, pp. 317–328.

Sandhu, R.S., Coyne, E.J., Feinstein, H.L. and Yourman, C.E. (1996): "Role-Based Access Control Models." *IEEE Computer*, February 1996, pp. 38–47.

Salzer, J.H. (1974): "Protection and Control of Information Sharing in Multics." *Communications of the ACM*, Vol. 17, pp. 388–402.

Satyanarayanan, M. (1989): "Intergrating Security in a Large Distributed System." *ACM Transactions on Computer Systems*, Vol. 7, pp. 247–280.

Sikkel, K. (1997): "A Group-based Authorization Model for Computer-Supported Cooperative Work." Arbeitspapiere der GMD 1055, GMD, Sankt Augustin, Germany.

Shen, H. and Dewan P. (1992): "Access Control for Collaborative Environments." *ACM Conference on Computer-Supported Cooperative Work (CSCW'92)*, Toronto, Canada, pp. 51–58.

Trevor, J., Koch, T. and Woetzel, G. (1997): "MetaWeb: Bridging the Gap between Synchronous Groupware and the WWW." *European Conference on Computer-Supported Cooperative Work (ECSCW'97)*, Lancaster, UK (these proceedings).

Trevor, J., Rodden, T., and Mariani, J. (1994): "The Use of Adapters to Support Cooperative Sharing." *ACM Conference on Computer-Supported Cooperative Work (CSCW'94)*, Chapel Hill, North Carolina, pp. 219–230.

Gatherers of Information: The Mission Process at the International Monetary Fund

Richard H. R. Harper
RXRC, 61 Regent Street
Cambridge, CB2 1AB U.K.
harper@europarc.xerox.com

Abstract: The paper reports findings from an ethnographic study of work practice at the International Monetary Fund, in Washington, DC. In particular, it describes the mission process, drawing attention to important aspects of social organisation in that process. These aspects, relating to social validation, ritual, and the moral (as against the arithmetical) transformation of numbers, are crucial to understanding the nature of missions and what role new technologies might play in them.

Introduction

This paper reports on a study of work practice at the International Monetary Fund, in Washington, DC. The goal of the study is to examine the organisational circumstances in which new groupware and CSCW tools might be introduced and to consider the potential changes that might be brought about by their introduction. The International Monetary Fund (or "the Fund" as it is more familiarly known) is a particularly interesting place for study for a number of reasons, not least of which is its high profile. But in addition, many aspects of its work practices seem highly amenable to collaborative technology, whether it be new document forms including hypertext and active documents (Harper, 1997), inforrmation accessing technologies like LOTUS NOTES (Harper, 1995), distributed information-sharing (Harper & Sellen, 1995), workflow technologies (Sellen & Harper, 1996), media space technologies (Kent & Harper, 1985) or portable document readers (Sellen & Harper, 1997).

The particular concern of this paper is the Fund's mission process and the issues that need to be considered in determining how new technologies may support that process. In brief, a mission involves a team from the Fund visiting a member

J. Hughes et al. (eds.), Proceedings of the Fifth European Conference on Computer Supported Cooperative Work, 361-376.
© *1997 Kluwer Academic Publishers.*

country and, over a period of about two weeks, preparing an analysis of that country's macroeconomic situation. This analysis, which may include recommendations for policy changes by the member authorities or for a loan by the Fund, is then presented to the Fund's Executive Board in a staff report.

On the face of it, mission activity would appear to be the kind work that new collaborative technologies might radically alter. With digital telecommunications, for example, multimedia meetings between Fund staff and government authorities could be undertaken on a dial-up on demand basis; with various new open information management systems, information and documents associated with meetings could be accessed from Washington. Consequently it might appear reasonable to suggest that new technology will eventually do away with the need for missions, at least that part of missions that involves travelling. But what I will show in this paper is that missions are much more complicated than they might first appear. It is not simply that missions involve ritualising events—which can be arcane and resistant to change at the best of times—it is also the case that mission work involves dealing with what participants themselves call "the facts of life". These facts of life beg questions about the character of the information gathered and discussed on a mission. My task in this paper is to elaborate just what some of these facts of life are, as well as some of the ritual and ceremonial aspects of missions. At the end of the paper, I will then discuss the relevance of these findings for the introduction of CSCW technologies into the mission process.

More specifically, I will describe how the elemental mechanics consist of an iterative process whereby a mixture of arithmetical, econometric, and meeting skills are used to create data that are reconciled and measured against the data collected by others within the mission team. Running through these basic mechanics are a number of key facts. For example, the broad set of skills and techniques used on missions enable the economists to produce a staff report *come what may*, i.e. irrespective of the incompleteness of the data they have access to and disregarding (more or less) any contingencies they have to deal with. But the task is not simply to collect *correct* data. Rather, a mission team has to create an analytic perspective which determines what is relevant and what is not. This is a laborious process. But it also is a *social process*. To begin with, the perspective is jointly developed between the mission team and the member authorities. In addition, though data may be found in a variety of different places (namely, different offices within the various institutions of the member government agencies), only certain persons within those offices have the rank to sanction data as relevant for the perspective in hand. These people provide the stamp of approval. A mission must seek these out. This process is, in some part, *ritual*.

This is not the only ritual element of missions. Another has to do with the process of agreeing a basis for policy concerns in discussions between the mission and the authorities that typically occurs at the end of missions. Here the mission chief will make fairly ritualised orations to the local authorities; these commence and sometimes terminate the discussion of policy. I will not be suggesting that these orations are merely ritual or symbolic showpieces, or that they have no analytic value. Rather, I will want to show that it is partly through their ritualising effects —and the partly ritualising responses they can generate—that the symbolic importance of the events are demonstrated. My thesis will be that without ritual, the essential characteristics of the events—in this case policy discussions—would be changed. This character ensures that the outcome of these meetings is treated as consequential; or, put another way, ensures that these are meetings that *count*.

Of course in this setting, the word "count" has at least two relevant meanings. The first meaning implies the significance of the meetings, and the second points towards the fact that these events are in crucial respects about counting numbers. My view is that such countings are not simply arithmetical (although they do involve a large amount of that), but are also the final stage of a social process that transforms *speechless* numbers into ones that have a *voice*. This voice is communicating something very specific: it enables the team to make warranted determinations of what the future will be. For, in the final analysis, the purpose of missions is (crudely speaking) to enable a mission team to divine the future in the shadows of the present. But such activities are not a kind of magic—something that is made-up on the basis of witchcraft or sorcery. Rather, this predicting of the future is undertaken on the basis of materials that can be demonstrated to be "reasonable", "warranted", "accurate" and "objective". This is not to say that a mission does in fact always predict the future precisely. It is to say that they get themselves in a position where making predictions is a reasonable thing to do. In this sense, the team's predictions consist of a kind of science. This science is a practical, "real world", hands-on skill. This is what the Fund's mission work is all about.

The International Monetary Fund

The Fund, based in Washington D.C., is a financial 'club' whose members consist of most of the countries of the world. Member countries contribute to a pool of resources which can then be used to provide low interest, multi-currency loans should a member find itself facing balance of payments problems.

The Fund has some 3,000 staff, of which 900 are professional economists. These economists analyse economic policies and developments—especially in the macroeconomic arena. They have particular interest in the circumstances surrounding the emergence of financial imbalances (including those that lead to a balance of payments crisis), the policies to overcome such imbalances, and the corrective policy criteria for making loans. This involves going on missions to the country in question.

The Fund is divided into a number of departments. The most important for my concern are the "area" departments which are responsible for particular member countries divided up into contiguous geographic blocks (Western Hemisphere, Middle Eastern, etc.). The area departments are divided into divisions, each with responsibility for certain countries. The divisions are populated by desk officers and chiefs. Desk officers are economists who develop and maintain expertise on any particular country. A chief will manage several countries and desk officers, and hence will be responsible for the information the Fund has about any particular set of member countries.

Method

The research consisted of six months ethnographic field work carried out by the author. This field work centred around the 'document career' of staff reports, from the first draft of the 'briefing paper' prepared before a mission commences, to observation of the mission process itself, to observation of the post-mission review cycle, and then to translation, printing, and circulation processes. (For further elaboration see Harper, 1997).

A Case Study of a Fund Mission

Limits of space force me to confine my exposition of a Fund mission by focusing on only some key parts or events of the mission I observed. First, I present a vignette of the team's first meeting. This will provide me with the opportunity to begin explaining how mission work is in large part a social process. It will also provide me with an opportunity to explain how members of the mission team assumed that the materials they gathered as part of this process have what one might call "understandable" problems: numbers get added up incorrectly, miscategorisation occurs, and spreadsheet tables get lost. These are part of the facts of life in mission work and these are the things that the team must deal with come what may. I will then characterise in general terms the data gathering activities undertaken on mission before providing a second vignette, this time of one of the meetings undertaken by two members of the mission with a key official in the authorities. Here I will point towards how a mission needs to get a perspective that can enable it to distinguish between usable and unusable numbers. Some numbers are good for certain tasks, but not for others. I shall provide some examples for illustration. I will then discuss how the chosen numbers have to be socially validated. This senior official could only sanction some and not all numbers. Finally, in a third vignette, I will describe one of the policy meetings that occurred at the end of the mission. Here I will want to draw attention to the ritualising effects of these meetings (desired but not always achieved), important not only in giving those meetings the status they have but in transforming the numbers that are presented in those meetings into ones that count.

Before I start my exposition, two remarks need to be made. First, the mission team consisted of a chief and his deputy, the desk officer responsible for the country in question, a fiscal economist, and a rookie economist called an "EP". Second, for the sake of confidentiality, I shall call the country in question "Arcadia".

Day One: A Vignette

The first meeting occurred an hour or so after the team had settled themselves in to their hotel in the Arcadian capital. The desk officer commenced the meeting by explaining that when he had arrived at the airport an official had given him two copies of the Arcadian budget and four sets of the national accounts. But he explained that although the national accounts had the same bottom line, they were made up of different numbers. He then said:

> "But I have sorted them out. I assume that (the Arcadians) must have included some early drafts. It is not a problem. It is the bottom line that matters at this point. Besides, I can see from the way they have been working which is the most recent so I will use that. I can clarify things with officials later on. Still, here are some materials that each of you can use to help build up your tables".

At which point he started sorting out the tables and giving them to the rest of the team, explaining as he did so: "These won't be completely right but you can use them to set up the spreadsheets. You can start entering them straight away. Here, use these numbers and these". The deputy then took over the meeting: "Okay let's not worry about that at the moment. Let's try and plan out what we have to do".

She then outlined what meetings had been arranged, and a list was handed out. She pointed out who amongst the team would be meeting which official and when. She turned to ask each economist:

> "Do you know what you can get out of this person? What information will you still need after this meeting? Do you know who you will need to meet afterwards? Can I have those meetings arranged for you now?"

She took particular pains to explain what the EP would be doing, listing the officials he would be seeing and explaining why he would see them:

> "The first person you meet tomorrow at the central bank will give you the latest figures on the monetary sector (the EP's concern) but you should get a lot from her because she knows more or less everyone you will need to deal with. She will give you a lot of advice on what you need to find out. She is easy to get on with so don't worry, you will be all right".

Comment

In many ways, this first meeting in Arcadia was fairly inconsequential. But there are two telling aspects of the meeting on which I want to reflect: first, the attitude of the desk officer to the materials he was given at the airport, and second, the deputy's concern with whom the mission members would be meeting.

As regards the documents given the desk officer and their apparent oddness, essentially what he found was that four sets of national accounts did not consist of the same individual numbers. I think it is extremely important to grasp his perspective on this. For example, a conspiratorial desk officer might have contended that the oddity was a reflection of deliberate obfuscation on the part of Arcadian officials. But this desk officer did not think this. Rather, his assumption was that the problem in the documents had to do with the nature of the informational material that is used in the Fund's work. To paraphrase, his view was that this material had to be worked up, crafted, and polished. Further, in this process mistakes can be made, sometimes simple and sometimes more complex. In this case, the oddness was actually the result of a clerical error: some early drafts of the tables had been picked up. In other words, he did not view the material of his work as existing in some tidy, clean and perfect world; a world say, akin to a scientific laboratory. Instead, he assumed that these materials are produced in the ordinary world of offices, over-filled with paperwork and filing cabinets. These materials were produced in the mundane world where simple mistakes get made for all too ordinary reasons.

Much turns around this. For, when one is trying to understand a "real world", practical activity, in this case the Fund's work, it becomes all to easy to make misleading comparisons between what one might call the "dirty facts" one finds in that real world and what one might call the clean, tidy facts one will find in the confines of, say, pure research. Such comparisons, wrong in my opinion, are commonplace, especially in relation to activities that involve numbers (Lave, 1986). It is important to note that this desk officer, and I would claim that this held for all members of the mission, did not have a contrast of this order in mind. It was rather that they knew there would be practical difficulties of this kind in their work. They did not bemoan this. Their "problem", if that is the right description for it, was not that these difficulties would arise, so much as they could not predict when they would show themselves. As this first instance indicates, these difficulties did indeed show themselves at unexpected times, this time even before they had managed to unpack their bags.

The second issue I want to raise also relates to another fact of life on missions. This issue has to do with how and why the mission team displayed a concern with the *social processes* underlying its work. The fact that the deputy wanted to talk about which meetings were arranged with whom, and therefore what would be the outcome of those meetings was not, I would argue, a reflection of the mere fact that data have to produced by someone. It is rather a recognition of the fact that in policy work, *numbers and persons go hand in hand*. In other words, the team was recognising and depending upon the relationship between an individual's role in an organisation and the understanding that individual has as a result of that position. This may seem a banal point, but it is fundamental to mission activity. The work is all about creating analysis through the social process of agreeing and determining the facts in question. What is of concern to members of a mission is what *in practice* this means: which people and in what ways can these things (agreement of the fact and determination of policy) be achieved in any particular instance.

This brings us to the problem of the rookie economist—the EP. One of his difficulties was that he was naive as regards these matters. He did not know who to ask about the relevant materials, and perhaps even did not know what would be the right questions to ask even if he did get to the right person. These things he would of course learn through the advice he was given and through the experience that he would slowly accumulate. But that would take time. In the beginning he found these things difficult. The point, however, is that these are just practical realities that have to be dealt with— these are just facts of life.

Ordinary Work

These arguments beg the question of exactly what economists ask and of whom. To elaborate, I will now describe some of the things that get done in the early stages of a mission.

The first few days of the mission were spent marching around the various buildings of the Arcadian authorities, gathering more information and more numbers, and discussing with those responsible for their production, issues to do with how to interpret those numbers, and on that basis, how to use them. Each member of the mission had their own "circuit" of meetings, numbers, and officials to work around. More specifically, the Fund separates economies into various sectors, and this is reflected in the organisation of the mission process. In this case, the desk officer concentrated on the national accounts, prices, and wages; the fiscal economist concentrated on public finance; and the EP concentrated on the monetary sector and financial reforms. The deputy chief had responsibility for the external sector and the balance of payments. The chief had the task of integrating these figures and of presenting them to the authorities in the policy meetings.

This data collection process consisted of various sections or stages. First, there was the collecting of the first set of data. This supplemented the data the desk officer had already collected over the year including data collected through a questionnaire he sent to the Arcadians. These data were collected in meetings at such places as the *Central Bank* for balance of payments and foreign currency holdings data, and the *Ministry of Finance* for fiscal figures. At the end of each day, each economist added the figures to their increasingly extensive spreadsheets. The figures for one sector were then be reconciled with the figures in the other sectors. When there was a problem of reconciliation between two or more sectors, the team tried to decide what might be the cause. They conjectured that the numbers collected for the fiscal sector were not up-to-date in comparison to figures from other sectors. To investigate this, the fiscal economist asked that they enquire into when the figures were calculated in his next round of meetings. This may be thought of as the further stage of the mission.

However, the division of labour on the mission consisted of more than simply a distribution of data gathering jobs. It was also bound up with the need to generate an analytic picture that could help determine what numbers to gather and what those numbers *meant*. This was reflected in the work the deputy chief and the desk officer undertook at the beginning of the mission. In particular, they arranged meetings with one key official in the Ministry of Planning. The deputy chief and the desk officer wanted to talk with this individual not only to gather certain figures as part of their data gathering, but also to get some guidance on how to read and interpret the figures that the team as a whole were gathering. The official in question had an almost unique insight into the economic position of Arcadia. This was based, in part, on years of work in various ministries and in part on his current role in the Ministry of Planning.

What they were after was two things. First, they wanted some advice on how to separate the flotsam from the main body of economic fact. For the figures that would be collected in the data gathering consisted both of long term trends or "underlying movements" and elements reflecting one–off events. The official in the Ministry of Planning could provide this "inside information".

The second purpose of these meetings related to the fact that the official could share with them the perspective the authorities had on current economic trends. Here the concern was for the mission to understand the weight given to some issues, and the indifference felt towards others. Ultimately there would be a good chance that these views would be shared with the team during the policy discussions that concluded the mission, but the team wanted to get an understanding before those events so as to tailor their investigations in such a way as to enable them to "talk to those views".

The trust between the official and the team was also such that the official could offer frank remarks that might be more difficult to make in the formalised and partly ritual events of policy discussion. For example, the official was quite willing to say the authorities "really didn't know" why some trend was manifesting itself in the figures whereas in the policy meetings, such admissions would be difficult. It is important to realise that such frankness was not pointing towards failings on the part of the authorities. By and large they had considerable knowledge about the matters at hand. It was just that there were a handful of issues that they were unsure about. This was a fact of life.

Essentially the process in question consisted of a series of meetings during which the numbers (in the national accounts, the monetary sector, and so on) were briefly analysed and discussed. These meetings went on throughout the mission as the team gradually revised and built up its own tables. The process itself involved going through the individual numbers (or category of numbers) one by one, while the official simply outlined what he thought the team ought to know about that category, presenting the Arcadians' view on those numbers. Sometimes the members of the mission raised their own concerns about a number, requesting the official to explain some issues there and then, or to investigate those numbers for discussion later on.

Discussing the Facts amongst the Facts: A Vignette

An illustration is provided by the first of these meetings, the topic of which was "the macroeconomic framework and review of overall developments". Once formalities had been completed, the desk officer said that the mission wanted to get some explanation as to why there had been a lowering of export volumes and an increase in imports over projections in the most recent quarterly figures. He pointed towards the relevant numbers in the tables. The official responded by saying the answer(s) lay not in the general but in the particular, and suggested that they go through each sub-category of exports and imports. This indeed was how they proceeded.

The desk officer commenced the discussions: "Mechanical and electrical goods: these are down on projections: why?"

The official replied:

"There is poor demand for these goods. It reflects the general weakening of demand in the world economy".

Desk Officer: "But if this is the case why has there been an increase in imports of raw materials given that there appears to be a slow down in the economy as a whole?"

Official: "Well, because there has been an increase in investments in tourism. This has caused an increase in imports of raw materials—building goods. This is seasonal: it is the time when many buildings need rebuilding. It is not a trend."

Desk Officer: "Okay, whilst on the subject of tourism, let's move down the table to numbers for tourism: how is that there has been a decline? Or rather, how is it that there has been a reduction: receipts for tourism are down."

Official: "Tourism? There are more tourists this year but they spend less. I think it is that we went down-market a bit. The tourists who are coming this year spend less than those who came last year. This is a potential problem: if the hotels go down too far the quality of the resorts goes down and the appeal to tourists reduces further. We are trying to ensure that we avoid that. We don't want to go through the crisis in (a nearby country). They found that they went down so far that the market for tourism collapsed. They built so many cheap hotels that they destroyed the reason for going there".

On certain categories of numbers the discussions became even more detailed. Partly this was a reflection of what numbers were available. For example, the imports numbers had the following categories which led the deputy chief and desk officer to ask for quite specific accounts:

Deputy: "Why has there been such large increase in agriculture and food stuffs? Look, this figure here: milk and yoghurt."

Official: "Well, it has become fashionable. I think it is to do with healthy eating."

Deputy: "But this is a huge increase, this is millions of litres. No, seriously!"

Official: "Yes, what can I say? People in Arcadia didn't used to drink milk. It's not traditional. This year everyone is drinking it. I think young people think it will make them look like athletes."

The official then patted his tummy and said: "I've not been drinking it!"

The desk officer and deputy chief looked at each other and laughed. "Okay, let's not worry about that one, it won't show itself in the final total anyway."

Sanctioning Numbers

As the week passed, so the focus of concern changed in these meetings. Gradually, the team began to build up a higher level picture where things like the oddities in the current accounts disappeared from view. I do not want to describe these discussions, however, since the main point I want to draw from these meetings with the official in the Ministry of Planning is how he was able to give inside information— information that derived from his location within the government and at the centre of information production. Meetings with him were an informal nexus whereby the team were able to sort out the "facts amongst the facts" and to learn about the authorities' perspectives.

It is important to note, however, that as the team moved toward completion of the data gathering stage of the mission and began to reconcile the tables they were generating (i.e., for the monetary, the real, the fiscal and the external sector), so they embarked on another cycle of activity. Here the role of this official changed. For though he was able to give very useful comment on many of the numbers in question, he was only able to *sanction* a sub-set. The team needed to get all of its figures sanctioned before they could start on the analysis of policy and prepare their efforts to discuss policy with the authorities.

By using the term "sanction", I am pointing toward the fact that the Arcadian authorities had to agree to a number being used by the mission. An illustration of this is provided by the fiscal economist's activities. He commenced his work with meetings with a senior member of the Ministry of Finance. During these meetings he set out some of the figures in the budget he wanted to discuss. The official nearly always directed the fiscal economist to other, more junior officials to discuss these numbers. During the meetings the economist had with these individuals, they explained why they had calculated the numbers and how. One might characterise this part of the fiscal officer's activities as a process of going to the horse's mouth: i.e. getting to the person who was responsible of the production of the numbers in question. Now going to the horse's mouth is not all that the fiscal officer had to do. For once he had understood the numbers in question, once he had revised his own numbers, once he had worked up the picture as he understood it, he then had to go back to the more senior official to get that individual to "sign off" the numbers.

There are a number of reasons why he had to do so. First, he had to make sure that the numbers he got from the junior official would not be contradicted by numbers generated elsewhere. A senior official may be more likely to know this. Second, some of the figures he ended up using in his tables were the product of calculation prompted by his own questioning. Therefore the more senior official would not necessarily have seen these numbers beforehand. Since this official would ultimately be held responsible for these numbers, it was therefore proper that *he* signed them off. Part of the protocol of this meant that the junior official showed the newly calculated numbers to his senior colleague before the fiscal economist did so. But third, and this reflected a more salient point, these signings off were a ritual display of social status and power. This was particularly obvious in relation to the senior official the fiscal economist dealt with since this individual was a political appointee. He had no interest in the numbers his more junior staff calculated nor very little understanding of why they were calculated. Nonetheless, his was the signature that was required before those numbers could be used.

By combining the product of all this work, the team constructed a basis upon which they could start making some concrete determinations of policy alternatives. The output of their work could not be measured on, say, the basis of completeness, comprehensiveness or accuracy. Rather, the product of their activities was a perspective from which to reason through policy alternatives. This is ultimately the purpose of missions: not description, not reporting, but enabling a mapping out of the implications of the current situation for the future.

That this is so is shown in the fact that the main event of the mission was the policy discussions that concluded it. As the deputy chief put it, these were "What it is all about," "The thing that matters".

I do not want to describe all the activities the team undertook to prepare themselves for the discussions. What I do want to do is present a third vignette, this time of one these meetings. My concern here is to provide a flavour of how these meetings could have ritualising effects, and in particular how the effects of these rituals transformed the numbers presented by the chief into ones that could be used for policy discussion.

A Vignette of Policy Discussions

When the team gathered in the hotel reception early in morning of the first day of policy meetings, there was an atmosphere of relief combined with tension. The economists knew that they would not be doing much during the discussions and that the chief would be the centre of attention. This was his day. But they knew also that the outcome of these meetings could either be the completion of the mission on schedule or the need for more work and delay.

On this particular day, there were to be two meetings: the first with the Ministry of Finance, the second with the Central Bank. I focus on this latter.

Officials were waiting for the delegation at the entrance to the bank, and led the team into a meeting room. The chief entered first, followed by his staff. Whilst waiting for the bank officials to arrive, the chief asked for his economists to sit either side of him. He took some spreadsheet tables from his briefcase and placed them on the desk in front. He began to move them around like a painter preparing his palette. He then asked the desk officer for one of the medium term projections tables, which he added to his collection on the table. Finally, he took some handwritten notes from his jacket pocket and placed them in the centre of his palette of documents.

An official then burst in and announced the imminent arrival of the bank's Governor. The team stood up. The Governor arrived with a flurry of officials and secretaries behind him. The Governor sat down directly opposite the chief, similarly surrounded by his cohorts. After formalities, the meeting began. The chief stood up and commenced his oration. He complimented the Arcadians on the work that had been achieved in the past year and the impressive performance in certain areas of the economy. He commented also on the continuing frailties in certain areas.

The chief then came to what the mission believed was the heart of the matter, for it was the team's view that the authorities were clearly exceeding their projected credit levels to the government. There were a number of reasons for this, including lower than expected growth in some sectors and, most noticeably, an unexpected growth in expenditure in agricultural stocks, particularly for olives. Related to this, there was a reduction in the revenues from the sale of olives in export markets—all of this in a year where the harvest had been unusually good. The chief explained that as a result of this situation, the Arcadian authorities would find their foreign reserves getting reduced to a very low level, little more than one week's imports, or even lower. This was, according to the chief, too little, and necessitated immediate corrective polices. Failure to adopt these policies could lead the Arcadians to seek assistance from the Fund in the near future. As he explained all this he would point at the documents in front of him, and would sometimes pick up a spreadsheet as if looking at an oracle.

When the chief finished his oration there was a long silence. Then the Governor turned to his officials and beckoned them to gather round his chair. For some minutes the Arcadians discussed matters quietly amongst themselves. All the mission could see was a wall of individuals with their backs facing outward. Gradually, officials started to peel off and return to their seats. Eventually, the Governor turned round to face the table again. After a pause, the Governor explained that his staff wanted to go through the numbers again. The chief repeated his figures. The Arcadians looked at each other, before the governor said that they concurred with his calculations. One of the officials then asked if he would tell them who provided each of the main numbers—i.e., which persons in which department had given them to him. The chief, with the help of his team, provided this information. The Arcadians again huddled together. Eventually, they returned to the table. After a pause, the Governor nodded to one of his officials who then announced that the "authorities did indeed agree with the figures that the chief had presented".

The next stage of the meeting involved investigating policy alternatives. The chief started this stage by continuing his oration during which he outlined what he thought were the main issues to be investigated. The investigations followed. In brief, these involved modifying certain variables in the *monetary tables* to see just what the impact would be on other variables. Different policies would affect different variables and so the hope was to eventually determine the "appropriate policy stance". These investigations took some time. By the time the meeting ended, the mission team and the staff of the central bank had spent nearly five hours together.

The Raw and the Cooked

There was obviously much more involved in this meeting (and others I have not discussed) than is conveyed in these brief remarks. My concern here is to focus on the fact that this meeting was one that turned out to be one that *counted*. There are two aspects to this. On the one hand, the meeting was about adding numbers; on the other, it had a particular and crucially symbolic aspect that made those countings matter. Both issues are intimately connected. But one has precedence over the other. Let me explain.

The meeting consisted of two main parts, with a watershed in the middle. The chief's oration flowed across both stages. His oration commenced with a presentation not just of what the team had been working on, but the team's final view—its output. Given that the team was invested by the Fund to act on its behalf, this view was effectively the Fund's view. Accordingly, it was presented with all the solemnity it deserved. This was not an opportunity for the discussion of opinions, or for jokes and levity. But nonetheless, this view *did not count* unless it was accepted by the Arcadians. For, though the Arcadians had been involved in its development—some individuals more than others as we have seen—the Arcadian authorities had not officially accepted it and were under no obligation to do so. The periods during which the governor and his officials turned away and discussed the chief's remarks were opportunities for them to decide whether to accept or reject it. These were therefore moments pregnant with tension for the mission team. It was only once the Arcadians had announced acceptance that the next stage of the meeting could occur. This second stage also involved the chief standing up and making a speech, but this time his remarks had a different character. If before they were descriptive, now they became an opportunity to outline issues to be investigated. It is in this respect that there was a watershed in the centre of the meeting. For after the Governor's acceptance, the chief's presentation became the common ground upon which both sides undertook subsequent analytical work. I shall say some more about that work in a moment, but before I do so let me make some more remarks about the significance of this watershed.

It might appear that I am proposing a view on missions that echoes the perspective of Lévi-Strauss (1962). Lévi-Strauss was an anthropologist who claimed (amongst other things) that what was essential to human society was the fact that objects in the world were transformed from their natural, "unsocial" status into social objects by the process of "cooking". Lévi-Strauss' argument was that it was the miraculous transformation that cooking brought about that displayed man's (for it was mostly man in Lévi-Strauss' work) God–like power over nature. Here it might be thought that I am suggesting that policy meetings involve a transformation of something that is, in a sense, *raw* into a thing that is *cooked*. In being cooked it is thereby touchable, clean, and, in the Fund's sense, useable for analysis. Although this will allow some light-hearted remarks about how missions are involved in the process of "cooking the books," I think the comparison is useful. For it draws attention to the *moral element* in the work that gets undertaken on mission, a moral element made conspicuous in the process of sanctioning numbers.

For the process of converting "raw numbers" into meaningful and "useable" information constitutes, in part, a *moral transformation* and not just an arithmetical or econometric one. In being accepted by the Arcadians, the numbers came to be ones that counted. This is in part a moral process because being accepted, or *passing the test* made no difference to the numbers as numbers. The difference made is to the moral status of the numbers.

I want to suggest that this does not just hold for the events within the policy meetings, albeit that they highlight the issues most clearly. I want to argue that mission work as a whole consists of a process of gathering data, subjecting these data to various assessments and sanctionings, and, if the data pass these tests, using them in analytical tasks.

This discussion of the moral basis of economic facts could lead one to think that economic reality is "merely" a social construct. It might lead one to believe that the concern of missions is not the real, hard, economic facts, but to ensure that the process of building a picture results in the local authorities agreeing to that picture. This would give the impression that the exact nature of the picture does not matter; the main concern being simply that the two sides (the mission and the authorities), agree to it. To be sure, certain sociological commentators would delight in such a notion, but this view is quite wrong[1]. The point I am making is that the business of economic fact and the analysis of policy are immersed in considerations of the social. It would be wholly incorrect to separate them.

This leads me back to the second stage of the meetings. For here the kind of analytical work undertaken was clearly empirical, hands-on science. But it was also social, wherein the various participants tested and corroborated their investigations with their colleagues. Of crucial importance, these meetings were populated by those people whose status and business was to determine what was the right way and the wrong way of doing these things, for these were experts doing their work. It is in this sense that there is an additional basis for the claim that mission work has a moral component: these meetings could only be undertaken if the "experts" in this field were there. The experts I have in mind are both those people who may have had technical training in economics and those whose social position, say as governor of the central bank, entitled them to be there. It was the determinations of *these* people that counted, and *their* assessments of what was the right way of doing things that mattered. This was why these meetings *counted*[2].

Conclusion

These arguments may seem quite distant from questions to do with technology in organisational life. But what I have been wanting to argue is that certain social processes enable certain sorts of information to be suited for organisational use. Information does not "sit out there" in the real world waiting to be caught up in the information net. The task of the Fund's missions is not simply to go and collect data. The practices of missions make information suitable for processing, and this is, in large part, a social process involving ritual and ceremony. But these practices are also practical, and the facts of life of this practical activity constitute the context in which mission teams have to undertake their computational and analytical work. In short, what I have been attempting to do in this paper is to look at how information is transformed into the kind of object that is suitable for practical action. Only

---

[1] See for example, Porter (1995).
[2] This is a difficult point and I think one that is often lost in most sociological descriptions of experts at work. For a good exposition see Button, G. and Sharrock, W. (1993) pp.1-25.

once we have understood that, can we turn to the design and specification of the technology that would support the mission process.

There are some important implications for the application of CSCW technology here. For—and as I noted at the outset—with only a cursory understanding of the mission process, one might think that computer networks and the capability to remotely transmit, access, and process data might help obviate the need for mission work, allowing member countries to make available the kind of up-to-date information the Fund is interested in. But in fact, this analysis shows that mission teams do not simply gather pre-existing data. Rather, they start their work with these data and then "work it up" through a complex social process to create an analytical perspective. This perspective only exists in the hearts and minds of the participants, and not in the numbers themselves. In essence, the experts involved constitute the perspective by participating in its development. That they do so means that the analytic perspective cannot be generated by the use of any sort of technological "knowbot" because such entities do not have the social validation and the expertise that comes from being part of the social process of mission work.

A second implication pertains to the use of video technology. We have seen that missions involve ritual transformations. One might think that the introduction of video technology would be strongly resisted by those involved in mission work if those ritualising events were somehow interfered with. However, I would contend that video technology might actually bolster these processes. For, many multiperson videoconferencing systems involve explicit protocols for turntaking. These could enhance the controls that chiefs and their equivalents in the local authorities might want to exercise. That is to say, the strictly hierarchical aspects of these meetings could be made technologically concrete. Further, such meetings can be planned for, and the participants pre-determined—another requisite for the use of most video systems. Given also that the meetings involve so many persons of high status, the cost for the video system can be justified by the time saved by not having those persons travel.

Of course, there may be a host of reasons why video may nonetheless be rejected, not least the unwillingness of member authorities to accept Fund recommendations for how those authorities might put "their house in order" when the Fund's senior staff haven't even bothered to visit the house in question. This is to put it glibly, but points towards the delicate balance of symbolic power between the Fund and its members. Space has precluded discussion of this (but see Harper, 1997). But perhaps more importantly given the materials I have been able to present, video technology may be unsuited to supporting those aspects of policy meetings that are analytical: i.e., after the ritual transformation of numbers has occurred. Here, the "talking head model" of social interaction, which appears to be the basis of most video technology, is antithetical to the flexible sharing of work objects (spreadsheets, lists of numbers, and so on) in the ad hoc, pragmatic, unpredictable way that is constitutive of how experts do their work together. (See Heath et al., 1995 for more detailed comments on these issues.)

In short, the conclusion of this analysis is that those very things that might appear most resistant to technological support and change—namely, ritual transformations—are the very things that CSCW technologies might best support. In contrast, activities to do with the analysis of numeric information may be much less suitable in this regard. This may seem paradoxical, given how numerical information is so suited for computation, and how essentially social phenomena like rituals would appear to be so alien. But this paradox is misleading. For in missions, analytical work and ritual go hand in hand. Numbers consist of the raw data, but these need to be transformed ritually into materials that are analytically useful. Only the human "experts"—whether they be Fund economists or officials in the member authorities—can determine what is acceptable from what is not. It is only they who can determine what numbers can speak for the future and which must remain silent. It has been the purpose of this paper to explain why.

References

Button, G. and Sharrock, W. (1993). "A Disagreement over Agreement and Consensus in Constructionist Sociology, *Journal for the Theory of Social Behaviour*, Vol. 23. No.1, pp. 1-25.

Harper, R.H.R., (1997). *Inside the IMF: An Ethnography of Documents, Technology and Organisational Action*, Academic Press, London & San Diego.

Harper, R. H. R. (1995). "The Faces of Information Work: Collaborative Tools, Information, and Organisational Symbols", *Proceedings, Colloquium on Workplace Studies*, King's College, London, August 7–8th.

Harper, R.H.R. & Sellen, A.J , (1995). "Collaborative Tools and the Practicalities of Professional Work at the International Monetary Fund," *Proceedings, of CHI'95*, Denver, Colorado, May 7–11th, pp. 122-129.

Heath, C., Sellen, A.J., & Luff, P. (1995). "Rethinking the Virtual Workplace: The Need for Flexible Access in Video-Mediated Communication." *Proceedings of ECSCW '95*, Stockholm, Sweden, pp. 83-100.

Kent, C. & Harper, R.H.R. (1994). *Portable Porthole Pads: An Investigation into the Use of a Ubicomp Device to Support the Sociality of Work*, Rank Xerox Technical Report EPC–1994—110, Rank Xerox Research Centre, 61 Regent Street, Cambridge, CB2 1AB.

Lave, J. (1986). "The Values of Quantification", in Law, J. (Ed) *Power, Action and Belief*, Routledge, London, pp. 88-111.

Lévi-Strauss, C. (1962). *The Savage Mind*. Weidenfield and Nicolson, London.

Porter, T. M. (1995). *Trust in Numbers: The Pursuit of Objectivity in Science and Public Life*, Princeton University Press, Princeton, New Jersey.

Sellen, A.J. & Harper, R.H.R. (1997). "Paper as an Analytic Resource for the Design of New Technologies", *Proceedings of CHI '97*, Atlanta, GA., March 25-27, pp. 319-326.

Sellen, A.J. & Harper, R.H.R. (1996). "Can Workflow Tools Support Knowledge Work? A Case Study of the International Monetary Fund," *Rank Xerox Technical Report*, Rank Xerox Research Centre, 61 Regent Street, Cambridge, CB2 1AB.

Index of Authors